Citizens
and the
Environment

Citizens
and the
Environment

Case Studies in Popular Action

Lynton K. Caldwell   Lynton R. Hayes

Isabel M. MacWhirter

INDIANA UNIVERSITY PRESS   BLOOMINGTON & LONDON

Published in Canada by Fitzhenry & Whiteside Limited, Don Mills, Ontario

Manufactured in the United States of America

Library of Congress Cataloging in Publication Data

Caldwell, Lynton Keith, 1913–
Citizens and the environment.

Bibliography
Includes index.
1. Environmental policy—United States—Citizen
participation.   I.   Hayes, Lynton R., 1943–   joint
author.   II.   MacWhirter, Isabel M., joint author.
III.   Title.

HC110.E5C3   1976   301.31'0973   75–31422
ISBN 0–253–31355–4   1 2 3 4 5 80 79 78 77 76

Contents: — Part I: Critical
areas ... — Land use —
Coastal zone ... — Part II. etc.

P. 481-435

CONTENTS

PREFACE

THIS BOOK DESCRIBES the ways in which citizens have organized and acted in response to perceived threats to their environments. The cases have been selected to illustrate the wide variety of issues in which citizens have felt impelled to organize to defend interests which were threatened by agencies of government or corporate enterprise. In many cases, the power of government and business combined to promote economic development in ways that disregarded environmental and social values. Agencies of government were frequently found to work at cross-purposes on environmental issues and were too often discovered to be indifferent or reluctant defenders of the public interest as the protesting citizens understood it.

This volume is a response to a need for real-life resource materials for learning or teaching about public response to environmental issues. The cases record successes, failures, and inconclusive outcomes of citizen efforts for environmental protection. Sixty-eight cases were examined to provide a broad coverage of issues and geographic representation. Detailed, in-depth case studies would not have been the answer to the need. Had analyses of organizational behavior or definitive studies of particular environmental controversies been the objective, no more than six or eight cases could have been reported in a volume of this size. But for illustrating the varied roles of citizens in environmental politics, the often critical role of concerned individuals, and the characteristically ambivalent responses of government agencies faced with conflicting demands, breadth in coverage was viewed as preferable to depth. The target audience includes students at the advanced secondary and junior college levels, and interested citizens generally. The style of writing is simple and direct, and a general uniformity of structure in the chapters facilitates the comparison of cases by students or teachers.

The book deals with the man-made urban environment as well as with the rural environment, wildlife, and nature protection. Its ten chapters deal respectively with land use, the coastal zone, inland waters, air quality and weather modification, natural areas and wildlife, energy, economic growth, health, the quality of urban life, and institutional arrangements. Although citizen action was most frequently found to be directed against the duly constituted authorities of government (at all levels), no single cause or set of institutions could fairly be held generally accountable for environmental dereliction. Some agencies were more responsive than others to citizen appeal and to quality-of-life considerations. But the cumulative effect of the sixty-eight cases should be a heightened awareness of the complexity and ramifications of most environmental issues and of the diverse, and often incompatible, concepts of the public interest, of professional and legal obligations, and of the fundamental purposes of government in American society.

It should be apparent that it is not possible to categorize the cases simply, under single-topic headings. For example, many energy problems involve land use, and almost every case has implications for economics. From an ecological perspective, everything is ultimately linked to every other thing. Because of the systemic interrelatedness of all aspects of the natural environment, it often happens that a particular environmental case could be classified among any of several topics, depending upon the aspects emphasized. For example, the controversy over the proposed nuclear power plant at Bodega Head, California (Chapter 6, Case I) was simultaneously an energy, land use, and coastal zone issue, with economic and institutional implications. Some cases could, with equal justification, have been placed under another topic, were a different aspect of the case to have been emphasized. The implication of this interrelatedness is *not* that environmental cases cannot meaningfully be classified, but rather that *their context is almost always complex*; no single set of considerations or values is sufficient either to understand or to cope with the factors involved.

There is also a dynamic quality to the cases that sometimes makes their outcomes inconclusive. When an environmental controversy enters the field of litigation, an extended process may ensue through state and federal courts with successive appeals and remands. Cases such as Scenic Hudson (Chapter 8, Case IV) or Reserve Mining (Chapter 8, Case V) have been in the courts for years, with the final environmental consequences still to be determined.

The authors have endeavored to provide an authentic version of each of their cases. But it is inevitable that the several parties to any case will not see the events from the same perspective or evaluate the outcome by the same criteria. Thus rarely, if ever, can there be a definitive version of a case. The principal sources of the authors' information are indicated in notes appended to the cases.

Although no chapter was wholly the work of any one individual, each author was chiefly responsible for particular chapters. Isabel MacWhirter wrote chapters 2, Coastal Zone; 3, Inland Waters; 4, Air Quality and Weather Modifications; 8, Environmental Health; and 9, Quality of Urban Life. Lynton Hayes wrote chapters 1, Land Use; 5, Natural Areas and Wildlife; 6, Energy; 7, The Economy and Growth; and 10, Institutional Behavior. Lynton Caldwell wrote the introductory chapter and edited the substance of the entire volume. Editing for style was done by John Muller and Nicholas Fattu, Jr. Manuscript typing was done by Professor Caldwell's secretary, Jan Lundy, and by Jolene and Manuel Cabral, Teresa McClary, and Grace Smith.

The authors gratefully acknowledge the assistance of the Office of Environmental Education, United States Department of Health, Education and Welfare, and of the Indiana University Foundation in the preparation and publication of these cases.

Earnings from the sale of this book, beyond the costs of publication, will be paid into a fund in the Indiana University Foundation for the support of further case studies in environmental policy-making.

INTRODUCTION

The People versus the Duly Constituted Authorities

THIS BOOK AFFIRMS and illustrates the vitality of self-government during a period when the feasibility of democratic self-government is being severely tested and questioned. It also illustrates its difficulties and limitations even in a political system favorably disposed, in theory, to popular participation. In a world of increasing complexity, change, and personal mobility, many people find it difficult to retain a sense of participation in public affairs. The big decisions of the present day appear to be made by, or through the actions of, vast impersonal aggregations of power such as corporations, unions, trade associations, and, especially, the agencies of government. These organizations are widely viewed as unresponsive to public opinion generally and indifferent to the needs or values of individuals. Their influence extends beyond their formal organizational structures and persuades or coerces individual citizens and local holders of public office to accede to their policies.

The specific activities of these great power blocs may not be inevitably harmful to the public welfare or subversive of responsible government. But their scope, impersonality, and economic strength and the momentum of their drives toward organizational goals, make them formidable destroyers should their actions tend toward destructive consequences. In recent years, as American citizens have sought to arrest the accelerating deterioration of their environments, they have time and again been brought into confrontation with these power blocs. The individual attempting unaided to oppose them encounters a juggernaut effect. The destructive action rolls on, oblivious of individual protest. Only in exceptional circumstances can an individual single-handedly arrest the course of environmental destruction by a government bureau or large corporate enterprise. But informed and purposive individuals, organized into active committees and coalitions, can multiply their influence out of proportion to their numbers.

The ten sets of case studies constituting this book recount the efforts of organized citizens to protect or improve the quality of their environments. In these efforts the citizens were forced to challenge the representatives of economic and political power. These challenges were not always successful or wholly effective. Nevertheless, the record of success is impressive and, in some instances, a partial victory was, on balance, significant, and was considered worth the effort. In many cases the citizen action was not, at least initially, hostile to the organization threatening the quality of the environment or to its general purposes. The citizens' objective was frequently limited to persuading or compelling the government agency or corporation to carry out its mission in a manner that respected or conserved environmental quality. Hostility to bureaucratic or corporate power developed when moderate efforts of citizen groups were ignored or rebuffed and when the juggernaut of economic and political power threatened to roll over the environment until checked by a greater force—often an injunction from a court of law.

Responding to the Public Interest

The rise of environmental quality as an issue in American politics has given renewed pertinence to a number of questions inherent in the practice of democratic government. Prominent among these are the following: (1) When public opinion is divided, to whom, and on the basis of what criteria, should government respond? (2) What is the public or social responsibility of private economic power beyond that required by law? (3) Is it realistic to assume that elected representatives of the people do, in fact, represent their wishes? (4) May the motives and actions of public officials legitimately be cloaked by the authority of public office? (5) Does the individual citizen or citizen organization have a realizable right to question public or corporate officials in matters of general public concern? and (6) Is citizen interference with the lawful acts of government or business (even though these acts may be irretrievably destructive) a threat to the orderly and responsible processes of government and the economy?

Environmental issues have not been unique in accentuating these questions. But popular concern for the environment has grown more rapidly than government and business and the assumptions underlying their missions have adjusted to the new environmental values, costs, and implications. As a consequence, government and business, being conditioned to respond affirmatively to almost wholly economic uses of the environment, have usually responded negatively to proposals that would subordinate economic development to ecological or aesthetic values. And because concern for environmental quality, although widespread, is unevenly distributed among the citizenry, the responsiveness of government and business to environmental questions may become complicated and problematic.

The public official—and more especially the business executive— necessarily has some notion of to whom he should respond. In fact, the constituency of particular government agencies or business firms can never be the whole people. All constituencies are to some extent limited, defined by a particular governmental mission or business clientele. In those instances where almost everyone is affected by the activities of an organization, only some particular aspect of people's lives is involved. For example, delivery of the mails and distribution of electric energy affect almost everyone but have little or no direct bearing upon a wide range of popular needs, interests, and values. In meeting the demands of one sector of the public, the needs or preferences of other sectors may be prejudiced. Especially in government, officials are popularly believed to be obligated to act in accordance with the abstract logic of law that defines public interest. But legal definitions of public interest often have a fictional quality and do not necessarily reflect the understanding, wishes, or even votes of a majority of a popular electorate. And yet the official can believe that his duly constituted authority is, by definition, exercised in the public interest no matter how many citizens disagree.

The cases reported in this volume repeatedly illustrate the conviction of public and business administrators that they represent the public interest. When acting within statutory or corporate authority, these officials characteristically assume a role of rectitude. Thus they tend to view the interposition of so-called public interest groups (e.g., on behalf of environmental protection) as obstructionist meddling. The acrimony characterizing many environmental disputes reflects moral indignation felt on both sides of the controversy. The environmentally concerned citizen sees the public or business official as sacrificing or betraying the interest of society at large for some special economic or political purpose that is substantively or morally wrong whatever its legality. The officials see the protesters as self-appointed troublemakers interfering with the orderly, lawful, and efficient processes of government or business. By what right, they ask, does this self-interested minority burden and delay the conduct of public business for which society, in its wisdom, has made them and not the protesters responsible?

The Meaning of Citizenship

By what right do private citizens seek to supersede the considered judgment of the duly constituted public authorities? Do the obligations of citizenship extend to more than voting, paying taxes, jury service, and a general obligation to obey the laws? Is there a significant distinction between citizenship as a legal status and citizenship as a social role? Except when manifest support is needed, public officeholders and politicians are usually happiest with a passive role for citizenship. It may be argued whether active participation in public affairs is necessary to the fullest expression of citizenship. But it is certain that active citizenship is necessary to the vitality of self-government.

As a source of guidance to public officeholders, "the people" is an abstraction. Especially in a heterogeneous society as diverse as that of the United States, there is no way of ascertaining the will of "the people." The divergencies of attitudes, interests, and values make it impossible for any group or individual to represent the popular will in other than a symbolic or abstract sense. Nevertheless, the public official, under the theory of government prevailing in the United States, is presumed to be guided by the public will, except where that will is subordinate to fundamental (i.e., constitutional) law. In the absence of clearly defined law or explicit evidence of public opinion, the official must rely on his own judgment and preference unless he can obtain guidance from some source which will afford support for his decision. This guidance is almost invariably available from the representatives of the so-called special interests. All interests are, in some sense, special, but the phrase "special interests" commonly refers to those persons or groups who seek a particular economic or political advantage for themselves to the relative disadvantage of the rest of society.

The fact that only a few members of society benefit directly does not mean that a special interest is necessarily bad. The quality of the society as a whole may be enhanced by public programs that directly assist only a fraction of the population. Random examples could include medical research relating to cerebral palsy, aid to the blind, high-energy accelerators, or assistance to the performing arts. The "special" quality in the special interests suggests an unfair or illegitimate advantage gained without commensurate benefit to the public generally, and frequently through the corruption or subversion of the processes of government. Although there are provisions in nearly all systems of government to prevent or expose such abuse, experience has shown that the official sanctions are not always effective. It has been a truism of democratic and responsible government that only the vigilance of citizens can insure the accountability of public officeholders.

Citizenship is therefore a status that enables those who possess it to play a role in civic affairs. In the earlier years of the American republic, this opportunity to participate in the formulation of public policy was widely held to be a moral obligation, notably expressed in the writings of John Adams and Thomas Jefferson. But the changing circumstances of American society, especially toward greater complexity, heterogeneity, and specialization, were accompanied by changing perceptions of the obligations of citizenship. The affairs of government were no longer as simple as Andrew Jackson believed them to be. Increasingly, effectiveness in voluntary participation in government required time and information that most citizens could not easily obtain. Increasingly, the citizen/amateur confronted bureaucratic professionals, specialists, and technicians who counselled their would-be, unofficial collaborators to refrain from interfering in matters to which they could not possibly bring competence or informed responsibility.

A characteristic official response to concerned and distressed citizen activists has been that the public officials have done just what the protesters would themselves do under similar circumstances. If you knew what we know, the officials would say, you would do as we have done. But, of course, we can't let you have our information, intended only for official purposes. Prior to the Freedom of Information Act and the Environmental Impact Statement Procedures of the National Environmental Policy Act of 1969, public officials could and did avoid public disclosure of the basis of their actions or of the factors considered in the making of official decisions. Public hearings, especially on environmental issues relating to highway locations, dams, airports, and electric generating plants and transmission lines, were legalistic rituals, necessary under the law but seldom affording real opportunity for meaningful citizen participation in the policy process. Citizens usually were presented with *faits accomplis*. The charade of the conventional public hearing was conducive to little more than public cynicism and discouraged citizens from pursuing active involvement in public affairs.

During the decade following the mid-nineteen sixties, several developments converged to give renewed impetus to citizen activism. Public disclosure legislation, the liberalizing of judicial doctrines regarding qualifications for bringing suit in the courts, and the example of political success by activists in civil rights and antiwar movements had a common effect in facilitating the organization of public interest activists across a broad spectrum of concern. The environmental quality movement was a major beneficiary of this development. New organizations such as Friends of the Earth emerged, and older organizations such as the National Audubon Society, the Sierra Club, and the Izaak Walton League grew in membership and in political effectiveness. Supplementing this growth of nonprofessional activism was the emergence of the public-interest law firm. Organizations such as the Environmental Defense Fund (EDF) and the Natural Resources Defense Council (NRDC) developed a symbiotic relationship with more general environmental protection groups. The cases in this volume frequently record the collaboration of local and national environmental action groups with public-interest law firms in suits against big government and big business.

The public-interest organization is a response to emergent changes in the quality of public life in the mid-twentieth century and affords an institutionalized means for citizen involvement in public affairs. It overcomes many of the traditional obstacles to effective citizen participation in public policy making and does so at a time when more people with the means to make themselves effective—educational, financial, and occupational—have discovered motivations for concern with the processes of public policy making. The cases in this volume are, in large measure, instances of this aroused concern among people who have come to believe that unless they effectively confront the political process, government (and business) will not serve their interests or the interests of the greater number of people in the society.

The Duly Constituted Authorities

As the writing of the following case studies developed, a pattern or characteristic sequence of events appeared that the authors and editor had not foreseen. The selection of case studies was based wholly on an effort to see how citizen groups had responded to environmental issues in a broad variety of instances. No attempt was made to develop a pattern of adversary situations between citizens and government. Although conflict situations were foreseen, the object of environmental protest seemed more likely to be the business community—the issue to be corporate profits versus the quality of the public environment. In many cases, economic interests were the perpetrators of environmental degradation. The Reserve Mining case (Chapter 8, Environmental Health) is an example. But even in these cases, government, at various levels, emerged more often than not as a partner, promoter, or protector of activities that diminished the quality of the environment. And with a frequency that surprised the authors, not only did government emerge as the primary culprit, but those agencies of the federal government to whom citizens, perhaps naively, looked for protection of natural resources and the environment were primary agents of environmental degradation. The United States Department of the Interior and its principal bureaus have been among the most frequent objects of righteous indignation.

The culpability of public officials, as seen by environmentally concerned citizens, differs with levels of government and with agencies. A plausible, but not wholly accurate, generalization would be that malfeasance characterizes a determined federal officialdom, misfeasance is more often a consequence of state government ineptitude, and nonfeasance describes the unwillingness of local officials to perform the duties of their offices to protect the environment from rapacious techno-economic despoilers. There is, however, some basis in fact in this trio.

The environmental malfeasance of federal agencies follows primarily from their commitment, by statute and also by bureaucratic and professional conviction, to economic growth and development. The tacit assumption underlying many federal programs for the management of natural resources has been that economic development brings the greatest good to the greatest number of people and should therefore take priority over all or most competing issues. These federal agencies, notably the U.S. Army Corps of Engineers, the Federal Power Commission, the Nuclear Regulatory Commission (formerly the Atomic Energy Commission), the departments of Agriculture, Interior, and Transportation, and the Tennessee Valley Authority, are armed with vast fiscal and legal powers, many with statutory custody over equally vast public assets in lands, waters, minerals, and strategic sites. Their missions were largely determined years, and even decades, prior to the rise of environmental concern among politically significant numbers of Americans. Their career personnel, especially the more senior, tend to equate their agency and professional mission with the public interest. They also tend to identify more readily with the economic interests that they serve or regulate than with environmental action groups whose objectives would restrict or reverse traditional agency policies.

Although exceptions appear to be increasing, the states traditionally have been indifferent protectors of the environment. In many environmental cases involving federal malfeasance, state governments are collaborators. State governments have often sought federal aid in projects that have had environmentally destructive consequences. But a frequent and often valid charge against state governments has been their lack of foresight, their tendency toward expediency, and their ineffective and inefficient management of environmental affairs. Few states have the capability of undertaking large environment-shaping programs such as the North Central Power Study, the Southwest Power Study, or the Tennessee Valley Authority. The environmental damage they engender has often been caused by blunders, delays, and divided counsels within state agencies.

Nonfeasance may be found at all governmental levels but is especially common among local officials, who have too often been revealed as yielding to behind-the-scenes pressures by economic and political interests whom they fear and respect. Lawsuits to force public, and especially local, officials to act, usually through a writ of mandamus, have often failed because the courts have found that action by the local officials was discretionary. A survey of local communities throughout the United States would show that ordinances governing outdoor advertising, real estate subdivision, air and water pollution, and solid waste disposal are frequently not enforced or are administered erratically and with more than occasional favoritism.

Few public officials, except those under indictment, could be expected to admit to dereliction of duty in protection of environmental values. Their duty, as they see it, is to serve *other* values. There is, moreover, a well-known historic tendency among public officials to see themselves as personifications of the public interest. (*L'état, c'est nous!*) Invested with the dignity of office and with certain privileges and immunities associated therewith, they cannot realistically be expected to suffer gladly the questioning of their decisions or their motives. Elected officials may concede that they must answer to the people, but they understand this to be a matter of principle that should not be pushed too vigorously in practice. A plausible but often evasive argument is that the government official cannot accede to the requests of any particular group of citizens, because government must be responsive to all the people equally. This proposition, however, would deteriorate into political science fiction because if the whole people is an abstraction, it would therefore follow that an official equally responsible to everyone would, practically, be responsible to no one.

The discomfiture of the duly constituted authorities can, in part, be explained by the rise of opposition from unexpected sources. The environmental (and consumer) protection movements have drawn heavily upon the middle class for leadership and membership. Groups that seldom became involved in politics, and could (formerly) be counted upon to support duly constituted authority, have begun to question the exercise of that authority. These middle class activists command informational and organizational skills that can be employed to challenge official explanations and alibis. Among the citizen groups are accountants, lawyers, teachers, business executives, farmers, scientists, and engineers. They are quite capable of dissecting agency budgets, of uncovering the fallacies of cost-benefit ratios, and of pointing out alternatives that government officials failed to explore. For these activists, public office holds no mystique; and they have no patience with the proposition that government knows best, that government must act as it does on information that the public cannot have.

Faced, as they sometimes are, with opponents who outclass them in knowledge, and in organizational, computational, and communications skills, public and business executives frequently seek the protection of official status. Committed to policies that can no longer be defended without exposing their arbitrary or special interest character, these officials take the bureaucratic equivalent of the Fifth Amendment to the United States Constitution. They refuse to respond, decline to be questioned, and rely upon the status of office or position to shield them from a querulous citizenry. Their posture, now familiar to thousands of citizen activists throughout the nation, may be summarized in the following homily: By what right do you question us? We, the duly constituted authorities, act upon the basis of authority conferred upon us through the orderly process of the law. If you don't like our decisions, take your complaint to the people on election day or to the legislatures who write the laws. But don't come here telling us, the duly constituted authorities, how we should discharge our official duties. With increasing frequency, citizen activists are taking this advice. Unresponsive state and local officials have been turned out of office in a number of recent elections, perhaps most dramatically in the 1974 elections in the state of Colorado.

It is easy to understand why elected officials, no less than professional public administrators, might tend toward a strong dislike of organized citizen activists. Unlike the professional lobbyist for economic interests, citizen activists are seldom in position to ingratiate themselves with politicians. Especially in the area of environmental policy, organized citizens frequently importune the government to do things displeasing to powerful backers of particular politicians. Possibly the reforms in fund raising for political campaigns may lessen the influence of wealthy and corporate donors to campaign funds. But practical political tradition tends to accord open-handed special interests a higher priority in political life than the more cautious, and usually impecunious, representatives of the public interest. Indeed, the United States Congress has used its power to tax to discourage citizen efforts to participate in, or even to influence, the law-making process. Tax exemption is denied to nonprofit citizen organizations that undertake to "influence" legislation!

Why the Adversary Process?

Politics has always involved competition for power and for a decisive voice in public decisions. It is thus an adversary process, especially so in the United States, where a high percentage of legislators and officeholders are lawyers. The American legal system is essentially adversary in character. And although verified knowledge may influence the processes of law and government, the orientation of the political system is toward the adjustment and resolution of group differences rather than toward discovery of ecologically optimal and enduring answers to questions of policy.

In a world in which the means to satisfy human wants are far more limited than those wants, an adversary politics is to be expected. The attitudes of people and their acquired behavior patterns, with respect to competitive or cooperative action, influence political style. Hence, the adversary character of politics might be modified by culture or experience to allow greater degrees of cooperation and a genuine search for the public interest. Such a search might take the form of problem solving, an approach especially applicable to difficulties in man's relationship to the environment. Possibly the most familiar example of this approach is the use of citizen committees or commissions on issues of public concern.

Of course, not all issues that divide public opinion are amenable to treatment as problems. Not all value choices can be resolved by rational methods based on adequate information and analysis. Nevertheless, a large number of man's environmental difficulties do have a problematic character. For example, control of agriculturally harmful insects without adverse side effects requires a problem-solving approach. Similarly, research is needed to understand the transformations of chemical substances in emissions from smokestacks and exhaust pipes. These and many other areas of environmental concern cannot be dealt with effectively merely by ascertaining the state of public opinion and awarding the official decision to the politically most influential point of view.

Toward Better Modes of Public Decision Making

The hazard of traditional adversary approaches is that they are not only insufficient to cope with a large number of man's environmental difficulties but, additionally, they may lead to decisions that make the difficulties worse. And if adversary approaches to political issues are inevitable, what hope is there that human society can cope with its environmental problems? The best hope may lie in a combination of adversary and problem-solving approaches which would help to avoid the most harmful effects of conflict situations without seeking the probably unattainable condition of a thoroughly rational and cooperative politics.

Two important properties of an ideal system of public decision making would be error detection and self-correction. Both are needed. Self-corrective mechanisms usually take the form of cybernetic or feedback loops. Information to the effect that a certain decision has been erroneous in relation to specified goals or human welfare may be too long delayed in the feedback process to prevent serious damage before the error is corrected. Moreover, the goal or policy toward which self-corrective action is taken may itself be intrinsically erroneous in the sense that if realized it would entail unwanted effects generally harmful to human well-being. Thus a means to detect error in advance of normal feedback would be highly desirable.

One practical means toward safer and wiser public decisions is through full disclosure of the information and considerations entering into the decision process. All human organizations, including government, show introvertive tendencies. Organizational commitments tend to be perpetuated and protected from possible adverse scrutiny. Organizational units and personnel have been shown to resist efforts to change a course of action once set. Agencies of government and business regularly invoke secrecy and practice subterfuge in order to avoid questions regarding their motives or the full range of probable outcomes of their actions. In the absence of well-developed means for examining the official processes of planning and decison making, the unofficial representatives of the public find themselves placed in a disadvantaged relationship to the duly constituted authorities.

The conventional public hearing has proved to be a generally ineffectual and misleading way of making public information about official action. The hearing format emphasizes the adversary relationships between proponents and opponents of official proposals. But public hearings have seldom been provided for purposes of full disclosure or critical questioning of agency plans. It is doubtful if more than a very small percentage of public hearings have ever directly or significantly influenced the decisons of public authorities, including legislative committees. For such hearings to be more than symbolic rituals, the conditions under which they take place must be reinforced by provisions such as the following.

First, means are needed to increase the responsiveness and accountability of individual legislators and the legislative process. Responsible self-government might be made more likely by statutory prescriptions regarding legislative procedures and the drafting of agency policies and programs. These should include, as minimal requirements, specifications regarding the methods to be used, the character of the information to be sought, and the parties to be consulted.

Second, means must be provided for citizens to examine the record of official decision making, to test its findings, and to question the authors of official proposals. These means should provide against self-interested abuse or uninformed obstructionist tactics. But they should also remove the cloak of official secrecy from the public business. They should provide against tendencies to evasion, timidity, or arrogance on the part of duly constituted authorities.

Devices to achieve these objectives include (a) reformed public hearing procedures (presently to be discussed), (b) a published flow chart showing the stages and major decision points in agency planning at which citizen input is appropriate, and (c) the right of access to the courts of law to challenge the legality of agency action. The last device is now provided by liberalized doctrines regarding class-action suits and "standing" to sue. But these liberalized provisions have been under attack by economic interests and judicial conservatives.

Many of the foregoing provisions are prescribed by Section 102 of the National Environmental Policy Act of 1969 (NEPA). This act, and especially the environmental impact statement and freedom of information provision that Section 102 of the act contains, has been so important in the following case studies on citizen environmental action that it seems desirable to print this section of the act in full:

> The Congress authorizes and directs that to the fullest extent possible: (1) the policies, regulations, and public laws of the United States shall be interpreted and administered in accordance with the policies set forth in this Act, and (2) all agencies of the Federal Government shall—
>
> (A) utilize a systematic, interdisciplinary approach which will insure the integrated use of the natural and social sciences and the environmental design arts in planning and in decisionmaking which may have an impact on man's environment;
>
> (B) identify and develop methods and procedures, in consultation with the Council on Environmental Quality established by Title II of this Act, which will insure that presently unquantified environmental amenities and values may be given appropriate consideration in decisionmaking along with economic and technical considerations;
>
> (C) include in every recommendation or report on proposals for legislation and other major Federal actions significantly affecting the quality of the human environment, a detailed statement by the responsible official on—

(i) the environmental impact of the proposed action,

(ii) any adverse environmental effects which cannot be avoided should the proposal be implemented,

(iii) alternatives to the proposed action,

(iv) the relationship between local short-term uses of man's environment and the maintenance and enhancement of long-term productivity, and

(v) any irreversible and irretrievable commitments of resources which would be involved in the proposed action should it be implemented.

Prior to making any detailed statement, the responsible Federal official shall consult with and obtain the comments of any Federal agency which has jurisdiction by law or special expertise with respect to any environmental impact involved. Copies of such statements and the comments and views of the appropriate Federal, State, and local agencies, which are authorized to develop and enforce environmental standards, shall be made available to the President, the Council on Environmental Quality and to the public as provided by Section 552 of Title 5, United States Code, and shall accompany the proposal through the existing agency review processes;

(D) study, develop, and describe appropriate alternatives to recommended courses of action in any proposal which involves unresolved conflicts concerning alternative uses of available resources;

(E) recognize the worldwide and long-range character of environmental problems and, where consistent with the foreign policy of the United States, lend appropriate support to initiatives, resolutions, and programs designed to maximize international cooperation in anticipating and preventing a decline in the quality of mankind's world environment;

(F) make available to States, counties, municipalities, institutions, and individuals, advice and information useful in restoring, maintaining, and enhancing the quality of the environment;

(G) initiate and utilize ecological information in the planning and development of resource-oriented projects; and

(H) assist the Council on Environmental Quality established by Title II of this Act.

Although the NEPA is a giant step forward in enabling the citizen to exact responsiveness from his government on environmental issues, it does not meet all requisites for responsible government. Public hearings are potentially more meaningful because of the criteria and written record required by the NEPA. But the act makes no significant provision to insure the good faith or procedural adequacy of public hearings. In an article entitled "Public Involvement in Government Decision," M. Rupert Cutler and Daniel A. Bronstein propose that:

Resource agency hearings would be more useful, both to the public and to the agency, if conducted by a person independent of the proposing function in the agency, and if this independent hearing officer were allowed to make his own report on the merits for the information of those empowered to reach a final decision. Hearings should be held early in the planning process at convenient, neutral locations, after at least thirty days' advance notice and adequate publicity. They should be conducted in a relatively unhurried manner, with reporters on hand to make *verbatim* transcripts of the proceedings. The product of these hearings, in addition to the transcript and a tally of proponents and opponents, should be a report on the merits of the issues to the decisionmakers. These reports should be based on a sifting of the worthwhile contributions of fact and philosophy from the rhetoric—much as a judge sifts the evidence—and should suggest an equitable decision or set of alternative decisions, supported by reasons much as they are offered in a court's opinion.

These authors also emphasize the need for sufficient lead time in the review process to permit citizen groups to make their own studies and arrive at their own policy conclusions. When government agencies schedule hearings at their own convenience, and often with a view toward minimizing public input or interference, the citizen is at a double disadvantage, lacking the staff and fiscal resources of the bureaucracy. A familiar strategy of the authorities has been to postpone hearings until projects are far enough along to make plausible the argument that so much time, effort, and money have already been invested in the project that it would be an irresponsible waste of public resources not to let it move forward.

The objective sought by these and other provisions and devices is not to hamstring or cripple public administration, but to make it more responsive and accountable in a practical way. This objective is based upon the unexceptional premise that the United States has been ideologically committed to democratic or popular government. It is also premised on the proposition that the best way to keep the public officials honest, diligent, and alert to the public interest is through procedures requiring full disclosure of all factors bearing significantly on official decisions. These procedures are viable, however, only to the extent that people make them so. Democratic self-government, in its representative form in the United States, is one of the most difficult kinds of social effort to undertake. It works well only when thousands of citizens cooperate to make it work through their study, organizing, questioning, and follow-through. It is a demanding form of government, and its fundamental component—the functional citizen—will be identified in the concluding section of this chapter. Meanwhile, however, an important factor in enabling the citizen to function effectively should be considered.

This factor is the continuing availability of competent legal counsel. In the late 1960s, following broadened interpretations by the courts of the right of citizens to sue, public-interest law groups developed rapidly and have gained demonstrable influence in the shaping of public policies. Evaluating this development, Burt Schorr, writing in the *Wall Street Journal,* observed that:

> True it's an uneven influence, frequently frustrated by bureaucratic recalcitrance and now hurt by recession-caused reductions in funds and manpower at the disposal of public-interest organizations, plus two recent Supreme Court setbacks. Yet the federal apparatus is feeling its impact at many points.[1]

The reductions in funds have followed largely from the financial pinch felt by foundations whose investments have declined in value. The setbacks in the courts have been, first, a somewhat stricter interpretation of rights to bring suit in the federal courts on behalf of particular classes of persons (class-action suits), and, second, a court ruling that attorneys' fees may not be recovered from the losing side in public-interest litigation unless specifically provided by the statutes under which the action has been brought.

These rulings tend to favor corporate and government interests, particularly with respect to the recovery of attorneys' fees. Both large corporations and government agencies retain legal counsel and expert witnesses that public-interest organizations, funded only or primarily by the voluntary contributions of citizens, are hard put to match. An effort to insure the continuing availability of legal talent to citizen-action groups has been undertaken through the Council for Public Interest Law, an organization co-chaired by Mitchell Ragonin and former Environmental Protection Agency Administrator William Ruckelshaus. Among possibilities considered are the funding of public-interest lawyers through federal, state, or local government treasuries, bar associations, and public subscription.

The problem is one of equity. In a society increasingly managed

---

[1] July 15, 1975, p. 1, col. 1

by large organizations, and in which adversary procedures are invoked in the settlement of policy disputes, the contest between organized corporate and bureaucratic power and volunteer citizen groups is so uneven as to invalidate the procedural significance of the right to judicial remedy for alleged abuses of public environmental rights. Some means of adequately representing the collective interests of "unincorporated" citizens is necessary to make the idea of functional citizenship fully meaningful.

It may, of course, be argued that representation of the public interest is the very purpose of government. But in a heterogeneous society in which value consensus is weak and pressure-group organization is strong, it may be unrealistic to expect the public agencies honestly to seek the public interest or to consider all alternatives in meeting public needs. The idea of public funding to represent the interests of citizens who are affected by environmental acts of government, but lack the financial means to pursue constitutional remedies, is surely not inconsistent with the American concept of a government of checks and balances.

Functional Citizenship

The role and responsibility of the private individual is critical to the effectiveness of democratic self-government. But the place of the citizen in the structure of American government has largely been neglected. Although the relationship of the individual to the state has been a well-worked theme of Anglo-American political theory, the citizenship function seems largely to have been taken for granted. The role of the citizenry has not begun to receive the attention lavished on the presidency, the Congress, and the courts.

The federal and state constitutions and statutes describe generally the roles and responsibilities of executives, legislators, and judges. Legislation regarding the individual citizen is, however, chiefly concerned with civil rights. The role of the citizen in the structure of government has been specified chiefly in relation to the right to vote; but not all citizens are allowed to vote. The other major attribute of citizenship, the obligation to pay taxes, is not confined exclusively to citizens. Jury duty touches comparatively few individuals. And so neither law nor popular theory of government provides a coherent or consistent concept of the functions of the citizen in American society.

It is curious that the roles and responsibilities of citizenship should be so poorly defined in a nation in which the importance of the individual and the rights of citizens have been strongly emphasized in political rhetoric and tradition. In part, an explanation may be found in the tendency of American politics toward tacit understandings and vaguely defined, but broadly held, general assumptions. In those decades of the nineteenth century characterized by Jeffersonian and Jacksonian political attitudes, it seems probable that there was a general consensus concerning the relationship between citizen and government. But that was an era of minimal government, with most public functions performed at local and state levels and of a character readily understandable to ordinary individuals. The nature of public office, and the capacity of the citizen to serve in it, were epitomized by the familiar assertion of President Andrew Jackson in his first annual message to the Congress:

> The duties of all public officers are, or at least admit of being made, so plain and simple that men of intelligence may readily qualify themselves for their performance.

This opinion is no longer plausible nor generally held. Technical and scientific expertise, requiring years of extensive preparation and experience, are required for the performance of a large number of public tasks. Regardless of their intelligence, persons cannot readily prepare themselves for the more demanding public functions like, for example, food and drug administration, aviation, nuclear reactor safety, or the analysis of flood control alternatives. The citizen can seldom offer expertise equal to that of the professional public executive or technician. How, then, can the concerned amateur assist, correct, or control the behavior of the expert?

There are obvious advantages in expertise that society cannot afford to lose. Yet this expert knowledge has often been used short-sightedly or unwisely. Environmental disputes have often been fought out between concerned citizens/generalists and mission-oriented technicians. How can citizen action play an appropriate and effective role, and avoid superseding informed and tested professional judgment?

Requirements of full disclosure and the threat of confrontation by informed citizens and their expert witnesses in public hearings and the courts appear to be having a salutary effect upon the planning functions of various federal and state agencies. Some recalcitrant bureaus and stiff-necked bureaucrats can still be found in Washington and in the capitals of the states. Nevertheless, knowledge that agency plans and projects are likely to be scrutinized and may be challenged encourages attention to the considerations specified in the National Environmental Policy Act as guidelines for agency planning. And the tie-up or defeat of agency projects in the courts is almost certain to feed back into agency planning procedures and decison-making criteria.

There is some evidence to indicate that public officials and technical experts have been learning from experience. There is a tendency for government agencies to go earlier to the public for opinions and reactions than was formerly the case. The Army Corps of Engineers, for example, attempts to communicate at much earlier stages in its planning with groups who it knows are concerned and who may be adversaries if these concerns remain unrecognized or unsatisfied. Even the major political parties have attempted to broaden their bases of popular support through more representation and input from the public at large. But the chief assurance that these changes will be lasting, and not merely tactical, is in the apparent movement toward institutionalizing functional citizenship.

Most of the groups whose actions are reported in this volume have been extemporaneous and *ad hoc* in nature. They have been formed in response to particular environmental issues. Many have not survived the resolution of the issue, others have become continuing organizations, maintaining a watch on the duly constituted authorities.

But it should not be thought that in environmental controversies the governmental authorities are always "wrong" and organized citizens always "right." Government agencies are often found on both sides of an issue, as, for example, in respect to Miami, Florida's proposed airport in the Everglades. There are cases in which the authorities risk political reprisal and high-level executive displeasure in defending the quality of the environment against exploitive local interests. To argue, as the following cases do by implication, that government too often aids and abets environmental exploitation, contrary to the general public interest, is not to contend that this is the invariable posture of government. The fact that citizens have repeatedly been compelled to organize to defend the environment against the agencies of government is a truth, but it is not all of the truth concerning the politics of environmental quality in the United States. That voluntary citizen action has been a positive and constructive force for more responsible government is, however, a generalization that we believe will stand without successful challenge.

The institutionalization of citizen action through generalized environmental action groups and especially through public-interest law firms, such as the Environmental Defense Fund and the Natural Resources Defense Council, imparts attributes of continuity and credibility that citizens, individually, can acquire only with exceptional personal influence or distinction. These organizations and the thousands of citizens who voluntarily support them and have caused them to work are perhaps our best hope that the United States of America may be governed more wisely, honestly, and effectively in the years ahead than it has been in the more recent decades of the past.

Readings

Caldwell, Lynton K. "Responsiveness and Responsibility: The Anomalous Problem of the Environment." In *People vs. Government: The Responsiveness of American Institutions,* edited by Leroy N. Rieselbach. Bloomington: Indiana University Press, 1975, 300–327.

Citizens Advisory Committee on Environmental Quality. *Citizens Make the Difference: Case Studies of Environmental Action.* Washington, D.C.: Citizens Advisory Committee on Environmental Quality, 1973.

Cramton, Roger C. and Barry B. Boyer. "Citizen Suits in the Environmental Field: Peril or Promise?" *Ecology Law Quarterly,* 26 (Summer 1972), 407–436.

Endres, Mary Ellen. "Environmental Protection: Citizen Action Forcing Agency Compliance Under Limited Judicial Review." *St. Mary's Law Journal,* 6 (Summer 1974), 421–443.

Katz, Joan M. "The Games Bureaucrats Play: Hide and Seek Under the Freedom of Information Act." *Texas Law Review,* 48 (November 1970), 1261–1284.

Large, Donald W. "Is Anybody Listening? The Problem of Access in Environmental Litigation." *Wisconsin Law Review,* 2 (1972), 62–113.

Mannino, E. F. "Strengthening Citizen Input Under the National Environmental Policy Act." *Pennsylvania Bar Association Quarterly,* 45 (June 1974), 411–422.

Sax, Joseph L. *Defending the Environment: A Strategy for Citizen Action.* New York: Alfred A. Knopf, 1971.

Winder, John S., Jr. "Citizen Groups, the Law and the Government." *Environment Law Review,* 2 (1971), 40–50.

Citizens
and the
Environment

I

CRITICAL AREAS OF THE NATURAL ENVIRONMENT

The chapters and cases in Part I focus on the impact of human activities upon the natural world. The interrelated aggregation of the basic elements of nature—land, water, air, and living things—constitutes the complex ecological supersystem called the biosphere. This sphere of life forms an envelope surrounding the entire earth, extending from beneath the surface of the soil and the seas to the upper reaches of the atmosphere.

Although life is unevenly distributed within this sphere, it is everywhere interconnected. Threats to the integrity or survival of any part or element of it could have ramifying consequences deleterious to other aspects, or to the planetary life-support system as a whole. Thus, deteriorating air quality could affect plant and animal life, modify weather and, ultimately, alter climate. Or misuse of land could cause the siltation, salinization, or contamination of lakes, streams, and coastal waters with destructive effects on marine life and, in extreme cases, could modify climate.

The quality and, indeed, the continuation of all life, not excepting humanity, depend upon maintenance of the life-supporting elements of the biosphere. Human welfare, comfort, and the satisfaction of material and psychological needs depend upon the continuing integrity of the natural environment. But the emergence during this century of a populous, urbanized, industrialized way of life has occurred with relatively little public awareness of its cumulative impact on the natural world. Early warnings by naturalists and environmental scientists were

3

largely unheeded until, by the nineteen sixties, the deterioration of the natural environment became obvious.

In the United States, the growth of public awareness of environmental damage was accompanied by efforts on the part of concerned people to stop or to reverse the destructive trends. In their efforts, they invariably became involved with government and, more specifically, with public officials at all jurisdictional levels—local, state, federal—and at all levels of the administrative bureaucracies and the courts. And although these concerned citizens characteristically sought to invoke the powers of government on behalf of environmental protection, they often found themselves confronting deeply entrenched bureaucratic powers programmed to serve the very activities that were impairing the natural environment.

The explanation of this conflict between environmentally concerned citizens and government agencies promoting the exploitation or domestication of the natural environment is, in a significant way, historical. The emergence of the environmental quality movement during the nineteen sixties is explained by the simultaneous upsurge of scientific knowledge, public information, and cumulative environmental damage. The extraordinary explosion of population and economic activity in the nineteen fifties was encouraged and assisted by governmental policies intended to promote expansive economic growth. The environmental impacts of long-standing programs in flood control, drainage, irrigation, power development, recreation, agriculture, road building, and housing were exaggerated by burgeoning public budgets and a booming economic marketplace. But these governmental activities proceeded under separate, and sometimes competing, administrations. No means were provided for coordinating their interactions or mitigating their impacts—direct or indirect.

A major step toward reorienting the programs of federal agencies with regard to their environmental impacts was taken in 1969 with the passage of the National Environmental Policy Act. This legislation marks the beginning of a systematic effort to reform the impact of government upon the environment. But it is only a beginning, and as many of the cases in this volume will show, there is a long way to go before the American people or their governments reach a consensus on the basic values and priorities to be served in the use, protection, and preservation of the natural environment. Yet, to some extent, the cases and controversies described in Part I represent the process by which accommodation, if not consensus, is achieved. They also illustrate the way in which bureaucratic arrogance and technocratic "tunnel vision" have aroused normally quiescent citizens to activist roles. Governmental unresponsiveness to values widely shared among the American people has created a functional citizenship that no amount of peacetime patriotic exhortation could have induced.

The cases in Part I illustrate action that citizens have taken to protect critical areas of the environment. In some areas, notably air and water quality control, coastal zone management, and protection of endangered species, legislative successes have been recorded. Land-use planning legislation, however, has been slow to win acceptance in Congress and in most states. Municipal efforts to protect environmental quality and control physical growth have been subjected to close surveillance by unpredictable courts. The development of special policies appropriate to the protection of particular environmental areas has, at least in principle, been accepted as a fact of American civic life.

1

Land Use

Introduction

In modern Western societies, land-use decisions have been based primarily on economic rather than ecological concerns. The economic value of land has depended either on its direct contribution to the production process or its attractiveness as a commodity in the marketplace. So, land has been used for mining, forestry, hunting, agriculture, and human settlements; if it had no exploitable economic value, the land was left as a wilderness. But land might also be acquired as an investment, either for speculative purposes or for security during periods of uncertain monetary values. Conceiving land-use policies from a perspective restricted to narrowly defined economic values has obscured the ecological and social values of land.

For instance, building cities adjacent to estuaries affects the adjoining coastal zone and continental shelf, usually in biologically destructive ways. Land used for an airport complex will have an impact on watersheds and the atmosphere of the locality. Policies which permit strip mining for coal have led to landscape degradation, disruption of traditional life-styles, and deterioration of the surrounding natural environment. Communities in neighboring areas may be affected as well. Visitors to Maine will be affected if oil refineries are built on popular coastal vacation sites. All Americans will be affected if areas of Alaska and Florida are designated as wilderness or if their natural endowments are disfigured or destroyed. If a city in Oregon limits the amount of land allowed for urban growth, it may affect citizens' mobility elsewhere. If the nation's land is viewed as a commons, then New Yorkers have a right to express policy preferences for land use in Texas. The pressure for changing laws to control the use of land in the United States has been increasing dramatically since the early 1970s. The need for an ecological basis for land-use planning has emerged gradually, and mounting pressures upon the limited land resources of the nation have prompted serious debate and new legislation.

It has been estimated that construction in the United States between the years 1970 and 2000 may exceed the total construction of the last two centuries. The U.S. Census Bureau projects that by the year 2000 the population of the United States will have risen to 220–285 million. But population growth and projections about construction account for only a part of the pressure for land use. Increasing affluence is also a factor. The Commission on Population Growth and the American Future has projected that per capita consumption expenditures will double in the next thirty years. This means more automobiles, recreation sites, travel, and second homes. Second home starts and rural lot sales number hundreds of thousands each year. Expanding urban areas consume an estimated 420,000 acres of land annually, according to the Council on Environmental Quality. These pressures, and many others, upon the use of land raise serious problems of priority for public and private lands of the nation and for the quality of life generally.

Of the two-thirds of the land in this country not owned by the federal government, about 3 percent is owned by state and local government and 2 percent is reserved for American Indians, although Indian lands have been repeatedly invaded for non-Indian activities. The remaining 1.3 billion acres is privately owned. Included in this private sector are most of the nation's urban areas, where 70 percent of the population lives. According to some forecasts, one-sixth of the continental land area of the nation will be urban by the year 2000. Private land is the subject of greatest controversy concerning land-use planning. Early American colonists brought with them a doctrine of the private ownership of land, and private ownership included rights to its exploitation in any form. But during the last century, public interest in the use of privately owned land has risen greatly. This public interest in land use has been expressed in various forms of control over private lands, such as zoning to control private developments, subdivision restrictions, scenic easements, public health laws and inspections, building codes and inspections, and planning for public amenities and improvements. Such efforts have most often occurred in urban areas. In rural areas, soil conservation programs and subsidy schemes have influenced land use. But today public control of private lands still presents many unsolved problems.

Land-use planning in the United States has traditionally occurred at the local rather than the state or federal level, and the wide diversity of local authorities is characterized by an equally wide diversity of legal powers. Used primarily for preserving property values or increasing assessed valuations for taxation, local land-use regulations have contributed to urban sprawl and unplanned development. Local governments, which are dependent on property taxes for revenue, find it difficult to resist development. Moreover, regional problems of environmental management are beyond the scope of local jurisdictions.

Although local and state governments have been taking an increasingly active role in the conflict of private property versus the public good, the use of police power to achieve orderly development and to protect natural resources and aesthetic values creates problems for which there are no simple solutions. For example, the "taking" of land from private owners presents many difficult legal issues. Landowners are entitled to "just compensation" when public restrictions on the use of their property is found by the courts to be a "taking" under the Fourth Amendment of the United States Constitution.

No state has enacted a comprehensive land-use program, but many have enacted separate statutes directed at specific land-use problems. Hawaii and Maine, for example, have provided for extensive control on a statewide basis. Some of the defined areas in which certain states have prohibited certain land uses illustrate trends. Coastal wetlands laws in eastern seaboard states such as Massachusetts, Rhode Island, New Hampshire, North Carolina, and others control dredging and filling. Delaware prohibits heavy industry and offshore bulk-transfer facilities in a specified coastal zone. The state of Washington prohibits surface drilling for oil and gas in certain coastal areas. Alaska, Hawaii, and Idaho have enacted innovative legislation that zones land against hazards near airports. Surface-water zoning, which regulates recreational activities on public waters, has been extensively applied in Minnesota, Vermont, and Michigan. Maine regulates land use for commercial and industrial developments in excess of twenty acres. Power plant siting regulations have relatively recently been put into effect in Vermont, Maryland, and New Hampshire. Land-use regulations for scenic rivers, transmission line routing, and the use of shorelands have increased dramatically since the late 1960s. New institutional arrangements for regional environmental management and land use also have been established. Of particular note are the Hackensack Meadowland Development Commission, the San Francisco Bay Commission (see Chapter 3, Coastal Zone), and the Tahoe Regional Planning Agency.

National growth problems and policies for land use are intimately related. Population growth as well as industrial and economic development lead to growth in the utilization of resources, in the size of communities, the number of airports, schools, highways, and hospitals and, ultimately, to growth in the development of land, much of it concentrated in the suburban belts around rapidly expanding cities. There are very few federal or state laws to control growth and many to promote it. Numerous federal and state laws encourage highway and road extensions, construction industries, and the development of sewer and water facilities far removed from main urban areas. (See Chapter 7, The Economy and Growth, for details on growth.) Prudent growth planning should calculate and coordinate population distribution, housing needs, urban development, agriculture, recreation, and open space in conjunction with the development of energy facilities and industrial production, water distribution, sanitation and waste disposal, and transportation. In recent decades, there has been some planning for specific land uses associated with growth, such as utility plant sites, utility corridors, recreation sites, sites for waste disposal, and urban expansion zones. But there has been little effort to develop clear goals or policy guidelines for national growth targets. Today, decisions concerning land use and growth are made by innumerable public and private agencies without guidance by a rational and comprehensive plan reflecting a broadly based public consensus.

The inadequacy of federal, state, and local laws and institutional arrangements for environmentally sound land-use control has been recognized particularly since the late 1960s. As of early 1976 no national land-use planning bill had passed the Congress, although several versions of the National Land Use Planning Act of 1970 introduced by U.S. Senator Henry M. Jackson have passed the Senate. Opponents of land-use legislation, including the ultraconservative Liberty Lobby, succeeded through a procedural maneuver in preventing a House vote on a bill in the 93rd Congress. The principal features of the proposed legislation were those embodied in S. 268 in the 93rd Congress, which would have assisted the states, within a specified period of three years, in establishing a state land-use planning process. States would prepare and continuously revise an inventory of natural resources, devise a method for identifying large-scale development projects, and identify areas of critical environmental concern, for example, areas impacted by major federal or industrial facilities. Within five years states would establish statewide land-use programs. The proposed act would not have preempted effective state land-use programs and existing and related federal programs. It would have returned to the states some land-use controls ceded to local governments through zoning acts of the 1920s, but the preemption of local authority would have been minimal.

Aldo Leopold, one of America's most famous conservationists, pessimistically predicted in the 1940s that ecologically sound land use was a century or two away. But a task force on land use and urban growth reported in 1973 that a new mood in the United States expressed a growing awareness of ecological dimensions of the land.[1] It seems that land use is gradually being viewed as more than solely a matter of economics. Growth and development proposals are increasingly being tested against environmental criteria. The treatment of land as a commodity and its evaluation in almost wholly economic terms is being modified on behalf of a broader range of human values.

CASE I   Preserving Open Space: Jefferson County, Colorado

The Colorado Division of Planning has estimated that the state's population may grow by 44 percent between 1970 and 1980. Migration

---

[1] William K. Reilly, ed., *The Use of Land: A Citizen's Policy Guide to Urban Growth* (New York: Thomas Y. Crowell, 1973), p. 318.

to Colorado, in pursuit of employment opportunities and beautiful Rocky Mountain living conditions, has made Colorado one of the fastest growing states in the country. The fastest growing county in Colorado, Jefferson County, has a population growth rate four times that of India, with the population density of the county quadrupling between 1950 and 1970. By 1971, citizens in the county were alarmed at the rate open areas were being destroyed to accommodate the uncontrolled growth of population, industry, and residential development. Urbanization threatened to destroy the beauty of the rocky foothills and rolling plains immediately adjacent to and partly encircling metropolitan Denver.

Fears of citizens, conservationists, and environmental groups were shared by some professional planners, representatives of municipalities, and officials of park and recreation districts. Many public authorities had attempted to plan for growth in Jefferson County. The county Planning Department, the Regional Council of Governments, the Regional Transportation District, and planners in a number of municipalities had provided for natural areas and some open space in master plans. But citizens discovered that, with the exception of the municipalities, none of the agencies had funds for purchasing open space. Open space was not being purchased by the county, it was not ensured in local plans, and it was not preserved by zoning. Natural landscapes were not going to be available for long. Convinced that the rampant growth rate would increase the degradation of the unique and relatively unspoiled mountain region, citizens organized to retain some of the remaining open space.

Realizing that county zoning laws were inadequate to protect the surrounding foothills, plains, and wetlands, and knowing that there were no public funds for the task, citizens had no option other than buying open space. In the fall of 1971, concerned citizens began to organize a campaign for educating the community toward the value of preserving open space. Led by the Jefferson County League of Women Voters, the citizens' group known as PLAN Jeffco was formed. PLAN Jeffco resolved, with the support of numerous conservation and public service groups, to have an open-space land proposal on the ballot of the general election of November 7, 1972. Through extremely efficient organization, communication, and research, PLAN Jeffco led a successful public education campaign that culminated in a majority county vote to tax itself to purchase and preserve some lands in a natural condition.

The Actors

The main participants in the case at the local government level were county officials and their agencies from both the unincorporated areas and the cities and towns. City managers and mayors, along with the Jefferson County Planning Department, the Regional Council of Governments, and the board of county commissioners participated in policy formation.

But it seems fair to say that PLAN Jeffco, the group that designed the county tax resolution and the detailed plans for implementing the open-space proposal, was the dominant participant. The Jefferson County League of Women Voters and more than thirty other organizations endorsed PLAN Jeffco's work and lent financial or organizing support. PLAN Boulder (of Boulder, Colorado) helped establish the organizational foundation of PLAN Jeffco and, therefore, had some indirect policy influence.

The U.S. Department of Interior's Resource and Land Information Program and the Federation of Rocky Mountain States indirectly contributed to the implementation phase of the policy process by cooperating in a computer modeling study. This study was generated by PLAN Jeffco, and its findings were accepted by the Citizens Open Space Advisory Committee as the core of operations.

The Policy Process

From the beginning, the general objective of PLAN Jeffco was to buy up open-space areas in Jefferson County and zone them to remain in a natural state. Special emphasis was given to a balanced growth for the county, and consequently land logically sought by developers was not sought by PLAN Jeffco. Marginal lands such as table mountains, hogbacks, and floodplains were generally the main sites for acquisition. Financing the plan was to be arranged through a proposed ½ percent county sales tax, which would raise an estimated $4 million annually. The open-space purchasing plan was to be implemented by elected county commissioners and a board of advisors and citizens. PLAN Jeffco, its volunteers, and supporting organizations attempted to achieve these general objectives in less than one year.

There were two major stages in the policy process. The first stage was drafting a resolution and supporting it politically. This resolution was accepted by the voters in an altered form in 1972. But the second stage, the implementation of the acquisition scheme, has developed slowly.

The policy process in this case can be understood best by examining the three steps of the first stage of the process: organizing the PLAN Jeffco group and drafting the open-space resolution, which revealed the specific objectives of the preservationists, were the first two steps. The canvass of registered voters to win local and national support for the cause of preservation was the third step, and it reveals the skill and efficiency of the citizens' planning. Finally, we will need to examine the second stage, the implementation of PLAN Jeffco's resolution during 1973 and 1974, to judge the effectiveness of the newly established policy.

Prompted by Carol Karlin, a prominent activist in the Jefferson County League of Women Voters, conservationists, civic groups, and homeowners' associations expressed increasing interest during the spring of 1972 in the concept of purchasing open space. PLAN Jeffco, created in January 1972, had undertaken elementary research and contacted interested persons and organizations. An open-space conference held in March formed a charter, elected directors, and discussed the problems of preservation in areas of rapid urban growth. More than 100 people participated in the conference: representatives from environmental groups, the general public, county and city planning agencies, and the federal Bureau of Outdoor Recreation. Members of PLAN Boulder explained how they had promoted and helped implement a city sales tax in 1967 for purchasing open space. The nature of land-use problems was illustrated by first showing slides at the conference and later taking a field trip through the county. The most important outcome of the conference was the formulation of a strategy to promote a political campaign. The objective of the campaign was to influence the voters of the county to adopt a tax-based land acquisition proposal on November 7.

For the first four months, PLAN Jeffco focused on efficiently employing the skills of the board members and resource people. An attorney helped draft the group's bylaws and a preliminary ballot resolution. The basic action plan was largely developed from the League of Women Voters' previous land-use study. Committees specializing in mapping, giving slide presentations, operating a speakers' bureau, writing newsletters and brochures, and handling press releases and public relations all generated public support. Representatives of PLAN Jeffco regularly participated in local environmental symposia and hearings. Some resource people focused on raising funds from individual membership subscriptions, homeowners' groups, recreation clubs, service groups, builders, architects, banks, and manufacturers. A thorough survey of nationwide open-space land purchase plans was conducted through agencies such as the United States Geological Survey, the Bureau of Outdoor Recreation, and the Colorado Game, Fish, and Parks Department.

The most crucial step in these early months was the drafting of the April 1972 PLAN Jeffco presentation. This rigorous and exhaustive five-page fact sheet revealed the depth of PLAN Jeffco's planning. Used in presentations to commissioners, community groups, and government agencies, the report itemized detailed statements on mapping, directions of growth, the deficiency of existing open-space plans, population density projections, and economic impacts of the open-space plan. The report also detailed property tax implications, the financing of the open-space plan, the availability of federal funds, the methods to obtain land, the potential areas for purchase, and potential uses of open-space acquisitions. The sophistication of this early planning and contact with the public enhanced the political power of PLAN Jeffco.

Drafting the ballot resolution was the principal task from May through July 1972. The resolution received valuable assistance from a legal counsel and professional administrators. The heart of PLAN Jeffco's proposal was the resolution which was to be presented to the county commissioners. Normally, these elected officials drafted their own resolutions. Because resolutions by boards of commissioners in Colorado have the same force as state laws and city ordinances, they may be changed only at subsequent elections. The PLAN Jeffco resolution was unique for a number of reasons: Jefferson County had never had a sales tax and was now called upon to institute a ½ percent sales tax for purchase of open space; the tax would generate up to $4 million annually in a county budget of only $20 million; the county had never purchased open space, yet the resolution called for this exclusively; funds were to be used for lands in a natural state and not for development projects such as swimming pools and tennis courts; a formula was included for distributing revenue equitably between cities and rural centers; and the resolution insisted on including a citizens' advisory committee to help officials establish priorities for purchasing land.

The citizens' group had to take into account many political and jurisdictional conflicts that could be expected from such a resolution. Many cities wanted to attend to their own priorities. Because 90 percent of the taxpayers lived in cities and towns, and a large portion of the open-space lands lay in the unincorporated areas of the county, PLAN Jeffco proposed an equitable revenue formula later accepted by the commissioners. Opposition came from low-income earners who, as expected, resisted extra tax levies. City governments did not want their own tax plans jeopardized, and some city officials and city dwellers opposed regional and rural land purchases with city tax dollars. But PLAN Jeffco worked skillfully to resolve many of these conflicts so that the resolution had a good chance of becoming law.

The impact that PLAN Jeffco had on policy can be measured by the details incorporated in the resolution. To counter city councils' objections, PLAN Jeffco pursued a highly effective campaign to woo their members. The press was invited to attend meetings between PLAN Jeffco and city councils. Compromises were drawn up, but conflict persisted. At first, the conservationists lost ground, but they responded by intensifying speaking engagements and soliciting favorable coverage in regional and national news. Open-space tours conducted by PLAN Jeffco, and well-planned conferences with city managers and mayors, seemed to increase public support for preservation.

In August 1972, the board of county commissioners agreed to place the issue of open space on the November ballot. From August to October, PLAN Jeffco increased publicity by distributing 76,000 brochures, numerous fact sheets, and newsletters, by using speakers, presenting slide shows, and drafting speech cards for its public relations people. A successful eight-week editorial release plan for metropolitan newspaper and television coverage brought enormous publicity to the PLAN Jeffco fight. A mammoth door-to-door campaign, involving 140,000 voters in 725 square miles, was successfully carried out in two months by more than 400 volunteers; in some precincts 60 percent of them were students. By November, the PLAN Jeffco proposal had the endorsement of thirty-four organizations. All the careful planning and strategies were rewarded by a favorable 51,140 to 42,309 vote on November 7.

At this point, the citizens of Jefferson County had successfully completed the first major stage in the policy process. The resolution was now law, and preservationists had legislative backing for their open-space purchasing program. In the second stage of the policy process, the implementation of the law, PLAN Jeffco turned its resources to acquiring land and establishing citizen input in decision making. To this end, task forces were established to compile a roster of qualified citizens for inclusion on the Citizens Open Space Advisory Committee (COSAC) which was responsible for selecting and purchasing sites, subject to the approval of the county commissioners. The citizens also considered creative ways of using the tax revenues that would be available in September 1973.

As early as December 1972, PLAN Jeffco had suggested specific sites for purchase, but citizens realized that a more comprehensive countywide plan was needed that would indicate alternative open-space purchase sites. The plan would require detailed maps and selection guidelines. For about four months, PLAN Jeffco concentrated on constructing maps and preparing a methodology for selecting sites. The maps identified crucial features of land in the county, such as the location of schools, landforms, highways, watersheds, and the proximity of residential areas to open-space sites. A ranking scale was used to weight priorities for purchase. PLAN Jeffco proposed to the Resource and Land Information (RALI) Program of the Department of Interior that it fund a computer modeling program for an open-space study. RALI agreed to sponsor the project in cooperation with the Federation of Rocky Mountain States. PLAN Jeffco participated in the creation of a new concept and methodology in a computer system for land planning and acquisition.

In April 1973, at the Colorado School of Mines, PLAN Jeffco coordinated a Land Use Open Space Symposium that included representatives from all county parks, planning experts, and geological and ecological experts. The newly appointed COSAC was also invited to attend. The symposium discussed the coordination of Jefferson County's open-space planning. PLAN Jeffco offered its new maps and tables of criteria and priorities to the participants. COSAC enthusiastically adopted both the citizens' concept and their methodology for planning.

Outcome

In August 1973, COSAC purchased its first open-space area of sixty-eight acres on a hogback near Red Rocks Park for an estimated $180,000. With the presentation of COSAC's First Interim Open Space

Plan to the county commissioners in March 1974, and a proposal for a land trust almost finalized in April, the citizens of Jefferson County seemed in a good position to accomplish their objectives of acquiring open space. Their success serves as a model of citizen participation in land-use policy.

CASE II   Wilderness Preservation: Mineral King, California

The valley floor of Mineral King covers roughly 300 acres. The larger Mineral King Basin of 15,000 acres surrounds the valley and is rimmed on three sides by Sequoia National Park, which was created in 1890. Mineral King Valley is the ecological focal point of numerous glacially formed hanging valleys and streams, but it was not included in Sequoia National Park because remnants of mining operations were incompatible with national park status. But in 1926, the 15,000 acres generally known as Mineral King were dedicated as the Sequoia National Game Refuge.

In 1898, John Muir, founder of the Sierra Club and famous American conservationist, proclaimed the value of Mineral King and called for its preservation. But perceptions of the values of the area differ. Mountainous wilderness prevails in the area, and conservationists wish to preserve it in a pristine state for its aesthetic values. Los Angeles and San Francisco, however, are only about 250 miles away, and developers see Mineral King as a prime site for mountain resort facilities. For more than twenty-five years, proposals for the development of Mineral King have provoked land-use conflicts over the site.

In December 1965, the U.S. Forest Service accepted a proposal from Walt Disney Productions for a $35 million resort complex in Mineral King. The proposed development would have affected roughly 13,000 acres surrounding the valley floor. Ski slopes, villages, restaurants, lodges, and facilities for 1.7 million visitors a year were proposed by Walt Disney Productions. A highway would have to be built to provide access to the region. Developers and government agencies agreed to build the road across a portion of Sequoia National Park, although roads not serving the park were prohibited by law. The controversy that ensued at Mineral King between conservationists, developers, the U.S. Forest Service, and the Department of Interior drew national attention. The Mineral King case is a classic illustration that definitions of the public interest may conflict in matters of land use.

The Actors

The U.S. Forest Service, a bureau within the Department of Agriculture, administers more than 186 million acres of public lands, including the national forest within which Mineral King lies. The main congressional mandate under which the Forest Service operates is the Multiple Use-Sustained Yield Act of 1960. This act stipulates the five alternative uses to which areas like Mineral King may be put: outdoor recreation, range, timber, watershed, and wildlife and fish. But this act does not specify how the Forest Service should choose between the five uses. It is within the discretion of the bureau to do what it wishes within the scope of the act to "best meet the needs of the American people." The public interest is defined as "the greatest good for the greatest number, in the long run." It is evident in the Mineral King case that the Forest Service was predisposed to develop the area: public interest was assumed to mean recreational facilities. Its decision-making process was almost closed to input from other public interests.

The U.S. Department of Interior and its National Park Service were also principal actors in policy formation for Mineral King. The only feasible route for a road to Mineral King ran parallel to the inadequate existing road. Since nine miles of Sequoia National Park would have to be crossed, the road could be constructed only with the permission of the secretary of interior. Congress had stipulated in 1961 that any use of parks would have to conform with the conservation of natural objects and scenery. Because the proposed road could not meet this stipulation, Secretary of Interior Stewart L. Udall strongly opposed the Mineral King project and for years would not grant Secretary of Agriculture Orville Freeman permission for the road. When the road was added to the California state highway system and with continued pressure from the Department of Agriculture, Secretary Udall reluctantly allowed the road through the park in late December 1967. It appears that the U.S. Bureau of the Budget, which was impressed with the economic boom Disney's project would stimulate in Tulare County, had also applied pressure on Secretary Udall.

Walt Disney Productions and associated resort-development contractors were the leading advocates for development. Their proposals were supported, as previously indicated, by the U.S. Forest Service. The role of the courts also had a significant impact on the eventual policy outcome. The Mineral King legal battle became a landmark case in American environmental law. The decision of the district court on July 23, 1969 in favor of conservationists held up development for more than a year, and subsequent events have continued to block implementation of the resort proposal.

Other principal participants in decision making for the use of land in the Mineral King case were conservationists from the local area, including the Kern-Kaweah Chapter of the Sierra Club, Mineral King District Association, and numerous individual and group protesters. The spearhead of local and national conservationists was the Sierra Club. It has represented those who feel that the public land unused for economic purposes should be preserved for more important public values.

The Policy Process

Public interest in federal policies for Mineral King was recorded in the 1920s when the Sierra Club urged the inclusion of the site in Sequoia National Park. But the Forest Service refused because of mining claims in the area from the silver rush of 1872–1888. Development interests became increasingly aware of the business potential of Mineral King after World War II, and by 1947, the Forest Service had determined the area should be considered for development. It released information on a development prospectus in September 1949. In March 1952, an investor made application to build a recreation complex worth $750,000. The Forest Service arranged a public hearing to discuss the issue in March 1953 in Visalia, California, under the auspices of the Tulare County Chamber of Commerce. Of the eighty-two persons or groups who were invited, only three were conservation organizations. No formal statement was made at this time by the Sierra Club, but the club was not opposed to modest development.

The problem of providing an access road to Mineral King blocked this early proposal. The National Park Service had to be asked for permission to cross Sequoia National Park and the state of California would have to authorize road construction. The Mineral King proposals lay dormant between 1953 and 1959 because of this problem. In 1960, Walt Disney Productions expressed interest in the site for a winter sports complex. By 1960, the Forest Service issued a new prospectus that outlined development worth $3 million, but did not include the cost of an access road.

This is the point at which citizens' groups and the conservationists publicly protested. The Kern-Kaweah Chapter of the Sierra Club had studied the valley and the proposals and notified the Forest Service of its intention to oppose development. Its view was that Mineral King should be preserved for existing uses such as hiking, fishing, and camping. The Forest Service, in turn, notified the conservationists that they had no influence in the decision-making process. There was no opportunity for the public to negotiate.

The addition of the Mineral King Road to the state highway system in July 1965, considered with great urgency by the state Highway Commission, helped convince the conservationists that the Forest Service had pressured the state into quickly attending to the road. Conservationists wrote numerous letters of protest to the Forest Service in 1965, but the Forest Service responded by indicating it felt the "public interest" lay in development. The Sierra Club requested public hearings in June 1965. It was told that the 1953 hearings in Visalia were sufficient. To all requests for hearings, the Forest Service answered that it knew where the "public interest" lay. Disney Productions' bid was accepted in December 1965 with a three-year development permit authorizing the developers to make surveys and plans. When Disney's master plan was submitted to the Forest Service in January 1969, it took only two weeks for approval. The Forest Service had not issued the thirty-year development permit because the contract for construction of the access road had not been awarded. Every request for participation in decision making by preservationists had been denied. The only alternative for the citizens' groups was litigation.

The conflict over policy from this point on was conducted in the courts. On June 5, 1969, the Sierra Club filed suit in the U.S. District Court for the Northern District of California in San Francisco to enjoin development. Plaintiffs directed one part of the suit at the Forest Service and secretary of agriculture and a second part at the National Park Service and secretary of interior. Resorts developed under lease on national forest land were limited to 80 acres by Congress. At Mineral King, the Forest Service had leased not only 80 acres but an additional 300 acres on a year-to-year basis. Plaintiffs challenged the Forest Service on three grounds: (1) the lease arrangement was a clear effort to circumvent the 80-acre limitation; (2) the use of the valley by developers would violate its status as a part of a National Game Refuge; (3) the Forest Service had violated its mandate by failing to hold public hearings on the development proposal.

The National Park Service and the secretary of interior were challenged by plaintiffs on three grounds: (1) only Congress could authorize construction of transmission lines within a national park; (2) the proposed highway through part of Sequoia National Park did not serve a park purpose and was therefore prohibited by statute; (3) the National Park Service had violated its mandate by failing to hold public hearings on the routing and design of the proposed highway.

On July 23, 1969, the district court granted a preliminary injunction. The court rejected the government's argument that the Sierra Club had no right to sue on behalf of the public. The government appealed the decision. On September 16, 1970, the U.S. Court of Appeals for the Ninth District overruled the injunction, stating that the Sierra Club had no legal standing to contest the actions of the federal agencies. The decision by the court was a shock to the preservationists since the U.S. Court of Appeals for the Second Circuit in New York had declared the right of standing to citizen interveners in the Storm King Mountain power case. (See Chapter 6, Energy.)

The Sierra Club appealed the decision to the Supreme Court where the positions were argued on November 17, 1971. Mr. Justice Stewart handed down the opinion on April 19, 1972. The Court held that even though plaintiffs claimed a special interest in Mineral King, the Sierra Club members would not be affected in their activities or pastimes by the project. Once again it was decided, in a four to three decision, that preservationists did not have standing. During June 1972, the Sierra Club returned to the district court with amendments to its complaint, including a claim under the National Environmental Policy Act (NEPA), which had been signed into law on January 1, 1970.

Outcome

The final outcome of preservationists' efforts to express their preferences in policy making has not been decided. The road scheduled to cross Sequoia National Park was deleted from the California state highway system. In May 1972, Disney Productions declared the size of their project would be scaled down. Congressmen from California and many other states have introduced legislation to add Mineral King Valley and the game refuge to Sequoia National Park. Citizen pressure for the opening of Forest Service and National Park Service decision-making processes to public scrutiny was not successful. But the relentless pressure from the conservationists generated state and national attention to the issues, and federal agencies received considerable adverse publicity. Moreover, although the Supreme Court refused "standing" to the Sierra Club on its 1972 appeal, the Court confirmed the right of appropriate groups of citizens to sue on behalf of environmental interests and laid down guidelines for such groups in future litigation.

CASE III   Landforms Degradation: The Northern Plains

A modern version of the California Gold Rush began in the late 1950s in the Buffalo, Wyoming area and in the late 1960s in the Bull Mountain area north of Billings, Montana. But this rush was for the coal and water resources of 250,000 square miles of the Great Plains. Beneath the surface of the land lay at least 1.5 trillion tons of coal. Experts initially claimed the reserves were of high quality and had a low-sulphur content. Although this claim was disputed by the mid-1970s, mining plans showed no signs of abating. Enough shallow seams of economically strippable coal existed to supply the United States at least until the year 2000. Government agencies and private industries who had been studying the reserves for a decade produced a number of reports in the early 1970s. One of the more influential reports issued from the office of Harold Aldrich, regional director of the U.S. Bureau of Reclamation, is known as the North Central Power Study.

The Bureau of Reclamation and thirty-five private and public electric power utilities proposed that forty-two generating plants located at the mines be constructed in the area. In combination, these plants could produce 200,000 megawatts of electricity annually, more than any country in the world except the U.S.S.R. and the United States. Each of the thirteen largest plants alone could produce five times the output of the Four Corners plant in New Mexico. An accompanying document dealt with the development of the region's water resources. Water requirements for the plants would exceed the municipal and industrial water requirements of New York City in 1970. The Bureau of Reclamation planned to approve a vast system of dams, reservoirs, and pipelines. Proposals for coal gasification, liquefaction, and petrochemical complexes raised the need for water to 2.5 million acre-feet annually. Transmission lines in the area would occupy more than 8,000 miles of mile-wide corridors across the landscape, carrying the power thousands of miles to eastern and western urban centers. A rapid influx of up to one million people was projected. The Great Plains were destined to become the coal and electricity-generating center of America.

The North Central Power Project threatened to overwhelm the land, its spacious beauty, and its semiarid ecosystems. The existing farming and ranching land-use patterns and rural life-style would be either drastically altered or removed in the interest of energy production. The project's study had only incidentally mentioned environmental, social, and economic impacts. The orientation of the proposal was not toward consideration of air, water, and noise pollution, strip-mine reclamation, the effects of river diversions, the impacts on semiarid ecology, fish and wildlife, or the quality of the human environment.

With little publicity and without public hearings, the federal government encouraged industry to exploit the Great Plains to provide energy to other parts of the nation. The coal fields seemed to provide a solution to diminishing national fuel supplies, dependence on Middle East oil, and power plant pollution in the cities. The proposal, however, almost ignored the interests of Indian tribes and local citizens, and developers did not foresee the conflict that was to develop over land-use rights and water rights. Threatened ranchers and farmers promptly organized associations of preservation-conscious citizens. The response of citizens to the formidable assault upon their land and way of life has been a model of effectiveness. By monitoring current developments, citizens have played a leading role in forming public policies for energy-related and land-use problems.

The Actors

Participants in policy formation in the Great Plains represented all levels of government, numerous industries, the Indians, national and state conservation organizations, and local citizens. The federal government was represented because it owned 54 million acres of land and held mineral rights to almost 75 percent of the coal reserves in the region. Most of the public domain is under the jurisdiction of the U.S. Department of Interior. Within the department, three separate bureaus —Land Management, Indian Affairs, and Reclamation—and the U.S. Geological Survey have principal authority for the administration of numerous aspects of development. Agencies at the state level participated in decision making through statutes for surface-condemnation policy and environmental policies. A Montana strip-mining reclamation act, power facility siting legislation, and reforms in the state's water resource policy further involved state agencies through 1971–73.

The nation's largest energy industries in oil, coal, and gas fields sought leases and bought land in the region. Worldwide construction firms and railway companies such as Union Pacific and Burlington Northern also contributed to industry's domination of the decision making. The looseness of federal and state regulations and the obvious neglect of the public trust, particularly within the Department of Interior, were quickly recognized by local citizens. Their reaction led to the prompt establishment of numerous grassroots organizations such as the United Plainsmen Association, the Tri-County Ranchers' Association, and the Bull Mountain Landowners' Association.

The Northern Plains Resource Council (NPRC) was formed in April 1972 as a regional coalition of farmers, ranchers, and conservationists from various grassroots groups. Acting as a coordinating umbrella for such groups, the council performed four major functions: research, communications, organization, and advocacy. The council has been the most effective nongovernmental body operating in the region on behalf of resource protection, and it demonstrates the significant influence citizens' groups can have upon policy formation.

The Policy Process

Citizen participation in decision making in the Great Plains has been significantly implemented by communications to the public, organized and scientific testimony at hearings, and research into existing statutes. The network of citizens' groups has been a successful watchdog of the public interest. NPRC has influenced the drafting of strip-mining legislation, such as the Mansfield Amendment to the Surface Mining and Reclamation Act of 1973. As passed by the Senate, the act would withdraw coal from strip-mining deposits owned by the federal government where the surface above the deposits is owned by someone else. If the Mansfield Amendment is adopted by the House of Representatives, NPRC will have helped protect Northern Plains' agriculture.

At the state level, the NPRC's lobbying efforts have been instrumental in the passage of coal- and water-related legislation. Coal was eliminated from condemnation statutes by amendment of a section of the Montana Eminent Domain Bill, enacted in 1961. Passage of the Montana Strip Mining and Reclamation Act of 1973 gave owners of surface rights more protection and established strong reclamation laws. Pressure from citizens' groups has been instrumental in setting up a Resource Indemnity Trust Fund, which helps restore environmentally degraded areas. The Montana Water Use Act and Utility Siting Act, both passed in 1973, emphasize public participation in policy making and strong local control. Early in 1974, the state of Montana approved a three-year moratorium on water allocations. There is now undisputed state and national recognition of the impact of citizens' groups on such legislation in the Great Plains in the early 1970s.

Besides influencing policy formation through lobbying, citizens' groups such as NPRC and others have also been instrumental in the enforcement of existing laws. In September 1972, the NPRC filed suit against the Montana Power Company and the state of Montana for the utility's failure to obtain the necessary permit from the Department of Health and Environmental Sciences for a power plant project. In this instance, citizens revealed the weakness of existing state laws and made siting act legislation, which followed in 1973, seem urgent and crucial. In another instance, a member of the Northern Plains Resource Council filed an affidavit, in May 1973, with the Department of State Lands concerning the Peabody Coal Company's violation of the Montana Strip Mining and Reclamation Act of 1973. On the basis of that affidavit, the Department of State Lands prosecuted Peabody. During the same month, the NPRC, the Montana Wilderness Association, the League of Women Voters of Montana, the Montana League of Conservation Voters, the National Wildlife Federation, and the Sierra Club filed suit to enjoin the Department of Interior, the Department of Agriculture, and the Army Corps of Engineers from further coal development activities in the region. The plaintiffs maintained that the federal agencies had failed to comply with the National Environmental Policy Act. Environmental impact statements had not accompanied lease applications or applications for prospecting permits for water and coal projects.

In October 1973, the Environmental Defense Fund was joined by NPRC and numerous citizen groups as coplaintiffs in a suit that charged agencies of the federal government with illegally selling water to industrial interests. Agencies such as the Bureau of Reclamation and the

Army Corps of Engineers were charged with violating a number of federal and state laws. In each of these suits, citizens' groups have intervened in the activities of government agencies. They have closely monitored agency and industry decision making, defending the right to public input into policy.

Through publicity and litigation, and by the drafting of more effective state legislation, citizens' groups have had some impact on policy. But federal agencies continually showed a lack of commitment to the demands for greater recognition of the environmental dimensions of their activities. Even more serious were the many discoveries by citizens' groups that statutes had been violated by numerous federal agencies. In March 1972, the U.S. General Accounting Office (GAO) began investigating matters related to federal coal programs in the region. The GAO sharply criticized the Bureau of Land Management for ignoring reclamation and environmental matters, and for not enforcing the law with regard to mining leases. In August 1972, the Bureau of Indian Affairs, responsible for the administration of leases for coal owned by Indian tribes, was also found by the GAO to have violated numerous laws.

The Department of Interior did not respond positively to the GAO accusations. In late 1972, the chairman of the Council of Environmental Quality and the administrator of the Environmental Protection Agency called for the department to take remedial steps in the Great Plains region. Citizens' groups urged state representatives to get the Department of the Interior to pay attention. When Secretary Rogers E. Morton refused to uphold a Senate resolution passed in October 1972 calling for a moratorium on coal leasing on federal lands in Montana, Senators Mike Mansfield and Lee Metcalf of Montana and Frank Moss of Utah protested. On January 12, 1973, Senator Mansfield conveyed to the U.S. Senate the views of citizens' groups about the environmental degradation of the Great Plains. Other complaints against the Department of Interior surfaced in 1973. The Native American Rights Fund of Boulder, Colorado, began to prepare data on the dereliction of duty by the federal government in handling Indian resource rights. Suits against the Bureau of Indian Affairs could be forthcoming. Also in 1973, conservationists prepared to examine in detail the nonobservance of regulations and lack of impact statements from agencies and industry. The Natural Resource Defense Council, the Environmental Defense Fund, the Sierra Club, and many other organizations have planned numerous legal cases. In April 1973, under the authority of the National Academy of Sciences and National Academy of Engineering, twelve prominent scientists began a study to determine "the potential for mined-land reclamation."

Outcome

The struggle for setting priorities in land use in the Great Plains is still unresolved.

CASE IV   Protecting Historical Sites:
Gettysburg National Military Park, Pennsylvania

In 1863, Gettysburg was the site of a critical battle of the American Civil War. Casualties in human life numbered 51,000. One hundred and ten years later, Gettysburg was the scene of a second battle. Commercialization of the property surrounding Gettysburg National Military Park had caused a casualty shared by all Americans. Conflict over land use on this historic site has been raging since late 1970, when a proposal was submitted to construct a triple-decked observation tower over 300 feet high beside the battlefield.

Situated in Adams County, with a population of 8,000, Gettysburg is very close to the densely populated northeast region of the county. Two thousand inhabitants are employed in Gettysburg's tourist industry which is supported by visitors to the park. The local travel council estimates that profits from tourism reach $25 million annually. Fifty million people are expected to visit the park during the decade of the 1970s. The surroundings of the park are heavily commercialized, and opponents of the commercialization view it as an affront to the "history-scape." Local government income depends heavily upon property and tourist revenues because the Interior Department's land holdings of approximately 4,000 acres are tax exempt. Gettysburg National Military Park is the pride of the Department of Interior's historical parks and monuments. It encompasses a large proportion of the battle site, the National Military Cemetery, site of the Gettysburg Address, and the Eisenhower National Historic Site.

The local people, and the nation generally, have viewed the park as a national treasure, and its preservation has been a national objective. When Thomas R. Ottenstein, a Maryland businessman, proposed building a $1 million "Tower for One Nation" overlooking the battle-field, he launched a modern battle for land use at Gettysburg. The tower project, proposed as a supplement to National Park Service facilities, was supported by many local groups: the Gettysburg Borough Council, county commissioners, local businessmen, and the chamber of commerce. But other interests opposed to the project were drawn into conflict over land-use policy. The goal of preservation was clear to most conservation groups and local representatives of the National Park Service, and blocking construction seemed possible with such united opposition. But the avenues of influence on policy making were not clear-cut.

The Actors

When construction of the tower began in the subdivision of Colt Park, its residents became distressed. On May 8, 1971, 150 homeowners filed a class-action suit against the developer on the grounds that the tower was a public nuisance. Local historical and veterans' groups resolved to oppose the construction, and the Gettysburg National Military Park administrators also opposed the intrusion on the landscape. Acting on legal advice, the park superintendent, some park administrators, lawyers, and local citizens formed Defenders of the Gettysburg National Military Park, Inc. This organization raised money in preparation to unite opposition to the project. A survey taken by a local newspaper of local attitudes toward the project showed that 82.9 percent of respondents opposed the tower.

From the state capital, the Pennsylvania Historical and Museum Commission and the Governor's Citizen Advisory Committee on Natural Resources urged the state administration to oppose the project. Late in 1971, the governor filed suit and won a temporary restraining order. But the role of the state in policy was to be preempted by the federal government.

The participant with the most policy-making potential was the National Park Service (NPS) within the U.S. Department of Interior. NPS has control of 283 field areas which include national monuments, parks, recreation areas, and many types of historic sites. The NPS has authority to help Americans learn, through direct observation, about the nation's historic heritage and how this heritage may be protected. It develops the recreational resources of parks while protecting the environment.

The Policy Process

To the public and all conservation interests, the National Park Service appeared to present a united front for preservation. Support for NPS was widespread as it adopted the leading role on behalf of preservationists. NPS had been developing a long-range master plan for the area in coordination with a pilot project financed by the Department of Housing and Urban Development. NPS had defined the tower project as a most damaging intrusion on this famous historical site.

Avenues through which NPS or citizens' groups could influence policy were very limited. The neighborhood class-action suit filed in May 1971 was the first attempt, but it was set aside later when the tower was proposed for a different site. The effectiveness of protests such as these was limited because the construction site was on private land. Even if the courts had upheld the case, the project could have been relocated at another undesirable site because private land was not subject to the same controls as federal lands. Moreover, the lack of zoning regulations in Adams County handicapped state and local actions on policy. The National Park Service preferred not to employ condemnation. This would not have prevented construction elsewhere on private land.

Local citizen and conservation groups could have used more planning and other strategies in pursuing their rights. Both the Historic Preservation Act of 1966 and the National Environmental Policy Act of 1969 were relevant. On May 18, 1971, Pennsylvanians had approved by a margin of four to one a constitutional amendment which declared the public right to the preservation of natural, scenic, historic, and aesthetic values of the environment. This created an opportunity for citizen or state action.

But in June and July of 1971, the National Park Service, assuming it knew the "public interest," decided to bargain in secret with Ottenstein, the tower developer. The NPS preferred not to await the outcome of the Colt Park nuisance suit or possible state action. Without conferring with its own local park administrators, master planners, Pennsylvania officials, or the citizens' groups, NPS announced on July 11 a compromise with the developer. Ottenstein had obtained approval of another site and had been granted right-of-way across federal property for an access road. This action has influenced the outcome of all subsequent efforts by the public to influence the course of policy.

Loyal supporters of the NPS and of preservation were astounded by the National Park Service's assumption of knowing the public interest when actually it was betraying public trust. There was strong public reaction against the arrangement, and partly in response to public demand, the state government took action. The governor of Pennsylvania immediately obtained a temporary restraining order against construction through a new environmental quality amendment to the state's constitution. Although public support for this action was widespread, the commonwealth's request for a permanent injunction on October 26, 1971, was rejected. The court decided that the NPS, with its mandate of working for "the benefit of all the people," had higher authority than the commonwealth, and accepted the agreement with the developers, which was seen as overriding state or private opinions.

The Commonwealth of Pennsylvania continued in 1972–73 to investigate the reasons for the sudden decision of the NPS to accommodate the tower builder. The office of the attorney general of Pennsylvania undertook an investigation of the business dealings and political connections Thomas R. Ottenstein had made in the state of Maryland. The investigation revealed that Ottenstein had at times been associated with organizations that had been involved in illegal dealings with former Vice-President Spiro T. Agnew, but no substantial evidence could be found to link Ottenstein to Agnew. In December 1973, the Commonwealth of Pennsylvania filed suit against the secretary of interior and the National Park Service alleging failure to comply with the National Environmental Policy Act, since no environmental impact statement had been prepared for the tower project.

Outcome

The courts resolved the conflict between the National Park Service and the combined opposition of local groups and the Commonwealth of Pennsylvania in favor of the NPS. The reasons why the NPS reversed its stand and worked out a compromise with the developer are still unclear. But the tower has now been built despite public opposition, and tourists are using the facility.

CASE V   Highway Building: Overton Park, Memphis, Tennessee

Overton Park has been a 342-acre recreational and cultural asset of central Memphis for over seventy years. It contains a municipal golf course, zoo, outdoor theatre, pathways, picnic areas, nature trails, a small lake, and 170 acres of forest. It attracts more than 2 million visitors annually. Widespread public support for its aesthetic and historical values had countered the pressures of urban growth upon its borders for decades. In 1955, the unveiling of a proposal to construct a six-lane expressway that would bisect the park sparked a bitter land-use conflict. The project would destroy 26 acres of park land and would occupy a tract 4,800 feet long and up to 450 feet wide. As part of the Interstate Highway System, the proposed expressway, known as I-40, had soon advanced to within one or two miles of both the western and eastern boundaries of the park. Public reaction to the plan divided the city. Citizen protest against the highway project met formidable opposition. But citizens' actions in the decision-making process for Overton Park have been instrumental in blocking construction for almost two decades.

The Actors

The Memphis City Council (formerly the city commission) held decision-making power over the park at the local level. Early in 1968, pressure by citizens caused it to oppose the expressway. Later, however, project supporters in the media and business community pressured the council into approving the routing. Memphis news media had always strongly supported the project. The Memphis Chamber of Commerce and the Downtown Association were active proponents of the expressway because of its business potential. At the state level, the Tennessee Highway Department encouraged construction of I-40.

The Federal Aid Highway Act of 1958, the Department of Transportation Act of 1966, and the Federal Highway Act of 1968 led to federal involvement in this highway issue. Thus, the U.S. Department of Transportation became a dominant policy participant. The Federal Highway Administration funded such projects and favored the I-40 routing. Section 4(f) of the Department of Transportation Act provided that the secretary of interior and others be consulted on matters of natural beauty in highway proposals. The Bureau of Outdoor Recreation exercised the authority of the Department of Interior.

The community tradition of pride in Overton Park generated the principal citizen action organizations. The first local organization that attempted to influence policy was the Committee for the Preservation of Overton Park. Formed in 1956, it had only limited influence because of a lack of sound leadership and organization. Forces favoring the highway were too strong for the committee, and it had no federal statutes to rely on. Another early opposition group was the Traffic Advisory Committee of Memphis. This group questioned the data used as justification in the proposal and the need for the route through the park. The Shelby Forest Council also opposed the expressway route. Not until the formation in 1964 of Citizens to Preserve Overton Park, Inc. (CPOP) were preservationists' views well organized. With amazing organization, expertise, and persistently effective tactics, CPOP established itself as the leading advocate of the "public interest" in policy. This group of citizens has played a dominant role in policy formation at each available opportunity.

The Policy Process

The process of decision making in this conflict over land use has been dominated by two sets of features. The first are the avenues for public participation provided by the federal statutes of 1958, 1966, and 1968 (discussed previously), and the National Environmental Policy Act of 1969. The second are the strategies and initiative which have been shown by the Citizens to Preserve Overton Park.

Prior to the formation of this group, citizens, through poor organization, had failed to impress highway planners at "corridor" hearings in 1961, which were required by the Federal Aid Highway Act of 1958. From its formation, the new citizens' group organized letter-writing and personal-contact campaigns with all the important and influential officials at federal, state, and local levels. The group drew national attention to the land-use conflict: they sponsored rallies, circulated a flyer entitled "Wake Up Memphis," raised funds, conferred with the governor of Tennessee, visited federal leaders in Washington, D.C., attracted federal administrators to Memphis for discussions, and built powerful allies in national conservation organizations.

In May 1969, the Tennessee Highway Department reluctantly held a design hearing which was specified by a new regulation in the Department of Transportation. Citizens to Preserve Overton Park, Inc. was supported in its protest by other groups, including the U.S. Bureau of Outdoor Recreation, the Wilderness Society, and the National Recreation and Parks Association. But the Highway Department prevailed, and the secretary of transportation granted approval for construction on November 5, 1969. At this point, government agencies made it clear that they were not open to further public input in decision making.

The Overton Park citizens were forced to use legal tactics. From December 1969 through 1970, they filed suits against the secretary of transportation and the Tennessee Highway Department in hopes of restraining construction. Having failed there, they turned to the Supreme Court and won a significant victory in early 1971. The secretary of transportation's approval was to undergo full review in the U.S. District Court of West Tennessee; as it appeared, he had failed to consider alternative routes. The district court was to make a substantial inquiry to determine whether the secretary had acted within the scope of his authority under the law. On January 19, 1973, the secretary of transportation refused to approve funds for I-40 in Overton Park because government studies had not adequately considered alternative routes. The state of Tennessee refused to accept his decision, and local officials persisted in seeking state funds to build the highway through the park.

Outcome

The conflict over rights to the use of this land was still unresolved in early 1976. Citizens have held that this public park is the common property of all the people of Memphis. It has been their democratic right to hold the local government accountable for the public trust. The citizens in this case have demonstrated the power of organized intervention in land-use decision making, but they have not yet won a decisive victory.

CASE VI   Limiting Urban Growth: Petaluma, California

Petaluma, a quiet city of 19,000 in 1965, grew to almost 30,000 in 1971. Situated north of San Francisco, Petaluma had traditionally existed on shipping, commerce, and agricultural activities; it had long been the egg-producing capital of California. Easygoing, small-town life had been the norm for many years. But the availability of Highway 101 for commuters to San Francisco, along with the expensive tax base and water shortage of nearby Marin County, brought rapid suburban growth to Petaluma. Springing up too rapidly to be planned, 14 percent of the city's housing was built in two years in only one-fourth of the city area; basic municipal services—streets, school systems, sewers and water systems—were severely strained. Demands for hospitals and parks could not be met. Rapid growth, and the numerous problems associated with it, aroused the concern of most of the community. Residents increasingly demanded slowing down the growth rate and drafting specific land-use designations. Petalumans protested the uncontrolled, rapid development of their environs and called for the right to determine the destiny of their city.

The Actors

Local demand for land-use control was soon translated into political action. During 1969, and particularly in 1970, the townspeople expressed their alarm to Mayor Helen Putnam and the Petaluma City Council about problems brought on by rapid growth. School systems were forced into doubling teaching systems to cope with the enrollment growth. Large areas of the city had their water restricted because supplies could not match demands. Thousands of citizens drew attention to these problems through correspondence with city officials and the local press and at community meetings. Responding promptly to the demands of a significant proportion of the community, the city council became a significant factor in policy formation.

Developers, builders, and some landowners became an influential force on the eventual outcome of policy. These interests were known as the Construction Industry Association of Sonoma County. Although activist citizens and the city council drafted regulations designed to control the growth of Petaluma, construction industry forces brought suit against the city. The construction industry had a significant impact on policy through its appeal to the courts. Judge Lloyd H. Burke of the U.S. District Court for the Northern District of California struck down the growth ordinance. In addition to its impact on local policy, the interpretation of the court in the Petaluma case is a landmark decision which, unless reversed, may influence the outcome of future litigation in similar cases in the United States.

The Policy Process

The original statement of development for the city was contained in the Petaluma General Plan of 1962, but by 1970 many of the land-use

designations in that plan needed revision. In that year, the Petaluma
Planning Department, in an effort to comply with increasing public
demands for growth control, presented to the city council some studies
of the impact of residential development on city facilities. The Planning Department forecast imminent tax rate increases would be required to accommodate necessary municipal services and recommended
a review of Petaluma's growth problems.

The city council responded to public pressure and the recommendations of the Planning Department early in 1971 by imposing a year-
long freeze on rezoning, development, and annexation. During that
freeze period, the city council, local citizens, the Planning Department,
and consultants prepared to establish new goals and policies for development. The Sonoma County Board of Supervisors met with
representatives of the public early in 1971, throughout a weekend in
a nearby Santa Rosa motel, to discuss the problems of economy, land
use, school systems, and public facilities.

In April 1971, utilizing the results of questionnaires that asked
thousands of city residents to identify their needs, the Petaluma Planning Conference considered policies for the city. Citizens were well
represented in this conference and contributed to recommendations
for development control that were to be included in the official statement of development policy adopted by the city council in the summer
of 1971. Some of the major policy recommendations were a greenbelt
encircling the city, a recommendation that growth be reduced to 500
building units a year, and requests for improvement to downtown areas,
beautification, and alternative modes of transportation.

Once the development policy alternatives were set, the implementation stage began. It was at this stage that the participation of local
citizens became more intense. The task of reviewing the first implementation program, the Environmental Design Plan, took several months.
Through this period, interested citizens participated with officials on
six committees, one for each main area of development: commercial,
industrial, residential, unincorporated areas, recreational areas, and
environmental land use. The plan specified land uses that would
achieve the goals of the council's development policy.

Planning regulatory measures for the development program continued with significant citizen participation throughout 1971 and most
of 1972. In August 1972, the Residential Development Control System
(RDCS) was announced and enacted by the city council. The RDCS

established a quota of 500 new residential units per year and allocated the quotas to east, central, and west areas of the city.

Under the RDCS, developers were directed to apply by September of each year for a share of the quota for development the following year, and applications were to be reviewed by the Residential Development Evaluation Board. The seventeen-member board consisted of six citizens-at-large, four members of local school boards, three professionals or businessmen, two planners, and two city councilmen. Citizen participation in growth policy for Petaluma was assured by strong representation on the evaluation board. The board would consider an applicant's general conformity to the city's plans and evaluate a proposal for development on two sets of criteria: the availability of municipal facilities and the proposal's quality of design, e.g., its contribution to the public welfare. Development proposals would be rated on a specified numerical scale. Public hearings would follow the rating, and the highest ratings were to be awarded development quotas. Residential quotas were also designed as the primary means of implementing the city's plans for a greenbelt park encircling the incorporated limits of Petaluma.

The Construction Industry Association of Sonoma County, representing builders, landowners, and developers, challenged Petaluma's residential quota system in the courts. The developers argued that the Petaluma ordinances violated the constitutional right to travel. The plaintiffs asserted that Petaluma could regulate its growth, but that the city should accept the demographic growth rate as given. The city should plan to accommodate whatever rate was in existence, according to the plaintiffs. Plaintiffs also challenged the policy of a five-year long denial of annexation and extension of public services to developments outside the limits of the greenbelt. Developers also alleged that the city of Petaluma's RDCS review procedures violated the applicant's right to due process of law, and that the growth policies had an exclusionary effect on low-income housing.

On January 18, 1974, Judge Lloyd H. Burke of the U.S. District Court for the Northern District of California accepted the home builders' argument that Petaluma's growth policy violated the constitutionally protected right to travel. The judge found that no city can regulate its population growth numerically so as to prevent residents of another area traveling in to establish residence. Judge Burke suggested that growth might be denied on traditional zoning and planning grounds, as long as the policies were not screening plans based on numerical quotas.

Outcome

Following Judge Burke's issuance of a temporary restraining order, the written findings of fact and conclusions of law, as well as a declaratory judgment and a permanent injunction, were issued late in April. In May 1974, the Petaluma City Council voted to appeal the court decision and request a stay of the orders issued pending the appellate process. Later appeals to Judge Burke and in the U.S. Circuit Court of Appeals to stay judgment were both denied. But in July 1974, as the result of a petition from the city of Petaluma, Supreme Court Justice William O. Douglas issued a stay of judgment pending arguments to be filed by the respondent.

On August 13, 1975, the U.S. Court of Appeals for the Ninth Circuit reversed the judgment of Judge Burke, thus sustaining the growth control measures of Petaluma.[1] In view of the importance of the issue involved, and the nation-wide concern of communities and of builders, the case may ultimately be resolved in the United States Supreme Court.

CASE VII   Land-Water Interface: Santa Barbara, California

On January 28, 1969, a drilling blowout on Platform A of the Union Oil Company began offshore at Santa Barbara, California. The blowout continued for eleven days, spewing up to 5,000 barrels of oil a day into the sea and onto the beaches. By February 7, it was substantially controlled but fissures continued to leak, and the ocean bottom is still leaking oil today. Since 1969, the leak has spilled an estimated 3 million gallons of sticky black crude oil. The blowout is now known to the world as the offshore oil disaster in the Santa Barbara Channel and has served as a dramatic illustration of conflict over policies affecting land use. This land-water interface issue has been a prototype for similar conflicts over rights to use coastal waters, the continental shelf, and the ocean floor.

The outer continental shelf of the United States, covering roughly one million square miles (more or less, depending on the boundaries

[1] Construction Industry Association of Sonoma County versus the City of Petaluma, 44 Law Week 20, 92.

used), is an enormously productive fishing area; it also contains millions of tons of minerals and billions of barrels of proven reserves of gas and oil. Jurisdiction over the continental shelf, and over tidelands and submerged lands on the coasts, has often been contested between states and the federal government. In 1947, the Supreme Court held that the United States had paramount rights over tidelands. Then in 1953, the Submerged Lands Act returned to the states all offshore lands lying three miles seaward from their coasts. But the states and United States have often been in court to establish ownership of lands beyond the three-mile limit. Currently, the Department of Interior, particularly the Bureau of Land Management and the U.S. Geological Survey, administers the provisions of the Outer Continental Shelf Lands Act with respect to leasing for oil, gas, sulphur, salt, and other minerals.

Situated on a naturally favored area of the California coast, Santa Barbara's attractions have led to the development of a successful tourist, convention, and retirement economy. The attractive environment was the cornerstone of economic prosperity. Oil had been discovered at the end of the last century in the Summerland area, and early drilling had been carried out from piers extending into the ocean, but it was not a major enterprise in the area. Santa Barbara has a tradition of environmental concern dating back at least to the turn of the century. The citizenry has had a reputation for intense community interest. As oil discoveries and drilling proceeded through the last seventy years, citizen concern for the welfare of the local environment increased. The record shows a continuous effort to legislate for the protection of tidelands and for the establishment of an offshore sanctuary.

The Actors

Between 1900 and the crisis of 1969, policies for offshore development were mostly confined to the state, which leased oil fields such as the rich Ellwood site. In 1955, the state legislature adopted the Shell-Cunningham Act to create a no-drilling sanctuary. After a Supreme Court decision in 1965, the Santa Barbara Channel outside the three-mile limit was placed under federal jurisdiction. Up to this time, the Santa Barbara issues had been dominated by participants such as oil interests, local citizens, county officials, and state agencies, in particular, the state Lands Commission. In 1966, a new actor entered the scene: the U.S. Department of Interior began leasing drill areas beyond the sanctuary.

Between 1966 and 1969, federal involvement increased because the Santa Barbara Channel beyond the three-mile limit now belonged to the federal government. The occasion for federal interest in promoting oil leases in the channel was the insistence of President Lyndon B. Johnson that more money be squeezed out of federal mineral holdings to help finance the war in southeast Asia. The president was under pressure from Congress to scale down the costs of his Great Society program to offset the escalating costs of an unpopular war. Johnson appears to have ordered the Bureau of the Budget to apply pressure to the Department of the Interior to grant the oil leases and to produce income that would ease the strain of war expenditures.

The U.S. Department of Interior, with jurisdiction over the development and conservation of mineral resources on federal lands, was inevitably a major actor, but it acted under motives that, to some extent, were in conflict. Santa Barbara County officials communicated their concern to the Interior Department about rapidly expanding leasing proposals. There were serious reservations by a few officials in the secretary's office concerning the wisdom of the leases, but presidential pressure proved stronger than departmental misgivings. Moreover, the interests of the oil companies have always been well represented within the Interior Department, and, with friends in Congress and the White House, these interests could challenge the authority of the secretary of interior himself. The mineral resources section of the Department of Interior has consistently promoted drilling and leasing, and has been viewed by some critics as tantamount to the agent of the privately owned oil industry. The oil industry placed the Interior Department under continuous pressure to approve drilling in the channel. The turning point for citizen involvement came with the formation of Get Oil Out, Inc. (GOO) two days after the January 1969 oil spill.

GOO rapidly grew to more than 2,000 members vitally concerned with retaining the beauty of the Santa Barbara Channel. It immediately supported the county and city in calling for a permanent ban on oil drilling in both federal and state waters in the channel. Through its efforts, more than 200,000 citizens in the United States and abroad petitioned the president to stop local oil development. In less than five years, it had an international reputation for being effective in a conflict in which citizen achievements had historically been negligible, for being politically astute, and for inspiring more than thirty anti-oil groups in the United States. GOO has been supported by the National

Audubon Society, the Sierra Club, the Santa Barbara Environmental Quality Advisory Board, other local protective associations, the League of Women Voters, the Community Environmental Council, and others. GOO has had an able board of directors including scientists, business executives, educators, attorneys, and retired oil executives. The organization has provided expert witnesses for hearings, who have testified on oil legislation, and it has used publicity and communications to advantage. It has often shifted its tactics from publicity to legislation, and from lobbying to litigation.

The Policy Process

The nature of citizen involvement in policies for the use of offshore land for oil drilling at Santa Barbara is best described by the activities of GOO. GOO supplemented and extended the work of county officials during the 1967–69 oil leasing permits activities of the Department of Interior. The county had asked for moratoriums on leasing in May 1967 and for buffer zone extensions to protect the oil-free sanctuary in the channel. Most of these requests, and the request for fewer drilling platforms, were not granted. Since the blowout in 1969, however, environmentalists have had significant, if limited, influence on the policies of the state and federal governments. Only one new platform has been installed in five years, and one platform, operated by the Phillips Petroleum Company, was removed from state waters in August 1974 as no longer economical to operate. It was near Point Conception on the west end of the channel.

Recently, the state Lands Commission has lifted its ban on drilling on state leases, but lifting the drilling ban is only part of the new policy. Developers must formally apply for drilling rights and present environmental impact statements; the applications are subject to public hearings. During 1974, Standard Oil of California and Atlantic Richfield applied for approval to resume drilling from existing platforms in state waters. The state Coastal Conservation Commission granted them exemptions from state permits, but these exemptions were challenged in superior court in San Francisco by GOO. The state Lands Commission, the final administrative authority, had the permits under review late in 1974.

The Department of Interior imposed drilling moratoriums of varying durations on federal leases at Santa Barbara after 1969. But late in 1973, reacting to the energy crisis, the department announced that it had withdrawn support for a bill that would have established an oil-free sanctuary in half the seventy federal lease areas in the channel. The impending energy crisis and intense pressure from oil interests inside as well as outside the government influenced the Department of Interior to favor development. Environmentalists anxiously awaited the department's decision on applications presented by Exxon Oil Company to drill in deep water in the Santa Ynez field. The approval was granted in August 1974.

Instances of litigation in the Santa Barbara case are numerous. Environmentalists, fishermen, pleasure-boaters, and beach-front property owners filed class-action suits, and most of these people have been awarded damages. The city and county of Santa Barbara, the city of Carpinteria, and the state filed suit against four large oil corporations in which the federal government was also a defendant.

Outcome

GOO has been more effective than anyone, including the oil industry, expected it would be when it was founded five years ago. Through the late Congressman C. M. Teague (R-California), GOO proposed H.R. 3177, which called for a moratorium on all federal leases until the Senate energy study is completed and technology is further advanced for drilling, producing, and containing oil. GOO influenced the president to deny applications in 1973 for two new platforms in the channel. GOO continues to monitor the actions of the city, county, state, and federal governments. The significance of its impact upon policies is unquestioned, but it has not gotten oil out of the Santa Barbara Channel, and unless there is a major shift in national priorities, it is not likely to do so.

Conclusion

In this chapter we have attempted to isolate some of the main problem areas of land use by presenting typical cases related to each problem. But it is also necessary to consider the interrelationships between the various problem areas in order to clarify the environmental dimensions of land use. The problem areas in these cases share common policy, institutional, and legal dimensions.

Institutional deficiency affected almost every case. The deficiency appeared in various forms. First, where protective laws already existed, government agencies seldom bothered to enforce them. In the Great Plains, Mineral King, and Overton Park cases, agencies had not carried out the full intent of the mandates on which their authority was based. Granting leases and permits to developers without requiring environmental impact statements or without investigating alternatives to proposals violates the law and the public trust. Second, government agencies often made decisions in secret and denied input from the public, or even overrode popular demand. This was especially true at Mineral King. Overton Park citizens, faced with similar treatment by government agencies, were forced to turn to the courts. In the Gettysburg case, another aspect of institutional deficiency was obvious: the National Park Service presumed to know the public interest, as it had in the Mineral King case, and tried to reconcile the conflict without public input. In each of these cases, the outcome of land-use decisions was hardly in the public interest. Finally, because so many cases have not been decided—only delayed—by court suits and appeals, the adequacy of judicial review for the ultimate resolution of land-use issues is questionable.

The lack of appropriate legislation also influenced the avenues citizens used to alter or establish land-use policy. At Petaluma, new ordinances and land-use plans had to be formulated. In the Gettysburg case, the lack of land-use regulations forced citizens to resort to litigation in the early phases of the conflict. Legislative developments at the state level during the controversy provided further avenues for policy reform at Gettysburg but were too late to be of use. Jefferson County citizens designed new ordinances and the fiscal means for protecting open space. On the Great Plains, activists promoted the drafting and enactment of new legislation that could become a basis for further environmental protection. These cases indicate that the need for comprehensive national land-use planning and policy is urgent.

The failure of federal and, to a lesser extent, state government to come to grips with the problems of growth has forced local governments to take action. Although most land-use planning has been implemented at the local level for fifty years, some of the techniques being used in the 1970s have been quite revolutionary. Some communities are implementing ordinances that specify building quotas, others restrict sewer connections, and some freeze all development for a period while planning can take place. The local level is perhaps the best point at which to institute growth controls. The trade-offs to be made between gains in tax revenues and losses in quality of life, or the ratio between the costs and benefits of growth, can best be decided in a case-by-case (or city-by-city) approach. The social, economic, and environmental variables to be considered are unique to each community.

Citizen involvement in the cases took many forms. Lobbying for the creation of new legislation was a basic strategy at Petaluma, in the Great Plains, and at Santa Barbara. The formation of communications networks, the development of lobbying expertise, and the creation of alliances with strong national conservation organizations were tactics in almost every case. Creating media support, gathering data from community surveys, and using research teams to generate factual evidence were valuable activities in other cases. In most cases, a key organization or an alliance of grassroots groups dominated citizen participation.

The majority of success stories in the fight to preserve historic landmarks and monuments can be attributed to the vigilance of citizens' groups. In many instances, such as at Gettysburg, citizens have not been successful. As the Gettysburg case demonstrates, some agencies entrusted with protection of the public interest violate their responsibilities. The National Park Service assumed it could act on behalf of the public interest, but it made crucial decisions without public participation. And those decisions invited suspicion that the service gave in to inappropriate, and possibly unlawful, pressures applied by persons at the highest levels of government. The scandals associated with Vice-President Agnew and President Nixon involving the improper use of political influence gave grounds for public mistrust. By arranging a secret deal with the developer, the National Park Service severed an avenue of approach to policy reform desired by the conservationists. The court held that a federal agency's decision would preempt the Commonwealth of Pennsylvania's authority. The National Park Service's actions were typical of numerous instances where agencies of government conspire clandestinely with development interests and present the public with a *fait accompli*. If citizens had had recourse to more effective land use and zoning laws in Adams County, or if they had been allowed by the NPS to participate in an open decision-making process, they might have been able to protect the historic landmark.

The impact of federal and state highway and transportation policies and the primacy of automobiles in American life have had widespread ramifications upon land use. The Overton Park case in Memphis raises many of the fundamental questions about values that are neglected in existing highway statutes and by the institutions administering them. The Three Sisters Bridge in Washington, D.C., the expressway-parklands controversy in San Antonio, Texas, and the Route 23 Bypass case in the Berkshire Hills, Massachusetts (see Chapter 5, Natural Areas and Wildlife), each demonstrate the reaction of citizens' groups to the devastating effects of obsessive highway construction upon the human environment.

The Great Plains case illustrates the poor record of government agencies in the region, and of federal agencies, in particular, to implement existing laws relevant to leasing, reclamation, or the environment generally. Agencies of the federal government have accommodated industrial interests. The problem of adapting old land-use laws to suit changing values was faced primarily by alert citizens' groups in the area. They assumed the challenge of bringing questions of economy and social impact before the public, administrators, and politicians. Public participation in policy appears to be the only assurance that fundamental value questions of the short-term and long-term public interest in energy and land-use policy will be asserted in the Great Plains conflict.

The Mineral King case has been recognized as a leading illustration of a recurring conflict between developers and wilderness preservationists, with government frequently playing an ambivalent role, and sometimes acting illegally to favor private interests contrary to established public policy. The Florida Everglades (see Chapter 5, Natural Areas and Wildlife), Franconia Notch in New Hampshire, the Cascades in the Pacific Northwest, and the Alaska pipeline case (see Chapter 6, Energy), also could have been examined as cases involving a common theme of opposing philosophies of land use. Wilderness areas have been increasingly recognized as a national heritage belonging to all Americans. Consequently, the policy conflict at Mineral King grew and involved not only local, but also state and national interests.

The land-use problem is only one of the fundamental issues addressed in the Mineral King case. Another issue is institutional accountability. Policy making for land use in the United States continually faces the problem of legal and institutional arrangements that are unresponsive to new societal needs. The Mineral King case reveals the failure of administrative agencies to implement the full intent of their authorizing statutes. The U.S. Forest Service assumed it represented the public interest, but the official arrogance of the service was the main block to policy reform. The National Park Service, for some years of the controversy, demonstrated a considerably different environmental orientation than the Forest Service, but the NPS eventually aquiesced to the dominant, mission-oriented arguments of the Forest Service and its supporter, the Bureau of the Budget. Because the public was continually refused the right of participation, it was forced to turn to litigation.

Coastal zones or land-water interface regions in the United States have been the sites of numerous land-use policy conflicts. (See Chapters 2 and 3, Coastal Zone and Inland Waters.) Proposed deep-water ports for supertankers and sites for oil refineries in Maine prompted citizen activity in land-use policy similar to the Santa Barbara case. A suit filed by Cordova fishermen in Alaska in an effort to protect their industry against oil spills also illustrates the conflict over the use of land beneath the sea. The Santa Barbara case illustrates the concept that the ocean floor, the beds of rivers and lakes, and surfaces above them, are all subject to land-use policy.

Perceiving the value of a region's environment has significantly affected both citizen participation in, and institutional response to, the land-use problems. Even though there is invariably a spectrum of views toward land problems in any one region, in the Petaluma, Santa Barbara, and Mineral King cases, Californians have shown remarkable concern about environmental questions. Public awareness of preservationist philosophy at Petaluma and Santa Barbara significantly influenced policy formation. The prompt response of citizen groups in the Great Plains and of PLAN Jeffco in Colorado suggests that a consensus on the quality of life and preservationist values is solidifying rapidly in these regions. The formidable opposition faced by Citizens to Preserve Overton Park in Memphis, and until recently the near absence of protective land-use regulations in Adams County, Pennsylvania, indicates that the environmental concern seen in the California, Colorado, and Great Plains cases may not prevail elsewhere.

Three fundamental aspects of the conflict over the right to the use of land have been identified by the cases: the problem of conservation versus development; the issue of private rights versus the public good; and the designation of public lands for private or public uses. Because decisions to develop or protect land resources affect every citizen, decision making for land use should include public participation. Increased citizen participation in policy making is needed to represent fully the public interest. Letting policy be set by self-styled experts in an era of rapidly changing values has not been successful; elected officials and government administrators seldom adapt quickly to the changing demands of the public they serve. The impressive contribution that citizen groups have made to the evolution of land-use policy in this country in recent years surely presages an ultimate shift from frontier values and economic assumptions to a more broadly based set of public attitudes regarding the ownership and uses of land.

Readings

Adams, Roger C. "The Land Use Policy and Planning Assistance Act of 1973: Legislating A National Land Use Policy." *The George Washington Law Review*, 41 (March 1973), 604–625.

Bosselman, Fred and David Callies. *The Quiet Revolution in Land Use Control*. Washington, D.C.: U.S. GPO, 1972.

Bosselman, Fred, David Callies, and John Banta. *The Taking Issue*. Washington, D.C.: U.S. GPO, 1973.

Caldwell, Lynton K. "Rights of Ownership or Rights of Use? The Need for a New Conceptional Basis for Land Use Policy." *William and Mary Law Review*, 15 (Summer 1974), 759–775.

Foss, Phillip O., ed. *Public Land Policy*. Boulder: Colorado Associated University Press, 1970.

McAllister, Donald M. *Environment: A New Focus for Land-Use Planning*. Washington, D.C.: U.S. GPO, 1973.

Reilly, William K., ed. *The Use of Land: A Citizen's Policy Guide to Urban Growth*. New York: Thomas Y. Crowell, 1973.

Roe, Charles. "Land Use: The Second Battle of Gettysburg." *The Appraisal Journal*, 42 (January 1974), 90–102.

United States Environmental Protection Agency. *Land Use and the Environment*. Washington, D.C.: U.S. EPA, 1973.

2

Coastal Zone

Introduction

The area where the land meets the sea is one of the most dramatic areas of the physical environment—the coastal zone. It is a region which differs greatly from one place to another and therefore is not easy to define. One of the best definitions of a coastal zone is that offered by the Woods Hole Oceanographic Institute in Massachusetts:

> The coastal zone is a band of dry land and adjacent ocean space (water and submerged land) in which land ecology and use directly affect ocean space ecology, and vice versa. The coastal zone is a band of variable width which borders the continents, the inland seas, and the Great Lakes.[1]

[1] B. Ketchum, *The Water's Edge*

47

The unique environmental characteristics of the coastal zone give rise to some equally unique policy problems. Because ecology and land use in the coastal zone directly affect marine ecology (and vice versa), environmental and resource decisions concerning any point in the area may have multiple consequences. For example, a dam built on a river emptying into an estuary will affect the estuary's marine life as well as the river's ecology.

The impact of coastal zone policy is felt not only by people who live in the coastal zone, but also by citizens who live in other areas. A good illustration of this fact is the controversy over superports, designed primarily for oil tankers. If these ports are built, they will have as important an impact on energy supplies for the interior of the United States as on the coastal zone. Many crucial functions are performed by the coastal zone which are enjoyed by people in all parts of the country. As a recreational area, a nursery for marine and other wildlife, a source of minerals and oil, and an area for ports, the diversity of services provided by the coastal zone is probably unequalled by any other area.

Coastal ecosystems, however, are constantly threatend by growing, man-made pressures. At the present time, approximately 75 percent of the population of the United States is living along the continental coastline and around the Great Lakes. Nine of the nation's largest cities are located in these areas. Population growth has put tremendous stress on the land and marine environment of the coastal zone. This stress has manifested itself in a number of serious problems involving the following activities:

1. dredging and filling
2. port construction and modification
3. drainage and pollution
4. offshore oil drilling and mining
5. development and construction
6. public access and use of beaches
7. power plant construction
8. transportation

A few examples will demonstrate the seriousness of the problems raised by these activities.

Dredging and filling: In the past twenty years, dredging and filling have destroyed over half a million acres of important fish and wildlife habitats in the United States. The increased turbidity of the water created by dredging kills organisms living at the bottom of the coastal floor, and the filling in of wetlands destroys an important source of food for marine animals and birds. These activities have greatly reduced the productivity of the coastal zone.

Drainage and pollution: Coastal areas have been especially vulnerable to pollution since they provide convenient access for discharging wastes into receiving waters. Both industry and expanding cities have been the major offenders in this regard. Drainage and pollution in the coastal zone have resulted in severe eutrophication of the water in some areas, deterioration of nursery grounds, health hazards, and reduction of recreational usage of many areas.

Power plant construction: As demands for energy increase, more and more power plants are being constructed in coastal areas. Power plants in these areas are threatened by flooding and earthquake dangers. Many otherwise promising sites in California, for example, lie along an earthquake fault. The tremendous amount of cooling water discharged in coastal areas from power plants alters the local ecosystems. Finally, there is a further problem of the aesthetic impact of construction in scenic areas.

The types of activities described above give rise to some difficult policy issues. Many of the problems which have developed in the coastal zone are industry related, affecting jobs and housing for the growing coastal population. Because attitudes and perceptions of the coastal zone vary from one sector to another, some of these problems make policy formulation even more complex. Technical solutions may be available, but their use depends upon public acquiescence to governmental action. Even though the National Coastal Zone Management Act was passed by Congress in 1972, its guidelines and protectional provisions have remained ineffective because of inadequate funding.

Coastal zone problems, then, have generally been entrusted to state agencies. Bordering states, however, have seldom integrated or coordinated their policies concerning coastal areas. Since the natural ecosystems along the coast are not affected by such man-made boundaries as state borders, attempts to solve coastal zone problems thus far have been inadequate.

A further problem for state agencies has been the handicap of competing with neighboring states to attract industry. The temptation, which frequently becomes reality, is to weaken environmentally protective controls so that industry will locate in the state. Due to the advantages of locating in the coastal areas, industry has often even predetermined state policy through high investment in particular projects. Such tremendous expenditures, prior to any official decision, limit the choices available to policy makers. Examples of this situation are the controversies over oil drilling in the Santa Barbara Channel, and the construction of the Alaska Pipeline. (See Chapter 6, Energy.)

As the population grows and the economic value of the estuarine zone rises, conflicts of interests and values will make policy decisions even more difficult. The problem facing decision makers to define the "public interest" in the coastal zone becomes apparent. Many services produced by the coastal zone may be called "public goods" to the extent, for example, that they are not normally bought and sold in the marketplace. There are also areas considered to be "common property" in the coastal zone, such as an estuary, which belong to everyone. How the citizen and industry are to use these public goods and common property is becoming increasingly important.

Uses of the coastal zone have largely been a question of value judgments. In the past, many citizens as well as developers and industrialists were not able to see beyond short-sighted goals in the coastal areas because the concept of "public interest" was closely associated with "economic growth." The average citizen, along with the policy maker, remained largely ignorant of the value and necessity of preserving healthy coastal ecosystems. Many looked on, and few protested, as beaches were covered with developments, marshes were filled in for new marinas, estuaries were polluted by industrial waste and local sewage, and oyster beds were destroyed by dredging.

Gradually, however, as the effects of these activities began to be apparent, concerned citizens started to view the coastal environment in a different perspective. This new perspective has usually resulted in conflicts of interest—and not always between the citizen and industry. In many cases, citizen has faced citizen, and industry has faced industry. The outcomes of these conflicts have resulted in both victories and defeats for citizen activists.

CASE I   Land-Use Problems: Filling In San Francisco Bay

San Francisco Bay is an estuary fifty miles long from north to south and one to twelve miles wide; it is surrounded by a population of over five million people. The Bay Area is renowned for its spectacular scenic beauty and recreational facilities. The bay also serves as an essential nursing ground for marine life, a haven for water fowl, one of the world's great harbors, and a center for a large commercial fishing industry. And, unfortunately, it has also served as an attractive piece of potential real estate for developers.

In 1850, the surface of the Bay Area totaled 680 square miles; today it totals only 430 square miles. While the major cause of this dramatic decrease was the diking off of salt ponds, filling in the bay for development threatened to surpass all previous uses when this case history began in 1961. Aside from the predicted reduction of the bay to a mere channel, the dredging and filling operations that were taking place all over the bay area were seriously threatening the estuarine system.

The Actors

There was no central policy-making organ for San Francisco Bay in 1961. At that time, political jurisdiction was fragmented throughout the nine counties bordering the bay, and they were free to act in their own economic self-interest. In most cases, the economic and political pressures for filling in the bay outweighed the advantages that would result from preserving the bay: the developers sought more profits, and the cities and counties needed the increased tax revenues offered by the new "territory."

A development scheme off the shores of the city of Berkeley prompted a concerned citizen to take action—Mrs. Clark Kerr, wife of the then president of the University of California. Mrs. Kerr discovered two other faculty members' wives who had similar concerns for the bay, so, with the help of a retired economist, they made a study of the planned development. Convinced that the future of the bay lay at stake, they invited a dozen or so conservationists to join them and formed the Save San Francisco Bay Association, which at the height of the two-stage battle included 18,000 members. They were later joined by the Sierra Club and various other conservation groups, as well as by two key figures in the California state legislature. In opposition to this group, of course, were the developers and most of the local governments in the Bay Area, who were opposed to regional plans for fear of losing their individual jurisdiction.

The Policy Process

Even though Mrs. Kerr and her supporters helped defeat the Berkeley plan, they realized that the whole bay had to be protected by some regional plan. The Save San Francisco Bay Association had already taken two of the key steps needed to set a new policy for the use and protection of the bay. The initial study of Mrs. Kerr and her friends prompted a further study by the University of California's Institute for Governmental Studies. The result was a book published in 1963, *The Future of San Francisco Bay,* which served as expert testimony as to the need for regional management of the bay. The groups also obtained the support of an aggressive and influential state senator, Eugene McAteer. The earlier attempts by Assemblyman Petris to pass legislation on the bay had failed, but McAteer was a more powerful member of the legislature and he pushed through a bill creating a commission to make an official study of the bay problems.

A massive public campaign then was organized to rally support for a regional protection plan. People wrote thousands of letters, went in busloads to the state capital to protest, and sent bags of sand and dirt to members of the legislature with notes that said:

> You'll wonder where the water went
> if you fill the bay with sediment.

The public campaign was further aided by media support, both from newspapers and the radio. The help of one particular disc jockey who was asked by McAteer to talk up the San Francisco Bay problem was tremendous.

The end result of these efforts was the successful passage in 1965 of a bill which established the Bay Conservation and Development Commission (BCDC). The commission had twenty-seven members from many fields. During their four-year tenure, they were entrusted to make a detailed study of the bay and to prepare a "comprehensive and enforceable plan" for the conservation of the bay's water and the development of its shoreline. Furthermore, anyone wishing to fill in any of the bay had to obtain permission from BCDC during this period.

Outcome

The final step in the creation of the new regional policy organ for San Francisco Bay was ensuring the permanence of BCDC in 1969. This was somewhat more difficult than establishing the commission had been because of the death of Eugene McAteer and because of the strenuous attempts by some local interest groups and industries to block the legislation. By using their previous tactics, however, citizens' groups managed to influence California legislators to pass one of the most comprehensive and powerful pieces of regional legislation that exists in the United States.

CASE II   Salt Marsh Conservation: Udall's Cove, New York

In contrast to the regional struggle to save San Francisco Bay is the struggle over Udall's Cove, a 100-acre salt marsh on Long Island, New York. This conflict dates back to 1960, but it really became an issue in 1969 when the village of Great Neck Estates, which owned half of the marsh, threatened to fill in its half of the cove to make a golf course.

Udall's Cove, like most salt marshes, does not have the dramatic scenic appeal or the multi-purpose utility which made public support for saving San Francisco Bay easy to obtain. Nonetheless, the small marsh, like others along the coast, was serving an essential purpose as a nursery for many species of marine life and as a nesting ground for birds. Since it is estimated that two-thirds of the ocean's sport and commercial fish either begin their lives in wetlands like Udall's Cove or feed on creatures spawned there, the fate of the cove was extremely important to those who knew its function and appreciated its unspoiled beauty.

The Actors

Incremental, but continual, dumping and filling in Udall's Cove had inspired the concern of Mrs. Aurora Gareiss, in particular. Mrs. Gareiss and her husband were one of a number of private property owners who lived around the marsh. Other landholders were the village of Great Neck Estates (fifty-seven acres), the city of New York (fifteen acres), and a construction firm, which owned a parcel of land and underwater rights for the cove. Since Great Neck Estates held the majority of land, their policy decisions on the use of the cove directly affected the interests of the other landowners and residents surrounding Udall's Cove. Other official actors, however, with potential policy-making abilities were the city of New York, the Nassau County Parks and Health Department, the state Conservation Department, the U.S. Army Corps of Engineers, and the U.S. Department of the Interior.

Private organizations concerned with the preservation of Udall's Cove were spearheaded by Mrs. Gareiss' Udall's Cove Preservation Committee. Further support was provided by the Great Neck Estates Marshland Preservation Committee and the Long Island Environment Council.

The Policy Process

In 1960, acting on her own, Mrs. Gareiss began to send out a barrage of letters to halt the filling of Udall's Cove. She wrote every conservation organization she had ever heard of, state legislators, congressmen, and the press. After no success, Mrs. Gareiss finally was directed to the mayor of New York's chairman of the Urban Task Force, Philip Finkelstein. Finkelstein advised Mrs. Gareiss to organize, so she and other conservationists formed the core of the Udall's Cove Preservation Committee, which later attracted members from all over the United States.

No clear cut avenue was available to these citizens wishing to influence future policies in regard to Udall's Cove. Unlike the San Francisco Bay Area citizens' groups, whose efforts were directed toward establishing a new regional policy and agency for bay protection, the citizens' groups concerned about Udall's Cove were primarily interested in preserving the salt marsh as a nature and wildlife sanctuary. This goal made it much more difficult for the Udall's Cove Preservation Committee to win public support, since the advantages of maintaining the cove in its natural state were not immediately clear to many citizens. Consequently, a variety of strategies were used in the struggle to set a new policy for the salt marsh.

Three key factors accounted for the conservationists' success. First, building popular support helped stop the proposed golf course fill. The Udall's Cove Preservation Committee led a campaign to inform local citizens, the press, and schools about the value of the salt marsh. They distributed reprints of a forty-page picture report on marshes from *Audubon* magazine, plus a covering letter, to every family of Great Neck Estates in December 1969. And finally, after a crisis in February 1970, when a band of local women locked arms for six hours to prevent huge dump trucks with fill dirt from entering the cove, the

Great Neck Estate Community Trustees voted to discontinue the golf course project.

Second, because the final disposition of the marsh was still uncertain, the committee decided to exert more pressure on the governmental agencies with policy-making jurisdiction for the cove. All the agencies, however, disclaimed responsibility. Mrs. Gareiss had contacted the Nassau County Parks and Health Department and the U.S. Army Corps of Engineers, who then referred her to the New York State Conservation Department. The department's involvement consisted of issuing a few ambiguous statements and refusing to take a positive position on specific threats to the cove. The Army Corps of Engineers finally decided to take some photographs but did not issue orders which would halt the illegal activities, even though such violations of federal law as the placement of wood fill on a navigable stream bank fell within its jurisdiction. The U.S. Department of the Interior told the committee that the marsh was "too small" an issue for them. Efforts to secure the support of official agencies did, however, bring the struggle even further into the public and official limelight.

Increasing awareness of the plight of Udall's Cove encouraged the support of New York City Mayor John Lindsay, a third major factor influencing the outcome of the conflict. With the support of the mayor and the influence of his Urban Task Force chairman, Finkelstein, as well as the continued pressure of citizens' groups, New York City and the town of Great Neck Estates finally agreed to create a wildlife preserve at Udall's Cove in 1972.

Outcome

Even though a wildlife preserve was established at Udall's Cove, the Udall's Cove Preservation Committee is still fighting plans for development in the cove area. This continuing struggle indicates that developmental policy and the public interest in environmental quality in this case have not been reconciled.

CASE III   Water Pollution: San Diego Bay, California

Water pollution is one of the most persistent problems of the coastal zone. Many states have established regional water quality control boards to control and abate water pollution problems. In California, San Diego Bay had been served by one of these regional boards since their establishment by state legislation under the 1949 Dickey Act. In spite of some enlightened efforts by the director of the local board, by 1963, San Diego Bay had become one of the most highly polluted bays of the U.S. coastline. Disposal of domestic wastes directly into San Diego Bay had begun as early as 1887. By 1961, this disposal totaled over 37 million gallons a day; by 1963, it had risen to 60 million gallons a day. Most of this disposal was inadequately treated sewage (in some cases, even raw sewage) or industrial discharges. Water clarity averaged only six feet, and bacterial contamination was so high that all the beaches had been quarantined. Needless to say, marine life had all but disappeared.

The Actors

The major policy-making organ in respect to water quality for San Diego Bay was the Regional Water Pollution Control Board. Under the Dickey Act, however, the board was unable to do much more than make recommendations. Responsibility for water policy enforcement thus fell to the local governments. Most of the local governments followed the lead of San Diego and dumped their wastes directly into the bay. Yet the city of San Diego and its citizens (primarily as voters) eventually became the major instigators of the plan to clean up San Diego Bay.

The Policy Process

In 1952, after examining environmental studies by the state Department of Health and the Department of Fish and Game, the Regional Water Pollution Control Board's first executive officer, Harold Miller, became convinced that the waste disposal problems of San Diego Bay could only be dealt with on a regional basis. The plan he supported, which was later adopted by the city and county of San Diego, was to construct a system which would collect all the area's sewage and take it to a primary treatment plant on a point of land where the treated effluent would be piped into the ocean.

This plan was proposed to the voters in 1954 in the form of a $16.5 million bond issue. Interestingly, there was no significant political or industrial opposition to the project because all actors realized that the state of the bay's pollution was extremely dangerous. Nonetheless, the bond issue was defeated. The defeat was attributed to three factors: the proposed plant was considered by many to be too close to a residential area; the method of paying off the bonds—through property taxes rather than by a standard monthly charge for each household—was not acceptable to many voters; and the ballot had also included a referendum on fluoridation of drinking water which attracted organized opposition. None of these negative reactions, however, reflected a lack of concern for the problem.

From 1954 to 1959, the city of San Diego developed an alternative plan for waste disposal which moved the plant almost to the end of the point of land previously suggested as a site, and also moved the pipe out two miles from shore and to a depth of 200 feet. This second plan was overwhelmingly approved by the voters in 1960 in a $42.5 million bond issue. The "metro" system became operational by 1965, serving seven cities and six sanitary districts. The final cost was $60 million, or $1.50 a month per household.

In addition to the almost immediate improvement in the quality of the bay water, the metro plan also provided for monitoring of the ocean quality off San Diego. The shoreline and offshore ocean were monitored the year before the metro system began operating. While some subtle changes in biological populations have been noted since the baseline year, the quality of the ocean environment has remained relatively stable.

Outcome

Thus, the citizens of San Diego, following the lead of a regional agency, adopted a regional solution to their water pollution problems which also safeguarded their immediate ocean environment. The key to citizen action in this instance was a recognition of the problem and a willingness to pay the costs to eliminate a serious water pollution problem.

CASE IV   A Continuing Struggle: Galveston Bay, Texas

Galveston Bay in Texas, like San Diego Bay, had earned a reputation as one of the most polluted stretches of water in the United States. In contrast to San Diego Bay, however, Galveston Bay still is stigmatized by the same reputation. Why the citizens of the Galveston Bay area have failed to solve their problems, while those in San Diego succeeded, is an interesting example of the role of perception, economics, and official agencies in determining the course of decision making. While water pollution remains the major problem of the Galveston Bay area, it really is symptomatic of the area's overall problem—uncontrolled growth.

Houston, at the center of the bay's problems, has been described as "Boom Town, U.S.A." It is predicted that Houston will become the second largest U.S. city in the next thirty years. The fact that there are no zoning laws reflects the extent to which the city is mesmerized by the growth ethic. Houston's prosperity has been largely the result of its becoming a seaport in 1915 when a ship channel, built by the Army Corps of Engineers, connected the city and the bay. This ship channel has since become a tremendous dumping ground for industries and the eight counties surrounding the bay. The corps has the legal power to control this pollution, but instead appears to have chosen to ignore the deplorable state of the bay for the benefit of industry and at the expense of the citizens.

The citizens in this case, however, do not seem to recognize their own interests. Because the bay lacks scenic appeal, and because it has been unable to offer the types of aquatic recreation found in other estuaries, the people in the Galveston Bay area have shown very little interest in its ecological preservation. Even such a profitable economic incentive as protecting a healthy fish and shellfish industry has produced almost no efforts to stem the staggering pollution. The municipalities around Galveston Bay continue to dump millions of gallons of raw, inadequately treated, or unchlorinated waste into the bay daily, to the point where parts of the bay are totally anaerobic. Projects which threaten to alter the very essence of an estuarine system, such as filling in all wetlands around the edge of the bay and altering the tidal flow from the Gulf into the bay, continue to be viewed optimistically as signs of further economic growth.

The Actors

The major policy implementation and enforcement agency in matters of water quality in Texas is the state Water Quality Board. This board, established in 1967, has strong legal equipment to carry out its policies, much stronger than California's at the time of the San Diego cleanup efforts. Other state agencies with areas of control over water quality in Texas are the Health Department and the Park and Wildlife Department. The state agencies, however, have failed to enforce their own standards. In fact, in two federal pollution control actions, initiated by the Environmental Protection Agency, the state sided with industry rather than supporting the federal action.

Municipal authorities, who have some policy-making jurisdiction as well, have also been delinquent in enforcing the state standards. Until 1971, Houston did not have even a single program for monitoring unauthorized sewage discharges. Harris County, in which the city of Houston lies, is the only one of the eight counties which has tried to use its inspection and enforcement powers. Its air and water pollution control officer, Walter A. Quebedeaux, Jr., has made himself quite unpopular with some political and industrial interests by his efforts to check the outflow of waste into the bay.

The Gulf Coast Waste Disposal Authority, a regional agency, has not yet been able to attempt constructive action to remedy water pollution. The only agency which seems to have complete authority to control water quality through its permit system is the Corps of Engineers; and it is more interested in pursuing its own projects, as noted earlier. Since other federal agencies are not allowed to bring suit against a polluter in Texas without the consent of the governor, federal efforts to protect the bay have been almost nonexistent.

Threading its way through this labyrinth of policy-making organs is a small group of concerned citizens who have to combat not only industry and government agencies, but the apathy of most of their fellow citizens as well.

The Policy Process

On two notable occasions, some citizens in the Galveston area have protested specific projects of the Army Corps of Engineers. One occasion involved the elite community of River Oaks, which wanted to stop a "rectification" project on the adjacent Buffalo Bayou; the other involved a suit to stop construction of the Wallisville Dam project. The first instance was one of the few victories won by conservationists in the Galveston area; the second effort was unsuccessful.

The significance of these two instances of citizen protest, however, is that both involved opposition to a particular project and neither was concerned with the general quality of water in Galveston Bay. The difficulty of finding out how the policy process works in the Galveston area, and which level of government is responsible for what area of control, makes it almost impossible for the concerned citizen to influence decision making, particularly when his opinion is the minority opinion.

A direct avenue open to the citizens in the Galveston area to influence water quality is the same one used by the citizens of San Diego: bonds to support the creation of a new regional sewage treatment facility. Houston had, in fact, made some attempts to improve its sewage collection and treatment facilities, but its improvement efforts were retarded by the voters' rejection of two large bond issues in 1968.

Outcome

In May 1971, a referendum was passed which allowed the state to increase the ceiling on water-development bonds to 6 percent and to increase indebtedness up to $100 million to assist the municipal and county governments with the cost of constructing treatment facilities. However, until there is a real regional effort to control water pollution, both on the part of citizens and the various agencies involved, it is doubtful whether cleanup plans for the bay will be as successful as they were in San Diego. Nonetheless, since 1972 there have been a few signs that industrial efforts to reduce pollution in the Houston Ship Channel are paying off. Seagulls, which apparently couldn't tolerate the area a few years ago, are back fluttering around the channel. A number of shrimp have also been found, one of the first indicators of improved water quality.

CASE V   Development versus Conservation:
Hilton Head, South Carolina

Hilton Head is an island off the South Carolina coast. It is part of an estuarine system called Port Royal Sound which is one of the few unspoiled areas left on the southern Atlantic coast. The island itself, which became the center of a development controversy in 1970, is largely an exclusive retirement community, while the county in which Hilton Head lies is an economically deprived area with about half of its population illiterate.

Because the area and much of the state is so poor, the governor of South Carolina, members of the state's Port Authority, and members of the Industry and Trade Commission made a trip to western Europe in the fall of 1968 in an attempt to attract more industry to the state. One company that was enticed by the tax and investment incentives to locate in South Carolina was the German company, Badische Anilin and Soda Fabrik (BASF). They proposed to build a $200 million facility for the production of dyes and plastics. From the site offered to BASF by the state, the company estimated it would be pouring 2.5 million gallons a day of waste water into the Colleton River, which flows into Port Royal Sound. The sound was not only the prime fishing grounds for the area (the major industry of the region), but its waters also lapped along the beaches of exclusive Hilton Head. This fact touched off the fight to save Hilton Head in 1970.

The Actors

The state agencies responsible for protecting Port Royal Sound were all in favor of the BASF plant. Considering the state's solicitation of the plant, this was no surprise. Further support of the proposed development came from business promoters and the county Chamber of Commerce, as well as from a prominent black citizen, John Gadsen, who was the director of a job-placement agency for the black community. Gadsen believed the only hope for the area was to industrialize, even though he was sympathetic to the potential plight of the fishing industry.

Opposition to the plant was led by Hilton Head's three main developers who controlled 17,000 of the island's 22,000 acres. They were primarily interested in protecting their investment. Aligned with the developers, although not happily so, were a group of conservationists, aided by the Audubon Society and the Friends of the Earth, who wanted primarily to preserve a high-quality estuary system. And finally, the Hilton Head Fishing Cooperative, which was run and operated by blacks, joined the protesters. The cooperative did an annual $300,000 business and was a symbol of black pride in the area, as well as a major employer. Over half the jobs in Beaufort County, in fact, were involved with fishing and tourism.

The Policy Process

Opposition to the plant arose primarily for three reasons: fear of pollution that would destroy the estuary as a recreational area and destroy the fishing industry; fear of further development after the BASF plant was built; and the realization that most of the economic benefits resulting from the plant would probably not filter down to those who needed them most. The opposition had reason to support the first claim since another plant recently built in the area had promised prior to its construction not to pollute, but within two years, it was discovered in gross violation of the state's already lenient standards. The second fear—further development—had already been confirmed by BASF's president who said that the company hoped to attract new industries to the area because of their plant. The final concern of some of the opposition could not be substantiated but was, nonetheless, a predominant feeling in some circles.

The first tactic of the opposition was to picket and demonstrate at the plant site and BASF headquarters. At the same time, the group secured the legal aid of the Audubon Society and Friends of the Earth. They also gained the support of one state legislator, Alex Sanders.

The group then demanded public hearings to air their views. The hearings centered around the potential pollution of the sound, and both sides produced a barrage of "expert" testimony on their behalf. As the hearings went on during eight weeks, BASF's position became more and more intransigent; the company's "face" or image was at stake, and the fishing cooperative sued for a moratorium on the plant's construction until extensive lab tests could be carried out.

Finally, a study conducted by the South Carolina Water Resources Commission questioned the company's pollution predictions. The issue ended up on Governor McNair's desk. The governor was, by then, also faced with immense political pressure since Secretary of the Interior Walter Hickel, who had learned of the conflict, warned BASF that his department would fight the project unless the firm guaranteed "nondegradation of the sound's water." Because of this pressure from the local level, and because of some observations in the commission's study, the governor abrogated the agreement with BASF.

Outcome

The proposed construction of an industrial plant at Hilton Head, a development encouraged by state and local business interests, was forestalled by the combined resistance of real estate developers and conservationists. Their objections were given additional force by pressure from the federal government. Temporarily, at least, the scenic and productive coast around Hilton Head has been protected. Further struggles over development will undoubtedly continue, however, unless local and state policy differences are reconciled. Implementation of the National Coastal Zone Management Act would do much to preserve areas such as Hilton Head from undesirable development projects.

CASE VI   Industry versus Environmental Quality: The Indiana Dunes

As early as World War I, efforts were made to protect from development that portion of the Lake Michigan shoreline called the Indiana Dunes. In 1925, a 2,100-acre Indiana Dunes State Park was created which included three miles of the spectacular shoreline. Demands to develop the remaining dunes area continued to grow, however, and by the early 1950s, plans to industrialize the area were beginning to be carried out at an alarming rate. Aside from threatening the unique ecological value of the dunes area, the plans were particularly alarming as a threat to public enjoyment of Lake Michigan. The Chicago metropolitan area, one of the largest urban areas in the United States, has ranked among the lowest in recreational acreage per 1,000 persons. Millions of people live within two and a half hours' drive of the dunes; thus, preservation of the area as a necessary recreational resource became a critical issue in the battle to save the dunes.

The Actors

Since the dunes were located in the state of Indiana, the Indiana state legislature and state agencies were theoretically in the principal position to protect the dunes. The governor and the state legislature, however, were adamantly in favor of development of the dunes and vehemently opposed to any preservation efforts. Save the Dunes Council, a citizens' group founded in 1952, decided to make the issue a national one after repeatedly failing to win support for protective legislation from Indiana politicians. Thus, the major policy-generating actors were extended to include a diverse group of individuals, scientific groups, and government agencies, among which the National Park Service was critical.

Another federal agency with jurisdiction in the case was the Army Corps of Engineers. The corps eventually opposed park preservation, along with two of the nation's largest steel companies, various land speculators, certain citizens of the area, and, of course, all the Indiana state and federal legislators.

The effort to establish an Indiana Dunes National Park was led by Mrs. Dorothy Buell of the Save the Dunes Council as well as by U.S. Senator Paul Douglas of Illinois. They were joined by a variety of national organizations, like the Audubon Society and the Izaak Walton League, and by a nationwide group of citizens. Local groups and municipalities were divided, as was organized labor. The steelworkers supported the lakeshore, and the building trades opposed it. Although its citizens would benefit from a national lakeshore, the city of Chicago remained strictly neutral.

The Policy Process

The original strategy of the Save the Dunes Council was to put pressure on the Indiana governor and legislators to force them to change their policy toward the dunes. Half a million signatures were collected all over the country toward this end, all of which were ignored by the governor and members of the Indiana General Assembly. Even support from the media in Indiana could not be obtained. When news of a proposal to build a deep-draft port in the middle of the dunes at Burns Ditch reached the council, a second strategy was adopted to seek national park status, and, at the same time, to win local support by pointing out the dubious rationale for building a port in the middle of the dunes.

In 1958, Senator Douglas introduced the first bill in Congress to create a 3,500-acre park called the Indiana Dunes National Seashore. His proposal would have taken the 4,000 acres purchased by Bethlehem Steel and some of the land proposed for the Burns Ditch Port. This first bill was not reported out by the Senate Interior Committee. The second and third bills, introduced in Congress in the early 1960s, managed to pass the Senate but got stuck in the House because of the efforts of Indiana Congressman Charles Halleck, who was then the powerful House Minority Leader. To make things worse, the Army Corps of Engineers, which had previously not supported the harbor proposal, came to the conclusion that the port would be economically feasible—justifying a $25 million federal investment. Their decision was based entirely on the findings of the Indiana Port Commission, which eventually was shown to have no documentation for its claims.

The Save the Dunes Council was gathering momentum, however, and began to gather the support of many influential persons across the country. The struggle had also gained the attention of President Kennedy, who, at the appeal of Senator Douglas, sent the harbor proposal to the Bureau of the Budget in 1963 to study the feasibility of the plan. The Bureau of the Budget, on behalf of the President, recommended that an 11,700-acre Indiana Dunes National Lakeshore be created (compared to Douglas's 3,500-acre suggestion), but at the same time, left the proposed site for Bethlehem Steel's finishing mill and the Burns Ditch Harbor outside the park area. This compromise administration bill had been drafted by the Department of the Interior and the National Park Service. Although the Save the Dunes Council was willing to accept this compromise, the battle went on for another three years because the park opposition was so determined to have its way in the dunes. Finally, growing legislative support in Congress enabled the bill to pass the House of Representatives and, on November 5, 1966, the Indiana Dunes National Lakeshore was established. The park included 6,500 acres not already in public ownership and totaled 8,600 acres. It became the only national park ever established against the opposition of the state in which it was located. By this time, however, at least one Indiana congressman, J. Edward Roush, had begun to support the lakeshore.

Outcome

The battle to save the dunes was not really over, however, because money to purchase the land still had to be appropriated. By 1972, 80 percent of the authorized land had been acquired, but not without some further leveling of dunes and additional conflicts over proposed projects, including three projected power plants. In 1975, several Indiana legislators proposed the addition of as many as 5,300 acres to the national park, while the National Park Service plan would increase it by 1,150 acres. These proposals are the center of further controversy, and it would appear that this pattern of struggle over every inch of sand in the dunes will continue with neither side emerging as the victor.

CASE VII   Planned Coastal Protection and Development:
Rookery Bay, Florida

Rookery Bay in Florida, like Hilton Head, was faced with the problem of development. At the time of the conflict, however, Rookery Bay was basically an untouched estuarine system with a minimal population. In 1964, a road into Rookery Bay was proposed, which was to be followed by further development. A number of the community's conservationists, fishermen, and other concerned citizens so vigorously opposed the planned road that the project was halted. The citizens realized, however, that their main problem was the need for a permanent solution to protect the bay from uncontrolled growth.

The Actors

The citizens banded together to form the Collier County Conservancy. They received help from the Nature Conservancy (a national group) and the National Audubon Society.

The principal government agencies with jurisdiction in Rookery Bay were the board of county commissioners, the county Water Management Board, the county and state health departments, and the state Air and Water Pollution Control Commission. These agencies were generally supportive of the conservancy's plan to protect the bay.

The Policy Process

The case of Rookery Bay is the story of how citizens attempted to plan for coordinated growth in their area with no major opposition to the project. The first step of the Collier County Conservancy was to seek advice from the Florida Board of Conservation biologists about the extent of the area which it was essential to maintain in a natural state if fishing, boating, and the overall estuarine system were to be protected. The major area identified for preservation was Rookery Bay itself, a 1,000-acre salt water lagoon. Since most of it was privately owned, the conservancy decided to purchase the property. The National Audubon Society agreed to participate and to take title to the lands after their acquisition.

The conservancy then proceeded to mount a successful drive to raise money and purchase the needed areas. From 1966 to 1967, 2,600 acres of privately owned land were purchased for $450,000. The area purchased surrounded 1,400 acres of state-owned land and became the Rookery Bay Sanctuary. The Collier Conservancy, in cooperation with the Nature Conservancy, raised more than $150,000 to purchase the land. Even though the drive met with a great deal of community support, as the president of the National Audubon Society pointed out, it was no easy task because of the astronomically increasing value of land.

In a third, far-sighted move, the conservancy realized that the establishment of the sanctuary itself would not be enough to protect the area. Since the sanctuary was part of the same estuarine system, damage to the areas outside the sanctuary would eventually have serious ramifications for the sanctuary itself. Acting on this realization, the conservancy sought the assistance of the Conservation Foundation, a nonprofit, private national organization. The Conservation Foundation decided to initiate a project to determine if conservation and development could be compatible in the area and, if so, to recommend a development program and suggest methods of implementing it.

The six-month study of the Conservation Foundation was completed in April 1968. It recommended a development strategy which would require "appropriate action both by private landowners and responsible government agencies." The significant point of the study, however, was the effort to show that development and conservation could coexist. Citizens confronted with what they see as no other alternatives to an existing growth policy often become totally opposed to any kind of development, as in the case of Hilton Head. Actually, the Hilton Head confrontation might have resulted in a compromise solution if the major agencies with policy jurisdiction in the case had not already made a prior policy commitment encouraging growth. Areas like Rookery Bay, however, which have as yet no development or population to speak of, offer a much wider range of policy choices to the decision maker, as well as easier access to decision-making channels for the citizen.

Outcome

Whether or not landowners and governmental agencies will together determine a growth policy for Rookery Bay is still uncertain. A

Conservation Foundation official noted that local officials seemed to have a lot of enthusiasm but no commitment to action. Moreover, some small landowners oppose the recommended development strategy. What happens to Rookery Bay will be important to observe because of Florida's rapid growth in recent years. If the Rookery Bay plan is a success, it will be a positive example for similar coastal areas to follow.

CASE VIII   Beach Preservation and Public Access:
The California Coast

Only 200 miles of public beaches remain along the 1,200-mile coastline of California. The rest of the coast has been ravaged by haphazard economic growth, bringing its population in 1970 to approximately 20 million. Access to the remaining beaches and coastal areas had become a major issue. At that time, protection of the coast was in the hands of no less than 200 different entities—46 cities, 15 counties, and a miscellany of state and federal agencies. Their efforts at protection had obviously been a failure. In 1970, at the instigation of conservation groups, legislators began introducing "Save the Coast" legislation. But because there were too many bills, none of them passed. This failure led to the formation of the California Coastal Alliance early in 1971, and it was this group that led the fight to save the California coast through a piece of protective legislation called Proposition 20.

The Actors

The major actors in the Proposition 20 conflict were initially the state legislature and various interest groups (including the California Coastal Alliance) and then, finally, the voters of California. The pre-Proposition 20 group was spearheaded by the California Coastal Alliance which, at its peak, included 700 organizations. The anti-Proposition 20 group was primarily composed of big business, developers, land speculators, and oil companies.

The Policy Process

The thirty-four organizations which initially joined together under the banner "Save Our Coast" had the support of a powerful member of the state legislature, Assembly Speaker Moretti. In March 1971, Moretti introduced a coastal protection bill designed to gain wide support among the legislators. At the same time, members of the California Coastal Alliance went from area to area in the state to solicit citizen support and to collect thousands of petitions in favor of the legislation. They organized a huge letter-writing campaign, special committees, and special events. The bill managed to pass the assembly by a fifty-six to seventeen vote, but then became stuck in committee in the senate. This delay was largely due to the effective lobbying of prodevelopment groups and the failure of a key senator to be present when the vote was taken.

In 1972, the alliance decided to try a new strategy. Again they lobbied for passage of coastal protection legislation, but this time they also quietly simplified the legislative proposals in order to take them directly to the voters in the form of an initiative in case the legislation failed to pass. In May 1972, when it became clear that all chances for passage of coastal legislation in the state senate had failed, the alliance began working to put an initiative measure on the November 7 state ballot.

Stage one of the alliance's plan was to collect all the necessary signatures and have them validated 130 days prior to the election—no small task in a state the size of California. Thousands of volunteer, rather than professional, signature collectors were used in the effort, and by June 1974, 418,000 validated signatures had been collected, enough to qualify the initiative for the state ballot.

Stage two of the campaign was even more difficult—winning voter support for Proposition 20 in the face of one of the most heavily financed opposition campaigns in the history of the state. The opposition's main tactic was to mislead the public with an advertising campaign designed to make the voter vote "no" instead of "yes" in order to "save" the coast. The California Coastal Alliance, however, put together a tremendous public relations campaign, winning support from celebrities, sixty state legislators, thousands of volunteers and, most important, much of the media. Every lead to a sympathetic supporter, every opportunity to gain media support, and every chance to advertise was utilized. The issue of public access to California's remaining beaches was emphasized in the campaign and gained many supporters. All of these efforts proved successful when on election day, November 7, 1972, Proposition 20 passed by a 55.1 percent majority.

Outcome

The new law created the California Coastal Zone Commission and six regional commissions. During the 1973–75 trial period, these agencies were directed to prepare a comprehensive plan for the orderly, long-range conservation and management of the state's coastal zone. This plan was released in January 1975; the battle to save the coast of California is now dependent on what happens in the state legislature. Unless the coastal plan is adopted, the coastal commissions will be disbanded in December 1976.

The plan proposed by the Coastal Zone Commission seeks to channel all substantial new development inland. The plan would also guarantee public access to the entire coastline, even privately owned land, and urges enactment of "open beach" laws patterned after statutes in Texas and Oregon. The plan calls for a moratorium on elimination of coastal agricultural land and urges tax credits for farmers to reduce pressures on them to sell such land for urban development. Mass-transit development would have priority over highway construction. The plan also encourages the use of unconventional power sources, including solar and geothermal energy, methanol, solid wastes, and wind power.

The debate over the plan, aside from some of the more controversial provisions, really centers on the authority of the Coastal Zone Commission to overrule local governments. Indications at the time of this writing are that the upcoming fight in the legislature will be the biggest political battle of the decade in California. The outcome of this struggle will, we hope, be the beginning of a new era for the state, as well as for the nation, in efforts to protect the irreplaceable coast.

Conclusion

The preceding eight case studies identify four major problems of the coastal zone: land use, water pollution, preservation and public access, and development. These are by no means the only important problems of the coastal zone, nor are they unrelated issues. All of the eight cases involved a variety of problems, even though one particular issue may have been more dominant than others in a given case. Just as considering the interrelationships between these problems is crucial to understanding the coastal zone as one part of the total environment, examining some of the implications of the cases presented in this chapter is helpful in understanding how policy is made and altered in relation to environmental decisions. The following are some of the critical points brought out by the coastal zone case studies.

Most of the coastal zone case studies indicate, first of all, some form of institutional deficiency, evident both in an initial failure to produce or enforce adequate policy guidelines for the existing ecosystem, and in a later failure to respond to citizen efforts to affect the policy process. Since individual states are generally responsible for setting coastal protection standards, the failure to produce adequate policy guidelines would indicate primarily a failure among the state agencies. Moreover, because enforcement of policy is usually the task of local agencies, most of the case studies in this topic reveal a failure of both local and state agencies in the creation and enforcement of coastal zone policy, as well as in their response to citizen initiative. In some cases, such as the Galveston Bay case, the federal agencies involved proved equally deficient.

Institutional deficiencies, though not the only factors affecting these coastal zone conflicts, definitely influenced the avenues citizens chose to alter or generate policy in each of the eight case studies. For example, in three of the cases—San Francisco Bay, San Diego Bay, and Proposition 20—failures at the local level to control particular coastal zone problems inspired a citizens' drive to create new agencies to cope with the issues on a broader level. Or in the Indiana Dunes case, the failure of the state legislature to respond to citizen efforts to alter policy brought the conflict to the national level. Despite institutional failure in each of these cases, however, the locus of responsibility in the policy-making process in each conflict was relatively clear. In a case such as Galveston Bay, where an essentially adequate policy to deal with the pollution of the bay existed but where the locus of decision making was very diffused, citizen efforts to alter policy in broad terms were unsuccessful.

The point at which an issue entered the political arena, therefore, greatly influenced the form of policy resolution in the coastal zone case studies. In the first four cases—San Francisco Bay, San Diego Bay, Proposition 20, and Indiana Dunes—where the general process of decision making was clear, citizens used the legislative process to effect a policy change. The remaining cases—Udall's Cove, Galveston Bay, Hilton Head, and Rookery Bay—did not use a legislative approach for several reasons, but particularly because the locus of decision making was unclear. As a result, the center of activity during the various conflicts was, in all cases, where the actors expected to have some impact upon the policy outcome. Thus, at Hilton Head, activists concentrated on demonstrations at the proposed plant site and other local displays of protest, since the state was already committed to the project. The strategy used at Rookery Bay was to create a plan in conjunction with a conservation organization that would combine conservation and ecology to prevent overdevelopment in what was still an unspoiled area.

A third crucial factor which influenced citizen involvement in the coastal zone case studies was the popular attitude toward, and perception of, the local environment. It was noted, for example, that the dramatic scenic appeal of San Francisco Bay and San Diego Bay was the major factor in arousing citizen concern about a local problem. Citizen appreciation of the scenery at Rookery Bay also inspired involvement when a conflict arose. These areas obviously had an added incentive for citizen participation in policy making, much more so than at Galveston Bay (a geographically unexciting place further marred by abuse), Udall's Cove, or the Indiana Dunes where many local citizens could not appreciate the value of maintaining these areas in their natural state. In an area like Galveston Bay, where public attitude was decidedly unconcerned about the state of the local environment, citizens were not in a position to alter or generate new policies, or even to enforce existing ones.

The initial perception by citizens of their local environment is consequently very important in affecting both citizen involvement and the manner in which institutions cope with coastal zone problems. Public attitudes toward any particular issue, however, were seen to be a product both of how the citizens perceived the environment of their area and how they viewed the issues at stake. At Hilton Head, for example, many citizens appreciated the aesthetic beauty of Port Royal Sound, but public attitudes were more affected by the economic issues raised by the proposed plant than by ecological ones. Or at the Indiana Dunes the controversy, which had been going on for several decades and had aroused a fair amount of conservationist interest, did not really arouse the general public until a harbor was proposed. In addition, almost all the cases revealed a tremendous diversity of interests in even those citizens taking the same stand on a particular issue. With the exception of the Rookery Bay and San Diego Bay case studies, where there was virtually no opposition to the proposed policy plans, citizen involvement took place on several levels and for numerous reasons.

The key to effective citizen involvement in the coastal zone case studies, however, appears to be establishing a large enough group which perceives an issue as essential to its own well-being. In each case, a variety of different tactics were used by citizens, but all the cases involved a key organization or alliance of groups which coordinated the efforts. Every case also used a particular strategy to win further public and media support.

The success of various tactics, however, cannot be viewed only in terms of victory or defeat, but must also be considered in terms of the long-range effectiveness of the conflict resolution. In general, it would appear that the timing of citizen involvement greatly influenced the resolution of a conflict. For example, in both the San Francisco Bay and San Diego Bay case studies, large-scale involvement was not primarily issue-oriented; citizens became involved because of the general condition of the bays, not because of opposition to a particular project. In both of these cases, conflict resolution resulted in basically effective long-term policies. On the other hand, in cases like Udall's Cove or Hilton Head, even though the citizens were temporarily victorious, completely satisfactory long-term policy results were not produced. Both of these cases were characterized predominantly by issue-oriented citizen involvement. Although focusing on a specific project obviously narrows possible policy choices, sometimes sufficient participation cannot be generated unless a conflict becomes issue-oriented. This was seen to be the case at Udall's Cove and the Indiana Dunes. In this situation, the resulting policy may be a compromise and not necessarily the most effective decision possible.

Compromise resolutions of conflicts emphasize the extent to which the policy-making process itself molds the demands made upon it. In every case in this chapter, the initial goal of citizens was altered in one way or another by the institutional arrangements and decision making that citizens came in contact with. In some ways, this alteration of goals serves as a moderating function in the policy process, but when the goals become diluted at every level of the process, as they did in the case of Galveston Bay, the benefits of citizen participation in decision making are almost totally eliminated.

If the problems of the coastal zone are to be at least ameliorated, wider citizen participation in decision making is essential. The kind of increasing public dissatisfaction with policy decisions (or lack of them) revealed in the eight coastal zone case studies itself indicates inadequate public involvement in the policy process. Effective citizen participation can help to both clarify and streamline the policy process, and to change the perceptions and attitudes of those who become involved in coastal zone issues.

This latter effect of citizen participation, a change in attitudes and perceptions, is perhaps the most important because, as the eight case studies show, policy is not just a set of legal dictums, but informal guidelines and practices as well. It is often these informal guidelines which appear to steer the decisions of policy makers and administrators, rather than the official policies. This was seen to be the case in Galveston Bay. If the policy-making process had been more open to citizens in the Galveston area, a change in attitudes toward the bay would probably have been evident, as well as a concomitant change in policy enforcement.

A final reason for increased citizen participation in coastal zone issues is that all the case studies involved essential questions of value and preference. For this reason, citizens should have the opportunity to have their opinions taken into account. Leaving the decisions totally to nonelected federal officials, removed from public opinion, or to state officials unresponsive to local needs, was shown to result in unsatisfactory policy decisions. The problems facing the coastal zone are urgent ones, and they are too important to be left solely in the hands of a slow and sometimes arbitrary bureaucracy.

Readings

Adams, Janet. "Proposition 20: A Citizen's Campaign." *Syracuse Law Review,* 24 (Summer 1973), 1019–1046.

Bailey, Gilbert and Paul Thayer. *California's Disappearing Coast: A Legislative Challenge.* Berkeley: Institute of Governmental Studies, University of California, 1971.

Bradley, Earl, Jr. and John Armstrong. *A Description and Analysis of Coastal Zone and Shoreland Management Programs in the United States.* Ann Arbor: University of Michigan Press, 1972.

Brahtz, J. F. Peel, ed. *Coastal Zone Management: Multiple Use With Conservation.* New York: John Wiley & Sons, Inc., 1972.

Hite, James and James Stepp, eds. *Coastal Zone Resource Management*. New York: Praeger, 1971.

Ketchum, Bostwick, ed. *The Water's Edge: Critical Problems of the Coastal Zone*. Boston: Massachusetts Institute of Technology, 1972.

Natural Water Commission. *Water Policies for the Future: Final Report to the President and to the Congress of the United States*. Washington, D.C.: U.S. GPO, 1973.

The Conservation Foundation. *The Decline of Galveston Bay*. Washington, D.C.: The Conservation Foundation, 1972.

United States Army Corps of Engineers. *Report on the National Shoreline Study*. Washington, D.C.: Department of Army, Corps of Engineers, 1971.

3

Inland Waters

Introduction

The nation's inland waters exist in many forms as rivers, lakes, bogs, swamps, ponds, and ground water. Large bodies of water such as the Mississippi River, the Columbia River, the Great Lakes, and the Everglades are well known, but whether large or small, inland waters are the nation's most vital natural resource. They are critical to the existence of all forms of life. They provide drinking water, habitats for aquatic wildlife, irrigation for crops, waterways for transportation, areas for recreation, and a wide variety of industrial uses such as power generation and cooling water. They also serve, unfortunately, as sinks for waste disposal. Although the importance of the inland waters

76

has long been apparent, only in recent years has an effort been made to develop a comprehensive and coherent national water policy. Because of the abundance of water in most parts of the country, national water policy has usually been formulated as if water were free and its availability unlimited. This was never true in the arid Southwest and, in fact, is no longer true in the nation generally.

Many areas of the United States now face critical water-related problems. Water shortages exist not only in the Southwest, which relies heavily on ground water for its supplies, but also in the Northeast, where the rapidly growing population has begun to overtax the available water sources. Most of our major river systems are grossly polluted, often to the point where they are unfit even for industrial purposes without prior treatment.

Yet polluted streams and depleted water supplies are really symptomatic of a larger problem: our pattern of land use. This larger problem encompasses critical issues affecting the environment, such as population growth (particularly intensified urban growth), economic development, and life-styles. Because of the complexity of interrelationships between water and land use, water policy is one of the most difficult areas in which to define the public interest and establish requirements capable of protecting existing water systems. While there are no easy solutions to the problems of formulating water policy, it is nevertheless evident that future policies must recognize the limited availability of water and the need to improve and protect its quality.

The nation's renewable water resources derive from an average annual precipitation of thirty inches or approximately 4,200 billion gallons per day (bgd). Seventy percent of this is consumed through evaporation and transpiration. Of the remaining 30 percent (approximately 1,260 bgd), the American people currently use 440 bgd. The remainder finds it way into the nation's reservoir of lakes, streams, and ground water. The National Water Commission estimates that by the twenty-first century, the nation will require somewhere between 720 bgd and 2,530 bgd for the purposes of agriculture, industry, and domestic consumption depending upon the policies adopted. The increasing demand for water is one of the major environmental problems that must be confronted by decision makers. Population growth has created some of the demand, but often water development projects themselves have spurred growth and, consequently, the demand for even more water. Population growth and economic development are, therefore, equally significant factors affecting both supply and demand of water. The fact that demands for water and water-related services are affected by a variety of other factors, and by policy decisions in fields quite removed from what is considered water policy, indicates the complexity of issues in water policy formulation. Yet, in the past, many policies have been made with little regard for these additional factors and, in effect, water policies have often been made through inadvertence.

One increasingly critical problem is the growing demand for water supplies due to accelerated energy production. There are currently 36 nuclear power plants in the United States; by the turn of the century, according to current estimates, more than 1,000 nuclear power plants will provide 50 percent of our electricity. If present trends in power consumption continue and technology remains unchanged, an estimated 20 percent of the nation's flowing water will have to be used to cool power plant condensers, both nuclear and traditional, by the year 2000. Other practices related to energy production, such as strip mining, shale-oil production, and coal gasification, also require tremendous amounts of water. Extracting oil shale, for example, could require an estimated twelve to eighteen thousand acre-feet of water supplies. Policy makers will have to seriously weigh the benefits of extracting these fuels and producing more energy against the environmental costs, including reduced amounts and quality of water.

A second major problem decision makers must face concerning inland waters is their deteriorating condition. Our water supplies are polluted by municipal sewage, storm water run-off, industrial wastes, animal wastes, thermal pollution, sediment, agricultural chemicals, mine drainage, oil spills, and so on. Industry, for example, uses more than half the total water withdrawals, mostly for cooling purposes. When returned to the natural environment, this heated water usually has a greatly reduced oxygen content. Heated waste water also carries with it a variety of chemical and other pollutants. Industry produces and uses several hundred new chemicals a year, most of which end up in our waterways, and the effects of these chemicals are largely unknown. The passage of disease organisms and chemicals through municipal purification systems into drinking water is no longer a potential threat; it is reality. Wild and marine life, of course, do not have the benefit of even inadequate purification of their water. Decision makers are thus being forced to recognize the necessity of maintaining a fairly high quality of water that not only will be adequate for both public and industrial needs, but also will be reusable. At the same time, environmental considerations, beyond purely economic ones, for maintaining water quality are increasingly becoming major policy issues.

Several other policy issues relating to inland waters have been sources of conflict for decades. These include irrigation of crop land, construction of dams for hydroelectric power or reclamation projects, channelization of stream beds for flood control or navigation, and drainage of wetland areas for agricultural use. These kinds of projects are controversial because they often encourage growth and industrial development on the one hand, but neglect ecological processes and environmental values on the other. Channelization, for example, has been particularly criticized because it destroys both fish and wildlife habitats as well as the aesthetic values of streams and rivers. Channelization also tends to increase rather than decrease the rate of erosion and the frequency and magnitude of downstream floods.

Water projects, water pollution, and water supply problems are governed by a variety of federal, state, and local laws and agencies. Initiation of water projects, largely under the control of Congress and federal agencies, has a long history dating back to 1818, when the House of Representatives passed a resolution granting Congress the authority to appropriate money for improvement and development of the nation's waterways. The initial concern of Congress was to improve navigability of waterways. Later, the two federal agencies responsible for designing, planning, and constructing water development projects (the U.S. Army Corps of Engineers and the Bureau of Reclamation) also concentrated their efforts on offsetting the variability of precipitation and streamflow and their effects upon water supplies. However, prior to the passage of the 1969 National Environmental Policy Act (NEPA), the processes for reviewing federal projects, with an agency or by members of the public, were not designed to consider environmental impacts of the projects. The NEPA requires the agency planning a project to circulate an environmental impact statement for comment to the other federal agencies which have "jurisdiction by law or special expertise with respect to any environmental impact involved." The states, which have their own laws pertaining to water projects, have usually failed to include any but economic considerations in their approval of federal water projects.

Federal involvement in water pollution policy has a much shorter history than its involvement in water projects. The first Water Pollution Control Act, passed in 1948, made it clear that states were primarily responsible for controlling water quality. Federal enforcement of pollution controls was restricted to interstate cases, and only at the request of a governor. The Water Quality Act of 1965 for the first time established a federal organization, the Federal Water Pollution Control Administration, set up in the Department of the Interior, to help control water pollution. Then in 1972, amendments to the 1948 Pollution Control Act further extended federal responsibility for formulating a broad policy on national water quality. These amendments made it a national policy to prevent the use of water bodies for any waste disposal by 1985. And finally, in December 1974, the first drinking-water supply act was enacted by the federal government. The responsibility for planning, implementing, and administering national policy, however, is still assigned largely to the states. Municipal governments are required to construct and operate their own waste treatment facilities. In spite of increased federal efforts to reduce water pollution and supply problems, there still remain tremendous difficulties in integrating and implementing policies among federal, state, and municipal governments.

CASE I   Channelization: Oklawaha River, Florida

The Oklawaha Valley ecosystem in Florida is one of the most distinctive semitropical areas in the United States. The valley forest is a tremendous, unspoiled hardwood forest, and the Oklawaha River, which runs through it, was a potential candidate for protection under the 1968 Wild and Scenic Rivers Act. The river has also been selected for a major project by the Army Corps of Engineers called the Cross-Florida Barge Canal. Authorized by Congress in 1942 by a one vote margin, the canal was conceived mainly as protection against possible Nazi submarine attacks. The war delayed the construction of the canal, however, and funds for the project were not appropriated by Congress until the early 1960s. With President Johnson's blessings, and in spite of the Department of the Interior's 1963 recommendation that the Oklawaha be preserved as a wild and scenic river, the corps began construction of the canal in February 1964. The threatened destruction of the Oklawaha River system because of the canal construction engendered one of the most intense conservation battles in the history of the United States.

The Actors

The key citizen groups involved in the Florida canal dispute were the Florida Defenders of the Environment (FDE) and the Environmental Defense Fund (EDF). The FDE formed the backbone of what became the National Coalition to Save the Oklawaha, which included the Florida and National Audubon Societies, Friends of the Earth, the Izaak Walton League, the Sierra Club, Trout Unlimited, the Wilderness Society, and the Wildlife Management Institute, along with the EDF. This coalition represented tremendous citizen pressure to save the Oklawaha.

The key government actor was, of course, the Army Corps of Engineers, but other government agencies were also involved: the Department of the Interior, the Forest Service, the Bureau of Sport Fisheries and Wildlife, and eventually the Department of Justice. The state agency with specific jurisdiction in this case was the Florida Canal Authority. Finally, the executive branch played a crucial role in the case: both the President's Council on Environmental Quality (CEQ) and President Nixon himself took part in halting further construction of the Florida canal in 1971.

The Policy Process

The initial stage of construction of the 107-mile canal entailed building two dams and a reservoir that flooded 13,000 acres of forest. By early 1966, public reaction against the first twenty-seven miles of the canal was strong enough to pressure the governor of Florida to hold a public meeting. At the widely attended meeting, citizens voiced their concern over the threat to the ecology of the Oklawaha River and, particularly, over the possibility that the region's aquifer could be polluted by porosity and leakage of the canal. The governor and the state legislators ignored citizens' protests, however, until the opposition reorganized and formed the Florida Defenders of the Environment in 1969.

The membership of the FDE included more than 300 scientists, lawyers, economists, land planners, and concerned citizens. William Partington, assistant director of the Florida Audubon Society, took a leave of absence from that organization to serve as president of FDE. The first step that the FDE took was to pool its scientific knowledge and publish a 115-page report entitled *Environmental Impact of the Cross-Florida Barge Canal with Special Emphasis on the Oklawaha Regional Ecosystem*. Released in March 1970, the report contains special studies contributed by geologists, ecologists, biologists, and hydrologists from various Florida universities. This support of the universities proved to be one of the key influences on the outcome of the initial canal conflict.

FDE used a number of other techniques in its struggle to stop the canal construction. The members sent a letter to President Nixon signed by over 150 scientists asking for a moratorium on construction; they urged a land-use study of the Oklawaha region to find alternatives to the canal; they made public appearances whenever possible; they enlisted the support of the media, particularly the cartoonists; they served as an information source for those who inquired about the issues; and, finally, they made a tremendous effort to brief the Florida delegation to Congress, the governor, members of the state cabinet, the heads of state and federal agencies, and the heads of conservation organizations about developments in the case.

By late 1970, most evidence favored halting construction. Secretary of the Interior Walter Hickel issued a report on the barge-canal project that referred to the FDE study and recommended a fifteen-month moratorium on the construction to allow for further research. The report on the canal from the Council on Environmental Quality (CEQ) recommended to the president that the project be terminated. Significantly, the Army Corps of Engineers' Citizen Advisory Board also recommended a "complete review" of the project based on the material that had been furnished by the FDE.

Also in late 1970, the FDE became one of the plaintiffs in a suit filed by the Environmental Defense Fund which sought a preliminary injunction to stop further construction of the canal, and eventually, a permanent injunction to completely halt the project. The judge ruling in the case granted the preliminary injunction on January 15, 1971. Four days later, President Nixon halted all work on the canal.

The struggle, however, was not yet over. In April 1971, the Forest Service recommended immediately lowering the water level of Rodman Reservoir to the normal river channel in order to save the remaining live trees in the reservoir. In May 1971, the Bureau of Sport Fisheries and Wildlife recommended to the CEQ (which, along with the Department of the Army, was making a study ordered by President Nixon of the future of the Oklawaha) that the Rodman pool be drained and the Oklawaha River Valley be returned to its natural condition. In September 1971, the Justice Department attempted to obtain a temporary draindown of the pool and was unsuccessful because of local judicial resistance. It tried again in the spring of 1972 and again was unsuccessful. Finally, in July 1972, a federal court authorized lowering the reservoir, only to have that authorization rescinded in February 1973 by a local court order increasing the level of the reservoir.

Along with the confusion of policy as to the status of the Rodman Reservoir, five suits connected with the Cross-Florida Barge Canal went to the district court in Jacksonville. One of these was the EDF suit for a permanent injunction against further construction of the canal, and another was the Florida Canal Authority's suit which disputed the president's right to stop by executive action a project authorized and funded by Congress.

Outcome

On February 4, 1974, U.S. Circuit Court Judge Harvey Johnsen ruled that the Cross-Florida Barge Canal project still existed and that President Nixon lacked the authority to halt the project. Judge Johnsen also ordered the release of $150,000 authorized by Congress, but impounded by the Nixon administration, for a new environmental impact study of the project. Finally, he ruled that the water level of Rodman Reservoir must remain at eighteen feet unless otherwise approved by Congress. The Justice Department is expected to appeal this ruling, and the opponents of the canal plan to continue the fight in Congress. Meanwhile, the impact assessment is being prepared by an inter-agency group lead by the Army Corps of Engineers. The final report is expected to be ready in September, 1976. This case is an excellent example of the difficulty of killing a project once it has been authorized by Congress.

CASE II   Dam Construction: Hells Canyon, Idaho

For almost 200 miles along the border of Idaho and Oregon, the Snake River has carved out the deepest gorge in North America, averaging 5,500 feet deep. The Middle Snake River, which runs through Hells Canyon, is one of the last free-flowing sections on the Snake

River. It supports an amazing variety of fish and wildlife, including some 150 species of birds and 25 species of fish. Like many of the nation's rivers, however, the untamed Snake is a potential source of hydroelectric energy. The battle to prevent the damming of Hells Canyon has been going on since 1954, when the first proposal for two dams was made to the Federal Power Commission. The struggle has highlighted the issue of whether the need for large-scale hydroelectric projects is genuine, or whether the power companies themselves generate much of the demand for their product. At the same time, the economic value of destroying one of the most scenic sites in the United States has been increasingly challenged as the public has become aware of the intended fate of Hells Canyon.

The Actors

The two federal agencies with major jurisdiction in the Hells Canyon case are the Federal Power Commission (FPC), which licenses all hydroelectric projects to private concerns, and the Department of the Interior, which also may authorize the construction of such projects by other federal agencies. U.S. Senators Frank Church and James McClure of Idaho and Bob Packwood of Oregon became the key figures at the national level when the conflict moved into the halls of Congress. The only state agency that has played a role in the Hells Canyon battle has been the Idaho Water Resources Board, which intervened with the FPC to build the High Mountain Sheep Dam itself.

The two private companies involved in the struggle over Hells Canyon were the Pacific Northwest Power Company (PNP) and the Washington Public Power Supply System (WPPSS)—both of which filed proposals to build dams in Hells Canyon. The citizens' groups which first intervened with the FPC to represent environmental interests at Hells Canyon were the Idaho Alpine Club, the Sierra Club, and the Federation of Western Outdoor Clubs. Later in the conflict, the major force to save Hells Canyon became the Hells Canyon Preservation Council, a small group of Idaho conservationists.

The Policy Process

The first applicant to file with the Federal Power Commission to dam Hells Canyon was the Pacific Northwest Power Company in 1954. Three years later, the examiner for the FPC recommended licensing the dam at Pleasant Valley, twenty miles farther upstream from the first proposed site. In 1958, however, the commission denied the license on the grounds that the full hydroelectric potential of the river would not be developed under PNP's proposal. PNP then reapplied, this time proposing a dam at High Mountain Sheep, about half a mile above the confluence of the Salmon and Snake rivers. At this site, the dam would be 670 feet high and would create a 58-mile reservoir in the heart of Hells Canyon.

Another company, Washington Public Power Supply System, then became interested in Hells Canyon and, in 1960, filed a proposal with the FPC to build Nez Percé Dam a mile below the Salmon-Snake confluence. Later the company amended its application, proposing to build either at High Mountain Sheep or at Nez Percé. The FPC, however, again recommended the issuance of a license to Pacific Northwest Power. At the same time, Secretary of Interior Stewart Udall decided the federal government should build the dam, if it was to be built at all, and he intervened with the FPC. Udall's intervention gave conservationists the reprieve they needed to organize an effort to save the canyon. The conservationists moved the battle into the courts; and after a five-year legal struggle, the Supreme Court ruled in June 1967 that the FPC had to reexamine more carefully all the arguments about the dam, including the case for no dam at all.

After the Supreme Court decision, the Idaho Alpine Club, the Sierra Club, and the Federation of Western Outdoor Clubs filed a petition of intervention with the FPC to represent the public interest in Hells Canyon. A few months later, the Hells Canyon Preservation Council was founded to help rally public opinion and to prepare for the FPC hearings in 1968. Working closely with other conservation groups such as the Sierra Club and the Wilderness Society, the council compiled an impressive amount of evidence against the dam. It also tried to find alternatives to the dam site. According to the power companies, the Hells Canyon site was selected because the dam would generate enough inexpensive electricity to meet the demands of the Northwest. However, even the power companies' figures differed as to how cheap the electricity would be, and many citizens began to question whether there was even a real need for the power. The power companies then switched tactics: they described the site as bleak and barren, devoid of any beauty, and they emphasized its economic benefits, such as the possibility of new jobs and increased tax revenues.

In the face of growing opposition to the dam, the two power companies (PNP and WPPSS) decided in early 1968 to join forces and to file jointly with the FPC to build at High Mountain Sheep. This tactic only intensified citizen opposition; and at the FPC hearings in Lewiston, Idaho, and Portland, Oregon, in September 1968, scores of people testified against the dam. The Hells Canyon Preservation Council presented petitions with 6,000 signatures, and hundreds of letters were sent from across the country. Yet in November 1968, the Department of the Interior announced that it had formed a coalition with the two power companies. According to the coalition plan, the utilities would prepay the department for fifty years' worth of power. Using these funds and a congressional appropriation, the Department of Interior would then build the dam at the Appaloosa site, twelve miles upstream. The coalition hoped to rush an authorization bill through Congress.

About the same time, however, Senators Len Jordan and Frank Church of Idaho had introduced a bill in Congress calling for a ten-year moratorium on dam construction in the middle of Snake River. Senator Jordan, a proponent of reclamation projects, apparently hoped that the moratorium would force power companies to pursue other alternatives, so that the canyon could be dammed for reclamation and irrigation schemes in southern Idaho. His proposal, supported by the Idaho Water Resources Board, was to build according to the old Nez Percé proposal, but then to pump the reservoir's waters back upstream to make southern Idaho bloom. Senator Church initially hoped the moratorium would at least give conservationists time to protect the canyon.

In the interim, the Hells Canyon Preservation Council had been working on a proposal to protect the canyon as Hells Canyon–Snake National River. The proposal, supported by the Sierra Club and the Wilderness Society, called for preserving some 714,000 acres, 400,000 of which were to be protected as wilderness. The bill was introduced by Senator Bob Packwood of Oregon in January 1970. In February 1970, the Senate Subcommittee on Water and Power held hearings on the Church–Jordan Moratorium Bill, but more than half the witnesses and people who had written to the committee supported Packwood's National River Bill over the moratorium. The moratorium did pass the Senate, but it died when the House took no action.

By this time, conservationists had become concerned that the moratorium would stall action on the national river proposal. Senator Church, however, remained adamant about his moratorium proposal, and he had the support of Senators Jordan and Hatfield as well. When the hearing was finally held on the National River Bill in September 1971, the lack of support from the three key senators spelled disaster for efforts of the conservationists. Continued public pressure, however, inspired the two senators from Oregon and the two senators from Idaho to compromise on a new bill, which they introduced in July 1973.

Outcome

The bill proposed a Hells Canyon National Recreation Area with 101 miles of free-flowing Snake River to be given a wild and scenic status under the 1968 Wild and Scenic River Act. The bill would also give instant wilderness classification status to 75,000 acres in Hells Canyon, and protect the rest (700,000 acres) in a recreation status. The Senate version of the bill now appears to have a very good chance of passage, but H.R. 30 has met with stiff opposition from industry and the Ford administration. Conservationists are cautiously optimistic that the House bill will pass in spite of these pressures. If not, the moratorium on dam construction in Hells Canyon ends on September 11, 1975, when the Federal Power Commission will be free to approve construction of the proposed dams. One hopes Hells Canyon will not meet the same fate as have many of the other beautiful free-flowing rivers in America. But there is now reason to hope that Hells Canyon may remain in the natural state. On January 14, 1976, the Hells Canyon National Recreation Area was established by law (PL94–199), protecting lands already designated as "wilderness" and providing for the study of additional areas for possible inclusion. So it appears that citizen perseverance, in this case, saved one of the very few remaining wild canyons from commercial development.

CASE III   Saving a Lake: Lake Washington, Washington

Lake Washington is Washington State's second largest freshwater lake, some twenty miles long and two to four miles wide. It lies just east of Seattle, which became a boom town in the Northwest during the 1950s and 1960s. As early as 1950, the pollution problem in the lake was already apparent. The population on the east side of the lake had risen dramatically; ten new towns were incorporated into King County in the 1950–60 period. By the mid-1950s, these towns were pouring 20 million gallons a day of treated and untreated effluents into Lake Washington. (Seattle disposed of its waste in Elliott Bay on the west side of the town, thereby destroying access to the beaches of Puget Sound which links the city with the Pacific Ocean.) Even though Lake Washington was not the major source of drinking water for the area, it was a prime recreation area and a source for marine life. The citizen effort to save the lake was so successful that Seattle won the All-America City Award in 1960. It is a classic story of effective citizen action.

The Actors

In 1955, more than thirty different agencies had sewage responsibilities around Lake Washington. The newly incorporated towns—eighteen governmental units with conflicting goals and lake policies—further fragmented jurisdiction. To complicate the situation even more, there was no legal mechanism by which the county, or even the state, could assume the task of halting the pollution.

A key figure who emerged in the early 1950s to outline a plan for Seattle's future was James Ellis, a young attorney and special deputy prosecutor who had tried to revise the King County Charter. This revision plan, sponsored by the Municipal League of Seattle and the Seattle League of Women Voters, was defeated at the polls in 1952. These two groups later inspired the movement which established in 1956 the Citizens Advisory Committee, a group appointed by the mayor of Seattle and the board of the King County commissioners. The committee was the key force in the effort to pass legislation controlling pollution of Lake Washington. Following the passage of the legislation (which was then to be approved by the voters), the major force which ran the campaign to establish the Metropolitan Municipal Corporation for the Seattle area was the Metro Action Committee, consisting of 400 members.

Strong opposition to the Metro plan was led by the Metropolitan League of Voters Against Metro. This group was supported by the Washington State Grange and Apartment House Owners and Managers, mostly on grounds that Metro would be costly and could become a "supergovernment."

The Policy Process

The Citizens Advisory Committee, consisting of seventy-five members under the chairmanship of Jim Ellis, studied various problems in the Seattle area besides the sewage-disposal problem. They recommended to the mayor and the county commissioners that the state legislature permit cities and counties in the area to join together in a metropolitan council. The Metropolitan Municipal Corporation Act, passed in 1957 by a one-vote margin in the legislature, specified six problem areas that were to be the concern of the proposed metropolitan agency—sewage, garbage disposal, water supplies, transportation, planning, and parks and parkways. With the referendum set for March 11, 1958, the Metro Action Committee was organized to run a campaign in support of the measure. Numerous other organizations endorsed the proposition, and the press, radio, and TV launched a public information campaign. In spite of success in Seattle, the suburban vote defeated the bill.

The Metro Action Committee then devised a new strategy. They invited suburban representatives to help prepare a new plan. Those cities too remote to be concerned were excluded from the proposed area to be covered by the metropolitan agency. The new plan also limited the agency's function to sewage disposal only, with the option to vote in additional functions later. A new election date was set for September 1958. This time the Metro Action Committee was supported by nine of the ten city councils involved and all ten mayors in the area. The committee was also supported by the Municipal League of Seattle and King County, the King County Medical Society, the King County Medical Auxiliary, the League of Women Voters of Seattle and Bellevue, the chambers of commerce, sportsmen's groups, and various other organizations.

Even though the opposition to the Metro plan was very strong, the determination and efforts of the committee volunteers were inexorable, climaxed by a "Metro March" in which 5,000 volunteers handed out 100,000 pamphlets door to door a few days before the election. The summer preceding the election had been particularly hot and helped emphasize the importance of maintaining clean recreational waters around the city. The September 9 referendum overwhelmingly established the municipality of metropolitan Seattle; the Metro plan was approved by 58 percent of the voters in Seattle and 67 percent in the suburbs.

Outcome

The original plan called for constructing sewage facilities over a ten-year period at a cost of $125 million, to be financed by selling revenue bonds. Later, extending the system to other suburbs raised the cost to $145 million, but even so the cost-per-month to the average residential home owner was kept to $2.00. The system currently consists of 170 miles of interceptor sewers and seven treatment plants. By the summer of 1966, all sewage and effluent disposal into Lake Washington had ceased, and by 1971, the water quality in the lake had returned to 1950 conditions.

CASE IV   Saving a River: The Willamette, Oregon

The beautiful Willamette River, which for 185 miles flows entirely in the state of Oregon, had become the Northwest's most polluted waterway by 1960. The Willamette Valley had long been the state's center of industry and commerce, supporting 70 percent of Oregon's 2.1 million people. By 1950, a huge complex of wood-pulp mills lined both sides of the river and poured enormous quantities of wood chips, sugars, and pulping liquors into the water. Other industries also dumped their wastes into the river, and some twenty municipalities poured their sewage into it. The river was a resource that Oregon could not afford to lose. Besides providing water for municipal and industrial purposes, the river served as a source of irrigation for thousands of acres of farmland, as a source of gravel, and most important, as a spawning ground for thousands of salmon and trout. The struggle to save the Willamette, which dates back as early as the 1920s, is an example of extraordinary citizen involvement in both water quality and land-use policies.

The Actors

The major state actor with policy-making jurisdiction over the Willamette was the state Sanitary Authority, established in 1939 and renamed the Department of Environmental Quality in 1967. At the federal level, the Army Corps of Engineers had jurisdiction under the Refuse Act of 1899 to issue permits for discharges into a navigable stream. The corps made no effort, however, to enforce this policy until 1971. Following passage of the 1965 Water Quality Control Act, the federal government finally began to help states, including Oregon, control water pollution. In the Willamette case, the Federal Water Pollution Control Administration played a significant role in the river cleanup.

Private citizens, both in groups and as individuals, were key actors in restoring the Willamette. Such groups as the Portland City Club and the Izaak Walton League were very important in eliciting citizen action on behalf of the river. The key individual in the Willamette campaign was Tom McCall, a former TV news commentator, who was elected governor in 1967 on a campaign promise of saving the river.

Finally, industry played a major role in the Willamette case. At many stages of the battle, industry opposed controlling pollution, but in numerous other instances, industry proved surprisingly cooperative.

The Policy Process

The Portland City Club, one of the first groups to study the condition of the Willamette, reported in 1927 that the river was "ugly and filthy" and concluded that its condition was "intolerable." Two years later, it was discovered that the river's dissolved oxygen level was less than 0.5 parts per million in certain places. The amount of dissolved oxygen limits fish and plant life which the aquatic system can support as well as the amount of waste it can assimilate. Five parts per million is considered the minimum amount of dissolved oxygen necessary to maintain a healthy river system.

During the 1930s, concern for the river increased. In 1933, the governor called a statewide conference about stream pollution. The state legislature finally passed a water pollution bill in 1937, but it was vetoed by the governor on grounds that it would cause financial hardship to cities and towns. By 1938, groups such as the Izaak Walton League decided to place an initiative measure on the ballot and bypass the legislature altogether. The measure, entitled the "Water Purification and Prevention of Pollution Bill," passed by a three to one margin. The act made restoring and maintaining the natural purity of all public waters a matter of public policy. It also authorized establishing water quality standards and creating a six-member state Sanitary Authority. The authority was directed to develop a statewide control program and to enforce the new requirements.

The Sanitary Authority, organized in 1939, formulated a policy requiring municipalities to provide primary treatment and chlorination of wastes. World War II delayed construction of treatment plants, however, and municipalities were not especially enthusiastic about being the first to comply with the requirements. In 1944, Portland took the lead, again as a result of a citizens' campaign. Under the leadership of a newspaper editor, the campaign won voters' approval of a $12 million bond issue to construct an interceptor system between the city's sixty-five sewer outfalls into the river and a new treatment plant. Other municipalities complied later, and by 1957, all cities on the Willamette were providing at least primary treatment of their wastes. This accomplishment was due entirely to public support since all construction costs for the plants were paid for by the cities.

But treating municipal wastes did not clean up the river. By 1957, pulp and paper mills had been directed to reduce their pollution discharges to maintain a minimum dissolved oxygen content of five parts per million. As more mills appeared, however, the river continued to deteriorate rapidly. The worst effect was seen in the decline of salmon runs. A 1967 report of the Federal Water Pollution Control Administration (now part of the Environmental Protection Agency) blamed the pulp and paper industry for the loss of the salmon. Its findings have never been refuted by the industry.

Finally, with the election of Governor McCall in 1967, and with broad public support, new legislation was enacted to strengthen the state Sanitary Authority's powers. The Sanitary Authority became the Department of Environmental Quality, and its chief enforcement tool is an annual permit system which allows certain "pollution quotas" for the year. As more industries develop, the allotted quota for each industry will become smaller. Failure to comply with the quotas can incur a $500-a-day fine or even the closing of polluting facilities. The 1967 legislation also requires mandatory secondary treatment for all discharges, making the Willamette the first major river in the country protected by such treatment.

Outcome

The 1967 program has reduced waste discharges into the Willamette by 90 percent. Since 1969, the dissolved oxygen level in the river has remained above the standard five parts per million, even in the summer months. The river is now safe for water sports and, most important, for marine life. In 1965, only 79 chinook salmon were counted going up the river; in 1972, the number had increased to 11,614. The cost of the new facilities has been about $150 million for municipalities and about $50 million for industry. The state paid 30 percent of the bill for the cities and has offered tax incentives to industry to help pay their costs. So far, the state has not had to bring suit against a single violator.

Citizens' concern for the Willamette River also spurred passage of a Greenbelt Bill in 1967 which preserves open space along the river's banks. State and local public lands currently preserve only 60 of the 510 miles of river bank, but another 156 miles is being purchased with combined state and federal funding. This greenbelt plan will eventually provide a system of recreation camps for boaters along the length of the Willamette, a series of recreation areas and boat-launching sites, a trail system for hiking, cycling, and riding, and other recreational features. It will be a fitting reminder of the value and importance of maintaining a healthy river system.

CASE V   Agricultural Water Supply: Kern County, California

Water supply issues in California entail geographical obstructions and political conflicts. The northern portion of the state has abundant sources of water, while supply is limited in the southern portion. The growing population—in already overpopulated California—has made the issue of water supply a critical one. In 1960, in spite of heavy opposition from the north, voters approved the state Water Bond Act which authorized a project to bring northern waters south via aqueducts. Authorized water agencies in the south were required to negotiate contracts with the state to get their water supply. This situation created some conflicts of interest, particularly in areas such as Kern County where the new water was to supply largely agricultural needs. The county's urban population, centered in the city of Bakersfield, was reluctant to subsidize the area's agricultural water needs. The efforts of citizens in Kern County to set equitable policies for distributing their water supply is interesting in terms both of policy-making and of the impact of prevailing attitudes about water on water supply decisions.

The Actors

The citizens of Kern County, primarily as voters, were responsible for setting water supply policies in this case. The major official agency involved in the conflict was the Kern County Water Agency, established in 1961. Citizens' groups included the Citizens' Campaign Committee and the local League of Women Voters.

The Policy Process

Kern County voters willingly approved the 1960 state Water Bond Act; the need for more water in the south was considered obvious, and the act did not commit Kern County residents to any decisions. The question of whether to set up a Kern County Water Agency to negotiate with the state for water met with much more opposition. The main resistance was against having a new governmental structure. The Kern County Board of Supervisors, however, supported the idea of establishing a county agency solely responsible for dealing with water problems. The agency proposal was passed in 1961, but with the provision that the entire voting population of the county would be called upon to approve the contract drawn up between the water agency and the state of California.

It took the agency's committee two years to reach an agreement with the state on the water contract. The Kern County Water Agency was potentially the largest contractor for agricultural water in the state, and the second largest water contractor of any kind. About 95 percent of the water to be purchased was for agricultural purposes. The contract was defended as the only way to increase economic prosperity in the area.

Residents of Bakersfield, however, were unconvinced. They did not object to the contract on the grounds that the area was already developed enough or that the water was probably not needed. Instead, their objection was that urban residents should not have to pay for water that would primarily benefit farmers and only secondarily benefit themselves. The split in opinion was largely between city residents and farmers, although a few farmers opposed the contract because more water would attract more farmers to the area.

Directing the campaign in support of the contract was the Citizens' Campaign Committee. The League of Women Voters also printed a fact sheet in support of the contract, obtained radio and television time, held meetings, and printed "Yes for Water" lapel tags. The opposition mailed a four-page flyer to every voter emphasizing the urban/rural split. On election day, November 12, 1963, 45 percent of the eligible voters turned out and approved the contract by a margin of 589 ballots, despite a fifty-cent jump in the tax rate. The vote essentially committed the area to further growth.

The water supply issue was not over, however, because the question of whether or not to form a greater Bakersfield water district was unresolved. All other areas in Kern County were already organized into districts. The problem for Bakersfield was that the incorporated city covered only one-third of the area of greater Bakersfield and included only one-third of the population; greater Bakersfield itself had no political or jurisdictional unity. The City Council was opposed to the idea of a water district because it felt that unincorporated areas would then be less dependent on council decisions about water supply. Opposing forces wanted the Kern County Water Agency to take on the responsibility of handling imported water supplies for greater Bakersfield. The agency, however, felt that this was not within its jurisdiction and that a local water district should be established. On the advice of the League of Women Voters, which had made a two-year study of the water situation in greater Bakersfield, the water agency adopted a policy of not making any long-term contract for water except with a duly constituted public agency.

A citizens' committee was formed to circulate petitions and collect the signatures of the 10 percent of the voters necessary to call an election. But the plan for a greater Bakersfield water district plan was not approved in the election and, afterwards, the Kern County Water Agency formed an improvement agency to meet the needs of Bakersfield.

Outcome

In the fall of 1971, citizens of Kern County did approve a bond issue totaling $17.5 million to finance the construction of a project to bring more water into the greater Bakersfield area. The cross-valley canal project should be completed in 1976. This project will deliver additional water to greater Bakersfield and to four agricultural districts in Kern County. By 1990, a maximum delivery of 1,153,400 acre-feet per year (one acre-foot equals 325,851 gallons of water) is expected in Kern County. This delivery is based on projected needs for the area. In this case, however, the actual needs of the area were not really the major issue in the citizens' efforts to define their water policies. Nor, for that matter, were the institutions involved in setting water policies for Kern County especially concerned about the environmental implications of their decisions, particularly their commitment to increased development.

CASE VI   Water Quality and Watershed Protection: Lake Tahoe, California

Lake Tahoe is nestled in the Sierra Mountains between California and Nevada. Many people consider it to be one of the three most beautiful lakes in the world, rivaled only by Crater Lake in Oregon and Lake Baikal in the U.S.S.R. Lake Tahoe is 22 miles long, 12 miles wide, 1,645 feet deep, and its water is so clear that sunlight supports plant growth 400 feet below the surface. It is also the major source of water for local residents. The Lake Tahoe Basin is the permanent home for 26,000 residents, but during the summer and winter months, the population may jump to 100,000. Estimates of future summer populations reach as high as 750,000.

The increased population living around the lake on a permanent or seasonal basis has created two critical issues that concern both local citizens and residents of other communities: the deterioration of the lake as a drinking-water source, due to sewage and sedimentation, and the overdevelopment of the lakeshore. Both of these problems threaten what many people consider the lake's chief asset—its recreational value. The Lake Tahoe case is, consequently, much more than a problem of community water supply. The method local citizens used to eliminate their sewage disposal problem is a particularly good example of effective, although limited, citizen action to prevent pollution of a water supply source. The Lake Tahoe case also illustrates how important local support is in coping with other problems, such as sedimentation, which may affect the water supply.

The Actors

Formulating public policy to protect Lake Tahoe presents special difficulties because the political jurisdiction of the lake is divided between two states. In California, the principal agencies concerned with the lake are the Department of Public Health and the Regional Water Quality Control Board, supervised by the state Water Resources Control Board. In Nevada, the state Department of Health has major jurisdiction over the lake, but the lake is further protected by a Nevada state law ("Relating to the Protection of Lake Tahoe and its Watershed"), which was originally passed in 1949 and amended in 1967.

Various federal agencies have also played a role in the Lake Tahoe case, in particular, the Federal Water Quality Administration. Less involved participants were the U.S. Forest Service, which owns half the land in the basin, and the Army Corps of Engineers, which may issue permits for shoreline construction.

Local government was not much involved in the case. There is only one developed city and four counties in the Tahoe area. However, eleven public special service districts have been created to provide sewer services.

One of the chief private actors at Lake Tahoe was the late Joseph McDonald, a former Reno newspaper executive. He headed the Nevada-California Lake Tahoe Association, created in 1957, and helped establish the Lake Tahoe Area Council in 1959. Other private groups concerned with Lake Tahoe have been the Sierra Club, California Tomorrow, and the League to Save Lake Tahoe.

The Policy Process

At first, area residents were concerned about waste disposal at Lake Tahoe. As early as 1945, the California Department of Public Health had prohibited direct discharge of sewage into the lake, and Nevada followed suit in 1949. Most sewage was disposed of in septic tanks. As the population increased around the lake in the 50s, residents began demanding sewer systems. Both the California Regional Water Quality Control Board and the Nevada Department of Health maintained their policy prohibiting discharges into the water, so alternate means of disposal had to be considered.

In 1963, the Lake Tahoe Area Council, at the instigation of Joseph

McDonald, asked experts to study sewage disposal facilities in the Tahoe Basin. On the basis of the study, the council recommended a new concept of waste disposal—waste export. The President's Advisory Committee on Water Pollution Control received the recommendations at a meeting held at Lake Tahoe in the fall of 1963. The seriousness of the problem spurred a conference between the governors of California and Nevada, and the result was the "California-Nevada Governors' Program for Progress," which outlined a policy of sewage disposal for Lake Tahoe based on the export idea.

This plan is now being carried out via four disposal systems which take the area's sewage out of the basin to Alpine County. Alpine County initially refused to cooperate, but then accepted the export plan under a multi-pact agreement made by California state legislators in 1966. To set up the system in the south lake area, a $1.8 million loan was granted from California and another for over $3 million from the U.S. Economic Development Administration. The north end of the lake has been much slower in developing its own system.

At both ends of the lake, the problem in implementing the sewage export plan was the resistance of the local populace. Many home-owners, particularly those who lived at Lake Tahoe only part of the year, were far from enthusiastic about a proposal which could cost an estimated $8,000 per household for sewer services. South Tahoe voters rejected three successive revenue-raising proposals before accepting one in 1966, and even this limited success was largely due to pressures from outside the community.

The majority of local citizens have also been reluctant to accept responsibility for the sedimentation problem of Lake Tahoe. It is now the most serious threat to the quality of the lake. Sedimentation is caused by various human and natural activities, but the major cause has been development of the shoreline. Most citizens have not realized that the sediment (rich in nutrients) and increasing turbidity encourage the growth of algae. In the last ten years, the growth of algae has increased by about 70 percent.

Those citizens who appreciated the seriousness of the sedimentation problem (and the concomitant development problem) tried to attack the problem by establishing a bi-state agency, the Tahoe Regional Planning Agency (TRPA). The agency was really the outgrowth of a concept proposed by Joseph McDonald and the Lake Tahoe Area Council that was first introduced in the California legislature in 1967.

After being passed back and forth between Nevada and California for two years, the plan was finally adopted in 1969 and ratified by Congress in December of that year. TRPA has ten members, five appointed by each state.

Originally, the agency was conceived as an instrument to prevent further degradation of the lake basin. The agency's success toward this end, however, has been limited. Following congressional ratification of the bi-state compact, several citizens' groups, including the Sierra Club, California Tomorrow, and the League to Save Lake Tahoe, joined in an appeal for a complete moratorium on all development in the Lake Tahoe Basin pending completion and adoption of a plan from the agency. This would have halted the sedimentation problem and rapid development along the shoreline. TRPA preferred, however, to leave the issue open while making its study.

Outcome

Finally, after a year of research, public hearings, and conflict, TRPA approved a basinwide, regional land-use plan in December 1972, but local resistance to this plan delayed its implementation. The agency was plagued by threats of inverse condemnation suits totaling $170 million by the owners of land deemed "ecologically too fragile for the type of development contemplated by the landowners." TRPA also had to raise the money, up to $150 million, to buy the estimated 34,000 acres to be purchased under the plan.

Furthermore, many California residents and legislators considered the plan too weak to protect the Tahoe Basin; and so in 1974, the California Tahoe Regional Planning Agency was reorganized and strengthened. In April 1975, the California agency revealed its own plan for controlling growth in the Tahoe Basin, which went far beyond that already adopted by the bi-state agency. Meanwhile, the bi-state agency's directors voted unanimously to relax draft regulations on three points of a proposed shore ordinance that had been considered too restrictive by certain developers. Both agencies' plans face public hearings and further agency consideration, but somehow a permanent regional plan must be adopted before the temporary controls of the bi-state agency expire in July 1976. A strong plan will do much to preserve the magnificent waters of Lake Tahoe and the scenic beauty of the surrounding basin.

CASE VII   Ecological Conservation: Thompson Pond, New York

Thompson Pond is a 100-acre lake about 100 miles from New York City. Little changed since the Ice Age, the pond is a favorite nesting location for waterbirds in the entire central Hudson Valley region. Red-tailed hawks, various species of ducks, coots, Canadian geese, osprey, and even a peregrine falcon have been residents around the pond. The pond also supports a thriving marine life. In addition to its value as a bird sanctuary and a fishing hole, the pond is also the head-waters for Wappingers Creek, the principal stream of Dutchess County where Thompson Pond is located. Although it is only a tiny body of water, the pond is critically important in the ecology of the county's chief watershed. The fifteen-year volunteer effort to save an ecologically essential water source and a valuable recreation and study spot is an important example of concerned citizen action outside the realm of government agencies.

The Actors

Private citizens were the chief actors in the fight to preserve Thomp-son Pond. Most of the pond and part of the shoreline were owned by a cattle rancher named George Brown. His support of the preservation plan was essential to its success. Other key citizens were Harry Shapiro, chairman of the Department of Anthropology of the Museum of Nat-ural History in New York, and Elting Arnold, secretary of the Nature Conservancy, a national group which sponsors land conservation through private action. It was Arnold's idea to save the pond (which had not yet been directly threatened by development pressures) by raising money to buy it for the conservancy. Finally, the chairman of the Thompson Pond Committee, Thelma Haight, and the committee's volunteers played important roles in the preservation efforts.

The Policy Process

When Elting Arnold conceived the idea in the late 1950s of pre-serving Thompson Pond by purchasing the land through the Nature Conservancy, he enlisted the support of the town supervisor, Robert Palmatier. They proposed the plan to George Brown, owner of most of the pond, who agreed to sell 173 acres. Half the cost for the land was covered by a purchase-money mortgage, and the remainder was covered by a loan from the Nature Conservancy.

The Thompson Pond Committee was then formed under the direction of Thelma Haight to raise the necessary funds. The twenty-member committee that assisted Haight included the town supervisor and his wife, the owner of the local newspaper, the president of a bird club, a state senator, a prominent attorney, several noted educators, and a few well-to-do benefactors. The committee used a variety of unique techniques to raise the money. One method was a list of "shares" of beauty that were sold under the slogan "Buy now, enjoy always." Items on the list included: "One black oak tree nineteen feet in circumference for $500"; "one acre of blue sky with silhouetted wood ducks for $100"; "one hollow tree with pileated woodpecker's nest for $10"; "one muskrat house (present occupant will remodel in fall) for $5." The committee was able to repay the Nature Conservancy's $20,000 loan after five and a half years of continuous efforts. Most of the donations came from 300 contributors and averaged about $65 apiece.

An additional 135 acres of the Thompson Pond shoreline became available in March of 1972. A well-known area conservationist, Kent Leavitt, handled the negotiations and acquired the tract for $55,000. Again the Nature Conservancy put up the money necessary to guarantee acquisition. The Thompson Pond Committee began work anew to raise funds. Most of the original members of the fifteen-year-old committee were again active in the new campaign. By the fall of 1973, only nine months following acquisition of the new parcel, the committee had raised more than half the required funds. This time a special leaflet was sent to hundreds of residents of the Wappingers Creek watershed area describing the urgency of preserving the pond because of its role in the ecology of the entire region. Contributions were also solicited from local business firms. This enlistment of local support for the conservation cause has been a major objective of the committee.

Outcome

The fifteen-year struggle to save a tiny lake created by a glacier millennia ago has not only protected the district's watershed but has also saved some beautiful acreage for the use and enjoyment of local citizens. While the opportunity to save most of our inland waters in such a fashion is not generally feasible, the determination of the citizens around Thompson Pond to set their own policy for the lake emphasizes that the attitudes of local people are important considerations in making environmental decisions.

Conclusion

Ensuring public access to clean water, recreational areas, and free-flowing rivers may often conflict with equally important public needs for water, such as sewage disposal, power production, irrigation, or development. It is difficult to establish the priority of these important and conflicting demands for water because we do not yet have effective mechanisms for rationally deciding which choices best serve the public interest. This is not to say, however, that the choice is never obvious; consider, for example, the obvious necessity of maintaining clean and healthful sources of drinking water. Yet other factors besides demands for water also influence decisions on water policy. The appeals of economic prosperity, conflicting land-use practices, or uncertainty about who controls the condition of water have often influenced water policy decisions. These conflicting goals and practices have resulted in many policies which are at best inadequate and often unnecessary—even harmful.

The difficulty decision makers have experienced in creating comprehensive water policies is indicative of two basic problems: institutional defects and conflicting perceptions of many water problems. As all seven cases illustrate, water problems generally are first perceived as local problems. The fact that a river runs by several cities, all of which require its use, is irrelevant to most citizens until their own use of the river is threatened. Instead of sharing the benefits and preserving the quality of a nearby water supply, small cities or towns which share the same river basin too often compete fiercely for water supplies; or a state, such as Arizona, which has severe water supply problems, may develop schemes to dam the Grand Canyon, giving little thought to the national implications of such a plan. Particularly in the case of water projects, which many citizens view as a means to immediate prosperity, the local nature of water policy decisions becomes clear.

The cases discussed in this chapter have emphasized only three specific aspects of water policy—pollution, supply, and development projects. Yet water policies dealing with these aspects will also have a much broader impact; water-related decisions affect where people move, how they live, and how they work. Equally important, these decisions also affect plant and animal life, often many miles from the problem being treated. Yet the basic mechanisms which resulted in the decision to dam Hells Canyon or to bring water to Kern County still appear to be operating today, so that the social and environmental consequences of water policies largely ignored by decision makers in the past are apt to be ignored by present-day decision makers. Fuller public participation in the formulation of water policies in recent years demonstrates that citizens have become increasingly concerned with these neglected social and environmental considerations. Yet not all citizen participation in decisions about our inland waters is generated by an environmental concern, as the Kern County case reveals. The case studies in this chapter illustrate both the varieties and degrees of citizen concern on environmental issues.

In order to consider some of the particular policy implications of these case studies, they will be reviewed according to the level at which the policy was formulated—national, state, or local. Water policy formulation at the national level is concentrated in the area of major projects—flood control, dam and channel construction, irrigation projects, and so on. The major federal agencies connected with the two case studies involving such projects—the Cross-Florida Barge Canal and the Hells Canyon Dam—were the U.S. Army Corps of Engineers, the Federal Power Commission (FPC), and the Department of the Interior.

These cases reveal, first of all, that on the agency level of policy formulation, attempted citizen participation has been limited or treated with outright antagonism. Although both the Corps of Engineers and the FPC have procedures for public hearings, the case studies indicate that the initial hearings have not adequately informed the public about the total impact of a proposal. In the Cross-Florida Barge Canal case, twenty years elapsed between the time the project was approved and construction of the canal began; but there was no second public review of the plans. This refusal to hold another hearing indicates that agencies consider public participation in the initial stages of the policy process valuable largely as a means to acquire public acquiescence to agency decisions, not as a means to incorporate public suggestions or criticisms in the project plans.

Second, both the Hells Canyon and Cross-Florida cases reveal that agencies make little attempt to question the real need for certain projects or their potential environmental impact. The Federal Power Commission relies on estimates by prospective builders of hydroelectric power facilities to determine the needs of the recipient area. Yet even when the Supreme Court ordered the FPC to reexamine this issue in the Hells Canyon case, the commission still recommended licensing the two power companies to build the Hells Canyon Dam. And in both the Hells Canyon and Cross-Florida cases, the initial investments of private companies and the Army Corps of Engineers became major obstacles to attempts at altering the agencies' policies, even though the need for the projects had been severely questioned by the public and the potential damage to the environment had been substantiated by scientific evidence. The passage in 1969 of the National Environmental Policy Act has had no certain effect, to date, on the probable outcome of these two cases.

Jurisdictional mixup is the third problem revealed by these two cases. This confusion exists at the various levels and between different agencies of the federal government. Moreover, the policies that do exist are often not integrated between these levels. For example, in the Hells Canyon case, two federal agencies, the FPC and the Department of the Interior, initially competed with each other to construct the dam. Then the Interior Department teamed up with the power companies in order to build the dam, while the Supreme Court suggested the possibility of not building the dam at all. Finally, the Department of Interior supported the moratorium proposal offered by two congressmen and apparently now supports the Hells Canyon National Recreation Area idea. The Florida Canal case is even more confusing: an initial policy established by Congress was later rescinded by the president at the recommendation of several federal agencies, and then it was reinstated by a district court judge ruling on a suit brought by a state agency. In both cases, citizens had difficulty in deciding where the appropriate arena for policy making lay in this tangle of multi-level decisions.

In the cases of the Willamette River and Lake Tahoe, citizen participation in policy making was centered primarily at the state level. Water policy formulation at the state level often involves the issues of supply and pollution, as these two cases illustrate. Unlike water projects, these two issues allow citizens significant participation in the decision process through the mechanism of voting. Often, however, the policy a voter is asked to adopt may involve increased taxes or other expenditures. As the Willamette River and Lake Tahoe cases demonstrate, local communities must be prepared to bear much of the cost for water pollution control and water supply programs. Judging from these two case studies, it would appear that a core group of concerned citizens, committed to a policy goal, is essential to convince local voters that the price for improved water services should be paid.

It is interesting that in both the Lake Tahoe and the Willamette River cases, a state agency was established as the result of citizen initiative to deal with specific problems of each area. The Lake Tahoe Agency (TRPA) was an innovation because it involved an interstate compact approved by Congress. The effectiveness of these agencies in policy enforcement, however, was like that in most states—dependent on municipal and industrial cooperation to ensure compliance. The extent of this dependency was evident in both cases, but especially at Lake Tahoe, where local citizens reluctantly had agreed to pay for the agency's sewer system proposal, but adamantly opposed the agency's efforts to regulate land-use practices around the lake.

At the local level, citizen participation in water policy formulation may occur on a variety of issues. The three case studies concerned primarily with local policy decisions are Lake Washington, Kern County, and Thompson Pond. Although at one point the Lake Washington case involved action by the state legislature, it was primarily a local policy issue. The major problem was pollution at Lake Washington, water supply at Kern County, and conservation at Thompson Pond.

Cases such as these, where the locus of policy formulation is essentially local, reveal how important public attitudes can be in the policy-making process. At the local level, when no institution exists to cope with the particular issue and where there is no other obvious arena of decision making, water policy is, by and large, an expression of local opinion which may be influenced by prior decisions—in Kern County, by the state's commitment to bring more water to southern California. For the most part, however, predominant local attitudes seem to govern water-related decisions made primarily at the local level.

Of the seven case studies, the Thompson Pond case is the only one which does not involve policy making through institutional channels of some kind. It has been included for this reason; it is a good example of various noninstitutional methods which citizens may use to formulate policy. Whether planning to save a local pond or fighting to save a nationally known river, citizen participation is an essential part of creating more comprehensive and effective policies for our inland waters.

Readings

Bronson, William W. "It's About Too Late for Lake Tahoe." *Audubon Magazine*, 73 (May 1971), 48–52, 61–64, 70–80.

Gleeson, George W. *The Return of a River*. Corvallis, Oregon: Water Resources Research Institute, Oregon State University, 1972.

Hull, William and Robert. *The Origin and Development of the Waterways Policy of the U.S.* Washington, D.C.: National Waterways Conference, Inc., 1957.

League of Women Voters. *The Big Water Fight*. Brattleboro, Vermont: Stephen Greene, 1966.

Meyers, Charles and Dan Tarlock. *Water Resource Management: A Casebook in Law and Public Policy*. Mineola, New York: Foundation Press, 1971.

Natural Water Commission. *Water Policies for the Future: Final Report to the President and the Congress of the United States by the Natural Water Commission*. Washington, D.C.: U.S. GPO, 1973.

Water Resources Council. *The Nation's Water Resources*. 7 parts. Washington, D.C.: U.S. GPO, 1968.

Wright, Jim. *The Coming Water Famine*. New York: Coward-McCann, 1966.

Zwick, David and Marcy Benstock. *Water Wasteland*. New York: Grossman, 1971.

4

Air Quality
and Weather Modification

Introduction

In order to understand some of the basic difficulties presently confronting both decision makers and citizens in determining air quality and climate modification policies, one must examine, first, the basic premises upon which our actions in this area have been based and, second, the nature and extent of current difficulties. Past policies and practices related to our atmospheric environment have usually ignored the fact that the atmosphere is not infinite. Like water or fossil fuels, air is a limited resource with a limited capacity to absorb wastes. Unlike water, air has no inherent self-cleansing properties, so chemicals

107

and particles must be washed away by rain or filtered by trees and other vegetation. Although wind may carry off pollutants in sparsely populated areas, they still remain in the air. As urban populations become more dense, however, the problem of "heat islands" arises, because energy-intensive cities are warmer than the surrounding countryside. This phenomenon creates atmospheric conditions that trap pollutants above the cities. Currently, the Public Health Service estimates that millions of Americans live in cities with a major air pollution hazard.

The Environmental Protection Agency (EPA) reports that in the United States 140 million tons of waste are pouring into the air every year. The major classes of identified pollutants are particulates, sulfur oxides, hydrocarbons, carbon monoxide, nitrogen oxide, and photochemical oxidants. Extremely hazardous pollutants include airborne asbestos, beryllium, mercury, and lead. But René Dubos, the Pulitzer prize-winning biologist, estimates that perhaps as many as two-thirds of the urban air pollutants have not been identified or analyzed by scientists.

The many sources of known air pollutants generally have been divided into two classes: stationary and nonstationary. Stationary sources include emissions from industrial processes, power generation, and waste incineration. Nonstationary sources include those connected with transportation vehicles such as automobiles, trains, and aircraft. Automobiles alone emit a larger tonnage of wastes than any other source. Measuring the total ton-weight of pollutants emitted from any one source, however, tells nothing of its geographical distribution, nor does such a figure suggest the harmful effect of polluted air upon the health and property of people or its effect upon the climate.

Most medical experts are convinced that breathing polluted air is a hazard to health. Gathering evidence as to the exact correlation of air pollution and certain diseases has been difficult because it is almost impossible to duplicate clinically all the pollutants in the air a person is exposed to. Sometimes the major effect of polluted air is to impair the body's mechanisms, making the individual more susceptible to certain diseases. Asthma outbreaks and air pollution levels have been clearly linked. Further evidence ties chronic bronchitis, pulmonary emphysema (the fastest growing cause of death in the United States), and increases in lung cancer in large urban areas to air pollution. The exact medical costs of human mortality and morbidity are not known, but the EPA estimates that it comes to at least $6 billion annually. The most crucial factor relating to this cost, however, is not merely the monetary sum, but the social significance of this figure. It is no surprise to the city dweller, particularly the inner city inhabitant, to learn that he receives the brunt of the assault from air pollution.

Air pollution is more than a health hazard. It threatens property and vegetation as well as humans and wildlife. As indicated previously, another effect of large-scale air pollution has been the alteration of climates in urban areas. The U.S. Weather Bureau reports that in the winter, cities have 100 percent more fog than rural areas. They also have 50 percent less ultraviolet radiation in the winter than country areas, 25 percent more wind, considerably more cloudiness, and as much as 10 percent more rainfall than the surrounding countryside.[1] The proliferation of dust particles in the air is one explanation for the increased cloudiness in urban areas in recent years, because dust is an effective cloud-forming agent. These conditions have significant economic and social consequences. For example, fog and clouds are a hazard of vehicular travel and add greatly to the incidence of accidents.

The climate of rural areas is also susceptible to adverse effects from air pollution. Studies by meteorologists suggest, for example, that dust particles suspended in the air over northern India and Pakistan have contributed to the spread of desert conditions. Also, jet airplane vapor trails have been observed to evolve into sheets of cirrus clouds.

Air pollution and jet vapor trails are inadvertent causes of climate modification. Man is also deliberately attempting to modify the weather. Most efforts to modify weather have been connected with increasing precipitation rates, but weather modification is far broader in practice than just rainmaking. Today there are operational programs for clearing supercooled fog at airports. Techniques to suppress lightning and hail storms are being investigated, and there are substantial research programs aimed at reducing the damage resulting from hurricanes. Even more ambitious weather modification projects include one proposal to dam the Bering Strait and pump water from the Arctic Ocean into the Pacific. This would induce an increased flow of warm Atlantic water into the Arctic Ocean, which would significantly reduce, or even eliminate, the area covered by sea ice.

The Bering Strait scheme would obviously have dramatic, and per-

---

[1] "The Polluted Air We Breathe," AFL-CIO *American Federationist* (February 1964).

haps drastic, effects upon the earth's climate. Yet even relatively harmless goals, such as increasing the snow pack for skiing, altering the course of a hurricane, or bringing rain to the desert regions, could have a significant impact upon the ecological balance of the affected area. The various effects of deliberate weather modification have not been thoroughly studied and, for most part, attempts to modify the weather ordinarily have excited little attention from the public. Most important, perhaps, is the fact that crucial social and environmental policy questions have not been answered.

Questions relating to climate modification are paralleled by similar questions about controlling air quality. The problem of reducing air pollution, for example, is partly technological, partly economic, partly political, and partly sociological. To illustrate: a policy designed to reduce sulfur dioxide pollution, by requiring the use of expensive low-sulfur coal in the United States, would not only raise the costs for the coal buyer (and ultimately the consumer), but would also present critical technological problems. For one thing, not all furnaces can burn low-sulfur coal. Second, since the amount of fly ash emitted during combustion is, in many cases, inversely proportional to the sulfur content, burning low-sulfur coal would require a plant to increase its precipitation capacity in order to catch the extra fly ash. Otherwise, reduced sulfur dioxide emissions would be exchanged for increased particulate emissions. Such a policy would also have political (not to speak of environmental) consequences: most low-sulfur coal comes from the western states and is obtained primarily by strip mining.

In the past, decisions relating to air quality have been made primarily at local or state levels. It was not until 1955 that the federal government first officially recognized the existence of an air pollution problem when it passed Public Law 84–159 (the Federal Air Pollution Control Act). This act authorized the Public Health Service to begin research programs on air quality and to offer technical assistance to state efforts to control air pollution. Two states, California and Oregon, had already moved toward control of air pollution in 1947 and 1951, respectively. Even earlier, in 1881, the cities of Chicago and Cincinnati had enacted legislation to control smoke. These early efforts, however, had little real effect on the growing air pollution problem.

In 1963, the federal government passed a new air quality act which initiated the policy of setting of federal air quality standards and created air quality control regions within states and interstate regions. The 1963 act allowed the federal government for the first time to intervene directly in interstate air pollution problems. Yet the 1963 act and all the legislation since 1963 including the 1970 Clean Air Act, have assigned to the states the primary responsibility for devising regulatory mechanisms to control air pollution. Thus, most of the day-to-day policy decisions on air quality are left to numerous municipal, county, and state agencies. While this practice has certain advantages, in that local and state agencies are theoretically best qualified to deal with their own particular air pollution problems, many decisions at these levels (as well as those at the federal level) have been criticized by citizens for their failure to serve the public interest, especially in relation to health.

Of course, one of the major problems local and state agencies often face is that they simply do not have the expertise available to analyze air quality problems and to formulate a policy that takes account of the total environmental impact of specific decisions. A second serious problem is that local and state agencies have been indecisive about enforcing the 1970 Clean Air Act due to the opposition of certain industrial interests.[2] In 1975, it appeared that the progress made toward improving the quality of air, at least in reducing air pollution, might be reversed under the excuse of an "energy crisis."

There may be provisions of the Clean Air Act which present difficulties of compliance because of time or technology. If specific changes prove necessary, it is important that they be made in the public interest and in a manner consistent with the objectives of the act.

CASE I   Dust Pollution: Fernley, Nevada

In 1964, the Nevada Cement Company constructed a single-kiln cement plant near Fernley, not far from Reno, Nevada, to take advantage of nearby limestone, clay, and iron—the basic raw materials for cement production. The kiln had been installed with a primary filtration system to trap dust created by cement production and a bag hose for secondary filtration. This equipment, considered the latest and most efficient antipollution equipment at the time, filtered 99 percent of the dust. Most of the 700 residents of Fernley agreed that the plant had been a model neighbor during its first six years of operation.

On September 5, 1969, the plant began operating a second kiln,

---

[2] See advertisements in *Time* magazine during the spring of 1974 by some electric utility companies. For example, the American Electric Power System advertised in the May 6, 1974, issue of *Time:* "It is absolutely imperative that the Clean Air Act be amended. There is no other way" (p. 9).

doubling production. The second kiln's antipollution equipment, however, filtered only 85 percent of the cement dust, which meant that 27,000 pounds of dust poured into the air every twenty-four hours. Local residents began complaining immediately, but the company refused to stop the flow of dust. The successful battle of the Fernley citizens against the cement dust could set a pattern for settlement of antipollution damage suits throughout the country.

The Actors

Eighty-five Fernley residents, led by Carl Pihlgren, were involved in the suit against the Nevada Cement Company. Their lawyer, Pete Echeverria of Reno, Nevada, decided to file a nuisance action because the Nevada air pollution regulations were just in the process of being developed. The exact agency jurisdiction for the case was unclear because of the proximity of the cement plant to three counties—each of which generally disclaimed responsibility in the controversy. The Lyon County Commission eventually agreed to participate in the case since the cement plant was actually located within the county lines, but not without initial resistance from the county district attorney. The seat of the county was fifty-five miles from Fernley, and most county officials preferred to ignore the pollution problem as long as the cement company continued to pay its taxes.

Nevada Cement Company, originally a cooperative member of the community, became totally intransigent in its attitude toward the public welfare after the second kiln was installed. After the citizens filed suit, Nevada Cement informed them that if it lost the case, the company intended to file a countersuit.

The Policy Process

The local residents initially attempted to stop the flow of cement dust by appealing to the company's sense of public interest. After their repeated attempts to persuade company officials to abate the dust proved useless, the Fernley residents, led by Pihlgren, went to the three county commissions. Even though dust from the plant was carried into two neighboring counties, the commissions in neither of these counties were willing to act on the complaint. They both felt it was up to the Lyon County Commission to do something about the pollution.

Because the Lyon County Commission was at first unwilling to help the Fernley residents, they appealed to the state Health Department, and even the governor, hoping to attract some support. With no support from any of these officials, the group sponsored a town meeting to which the media and the Nevada Cement Company were invited. The meeting convinced Fernley residents that Nevada Cement had no intention of stopping the pollution. They passed the hat and collected $1,100 to help pay for a lawyer. Carl Pihlgren and two of his friends went to Reno to hire Pete Echeverria.

After the group had filed suit against Nevada Cement in November 1969, the Lyon County Commission finally decided to seek a restraining order against the company. The Fernley group, however, did not want a restraining order at that point, since they had decided it would involve too much time and postpone their suit. But the county persisted, and in May 1970, the commissioners of Lyon County filed suit to abate the dust emissions. On September 2, 1970, the district judge found that the second kiln was causing damage to the property and health of the local residents, and that the dust emissions did constitute a nuisance. However, as is usual in nuisance cases, the court "balanced the equities" and concluded that shutting down the new kiln would impose hardships in "excess of any benefit" to be derived by the residents of Lyon County. The court consequently granted Nevada Cement a six-month period (from October 1, 1970 to April 1, 1971) to correct emissions from the kiln. Nevada Cement continued to emit 27,000 pounds of dust daily until 9:00 P.M. on March 31, 1971. An electrostatic precipitator was then installed, almost two years after the second kiln had been completed.

With the Lyon County suit concluded, the complaint of the Fernley residents began to be tried in April 1971, but when Echeverria decided to seek punitive damages, it was postponed again. During the four-week trial in November 1971 at the Lyon County District Court, Judge Waters heard testimony from seventy-nine Fernley residents about the dust damage to their property and about their unsuccessful, frustrating efforts to persuade the company to do something about it. One resident summed up the company's attitude: "I guess they thought we were just a bunch of hicks out here and they could do as they damn well pleased." Almost every testimony emphasized the difficulties of removing the dust, which settled in all parts of the house. Apparently the dust was so difficult to remove from windows that local sales of a particular toilet bowl cleaner boomed because it was the only thing that could remove the cement particles.

Nevada Cement contended it had been studying ways to solve the dust problem from the beginning. The company also attempted to demonstrate that the dust accumulation was not illegal, because of an alleged absence of proper state and county standards for such emissions. On November 28, 1971, Judge Waters ruled that the eighty-five Fernley residents should receive 5 percent of the company's net worth in punitive damages as well as general damages, totaling $1,885,120 or over $21,000 for each of the plaintiffs. The judge accused the Nevada Cement Company of "deliberate, wanton disregard of the property of others."

Nevada Cement appealed the decision to the Nevada Supreme Court in January 1973, to dispute the award of identical general damages to each plaintiff and the award of punitive damages. The Nevada Supreme Court's decision on October 15, 1973, affirmed the special damages awarded by Judge Waters and remanded the case to the trial court for a redetermination of the amount of punitive damages. In the interim, however, Judge Waters had died. A new judge was appointed but Nevada Cement, wishing to avoid possible legal entanglements over the issue of a new judge, settled the case before the trial began.

Outcome

Nevada Cement agreed to pay punitive damages of $1,050,000 and general damages of $175,000. The award of over one million dollars in punitive damages, which Echeverria had insisted upon, established a standard for other cases.

CASE II   Industry Resists Controls: Chicago, Illinois

The Chicago area is one of the nation's largest steel-producing regions and a major industrial center. The United States Steel Corporation has its South Works plant within the Chicago city limits, near the Illinois-Indiana border. In 1963, South Works came under a new Chicago air code which placed it in violation of the law. After negotiations with U.S. Steel, the Chicago Air Pollution Appeals Board in 1965 granted U.S. Steel (and the other three steel companies in Chicago) a six-year variance from the air code, provided that they install certain air pollution abatement equipment. U.S. Steel agreed to control emissions at its South Works plant from the open hearths, the electric furnaces, and the sinter plant by the end of 1971. Other sections of the mill were not included in the variance program.

During the first five years of the variance program, the emissions from South Works had been reduced by only 3,000 tons per year—from 54,000 tons to 39,000 tons. Total emissions from the sections of the plant included in the variance program were still 2,500 percent above permissible limits under the city ordinance. Furthermore, a 1970 report had determined that the South Works plant was the largest single source of particulate pollution in the city of Chicago. These data provoked an intense battle between U.S. Steel on the one hand and various citizens' groups and the Chicago Department of Environmental Control on the other.

The Actors

The citizens' groups involved in the South Works controversy were the Campaign Against Pollution (CAP, now called the Citizen Action Program) and the Clean Air Coordinating Committee (CACC), a coalition of sixty environmental and civic organizations. CAP is a particularly interesting citizens' group because it evolved from the efforts of the late Saul Alinsky, the noted community organizer, and his Industrial Areas Foundation Institute. Joining the battle against U.S. Steel on the side of the two citizens' groups was the Chicago Department of Environmental Control, which had major jurisdiction in the case. Later, the U.S. Environmental Protection Agency also became involved in the controversy. The efforts of the government agencies and the two citizens' groups were helped tremendously by the media, which found the CAP tactics especially good for news coverage.

U.S. Steel proved to be a formidable opponent. The company's attitude was to avoid any cooperation with the citizens' groups or the Chicago Environmental Control Board. The company had been under constant legal and civic pressure to clean up their South Works plant since 1965, but the company policy appeared to be to install pollution abatement equipment only as a last resort.

The Policy Process

In December 1970, CAP, CACC, and the Chicago Department of Environmental Control initiated a campaign to revoke the variance of U.S. Steel because it was not making sufficient effort to reduce emissions. On December 24, the commissioner of the Department of Environmental Control asked the Environmental Control Board to rescind the variance. At the same time, CAP attempted to negotiate with the local management of U.S. Steel. The attitude of the company, however, was that "the proper forum for negotiations is with government officials."

From February 1 to August 31, 1971, twenty hearings were held before the appeals board to consider rescinding the variance. The Clean Air Coordinating Committee took the most active part in the hearings, offering extensive testimony. CACC had also supported the city's request for revocation of the variance by filing a motion with the appeals board. In April 1971, CACC asked the city to issue citations to U.S. Steel for air pollution violations from plant equipment not covered by the variance program. The group's contention was that these sources of air pollution were not immune from prosecution for violations of the air code and should be fined as violations occurred.

On May 18, the appeals board adopted part of the CACC motion and rescinded the variance for the sinter plant. A few days later, the city, supported by the U.S. Environmental Protection Agency, began to ticket U.S. Steel for violations of the air code, as requested by CACC. By the end of 1971, when the variance expired, accumulated fines totaled over $30,000. While the effect of the fines was limited, U.S. Steel did become very active during the last year of the variance in reducing emissions from those sections of the plant included in the variance program. Whether this change in attitude was due to the badgering by citizens' groups and legal agencies, both in and out of the appeals board hearings, remains uncertain. There is no doubt, however, that CAP's tactics must have annoyed the local management of U.S. Steel.

During the hearing period in 1971, CAP adopted an Alinsky-style strategy of personalizing the conflict. CAP examined the Board of Directors of U.S. Steel and found that one member, Gordon Metcalf, was the chairman of the board of directors of Sears, Roebuck and Company. When Metcalf refused to cooperate with CAP, the group picketed two Sears stores and distributed leaflets explaining its campaign against U.S. Steel. CAP then went after the president of U.S. Steel, Edward Logelin. CAP discovered that Logelin was one of four candidates for the post of moderator in the United Presybterian Church. It also discovered that the church's general assembly had passed a resolution in 1970 recommending that "all Presbyterians raise environmental issues with employers." CAP charged that Logelin was avoiding his "moral responsibility for pollution" and that he was consequently unfit for the church post. CAP members pressed the campaign against Logelin even at the church's annual meeting in Rochester, New York, in May. Whether this effort was influential or not, Logelin was badly defeated for the post.

While attacking Logelin, CAP opened a new front in the battle with U.S. Steel on April 13, 1971, by charging that U.S. Steel's South Works were "grossly underassessed" for tax purposes. CAP claimed that the Cook County taxpayers had lost, on the average, between $10 and $15 million a year for the previous fifteen years, totaling $149.5 million. CAP also criticized the Real Estate Research Corporation, which had appraised the South Works, because a director of U.S. Steel was also a board member of the bank which owned the Real Estate Research Corporation.

Failing to elicit any response from U.S. Steel or from the county assessor, P. J. Cullerton, CAP began a campaign of publicity and demonstrations, including a rally on September 1, the quarterly tax collection day, featuring the distribution of large million dollar bills with Cullerton's picture and sarcastic notations printed on them. Later, CAP won the support of the Parent Teachers Association in its campaign against Cullerton.

Outcome

CAP members joined with CACC at the 1971 hearings, although mostly as spectators. Throughout the hearings, U.S. Steel attempted to delay the proceedings and obstruct the efforts of the Department of Environmental Control. When the appeals board subpoenaed six officials from U.S. Steel to testify, for example, the company challenged in circuit court the right of the board to issue subpoenas. While some progress was made in 1971 in getting the company to reduce emissions, pollution from the South Works plant still remains high. Even the reduced amount of emissions from the sinter plant is above the legal limits.

Though CAP and CACC continue to press for improvements at the South Works plant, no further legal action with regard to air pollution has been taken against the mill since 1971.

CASE III   Air Quality and Rail Transportation: Harlem Valley, New York

Between 1920 and 1940, the United States had one of the best passenger rail services in the world. After 1940, the railroads began a deliberate attempt to eliminate most passenger service on the alleged grounds of economics. The worst blow to passenger service was probably the 1956 Federal Highway Act. The effect of this act was essentially to create a highway system that duplicated the national railroad network; it thereby encouraged abandoning various railroad lines.

The northeast quadrant of the United States has been particularly affected by the almost continuous reduction of passenger rail service since the 1940s. The petition of bankruptcy by Penn Central Railroad in 1970, resulting in the creation of the government-sponsored corporation called Amtrak, is illustrative of the kind of difficulties faced by the railroad companies and the traveling public. Penn Central, which continues to operate because of federal support, serves many small communities which use the rail lines as their major means of transportation. In the New York City area this service is extremely important.

In the fall of 1972, Penn Central filed claim with the Interstate Commerce Commission (ICC) to abandon part of its rail service on the Harlem Valley Line, a 127-mile line running north from Grand Central Station in New York City. This action led to a suit by a group of citizens against the ICC on the grounds that removing train service would increase air pollution by forcing a shift to truck and auto traffic.

The Actors

The key group in the fight against the ICC was the Harlem Valley Transportation Association (HVTA), led by Lettie Carson. The group, a coalition of farmers, businessmen, and commuters, had been formed in 1960 to oppose the New York Central railway's proposal to reduce Harlem Valley passenger service. Joining the HVTA as legal aid was the Natural Resources Defense Council, a group of New York-based lawyers.

In 1965, New York state legislation established the Metropolitan Transportation Agency (MTA) and gave it authority to run passenger service in seven counties, including Dutchess County where the Harlem Valley is located. MTA, however, chose to limit its service to Dover Plains until June 1, 1972, when MTA became responsible for the operation of passenger service along all the Harlem division. Financed by public funds, MTA operated the Harlem Valley line by contract with Penn Central Railroad. When Penn Central recommended MTA abandon the 30.5-mile segment from Millerton to Ghent, New York, MTA agreed. Because MTA decisions are not subject to review or public hearings, HVTA had to file protest in the federal district court and with the Interstate Commerce Commission. All railroad companies must receive a permit from ICC to withdraw services. When ICC refused to cooperate with HVTA, Mrs. Carson and her supporters filed suit.

The Policy Process

Harlem Valley Transportation Association's fight against ICC in 1973 must be considered in light of its previous efforts to protect passenger rail service. From 1960 to 1972, the group had waged numerous struggles against the abandonment of rail service in Harlem Valley and against poor service on the tracks that were left. Some of the cases were won, others were lost. To inform the local public of the need to protect their train service, HVTA sent out a monthly newsletter, distributed materials to local high schools, and printed posters and bumper stickers. They continuously pressured the ICC and New York City's Metropolitan Transportation Agency on behalf of improved rail service. The group also kept the media informed by distributing press releases to newspapers, radio stations, and TV stations. Following a defeat for passenger service at Dover Plains, New York, HVTA petitioned Lewis Mumford to write an article on railway problems. An internationally known authority on urban technology and development, Mumford eloquently defended railway passenger service in the August issue of Harper's.[1] This article was distributed to all members of Congress and to many federal agency officials, as well as to all members of the New York state legislature.

[1] "In praise of trains: a revisionist theory of progress," Harper's 245 (August 1972), 22–26.

HVTA tried other tactics as well. In 1971, they had tried to obtain passage of a bill in the state legislature which would have required MTA to continue existing passenger service in the Harlem Valley. The bill passed both houses of the legislature but was vetoed by Governor Rockefeller. HVTA then attended six public hearings concerning transportation in the valley, from 1971 through 1972, in an effort to maintain adequate rail service in the area.

In August 1972, ICC posted notice in an abandoned railway passenger station that it intended to discontinue service along the 30.5-mile stretch from Millerton to Ghent, New York. Mrs. Carson wrote three letters to ICC asking when the commission intended to hold a public hearing, but she received no reply. Then she wrote to Senator Jacob Javits, who wrote to the ICC himself, and she finally received a reply from the ICC in December stating that the ICC eventually planned to hold a hearing. Mrs. Carson wrote back inquiring whether the ICC had written an environmental impact statement. The ICC replied that, according to the commission's procedures, it was not required to produce an environmental impact statement. Mrs. Carson fired back that the ICC was indeed required to do so under the National Environmental Policy Act (NEPA) of 1969, citing another case in which the Federal Power Commission had been successfully sued for failure to observe NEPA regulations. The ICC's answer was that it had no facilities to prepare an impact statement.

Prompted by this reply, Mrs. Carson decided to sue. She recruited the aid of the Natural Resources Defense Council (NRDC) and asked for the intervention of the New York Department of Transportation, the Department of Commerce, and the attorney general. New York City and New York State decided to join the suit, but their petition of intervention was thrown out by the district court hearing the case.

The case was given two hearings in June 1973. NRDC lawyers argued that the cessation of service would increase air pollution as well as create other conditions which should be considered "environmental damage." These included grain price increases, which would raise the cost of the region's dairy goods, and the consequent disruption of transport patterns, which would bankrupt a number of businesses. On June 21, Federal District Judge Marvin Frankel ruled that the ICC could not approve abandonment of any rail service unless it showed that such action did not "significantly affect the quality of the human environment."

He agreed that the alteration of railroad service—like the alteration of a river course—should conform to the provisions of NEPA.

Outcome

The ICC appealed Frankel's decision, but Mrs. Carson again won the case in the court of appeals in June, 1974. The victory was short-lived, however, with the announcement of the establishment of the United States Railway Association, Conrail, in the spring of 1975. On March 1, President Ford signed two bills providing the railroads with federal assistance of approximately $3 billion. This will be the first significant federal aid to the railroads since the land grants of the nineteenth and twentieth centuries. While this aid is desperately needed, the preliminary plan for Conrail included the abandonment of 6,200 miles of track. The new legislation authorizing Conrail allowed it the authority to supersede the courts until the final plan is approved, so Penn Central applied again to abandon the Harlem Valley Line. For-tunately, the rail legislation also allows the states the right to protest any abandonments before July 1975; and because the New York State De-partment of Transportation objected to Penn Central's decision, the tracks are still down along the Harlem Valley.

Many members of Congress and governors from the seventeen affected states in the Northeast and Midwest are adamantly opposed to the Conrail plan because of the proposed abandonments, and it is possible that the U.S. Railway Association's final plan will not be approved in Congress. Such a defeat will do little to alleviate the crisis in the Northeast and Midwest, however, until Congress recognizes the necessity of subsidizing rail service in the United States. While $3 billion is a considerable figure, it is less than 4 percent of the federal expenditures since World War II on other modes of transportation. Federal expenditures on the interstate highway system alone have amounted to $56 billion since 1956.

The Northeast and Midwest account for 44 percent of the nation's freight movement, and 48 percent of the population. Railroads are four times as fuel efficient as trucks in moving freight, and almost three times as fuel efficient as airlines in moving passengers. In a period when energy is at a premium, these advantages in fuel efficiency and other environmental considerations, such as reduced air pollution, give rail service a social utility that should be exploited and protected.

CASE IV   Air Quality and Road Construction: New York City

The lower Manhattan area of New York City has suffered from chronic traffic congestion since the 1920s. The first professional solution to this problem was proposed in 1927 by the Regional Plan Association (RPA), a private organization of planners. The RPA advocated a highway across Manhattan to connect the east side bridges and the west side Holland Tunnel. Postponed by the depression from official consideration, the plan gradually faded from public view until 1956, when Congress passed the Federal Highway Act. Under this law, certain approved highway projects could receive 90 percent of their funding from the federal government. The bill suddenly made financing the Manhattan Expressway project possible, because the new road would bring traffic to and from New Jersey. The project was quickly approved by New York City, but when the Department of Real Estate released an economic study in 1962 indicating the expressway would displace 2,000 families and industries employing 10,000 people, Mayor Wagner rejected the proposal. The proexpressway forces continued to exert influence, however, and Mayor Wagner reversed himself in early 1965.

When John Lindsay was elected mayor in 1966, he was known as an outspoken opponent of the expressway, yet by October 1967, Lindsay had changed his position. He decided to support a proposal for a depressed (rather than elevated) expressway, which would remove "only" 1,250 families and 400 businesses. Lindsay enthusiastically called the proposed expressway "probably the most dramatic, dynamic breakthrough the nation has yet seen in the planning of highways through congested urban areas."

When news of a study conducted by New York City's Department of Air Resources was leaked to the public in 1968, the battle against the longest debated road in the nation's history reached a climax. The study indicated that carbon monoxide levels near the expressway would be dangerously high. Using the battle cry of air pollution, opponents of the expressway waged a successful struggle against the prohighway forces.

The Actors

The conflict over the lower Manhattan expressway involved a variety of local agencies, all holding jurisdiction over some part of the proposed project. The main advocate of the expressway was a semi-public body, the Triborough Bridge and Tunnel Authority (TBTA), led by its chairman, Robert Moses, the progenitor of the post-World War II revival plans for the expressway. TBTA was supported by the Port of New York Authority, the Metropolitan Transportation Administration, and the mayor. Two other city agencies played a key role in the dispute, the Board of Estimate and the New York City Planning Commission.

The city's Environmental Protection Agency (EPA) became the chief agency opposing the expressway. Other city officials joined the EPA, including two borough presidents, two city councilmen, and two members of Congress. Opposition also came from a tremendous variety of citizens' organizations and private individuals. The business opponents of the expressway called themselves Citywide Organizations Against the Lower Manhattan Expressway. Groups of architects, artists, and local residents also formed a union against the project. Two key individuals in the struggle were Jane Jacobs, a prominent writer on urban problems, and Mary Perot Nichols of *The Village Voice,* who wrote numerous articles against the expressway in the local weekly.

The Policy Process

When the proposal for a depressed expressway surfaced in 1967, all that was needed to initiate the project was the approval of the Board of Estimate. In spite of an attempt by the opponents to kill the proposal at the board's meeting in March 1968, a sixteen to six vote opened the way for official federal approval. Since the state and federal agencies involved had already given tentative approval, official acceptance of the $150 million project was assured. The most remarkable feature of the expressway plan was that it had been reviewed, approved, and promoted with no significant alteration of the route (nor of the concept) proposed almost forty years earlier.

In April 1967, a required public hearing on the proposed expressway was held at a local high school near the construction site. The hearing was packed with opponents of the expressway and, by the end of the tumultuous meeting, Jane Jacobs had been charged with disorderly conduct (later changed to second-degree riot), inciting to riot, and criminal mischief. In spite of obviously vehement opposition to the plan, the city went ahead with the proposal, developing an even more elaborate idea to exploit its air rights over the expressway for various municipal facilities. The first proposed building planned for construction over the expressway was an annex to the Seward Park High School.

While the controversy was going on, the city's Department of Air Resources had been quietly carrying on a study of the effects of the road on air quality. This study revealed that people living near or over the proposed expressway might be subjected to as much as 300 parts per million (ppm) of carbon monoxide (CO) if the partially covered design were used. Predictions in ppm of CO, however, were meaningless to the public, and the New York Scientists' Committee for Public Information was asked for an interpretation. Its brief report estimated that the carbon monoxide levels forecast by the Department of Air Resources would be sufficient to cause the physical collapse of some people near the expressway. This shocking conclusion, however, did not prevent New York City's Educational Construction Fund from offering to construct a $19.5 million, doughnut-shaped, school-and-housing structure at the end of the Manhattan Bridge. The plan called for wrapping the access ramp around the building in a special funnel, and the middle of the doughnut would be a playground for elementary school children.

Finished in November 1967, the report was not made public but was given to several city agencies. Word of the study got out, however, and pressure from citizens, the press, and Congressman Edward Koch, who represented the Seventeenth District in Lower Manhattan, forced its release. Finally, the city's Environmental Protection Agency announced in December 1967 that controlling the fumes that would be emitted from the 15,000 vehicles expected to travel the expressway each hour would make the cost of the road prohibitive.

Local opposition became so strong that during the May 1968 public hearings, Mayor Lindsay announced the suspension of planning for the expressway. In June, Lindsay lost the Republican primary and, faced with opposition from all sides, he decided to try to win the support of the liberal Democrats, who were generally against the lower Manhattan project.

Outcome

On July 17, 1968, Mayor Lindsay announced that plans for the expressway were dead "for all time." In August, the New York City

Planning Commission ratified Lindsay's decision, and shortly thereafter, the Board of Estimate removed the expressway from city maps. The 1,250 families and 400 businesses threatened by the expressway received their second reprieve, one which they hoped would be final.

CASE V   Controlling Automobile Emissions: Two Legal Actions against Lead Pollution

In the two preceding case studies, citizens attempted to attack the problem of air pollution from automobile emissions in a somewhat circuitous fashion by opposing policies which would have increased the number of automobiles in the areas of conflict. Yet the problem of emissions, particularly lead, from an ever-increasing number of automobiles is an extremely serious one that cannot be solved by merely rerouting expressways or guaranteeing access to commuter trains. The 300,000 tons of lead added to gasoline annually in the United States are responsible for 90 percent of the airborne lead in America, and concentrations of lead in the air and soil near highways and in cities can reach dangerously high levels. It is estimated that 25 percent of urban children and 3 percent of urban adults have blood-lead levels above those considered safe even by the manufacturers of lead additives.

In an effort to control, and eventually decrease, amounts of lead in the atmosphere, a citizens' group called the Environmental Defense Fund (EDF) used two different approaches in the fall of 1969 and spring of 1970—one at the state level and one at the federal level. The outcome of their efforts illustrates the difficulty citizens face when they attempt to challenge the automobile and fuel industries.

The Actors

The Environmental Defense Fund is a group composed of scientists, lawyers, and other citizens concerned with the environment. EDF's first action challenged the California Air Resources Board (CARB), because CARB had the jurisdictional power to set ambient air quality standards in California. A few months later, EDF petitioned the Department of Health, Education and Welfare (HEW), under the Air Quality Act of 1967 and the Clean Air Act of 1963, to control automotive lead pollution in the atmosphere. Both of these actions were initiated prior to passage of the Clean Air Act of 1970.

The Policy Process

EDF filed its petition with the California Air Resources Board on October 30, 1969. The petition requested that CARB establish an ambient air quality standard for lead at 1.5 micrograms per cubic meter, establish an exhaust emission standard for lead at zero grams per mile by 1973, and prohibit the sale of motor fuel containing more than 0.5 grams of lead per gallon beginning January 1, 1972, and zero grams per gallon by January 1, 1973.

CARB did establish the requested ambient air quality standard, but it refused to act on the exhaust emission standard on the grounds that it did not have the authority to regulate the amount of lead added to gasoline. EDF then decided to file suit against CARB on July 1, 1971, claiming that the California air pollution control legislation gave CARB ample authority to regulate the lead content of fuel.

During the case, it was agreed that the only way to reduce the amount of lead in exhaust fumes is to regulate the lead content of motor fuel, but even so, the court decided against EDF. It upheld the view that determining the lead content of gasoline was not within the authority of CARB. EDF appealed the case on June 29, 1972, but the appeal was denied. In April 1973, EDF submitted a petition for a hearing before the California Supreme Court, hoping to convince the court that CARB had the authority to regulate the amount of lead added to gasoline. EDF's California case ended unsuccessfully on May 9, 1973, when the California Supreme Court denied EDF's petition for a hearing.

While pursuing the California action, EDF also submitted a petition to the Department of Health, Education and Welfare seeking federal remedies for automotive lead pollution. On May 5, 1970 EDF requested, on behalf of its membership and the general public, that the secretary of HEW take the following actions:

1. The immediate formulation and announcement of atmospheric lead air quality criteria;
2. The establishment of an automotive lead emission standard that would make it unlawful to emit lead from automotive exhausts;
3. The immediate issuance of a directive to automobile manufacturers instructing them to disclose prominently to the consuming public the octane requirements of new and old automobiles and the disadvantageous environmental and economic consequences of using excessively high octane gasoline;

4. The immediate prohibition of the use of leaded gasoline in vehicles owned or operated by federal departments and agencies; and
5. The immediate implementation of the Fuel Additives Registration Provision of the Air Quality Act (1967).

In support of their petition, EDF attached a memorandum which outlined the seriousness of the lead problem in terms of health and the further aggravation of other automotive pollution problems, such as increased hydrocarbon emissions, caused by the use of leaded gasoline. The memorandum demanded HEW take action under the mandate of the National Environmental Policy Act (NEPA), which had just been passed a few months earlier, and also under the 1963 Clean Air Act, which authorized the secretary to control pollution.

Outcome

HEW never acted on EDF's petition, but passage of the 1970 Clean Air Act has enabled the administrator of the Environmental Protection Agency to prescribe standards of emission for "any air pollutant from any class or classes of new motor vehicles or new motor vehicle engines which, in his judgment, causes or contributes to, or is likely to cause or to contribute to, air pollution which endangers the public health or welfare." Under this section (201) of the 1970 Clean Air Act, EDF and several other citizens' organizations continued to press for the removal of lead from gasoline. This section, however, did not specifically cover lead emissions. In 1974, the EPA decided to establish regulations phasing out the lead content in gasoline. These regulations have been described as one of the most important health regulations passed by the environmental agency. They would have required the over-all content of lead in the gasoline supply to be reduced approximately two-thirds by 1979.

The refiners argued in court that the EPA had used an improper legal basis for drawing up the regulations, that the evidence did not support EPA's concern for public health, that the case against automobile lead emissions "is a speculative and inconclusive one at best." The majority opinion of the court agreed in early 1975, although dissenting U.S. Circuit Court Judge Wright suggested that the opinion was related to the energy crisis "and a reluctance to 'waste' a single gallon of gasoline for reasons of health when extra gallons might prove to be in short supply."

CASE VI   Offensive Odors: Bishop, Maryland

Air quality is often considered a predominantly urban problem. Rural areas, however, are not exempt from air pollution as the residents of Bishop, Maryland, are well aware. In 1955, a small chicken feed and fertilizer plant was opened in Bishop, and from the outset, the stench from the plant was overwhelming. The odor drifted across the state line and offended inhabitants of the small town of Selbyville, Delaware. Apparently the stench was so bad that a federal engineer who tried to measure it became ill and had to leave. The events that followed the initial suit to enjoin Harold Polin, owner of the Bishop Processing Company, are a striking example of the ability of a private individual to circumvent and defy local, state, and federal efforts to maintain satisfactory air quality prior to the passage of the 1970 Clean Air Act.

The Actors

Every level of government became involved in the Bishop, Maryland, case. Initially, the county government attempted to help the community. Then the Department of Health, Education and Welfare and the Justice Department joined the local citizens attempting to stop Polin. The case soon became complicated, involving two state governments as well as the federal agencies.

The private citizens involved in the Bishop case acted primarily as plaintiffs in the numerous legal battles that ensued in the fourteen-year struggle against Bishop Processing.

The Policy Process

In 1956, the year after Polin started operations in Bishop, six concerned citizens, with the help of the county, obtained a court order permanently enjoining the Bishop Processing Company from releasing "noxious and offensive gases and odors." Polin appealed the case, lost, continued to pollute, and was fined $5,000 for contempt of court. The fine was effective for about three months, and then Polin returned to his former procedures and the noxious odors returned.

The citizens of Bishop, Maryland, and Selbyville, Delaware, suffered for another eight years before a second effort was made to stop Polin. After the first federal Clean Air Act was passed in 1963, the federal government held its first air quality conference in Bishop. On November 9 and 10, 1965, the Bishop, Maryland-Selbyville, Delaware Interstate Air Pollution Abatement Conference took place. The federal government was eager to prove its power of enforcement, and the Bishop case seemed a likely place to do so. The pollution problem came from a single-source polluter, the case was an obviously serious interstate problem, and the local residents were incensed. After two days of testimony, the conferees unanimously recommended an immediate cleanup of the plant premises at Bishop Processing and ordered Polin to submit an odor-control plan to the Maryland Department of Health by March 1, 1966. He was then given until June 1 to present evidence to the state of purchases or commitments for purchase of control equipment. The equipment was to be installed and all odors to be controlled by September 1, 1966.

The performance of the National Air Pollution Control Administration (NAPCA) at the conference appeared impressive, particularly to the members of several industries who had come to observe the proceedings. It took NAPCA two months before its recommendations were made official, however, and because of this delay, the state of Maryland, without informing HEW, told Polin that he could ignore the March 1 deadline. Polin, of course, was more than happy to do so. On September 1, 1966, no progress toward control of the odors had been made.

It was not until eight months later that a hearing board was finally set up to consider Polin's defiance of the cleanup order. When the hearing board convened on May 17, 1967, Bishop Processing was again ordered to abate the odors within six months. Polin then decided to file his own lawsuit, which challenged both the recommendations of the hearing board and the constitutionality of the Clean Air Act. Even though his suit was dismissed several months later, Polin continued to operate his plant with no odor controls at all.

In December 1967, NAPCA threatened Polin with a possible suit in the U.S. district court. Polin's next tactic was to agree to negotiations which proceeded for eleven months. Finally, both parties agreed to a consent order which "permanently enjoined and restrained the plant from discharging malodorous air pollutants into the state of Delaware." The federal government assumed the case was closed, and on January 17, 1969, HEW Secretary Wilbur Cohen reported to Congress that the successful conclusion of the case would be an important precedent for federal abatement action.

Bishop Processing returned to full operations of its plant after only a few months of limited operation. On February 7, 1969, the Justice Department asked the district court to shut the plant down. The court refused on the grounds that it needed "more evidence." The Justice Department tried again, but forgot to file an affidavit from the director of Delaware's Air Pollution Agency as required by the consent decree. After a third attempt, in November 1969, the court finally ordered Polin to cease all manufacturing and processing operations by February 1970. This time, Polin became discouraged and changed the operation of his plant from chicken processing to the production of vegetable oils.

Outcome

Citizens and government agents finally were successful in halting the pollution emitted by the Bishop Processing Company, but their success is far from reassuring. The procedure required fourteen years and the expense of several court cases.

CASE VII   Pollution Standards: Allegheny County, Pennsylvania

In the summer of 1969, the state of Pennsylvania made its proposed air quality standards available for public review in advance of the hearing scheduled in Pittsburgh on September 9. The proposed state standards were carefully examined by various community leaders who decided that they were inadequate. Of particular concern was the Air Pollution Commission's proposal to allow an annual average level for particulate matter of 100 micrograms per cubic meter of air, with a long-range goal of 80 micrograms. Evidence had shown that the death rate substantially increased for people over fifty when particulate levels in the air exceeded 80 micrograms in the presence of sulfur dioxide. The data inspired citizens to fight the state's proposed standards, and the outcome of the battle led to the formation of a citizens' group called GASP (Group Against Smog and Pollution), which in turn led a struggle to strengthen the Allegheny County air pollution code. GASP has since become one of the most effective citizens' groups attempting to combat air pollution.

The Actors

GASP was the key citizens' group in the fight to formulate strong air quality control legislation in Allegheny County, where Pittsburgh is located. Founded in October 1969 by 43 concerned persons who had attended or testified at the state air pollution hearings, GASP now has a membership of over 5,000. The GASP newsletter reaches a broadly representative group of over 100,000 people.

The key agencies involved in the legislative struggles were the Pennsylvania Air Pollution Commission, the Allegheny County commissioners, and the Allegheny County Health Department. The state and county commissioners did not strongly resist public participation in formulating air quality standards. Like their counterparts in many government positions, the commissioners were limited by bureaucratic procedures and a narrow agency perspective which made them initially unwilling to alter their proposed standards. The governor played a key role in obtaining the state commission's reconsideration of its proposed standards. Later, the county commissioners became quite open to the suggestions of GASP. The Allegheny County Variance Board has had the critical role of enforcing standards, and their cooperative attitude toward GASP has been noteworthy.

The Policy Process

Citizens' activity to strengthen the state air pollution standards was effective. Citizens deluged the governor and the state commission with letters of protest and personally contacted members of the legislature. A bipartisan group of fourteen congressmen wrote to the governor, urging him to reconsider the proposed standards. On September 9, 1969, the day of scheduled hearings in Pittsburgh on the state standards, 500 people showed up. Startled officials hastily moved the hearing from a small state office to a large auditorium. Public pressure continued after the hearing, and within a few days, the governor asked the state commission to reconsider its proposed standards. The commission decided to do so, and substantially upgraded its standards. The annual average for particulate matter, for example, was set at 65 micrograms per cubic meter—far below the 100 micrograms originally proposed.

Shortly after the hearing, GASP was founded. The group sought help from knowledgeable people such as Mortimer Corn of the University of Pittsburgh School of Public Health, and soon other scientists and engineers joined providing needed technical guidance. Allegheny County, containing the city of Pittsburgh and surrounding industrial communities, is a major center for steel and coal production and other heavy industry. The scientists and citizens in the GASP nucleus felt that a strong, enforceable set of air pollution regulations was crucial to the future of the city, listed as one of the top five in terms of air pollution in the United States.

Since the county commissioners were already considering the adoption of Article 17 to establish county air quality standards, the newly formed group had very little time to act on the proposed standards. To be most effective in a short period of time, the core members of GASP decided to organize a scientific committee and a legal committee and to recruit committee members from the Pittsburgh scientific and legal communities; many were faculty members from the University of Pittsburgh. The scientific committee, after evaluating technical aspects of Article 17, provided GASP with recommendations for developing stronger air pollution regulations. The legal committee, utilizing these recommendations, made proposals for the enforcement of Article 17. The work of these two committees, and the energy members of the fledgling GASP organization devoted to recruiting, public relations, and political activity, resulted in the adoption of a revised version of Article 17. Allegheny County established one of the strongest sets of air pollution regulations in the nation at that time.

The attention of GASP then shifted to ensure that the air pollution legislation was enforced. The legislation establishing ambient air quality standards also allowed for a variance board to hear appeals from polluters applying for an extension on cleanup deadlines. To ensure that the variance board would have an adequate representation of citizens, GASP polled the community and interviewed applicants before submitting its recommendations to the county commissioners who were authorized to appoint the board. Four of five appointees chosen by the commissioners were selected from people GASP recommended.

Since the inception of the variance board, GASP lawyers have attended almost every hearing. Polluting companies seeking to be excused from compliance with the law, often for indefinite periods of time, have objected strenuously to GASP's intervention in these hearings. But in 1970, when the variance board upheld GASP's right to participate in the hearings, the citizens' group won a major victory. Since the variance board began its work, variances have been granted only if the company submits a specific plan to bring its operation into compliance within a reasonably short time. GASP's efforts have also encouraged the public to attend variance hearings and generated media support.

GASP has been particularly effective in fighting air pollution from two United States Steel Corporation plants in the Pittsburgh area. For the variance board hearing in the summer of 1970 on emissions from U.S. Steel's Edgar Thompson Works in Braddock, an industrial community adjacent to Pittsburgh, the scientific committee of GASP prepared a document that described the history of the plant, the processes involved in its operation, and the control methods applicable to the industry. GASP's medical committee obtained testimony from physicians familiar with patients living in the vicinity of the plant, and the legal committee provided competent legal representation for GASP as an intervener. The leaders of GASP attended every hearing and, when necessary, they organized public participation. GASP's efforts resulted in the denial of a variance for the Edgar Thompson Works. GASP was equally helpful to the state and county when they filed suit against U.S. Steel's Clairton Coke Works in 1972.

Outcome

The group's activities in other areas have achieved notable success. GASP's public relations committee introduced clean-air buttons, cans, bumper stickers, decals, and created "Dirty Gertie," the dirty bird that became the symbol of the group. Dirty Gertie gives awards to the worst polluters in Pittsburgh. The group also awards certificates of merit to major emitters of pollutants who have made significant efforts to reduce their emissions. The GASP "Hotline" serves as a means of informing its members about activities in the Pittsburgh area and as a focus for discussion. In addition, GASP operates its own complaint department and forwards citizens' complaints to the control agency.

While air pollution has by no means been eliminated in the Pittsburgh area since the formation of GASP, the group's efforts have contributed enormously to the progress that has been made in improving local air quality. Well-organized citizens' groups can influence the legislation and enforcement of clean-air regulations, as well as call public attention to problems of air quality.

CASE VIII   Rainmaking: Two Cases—New York and Texas

Rainmaking is the one area of weather modification in which citizens have become actively involved in policy conflicts. As stated in the introduction to this chapter, rainmaking is only one procedure in weather modification technology, and it is a relatively insignificant one when compared to probable future efforts to control the weather. Nonetheless, to the orchard farmer, whose crop can be ruined by heavy hailstorms, controlling precipitation is crucial. The nearby rancher is equally concerned about rainfall, but he is worried about getting enough.

There have actually been very few cases of citizen involvement in weather modification conflicts, and in all of these, judicial procedures settled the differences. Farmers, ranchers, and resort owners—people whose livelihood depends on the weather—have been the largest segment of the population taking part in these controversies.

The Actors

In a New York case, *Slutsky* v. *City of New York,* the plaintiffs, resort owners in the nearby Catskill Mountains, sought to enjoin New York City from engaging in rainmaking activity to alleviate its water shortage crisis. In a Texas case (actually two cases which had been consolidated), *Southwest Weather Research, Inc.* v. *Duncan,* ranchers brought suit against a rainmaking company which had been hired by farmers to conduct cloud seeding for hail suppression. Both states have statutes dealing with weather modification, but they do not prohibit the practice. Because the cases relied on the opinion of the courts, however, the issue of state or federal policy on weather modification was not involved.

The Policy Process

In *Slutsky* v. *City of New York,* the trial court denied Slutsky's petition for an injunction on the grounds that damage to his property in the Catskills was speculative, but that New York's water crisis was real.

This court must balance the conflicting interests between a remote possibility of inconvenience to plaintiffs' resort and its guests with the problem of maintaining and supplying the inhabitants of the City of New York and surrounding areas, with a populace of about 10 million inhabitants, with an adequate supply of pure and wholesome water. The relief which plaintiffs ask is opposed to the general welfare and public good; and the dangers which plaintiffs apprehend are purely speculative. This court will not protect a possible private injury at the expense of a positive public advantage.

(97 N.Y.S. 2d at 240, 1950)

In the Texas cases, however, the plaintiffs were more successful. The trial court issued a temporary injunction restraining seeding operations in the entire area, but the appellate court modified the decision so as to apply only to activities over the plaintiffs' land. The court's decision directly contrasts with the Slutsky case:

We believe that under our system of government the landowner is en-titled to such precipitation as Nature deigns to bestow. We believe that the landowner is entitled, therefore and thereby, to such rainfall as may come from clouds over his own property that Nature, in her caprice may provide. It follows, therefore, that this enjoyment of or entitlement to the benefits of Nature should be protected by the courts if interfered with improperly or unlawfully.

(319 S.W. 2d at 945)

The Texas Supreme Court affirmed the decisions of the intermediate appellate courts.

These two cases reveal serious deficiencies in policy relating to weather modification. First of all, the courts have not developed a con-sistent body of principles by which to judge weather modification controversies. The dozen or so decisions already handed down by the courts have all depended on the different attitudes and regulations in the state concerned, as well as the opinion of the judges. Second, the plain-tiffs in these two cases had an almost overwhelming burden of proof. In the Slutsky case, for example, the judge was not convinced that the cloud seeding had any correlation with the subsequent meteorological events and, in any case, the damage was only speculative. Damages may be more easily proven by ranchers and farmers, but proving that cloud seeding caused a particular storm is much more difficult. Finally, these legal cases do not really deal with the fundamental concerns of weather modification efforts, nor are the courts the place to consider the pervasive effects of large-scale weather modification in either envi-ronmental or sociological terms.

Outcome

Efforts to modify the weather are increasing in the United States. Unless citizens become involved in policy decisions in this critical area of technology, more than a few isolated rain showers may be at stake.

Conclusion

Air pollution, which is not a recent phenomenon in many American cities, has provoked more citizen involvement in the decision-making process than perhaps any other environmental issue. The case studies in this chapter have emphasized citizens' actions in conflicts concerning air pollution, and have significant policy implications in that they reveal the following key points:

1. The perceived conflict between economic growth and air quality, especially from the viewpoint of industry;
2. The frequency of citizens' reliance upon the legal process in air quality controversies; and
3. The impact of decisions in other areas of policy on the quality of the atmosphere.

There are two underlying policy questions raised by each of the eight case studies dealing with air quality: What price are we willing to pay to achieve clean air? Who shall pay the costs? These are two of the most difficult questions faced by policy makers today, and the crucial decisions that must be made involve significant policy choices. Should the citizen be taxed to help pay the costs of air pollution control? Should industry be penalized for pollution and, if so, to what extent? The difficulty in deciding these types of critical questions lies initially in the delineation and interpretation of national air quality standards as they apply at federal, state, and local levels of government. As many of the case studies reveal, the lack of specific state and federal air quality standards, prior to 1970, severely limited both the ability of local and state agencies to protect the public interest and the number of avenues open to the public to protest air pollution.

With the passage of the National Environmental Policy Act of 1969 and the Clean Air Act of 1970, the public's right to a healthful environment was reinforced, at least temporarily. Yet the two key questions—who should pay and what price we are willing to pay to achieve the goals of clean air—are even more pressing at the present time.

In a recent report, the White House Council on Environmental Quality estimated that the annual costs of air cleanup would rise from $3 billion in 1973 to $20.3 billion in 1982. The latest EPA estimates, however, indicate that air pollution abatement efforts save $11.2 billion annually because of better health, less crop damage, and less deterioration of property. It now appears that neither the public nor Congress understood the full implications of the 1970 Clean Air Act. While many people continue to acclaim the legislation, it has undergone an onslaught from both industry and the Nixon and Ford administrations in the face of the "energy crisis." Even though the bill has withstood most efforts to weaken it so far, the nation's energy policy will undoubtedly play the crucial role in determining the course of air quality policy. The relentlessly growing demand for electric power and the generally uncooperative attitude of industry do not augur well for the future.

The intransigence of industry in many air pollution cases is one of the major factors which has forced citizens to rely on the legal process in order to ensure that the public interest be considered. At Fernley, Nevada, no amount of public appeal was able to arrest the flow of cement dust from Nevada Cement's plant. At South Works in Chicago, U.S. Steel actually flaunted its defiance of public policy. At Bishop, Maryland, Bishop Processing made a joke of state and federal enforcement efforts. The Harlem Valley transportation case in New York showed that industry was equally willing to disregard public need. In all of these cases, citizens first approached the industry prior to seeking a legal remedy; but in every instance, industry responded in basically the same way as a U.S. Steel official in Chicago: "The proper forum for negotiations is with government officials." What this statement really meant was that industry had no intention of altering its course of action until forced to do so by the government.

Although most of the controversies forced citizen activists to seek a legal remedy to their problem, three different types of approaches were used in the eight case studies. In the Fernley, Nevada, Chicago, and Bishop, Maryland, cases, citizens took what might be called a "punitive" legal approach—making the polluter pay in compensation for damages. This method was effective in the small industry case at Fernley, where over a million dollars in damages was awarded to the citizens. At both South Works in Chicago and Bishop, Maryland, however, the fines were basically an ineffective deterrent. In the rainmaking cases, the plaintiffs also attempted to seek damages and/or enjoin the activities of the two defendants.

A second legal approach is illustrated in the Harlem Valley case, where citizens utilized a "preventive" approach—halting an intended act of industry on the grounds that it would result in air pollution. This approach has been used successfully in other cases of citizen action throughout the country, such as *Clean Air* v. *Army Corps of Engineers* in New York.

A third approach, used in two of the studies of this chapter, is what might be called the "implementation" approach—pressing for implementation of existing laws or alleged jurisdictional powers. This approach was used by the Environmental Defense Fund in California and GASP in Pittsburgh. The only case study not directly using the judicial process at all was the Lower Manhattan Expressway case in which the opponents of the expressway relied on confrontation and pressure tactics.

One legal remedy not included in this chapter, which is used to overcome difficulties connected with nuisance suits, is the class-action suit. A Los Angeles lawyer, for example, filed a class-action suit for the people of Los Angeles against General Motors and several hundred other industries for air pollution in that city. This particular suit was thrown out of court, but other class-action suits have been more successful. In May 1974, however, the Supreme Court made it considerably more difficult to press lawsuits on behalf of a large group. The Court ruled that those who file class-action suits must notify individually everyone they intend to represent in the suit. In addition, the person or group of people who files the suit must pay for notification. Even though this decision applies only to groups seeking monetary damages rather than injunctive relief, it is expected to curtail substantially the number of class-action suits filed in federal court.[3]

Even if other legal approaches are used, however, court cases often take years and cost a tremendous amount of money. And perhaps the main weakness of depending upon the courts for solving air pollution issues is that legal cases do not generally affect public attitudes, nor do they stimulate the interest of the average citizen to participate in the policy process. Thus, the public involvement generated by the Lower Manhattan Expressway controversy may have done more to educate a significant number of citizens about the importance of the citizen's role in the policy process than would a dozen legal cases such as the two involving rainmaking. In the long run, organizations like CAP,

---

[3] "High Court Limits Availability of Class-Action Suits," *Louisville Courier-Journal* (May 29, 1974).

GASP, and HVTA can direct effective community involvement in important issues as well as influence community attitudes.

Not only industrial intransigence, but various weaknesses at the institutional levels of government have forced citizens to resort to the legal process in air pollution controversies. One common problem confronting citizens is trying to gain the support of the local agencies of government. This was seen to be the case at Fernley, Nevada. Sometimes local agencies simply do not want to challenge industry, particularly if the industry is the community's sole or major employer. This is especially a problem in small towns. Frequently, however, local and state agencies are reluctant to support citizens because the agencies are unsure of the extent of their jurisdiction, as in the Fernley and EDF case studies.

Another institutional problem noted in these case studies was the conflict between various levels of the government. In some cases, a local agency conflicts with another local agency (the Lower Manhattan case), in others, a state agency conflicts with a federal agency (the Harlem Valley case). Confusion between state and federal agencies over matters of policy enforcement is now rampant. Many communities now question the value of such specific national standards as those in the 1970 Clean Air Act because different areas of the United States have different types of air quality problems. Often communities are unsure if local standards more rigorous than federal standards should be enforced.

Until America's national goals for air quality become more clearly established in the minds of the public, in industry, and in the government, interagency conflicts will continue to hinder the creation of effective air quality policies and the enforcement of existing ones. Unfortunately, air quality control is rarely seen by either the public or the policy makers as part of a total environmental-management problem. Decisions to construct a freeway or to cease railway service must consider the potential impact on air quality, as the Lower Manhattan Expressway and Harlem Valley case studies effectively illustrate. The other side of the coin is equally significant; air pollution abatement efforts themselves have a broad impact on the environment. A commitment to clean air, for example, may mean increasing the solid waste generated by the new sulfur-dioxide-control technology. Decisions on the technological feasibility and advantages of various solutions to air quality problems must be accompanied by a broader perspective on the environment than is now prevalent. This is especially true when considering the apparent advantages of weather modification.

An informed public is always one of the most effective safeguards of the public welfare. Air pollution policy issues have inspired a considerable amount of public involvement because the problems are usually quite visible and often critical. Perhaps the most important tactical point to glean from the case studies in this chapter is the importance of converting scientific data into language that is meaningful to the public. This tactic was extremely advantageous to GASP's cause in Pittsburgh and to the opponents of the Lower Manhattan Expressway. Knowledgeable members of the community must be asked to interpret technical data that describe critical aspects of the general well-being.

Citizen involvement in the formulation and enforcement of local and state air quality legislation is especially vital in the struggle to create clean air in the United States. Continued citizen participation in all types of decisions affecting air quality will, we hope, make industry and government more responsive to the necessity of maintaining a healthy atmosphere.

Readings

American Association for the Advancement of Science. *Air Conservation.* Washington, D.C.: American Association for the Advancement of Science, 1965.

Crenson, Matthew A. *The Unpolitics of Air Pollution.* Baltimore: The Johns Hopkins University Press, 1971.

Edelson, Edward. *The Battle for Clean Air.* New York: Public Affairs Committee, 1967.

Esposito, John. *Vanishing Air.* New York: Grossman, 1970.

Fleagle, Robert G., ed. *Weather Modification: Science and Public Policy.* Seattle: University of Washington Press, 1969.

Hagevik, George H. *Decision-Making in Air Pollution Control.* New York: Praeger, 1970.

Massachusetts Institute of Technology. *Inadvertent Climate Modification.* Cambridge: Massachusetts Institute of Technology, 1971.

Taubenfeld, Howard J., ed. *Controlling the Weather.* New York: Dunellen, 1970.

Wollan, Michael. "Controlling the Potential Hazards of Government-Sponsored Technology." *The George Washington Law Review,* 36 (1967), 1105–1116.

5

Natural Areas and Wildlife

Introduction

The history of the United States is also a record of westward expansion—rolling back the frontier and conquering the wilderness. To pioneers, the wilderness and natural areas were so vast they seemed inexhaustible. These lands existed to be developed; they were cleared for agriculture and exploited for their resources. Most of the wildlife was not considered a resource, however; the only useful species of fish, bird, and animal were commercially valuable ones, such as the beaver, or species that were game. During the years of westward growth, the basically agricultural economy extracted commodities from prairies, rivers, and forests and altered the waterways and wetlands indiscriminately. Typical agricultural practices—for example, planting vast tracts of land with a single crop like wheat—fundamentally changed many of the nation's ecological systems.

The nation's industrial development was even more exploitive of

141

natural areas than was agriculture. Economic growth and population growth generated sprawling urban areas, and the landscape between them was laced with highways, railroads, transmission lines, and pipelines. Natural habitats were destroyed by building, disturbed by noise, and degraded by air and water pollution. The remnants of the original, wild America have been compressed into isolated pockets, and even these are continually threatened by pressures of human occupancy and economic development.

Protecting natural areas and wildlife *for* the people has been made more difficult by a recent problem: protecting the wilds *from* the people. Recreational use of forests, ski slopes, swamps, meadows, open beaches, offshore islands, and parklands has increased dramatically. Visits to national outdoor areas doubled between 1960 and 1970. In 1970 there were 837 million visits to federal recreation areas, 482 million visits to state areas, and an estimated 1.5 billion visits to county and city park areas. American families, with increasing disposable income and leisure time, bring cars, campers, boats, off-road recreational vehicles, and tons of solid wastes into natural areas. Facilities to serve these visitors spring up near most outdoor areas; highways, motels, and eating establishments are familiar signs of development on the edges of state and national parks. This development encourages overcrowding by visitors and inevitably disrupts wildlife. In many instances, certain predators (lions, bears, or wolves) are removed from parks as a consequence of tourism and development.

Public appreciation of wildlife and wilderness has gradually increased. More and more people now recognize the educational and scientific value of wilderness and wildlife. Natural communities and ecosystems are living research laboratories that may reveal how man can live in harmony with his environment. The solitude and scenic grandeur of wild natural areas are in greater demand than ever as more and more Americans are seeking an escape from vast suburban shopping centers, high-speed freeways, monotonous housing, and the noise and contaminated air of growing urban areas.

The nation's officially protected natural areas and wildlife habitats have been established through a number of different federal, state, and local programs, although the purpose of many of these programs has not been specifically to preserve wildlife habitats. A little more than a century ago, there were no formal natural areas such as national, state, or county parks and no national forests. Today the U.S. Forest Service has almost 181 million acres in national forests and 6 million acres in national grasslands, but only about 14 million acres of this land has been set aside as wilderness in which there can be no commercial exploitation or road building. The U.S. Bureau of Land Management (BLM) has more public land—453 million acres—to manage than any other federal agency. Although a great deal of this is leased to graziers, more than 70 million visitors annually hunt, camp, and picnic in BLM natural areas. The U.S. National Park Service manages 30 million acres, including sites such as national monuments, historical parks, historical landmarks, and national seashores. The U.S. Bureau of Reclamation manages nearly 200 reservoirs and lakes as recreation areas in more than twenty states. The U.S. Bureau of Sport Fisheries and Wildlife administers the National Wildlife Refuge System of 330 protected areas on 30 million acres. These areas provide a combination of recreational and wildlife protection uses. In addition to federally controlled land, state forests occupy 20 million acres, and there are also substantial acres of state and county parks, although these are unevenly apportioned among the states.

Both state and federal governments have jurisdiction over the management of wildlife populations and habitats. State protection of wildlife has traditionally commenced with game birds and animals. Only a few states have extended wildlife protection laws beyond game species, but in recent years, a number of states have implemented programs to protect some nongame species and a few have passed legislation to protect endangered species. Alaska, Florida, Massachusetts, and Connecticut already have laws protecting certain endangered species, and other states—Nevada, Minnesota, Wisconsin, New York, Oregon, and California—have recently begun to inventory endangered species.

Historically, states have regulated the population of game wildlife while the federal government has managed habitats on public lands, but even so, jurisdiction over wildlife protection and natural areas has not been clearly established. Federal laws have been enacted from time to time to deal with isolated parts of the complex problem of managing wildlife and natural areas. The Lacey Act, Black Bass Act of 1926, Migratory Bird Conservation Act of 1929, Fish and Wildlife Coordination Act of 1934, and others are examples of the incremental approach to wildlife and natural area management during the twentieth century. The Pittman-Robertson Act of 1937 and the Dingell-Johnson Act of 1950 are examples of attempts at federal-state cooperation in facing a common wildlife problem. More recently, the Fish and Wild-life Act of 1956, the Wilderness Act of 1964, the National Wild and Scenic Rivers Act of 1968, the Marine Sanctuaries Act of 1972, the Coastal Zone Management Act of 1972, and the Marine Mammal Protection Act of 1972 have been legislative efforts to establish policy at the federal level. The first attempt by the federal government to protect all native game and nongame endangered species was the Endangered Species Preservation Act of 1966, subsequently amended by the Endangered Species Conservation Act of 1969, which was aimed at giving aid to threatened species abroad.

National laws against the killing of endangered species are inadequate. For instance, the Endangered Species Conservation Act of 1969 lists only those species threatened with worldwide extinction. Domestic relatives or subspecies of endangered species are not protected, and there are no federal penalties for killing endangered species. Moreover, few wildlife laws are effective tools for protecting wildlife. Loopholes, administrative delays, excessive administrative discretion, and limited procedures for public participation in decision making detract from the effectiveness of many of these laws. Also, certain species of wildlife have been easier to protect than others; protecting species with little commercial value, such as wild horses, is easier than protecting dolphins, which are killed by the tuna industry's purse seine fishing methods.

Comprehensive policies for the protection and management of natural areas and wildlife are urgently needed in the United States. Although many federal agencies have extensive backlogs of authorized natural area acquisitions, Congress has not appropriated funds for them. Opposition to the establishment of natural areas is inherent in a society with unregulated growth in industry, population, and technology, and with a strong tradition of private ownership of land and its associated resources. Powerful threats to the remaining natural areas of the nation come chiefly from the private sector—mining interests, livestock graziers, road construction firms, real estate and recreation developers, loggers, airport construction contractors, and the fishing industry. But these economic interests are often assisted and protected by governmental agencies, some of which were established for this purpose.

Other government agencies, responsible for natural areas, have mandates that promote conflicting activities. For instance, the dilemma of the National Park Service is that it must conserve the timeless natural assets of wild areas and at the same time promote a parks-for-people policy. The U.S. Forest Service, which has a mandate for multiple-use management of its lands, is constantly under pressure from lumber, mining, range, and recreation interests not to extend preserves for wildlife and wilderness. Increasing political pressures urge these agencies and others at both federal and state levels to reduce natural areas and relax wildlife controls as population increases and economic development grows.

There is an urgent need for a uniform approach to the common problems facing both state and federal authorities. State and federal programs for wildlife and natural area preservation often pose jurisdictional problems. Although the use of certain poisons was banned on federal lands in February 1972, some states have been under considerable pressure from livestock interests to continue using them. State and local governments frequently have not appreciated the needs, values, or benefits of natural areas; they have failed to see the interdependency of wildlife and ecosystems that stretches beyond artificial territorial borders. State and municipal governments have often resisted the establishment of public seashores, wildlife sanctuaries, free-flowing rivers, or the creation of wilderness areas because reclassification of these lands would mean a reduction in tax revenues. Even though public and governmental efforts to preserve natural areas and wildlife have increased dramatically during the last quarter century, integrating policy between levels of government and between agencies is a serious problem that remains unsolved.

Concerned people have not always waited for government to act on behalf of the public interest in nature preservation. Many privately owned natural areas have been established through private funding or in many instances by volunteer citizen action. Many of these lands preserve wildlife habitats and protect endangered species. Half of the outdoor recreation areas of the nation, about 490 million acres, are owned privately. The Nature Conservancy has acquired more than 100 areas in almost thirty states; it supervises some, others are transferred to government or other suitable custodians for management as natural preserves. The National Audubon Society has numerous wilderness holdings and wildlife sanctuaries in salt marshes, swamp lands, river valleys, and on offshore islands. Private landowners throughout the nation have set aside remnants of open space for educational purposes, for scientific research, and for sightseers and picnickers. Groups of citizens in booming residential areas and in small rural towns have, to some extent, preserved natural areas, wildlife preserves, and pockets of open space in their communities. Conservation groups and preservation-conscious individuals have been the principal advocates of state and federal legislation preserving wildlife and natural areas.

CASE I   Wild and Scenic Rivers: Tennessee

Between the cities of Nashville, Knoxville, and Chattanooga, Tennessee, the Obed River and its tributaries form a canyon system of outstanding aesthetic, scenic, and recreational value rarely found elsewhere in America. Forming a watershed through the ancient Cumberland Plateau of eastern Tennessee, the Obed system comprises 140 miles of free-flowing streams. The forested mountains and scenic river gorges surrounding the Obed are far removed from the urban populations of Tennessee cities. Still sparsely inhabited, the counties of this area are up to 80 percent forested. Some of the most rugged scenery of the Southeast has survived in spite of development mainly because many of the river environs of the Obed are inaccessible to loggers and agriculturalists.

Forming innumerable rapids and stillpools, the Obed's waterway cuts through 250 feet of sandstone canyon walls, spectacularly colored in hues of grey, yellow, deep red, and green. Besides the geological uniqueness of this river system, the diversity and richness of its vegetation render it a priceless natural area. The valleys of the Obed and its tributaries, which pass through part of the 80,000-acre, state-owned Catoosa Wildlife Management Area, are a crucial part of the habitat of nationally known wildlife. The rare and endangered red-cockaded woodpecker, the wild turkey, the peregrine falcon, ruffed grouse, and golden eagle live within the area. Virginia whitetail deer, raccoon, oppossum, and many other game animals are abundant. The Obed is almost unique for sportsmen in the South because the native muskellunge and numerous other sport fish still thrive there. The wilderness aspects of the Obed River—varied terrain and waterflow—make it an increasingly popular recreation area. Conservationists fighting to preserve this wilderness, one of the few remaining unspoiled natural areas of free-flowing river in the country, have emphasized the need to protect the region from exploitation as a commercialized recreation facility.

The Actors

The Wild and Scenic Rivers Act of 1968 gave the U.S. Department of Interior and Department of Agriculture jurisdiction over a number of the rivers in the nation selected for study, including the Obed, but the Tennessee Valley Authority (TVA) was the dominant federal agency in most Tennessee resource matters. The southeast regional office of the Bureau of Outdoor Recreation in Atlanta had the immediate responsibility for the study of the Obed. A number of senators and congressmen became involved on the national level when conservationists turned the issue toward Washington, D.C. A number of state agencies played a role in the scenic rivers dispute, the Tennessee Game and Fish Commission and the Tennessee Department of Conservation in particular. State assemblymen also played a central role in introducing legislation in Tennessee on behalf of the conservationists.

The citizens' groups which led the fight to save the wild, free-flowing character of Tennessee rivers were the Tennessee Citizens for Wilderness Planning (TCWP) and the Tennessee Scenic Rivers Association (TSRA). These groups were supported later on by many other state groups, such as local chapters of the Audubon Society and Sierra Club, Save Our Cumberland Mountains, and by national groups such as the American Rivers Conservation Council, the Wilderness Society, and the Izaak Walton League. Conservationists stimulated the press throughout Tennessee and gained significant favorable publicity through editorials.

The Policy Process

As explained earlier, the citizens' groups had one specific goal for the Obed River and its tributaries: its preservation as a "wild river." The decision to achieve this goal through legislation by the state of Tennessee or through federal scenic rivers legislation gave the conservationists two avenues of approach to policy formation. An examination of the policy process for each avenue begins with efforts to establish a wild and scenic rivers system in Tennessee. With incredible organization and skill, the conservationists prompted the enactment of laws providing for a scenic rivers system in less than two years.

With the formation of the Tennessee Citizens for Wilderness Planning in June 1966, the goals and patterns of operation for the citizens' group were set. Opponents of river preservation were quickly identified. The Tennessee Valley Authority (TVA) had developed a plan to dam the Obed—a plan supported by the Emory River Watershed Development Association (ERWDA), a local group formed under TVA's Tributary Area Development Program which worked under the guidance of TVA's staff. The citizens' groups, TCWP and TSRA, combined forces to monitor opponents' activities as well as to generate support and publicity for preservation of free-flowing streams and natural areas. The groups concentrated on developing support among public officials. They took Congressman John J. Duncan, at that time the leading proponent of wilderness in Congress, on a canoe trip in the Obed River Gorge, sought the assistance of Congressman John P. Saylor and Supreme Court Justice William O. Douglas (along with Tennessee congressional and gubernatorial candidates generally), introduced the Tennessee Department of Conservation and the Game and Fish Commission to the aims of the groups, and presented numerous slide shows to civic groups, church groups, and school groups. When TCWP/TSRA learned that the prodam Emory River Watershed Development Association was going to hold its annual meeting in November 1967, they promptly mobilized an outpouring of antidam sentiment to Congressman Joe L. Evins, the ERWDA's guest speaker.

Other tactics of the citizens' groups included uniting scattered citizens' groups and generating press coverage. The groups analyzed the previous failures of citizen's organizations in other states and mobilized the support of fifty other organizations which opposed indiscriminate damming of stream after stream. A one-hour cable television program on the values of a scenic river system in Tennessee was arranged in March of 1967. After submitting testimony at the Senate Committee on Interior and Insular Affairs debate on the national scenic rivers system in May 1967, TCWP and TSRA issued their testimony as a news release in Tennessee. More than ten prominent newspapers published it. The citizen efforts for both state and federal legislation went on simultaneously.

The TCWP and TSRA goals of seeking political, popular, and press support were highly successful, and by July 1967, they had impressive political support from a number of state politicians. Citizens then tried to get TVA to drop the dam plans and adopt a policy of preservation. After guiding some TVA staffers and consultants on a field trip, showing slides, and submitting a report, a delegation from TCWP confronted TVA leadership in Knoxville to discuss that agency's plans for the Obed. The TVA plans were not clear, and although there were some hints that TVA had abandoned its plans for a dam, the citizens' group announced that it was not satisfied that administrative action would permanently preserve the Obed. Convinced that legislative protection was necessary, TCWP and TSRA increased their activity toward establishing a state river preservation system.

The TCWP invited a number of prominent people to their meeting of January 15, 1968, including several legislators and the parks naturalist of the Tennessee Department of Conservation. They discussed a report prepared by TSRA of river segments that were worthy of inclusion in a state scenic rivers system. One of the guests, State Representative William Pope, a member of the Tennessee General Assembly, promised that if the proposal could be drafted into a bill, he would introduce it in the legislature. Three members of TCWP and TSRA devoted three weeks to prepare this Tennessee Scenic Rivers Bill. The bill proposed three classifications of river areas—natural, pastoral, and partially developed—with specifications for the degree of protection given to streams and the nature of land-use controls for surrounding areas.

When the bill was passed on April 3, 1968, Tennessee became the first state in the union with a scenic rivers system. TCWP and TSRA had contributed significantly, not only by proposing and drafting the legislation, but also by arranging for positive testimony from the Tennessee Conservation League (100 affiliated clubs), the Middle Tennessee Conservancy Council, the eleven-county Hull-York Lakeland RC and D Association, and the Bluff City Club of Memphis. But groups favoring the Obed dam had removed the Obed from the system through an amendment in the house on March 18. At this point, TCWP focused on getting the Obed reinstated by senatorial amendment. TCWP quickly collected 1,000 signatures on a petition in five days and generated 130 comments and mailings from twenty-three localities. Although the amendment strategy failed, the citizens were satisfied the Obed and other rivers could be added to the system in a short time.

The necessity to add the Obed to the state's river system, however, was removed when the Obed was included in the study category of the federal system. In subsequent years TCWP and TSRA did add rivers to the state system, but some river segments were deleted due to pressure from a handful of legislators representing these areas, to whom the Tennessee General Assembly extended "local legislative courtesy." In 1972, even though TCWP mobilized thousands of conservationists, won major editorial approvals, and coordinated phone calls to thirty-three state senators, sections of the Harpeth River were deleted. The implementation of the state scenic rivers law also moved very slowly; it was not until 1973 that constant pressure from TCWP/TSRA and others had culminated in pilot studies of several rivers.

At the same time they were pursuing efforts to preserve the Obed and other scenic rivers at the state level, TCWP/TSRA members also spearheaded other attempts to affect policy in Washington, D.C. The dynamism of the Tennessee groups' participation is illustrated in two phases of developing a federal scenic rivers policy: first, the groups' involvement up to the signing of the Wild and Scenic Rivers Act, and second, the TCWP/TSRA role in the subsequent implementation of the act.

Early in 1967, TCWP and TSRA members had testified at congressional hearings in Washington, D.C., to advocate including Tennessee rivers in a national system. The groups' testimony advocated moratoriums on dam building and channelization of rivers under study and the classification of rivers to restrict use depending on their class; in general, they supported the legislation contained in Congressman John Dingell's H.R. 493 and Congressman Saylor's H.R. 90. The groups wrote to Secretary of Interior Stewart Udall to criticize several other proposed bills, particularly Congressman Wayne Aspinall's H.R. 8416. This bill was unacceptable to Tennessee conservationists because its moratorium on licensing dam projects applied only to the Federal Power Commission, not TVA.

In 1968, TSRA and TCWP testified at House hearings. They had obtained the endorsements of other citizens' groups, such as the East Tennessee White Water Club and Anderson County Young Democrats, and several members of the Tennessee congressional delegation also endorsed the advocacy of the citizens' groups. When the House Committee on Interior and Insular Affairs reported out the Scenic Rivers Bill in late June 1968, the Obed River and others were included in the study category. The citizens were well satisfied with the strategies they had used. At least five of the strategies had been influential: oral testimony in Washington, repeated contacts with congressmen, winning the endorsement of Tennessee representatives, the report on cost estimates prepared by TSRA, and winning the endorsement of many other citizens' groups for TCWP testimony. The prestige attributed to TCWP in the state, across the nation, and in government circles helped its impact on policy. The Obed River was still in the study category of the Wild and Scenic Rivers Act (PL 90–542) when it became law on October 2, 1968.

Even so, the river was not yet protected. Pressures still existed which were working against including the Obed in the national system. TCWP alerted its members and associated conservation groups that the rivers being studied, including the Obed, were not safe until the Bureau of Outdoor Recreation (BOR) examined and then formally included them in the act. Studies of the Obed by the BOR were delayed for more than a year by severe budget and staff reductions. The TCWP offered its expert assistance to the BOR, which was required to consult with government agencies at all levels and to make its study findings available to the public. The main goal of TCWP at this time was to help state and federal agencies implement the new legislation.

The TVA, however, ignored the position of Congress concerning the Obed River. In May 1969, it distributed its publication, "A Quality Environment in the Tennessee Valley," which proposed a dam on a tributary of the Obed system. Furthermore, the TCWP learned in November that TVA planned to connect Knoxville and Nashville with a 500-kv powerline that would cross the Obed and a major tributary. These plans of the TVA clearly violated the intent of the Wild and Scenic Rivers Act. TCWP also discovered that TVA was violating Section 7 (c) of this act by not informing the secretary of interior before commencing its studies. The citizens' group immediately communicated its information to the secretary of interior. The Department of Interior instructed the BOR to study the conflict, and TVA agreed not to jeopardize the intent of the Wild and Scenic Rivers Act.

After resolving the powerline crossing problem, mainly by its alertness and advocacy, TCWP faced two more threats to the wildlife and natural resources of the Obed River. In early 1970, TVA received a request from local communities in Roane County for a dam on the Obed, even though it would protect only 200 acres of flood plain. After restudying its 1965 dam proposal, the TVA came out with an even lower cost-benefit ratio than before, indicating that construction was economically unjustifiable. In this instance TCWP wrote to congressmen in defense of the TVA. Gradually TCWP convinced residents of the watershed area that wild river status for the Obed would benefit the whole area.

Soon after the flood plain issue, TCWP learned that the TVA had recommended strip mining for coal in an old site on the north bank of the Obed river. They immediately notified BOR, the state of Tennessee, and the chairman of TVA of this disfiguration in an area that Congress had authorized to be studied. TCWP and TSRA conducted photographic expeditions and field trips to the mining area to gather data, and they took with them representatives of other conservation groups and TVA officials. Soon after these trips, TVA agreed to cancel the contract with the operator, and also promised not to enter into new contracts for mining coal on the Obed or its tributaries. Once again TCWP's watchdog activities significantly influenced policy during 1970.

In the fall of 1970, the southeast regional office of the BOR began studies of the Obed. Not only did TCWP officials guide study teams in the field, they also contributed information on specific features of the Obed system such as river uses and history, waterfalls, caves, geological formations, vegetation, fish, and wildlife. Throughout this period of study and particularly in February 1971, citizens' groups made sure the attention of government offices was firmly directed toward continually evolving Obed issues. The TCWP and TSRA, along with representatives from a number of other clubs, held conferences with the state Conservation Department and the division chiefs of planning and strip mining. The Stream Pollution Control Board was alerted to proposals for coal washing on the Obed, and the TCWP was quick to protest proposed real estate projects close to the Obed.

As the frequency of such threats to the Obed River increased, the preservationists became convinced that immediate completion of the BOR study was imperative. They therefore contacted the entire Tennessee congressional delegation and urged them to promote a speed-up of the study. By June 1972, the BOR completed its study and was circulating it among task force members for comment. TCWP kept close watch on the study as it progressed to the secretary of the interior for his scrutiny.

Once the BOR set May 24 and 25, 1973, for hearings on the Obed River, TCWP was able to coordinate strong conservationist representation at the meetings in Crossville and Wartburg. When BOR attempted to cancel the hearings temporarily, TCWP pressure reopened them. At the hearings, alternative proposals for the amount of river area to be included were presented, and the respective costs of each were debated. The members unanimously preferred to have the National Park Service help with management rather than the TVA. While waiting for the BOR to announce the second set of hearings, TCWP and the American Rivers Conservation Council worked vigorously to submit recommendations to the Senate subcommittee that was holding hearings in Washington, D.C., on amendments to the 1968 National Wild and Scenic Rivers Act. The citizens' groups advocated extending moratoriums on water resource projects in the study category and increasing the amount of land to be required for each mile of river included in the scenic system. Before the second set of Obed hearings began in September 1973, the TCWP arranged to transport participants, provided readers for the written testimony of those who could not attend, and prepared for the strong opposition expected from antipreservationists. The antipreservationists, mostly those interested in strip mining and real estate developers, were heavily outnumbered at the hearings. The proposals were carried fifty-seven to ten.

Prior to the second set of Obed hearings, the BOR had issued an information brochure summarizing the main features of its proposal. About 100 miles of the Obed and its tributaries were to be added to the national system, mostly in the "wild" category. Written and oral testimony from citizens' groups generally praised the proposal and continued to emphasize the aesthetic qualities of natural areas on the Obed and its tributaries. In addition, they recommended purchasing buffer strips along scenic easements, urged that over-visitation be avoided, and strongly favored management by the National Park Service. By informing other state and national conservation organizations of the proceedings, TCWP was able to obtain the support of twenty-one organizations on a written resolution asking for the Obed system to be managed by the National Park Service.

The BOR announced that any modifications made to its report would be in response to public comment presented in both sets of Obed hearings. But in February 1974, it was discovered that the BOR had recommended that the scenic river areas be managed by TVA—a recommendation diametrically opposed to the publicly expressed desires of citizens. The report recommended a visitation figure of 580,000 annually on a mere 15,644 acres. This figure was four times greater than the per acre figure of the heavily visited Great Smoky Mts. National Park. The visitation recommendation was three times larger than the

175,000 figure contained in the BOR information brochure—a recommendation which had been criticized unanimously at the hearings for being too high. It seemed that BOR and TVA had betrayed the public trust and were recommending policies that would destroy the wildlife habitats and scenic values of the Obed.

Outcome

Despite the passage of both state and national legislation to protect wild and scenic rivers, the Obed was still threatened. TCWP and associated groups protested the BOR recommendations strongly to the Department of the Interior, to the BOR itself, and to various congressmen. The citizens then applied pressure to Tennessee's senators and congressmen who would introduce bills in Congress once the secretary of interior made a recommendation to have the Obed included in the National Wild and Scenic Rivers System.

CASE II   Wildlife Refuge: Great Swamp, New Jersey

The Great Swamp, one of the largest unspoiled areas of open space and wetlands between Maine and Virginia, is a remnant of the original wilderness of the Northeast. The Great Swamp is unique because it has survived in the most densely inhabited portion of North America. New York City is only twenty-five miles away, and on a clear day a visitor to the swamp can see the twin towers of the World Trade Center. More than 30 million people live within an hour's drive of the swamp, and the population in surrounding Morris County, which doubled between 1945 and 1963, will double again by 1976. This rapid population growth and industrialization in areas surrounding the swamp have always threatened it, but the most direct threat came in 1959, when the Port of New York Authority announced that the Great Swamp was a feasible site for the world's largest international jetport, a $220 million project to be operational by 1970.

The Great Swamp, 10,000 acres of undeveloped wetlands and forests, is the remnant of the ancient Lake Passaic, which geologists estimate is 15,000 years old. The woodlands, which contain 40 varieties of trees and at least 1,000 plant species, are the natural habitat of deer, mink, otter, fox, and raccoon and almost 200 species of birds. Because the Hudson River and Great Atlantic Flyways converge on the swamp, the area is a crucial sanctuary for birds. The Great Brook and Passaic River, both well stocked with fish, are part of the drainage system flowing from the wetlands. Great Swamp has been recognized for a long time as a wilderness refuge in the midst of a dense tangle of people, factories, railroads, highways, powerlines, bridges, billboards, storage tanks, and junkyards. For many years, professional and amateur naturalists had enjoyed the unique ecosystem of the swamp, and nearby schools and universities had used it as a field laboratory.

When the Port Authority announced its site plan in 1959, the community reaction was stunned surprise and despair. Even though the Port Authority was the most powerful interstate agency in the country and had a reputation for being tough-minded, local citizens nevertheless promptly organized to preserve the Great Swamp as a wildlife refuge. During the next three years, citizens' groups set a precedent by purchasing an area of national value with over $4 million in private funds. To conservationists, the rescue of the Great Swamp of New Jersey from the land developers and jetport planners may have been the greatest victory in the state since George Washington crossed the Delaware and took Trenton from the British.

The Actors

The work of conservationists was supported at the federal level by Secretary of Interior Stewart Udall and by the regional office of the U.S. Fish and Wildlife Service, whose director, John S. Gottschalk, endorsed the efforts of conservation groups and gave the support of his staff. At the local level nine citizens formed the Great Swamp Committee in December 1959. Among the group's original members were John T. Neal, president of the New Jersey Audubon Society, Mrs. James Hand, original chairman and member of the Summit Nature Club, and Mrs. R. L. Lloyd, a commissioner of the Morris County Park Commission. The committee was supported by a sister group, also formed at that time, known as the Jersey Jetport Site Association. The local government in Morris County and in surrounding towns helped the Jersey Jetport Site Association in its research work, and the Morris County Park Commission, in particular, supported the conservationists.

The North American Wildlife Foundation was perhaps the most significant participant in policy formation. Since 1911, this Washington-based, nonprofit, tax-exempt organization has worked for conservation, restoration, and improved management of wildlife and related natural resources. This organization helped the Great Swamp Committee cooperate with state, federal, and private agencies to promote the Great Swamp resource program in the public interest. Many conservation groups nationwide joined with local groups such as the New Jersey Audubon Society, the Summit Nature Club, New Jersey State Federation of Women's Clubs, and the Somerset Hills Garden Club.

The Policy Process

Naturalists had known of the resources of Great Swamp even before it appeared on government maps in the late eighteenth century; and as early as 1932, a government report suggested it was suitable for a waterfowl preserve. But the swamp was threatened by other plans including flood control and drainage projects. Since 1939, when Arthur Babson's book *Modern Wilderness,* called for preservation of Great Swamp, conservationists have tried to preserve the area. In 1951, 450 acres of the swamp were given to a conservation organization, but no land was added to this area until 1959. The Port Authority jetport proposal began the final chapter in the story to preserve New Jersey's last wilderness area.

The Great Swamp Committee (GSC) and the Jersey Jetport Site Association (JJSA), created in response to the Port Authority's plans, were the key organizations in most policy developments and the eventual defeat of the jetport plan. Although these two groups shared common objectives and kept in close communication throughout the controversy, their organizational structures and memberships were entirely different. The GSC was a tax-exempt organization which could not and did not lobby for legislation, but the JJSA was a nonexempt, politically oriented organization whose funding was not deductible. For the sake of efficiency and effectiveness, it was decided that each should concentrate on separate aspects of the problem.

The Great Swamp Committee concentrated on publicizing the conflict and raising money to purchase land. Subcommittees were set up to form a speakers' bureau and to negotiate a land sales' bureau. The committees and hundreds of volunteers mailed literature, stimulated editorial support, and gave slide presentations throughout the county and the state. Their work raised hundreds of thousands of dollars for land purchases. The Jersey Jetport Site Association did basic research on the problem by preparing a series of professional studies of the social and economic impacts of the jetport upon the region. It also monitored Port Authority activity and publicized new developments. By working closely with the New Jersey legislature, the JJSA also kept track of significant political developments. Between them, the GSC and the JJSA kept in close communication with all levels of government, private agencies, the news media, and the public.

The fundamental strategy of the citizens' groups was to buy the land and keep it out of reach of condemnation by the Port Authority and out of the reach of the state legislature. Once the land was purchased (at $200 an acre) and deeded to the U.S. Fish and Wildlife Service, only Congress or the president could restore the land to its former owners, and the secretary of the interior could make decisions about the swamp in the national interest. The North American Wildlife Foundation established the Great Swamp Fund, and in March 1961, the foundation invested the GSC with official committee status so that gifts of cash and land could be tax deductible. Affiliating itself with the Wildlife Foundation was an important step for the GSC because it enhanced fund-raising potential and established the group's credibility with the public. Later in 1961, the GSC was given extra support when nine nearby colleges and universities wrote to the regional director of the Fish and Wildlife Service and pointed out the scientific and educational value of Great Swamp as a laboratory site. Nineteen representatives from these institutions later met with the Fish and Wildlife Service to discuss preservation.

By late 1961, the Great Swamp Committee and its supporters had accumulated so much financial support and generated such publicity favoring conservationists that the Federal Aviation Agency officially lost interest in the area. But the Port Authority had not amended or withdrawn its original plan. Citizens' groups, however, were still committed to deed to the U.S. Fish and Wildlife Service 3,000 acres of the Great Swamp, the minimum area necessary for the Department of Interior to designate it a national wildlife refuge. The main objectives of the GSC at this time were still to purchase land and to educate the public.

In October and November 1962, the Great Swamp Committee continued to conduct meetings which drew favorable publicity. In October, the Summit Nature Club sponsored a meeting, at Lincoln School in Morristown, at which John S. Gottschalk, regional director of the U.S. Fish and Wildlife Service, was guest speaker. On November 27, Secretary of Interior Stewart Udall spoke on the "Urgent Need to Preserve Open Space" at a dinner meeting arranged by the Great Swamp Committee for prominent conservationists. The GSC hoped that this dinner meeting at Far Hills Inn in Morristown would elicit donations and widespread publicity. Sure enough, national newspapers and magazines published favorable editorials following this event. Even conservationists on Martha's Vineyard, south of Cape Cod, were alerted to the successful strategy by an editorial in an island newspaper.

Then in March 1963, the Texas Eastern Transmission Corporation threatened to construct a gas pipeline across the swamp, but the threat only spurred conservationists to increase their efforts. The Jersey Jetport Site Association announced publicly that it would oppose the proposal, and the Great Swamp Committee promptly sponsored an exhibit entitled, "A Nature Showcase: Our Wildlife Heritage Today and Tomorrow," that was held in the mall at Short Hills, New Jersey. Featuring painting, sculpture, photography, science displays, and a botanical garden, the exhibition attracted over 8,000 people and stimulated further public interest which, in turn, led to more donations. The increasing political influence of the work led by the GSC and the JJSA through the previous two years had now begun to show. In March, the House Appropriations Committee requested congressional approval for $310,000 to draw up a master plan for Great Swamp that could be completed by June 1964.

By the end of October 1963, both the government and the Port Authority were willing to admit the citizens were indeed serious. After presenting more than 400 slide shows, the GSC had raised well over half a million dollars and had purchased all but 919 of the required 3,000 acres. Nearly 4,000 contributions had been sent from over 200 different communities in 25 states and even Canada. Conservationists were confident that the secretary of the interior was prepared to make a national issue out of preserving Great Swamp as wild land.

With the dedication of the Great Swamp Wildlife Refuge on May 29, 1964, the major battle had been won. By June of that year, the GSC had donated 2,446.78 acres, and it added another 427.35 acres by August 1969. In March 1965 the first public money, $2.8 million, was allocated for acquisition of an additional 3,267 acres. In 1966, the National Park Service recognized the value of Great Swamp by designating it a Registered Natural Landmark, "possessing exceptional value for illustrating the natural history of the United States." On September 28, 1966, Congress designated 3,750 acres in the eastern portion of the swamp as the Great Swamp National Wildlife Refuge Wilderness Area, the first area in the East to be included in the National Wilderness System.

Early in the promotional work to save Great Swamp, the GSC recognized that public use of the area had to be controlled so that private rights were not violated and the natural values of the swamp were not impaired. GSC also realized that the areas adjoining the refuge and the water courses had to be protected so that the swamp would not be destroyed by forces outside its immediate boundaries. Working with the Somerset and Morris County park commissions, the GSC encouraged and helped finance the establishment of large county parks abutting the refuge to serve as buffer areas and primary visitor centers. Each county park system established a nature education facility to provide the information necessary to understand the ecological, archeological, and historical values of the Great Swamp Basin. The Morris County Great Swamp Nature Center was established first, even before the area was formally accepted as a National Wildlife Refuge.

Outcome

The struggle to preserve Great Swamp was characterized by inter-governmental and public coordination and cooperation. This sense of responsibility and cooperation continues in effect to this day, guiding land-use practices to protect natural values of the refuge.

As of September 1973, 5,900 acres had been acquired, including land condemned by the Fish and Wildlife Service. The Department of Interior plans to provide both a wilderness environment for people to enjoy and a natural habitat for wildlife. The western part of the Great Swamp wetlands and open space area will be managed, with certain areas labeled as nature trails, bridle paths, and observation towers. Some wetlands will be impounded, and forage crops will be planted in these for the benefit of migratory water fowl. The eastern three-fifths of the swamp will be maintained in its natural state as a wilderness area for field studies.

CASE III   Wetlands Preservation: The Everglades, Florida

In the southern tip of Florida lies a 4,000-square-mile swamp wilderness known as the Everglades. Called "pahayokee" ("river of grass") by the Seminole Indians, the Everglades is actually a vast, shallow, slow-moving river of fresh water flowing from the head-waters of Lake Okeechobee south through the sawgrass marshes, Everglades National Park, and into the Gulf of Mexico. The Everglades ecosystem supports a great variety of wildlife, dependent upon the unique environmental properties of the slowly moving water.

Man, too, depends on the Everglades' water resources for agricultural, industrial, and urban development. The large agricultural area south and southeast of Lake Okeechobee is one of the most intensively cultivated in the world. The incredibly fast growth of southern Florida has increasingly polluted the Everglades with pesticides, agricultural fertilizers, and industrial and urban sewage. Extensive channeling and flood-water projects have reduced the quantity and deteriorated the quality of fresh water resources. Today, rampant land developments in Florida's southern counties—Dade, Brower, and Miami—threaten the existence of this unique wilderness area.

The Everglades National Park, always a popular wilderness area, in recent years has attracted more than one million persons annually to see its 300 species of birds, mammals, fish, and reptiles. The third largest park in the United States, the Everglades was first authorized by Congress in 1934, but it was not dedicated until 1947, after protracted negotiations. Occupying the southern tip of the Florida peninsula, the park is the farthest point downstream in the "river of grass." The increasing disruption and pollution of the flow of water threaten to destroy the park's wildlife and endanger the fresh water resources of coastal cities.

The most dangerous single threat to the park and the surrounding wilderness occurred in 1968 when the Dade County Port Authority proposed to purchase thirty-nine square miles of Big Cypress Swamp for a jetport. The southern boundary of the proposed jetport site was only seven miles north of Everglades National Park. The conservationists' challenge to the county Port Authority resulted in one of the most intense conservation controversies in the United States; ultimately it involved the national media and the highest levels of the federal government. More than a park was at stake; it had become a symbol of wilderness. Finally, during the autumn of 1969, President Nixon announced that a commercial jetport would not be built at the Big Cypress Swamp site because it would pose too severe a threat to the park.

The Actors

Local government in the Everglades was fragmented; there was no effective regional authority to control the largely unregulated activities of special interests. Neither the state's planning department nor a regional government coordinating body for Florida's southeastern counties assumed such a responsibility. In the absence of governmental controls, the Dade County Port Authority (Port Authority), a highly autonomous organization, was able to play a dominant role in the conflict. Because the Port Authority was made up of the same people as the Dade County Commission, it presumably had a broad mission. But the Port Authority, independent of the rest of county government, had a hostile relationship with county government. Therefore, despite its seemingly broad powers, the county Port Authority had a narrow mission; it created the jetport proposal and led proponents of its construction.

The Central and Southern Florida Control District (FCD) was one of the agencies with authority to supervise the proposed transportation corridor from the jetport to nearby urban areas. The FCD sparked the controversy by alerting conservationists and government agencies to the minimally publicized Port Authority plans. The Florida Road Department also had jurisdiction in the proposal for a transportation corridor, but like most of the state government, it favored the project until at least late 1968.

The main federal agencies with policy-making authority in the issue were the Department of Transportation's Federal Aviation Administration (FAA) and the National Park Service (NPS) of the Department of Interior. The Everglades National Park management, due to a lack of autonomy, was slow to perceive the threat which the jetport and supporting developments posed to the park's wilderness and water supplies; it did not assume a major role in protecting the park. The Port Authority and the FAA had formulated policies for development long before the NPS and Interior Department entered the struggle.

Because no regional authorities were available to reconcile competing interests and because the Port Authority was unresponsive, conservationists had no alternative other than to take their argument to federal powers in Washington, D.C. The national news media therefore became dominant forces in conveying the issues to the American public, and the majority of the media supported preservation of the wilderness. Local and state conservation organizations, but primarily national ones, led the fight to preserve the Everglades wilderness.

The Policy Process

Although nationwide public opposition to the jetport was not organized until late in 1968, suspicion of the jetport's impact on the park surfaced locally almost immediately after the Port Authority announced its plan on November 9, 1967. Joseph B. Browder, a radio newsman and officer of the Tropical Audubon Society, informally questioned both the director and deputy director of the Port Authority about the jetport's potential threat to the park. Browder's initial concern was allayed by the authorities. Soon after this, however, a prominent local attorney, Dan Paul, wrote a letter to the editor of the *Miami News* criticizing the Dade-Collier jetport plan. The newspaper responded by supporting the project and its two main advocates, the Port Authority and the state Road Department.

The early decisions and the selection of sites were the sole responsibility of the quasi-public Port Authority and the special constituency it served. At no time did it request the Everglades National Park management to appraise the impact of the jetport on the park. The Port Authority chose the Dade-Collier site before its first formal coordination meeting on February 16, 1968, with cognizant state agencies, the Game and Fresh Water Fish Commission, the Florida Board of Conservation, and the Florida Control District (FCD). This meeting and subsequent correspondence with the Port Authority mitigated the initial skepticism of the FCD's executive director. But by July 1968, the FCD was again alarmed about the impact of proposed ground transportation routes upon water conservation areas in its jurisdiction. After meeting with Robert Padrick of the FCD, Joe Browder, who had left the news business in April to work fulltime for the National Audubon Society, alerted his superiors in the Audubon Society to the impending threat to the park. Both men resolved to inform other state conservationists of the dangers.

Meanwhile, in July and August 1968, the Port Authority carried out eminent domain procedures in the Big Cypress Swamp area. At site-breaking ceremonies in September, the governor and representatives of all levels of government praised the jetport proposal. Even though the

Bureau of Outdoor Recreation, the FCD, the Bureau of Sport Fishing and Wildlife, and the park management increasingly voiced skepticism, most public officials in Florida supported the Port Authority and the state Road Department.

In November, Padrick wrote letters sharply critical of the jetport and its transportation corridor plan and distributed them to over 100 conservationists around the state. He successfully publicized the issue and seriously jeopardized the credibility of the Port Authority. Immediately afterward, the FCD proposed to hold a meeting on December 13, 1968, of local, state, and federal government agencies and conservation groups concerned about the jetport project. This meeting turned out to be a crucial point in the policy process. Because of the meeting and because conservationist citizens directly challenged the Port Authority's planning and objectives, the governor's office became involved in the issue and, surprisingly, supported the conservationists. The governor's office suggested that all agencies at the meeting should prepare detailed environmental questions to address to the Port Authority, and that thirty days after it received the lists, a mass meeting would be held to hear the responses.

By this time local and statewide conservationists had begun to organize effective opposition. But it was not until February 1969 that the scattered conservationist opposition was finally unified into an effective coalition at the national level. The idea for a coalition originated at a top-level staff meeting of the National Park Service (NPS). Present at the meeting was Frank Masland, a wealthy industrialist and member of the National Parks Advisory Board. Masland used his influence and experience in the national conservation movement to propose that major national conservation groups form a coalition. As a result of the NPS meeting and Masland's work, a national coalition was planned in April 1969 at the office of the Wildlife Management Institute in Washington, D.C. Over a two-week period, twenty-two national conservation organizations and the United Automobile Workers of America banded together to form the Everglades Coalition.

The Everglades Coalition turned out to be the most important influence in the successful fight against the jetport. Members of the coalition who published influential magazines printed editorials and articles opposing the destruction of the Everglades. With its significant political influence, the coalition was able to lobby successfully at local, state, and federal levels; it also distributed letters and telegrams of opposition to the secretary of transportation, the president, and cabinet members; and it conferred with federal departmental officials and even White House advisers.

Another critical step in the policy process took place while the coalition was being planned. On February 28, 1969, over 200 representatives of public and private conservation organizations and individuals met in Miami Springs to hear the Port Authority's response to questions drawn up as a result of the December meeting at the governor's office. At this first public confrontation between both sides of the issue, the Port Authority gave evasive answers to many of the environmental questions, and its ecological planning was shown to be inadequate. To conservationists, the most important result of the meeting, so it seemed, was the decision to establish a regional tri-county planning authority and an inter-government environmental study group to oversee the jetport plan.

But over two months passed before these groups were organized. By June 1969, when the planning director refused to invite the NPS or conservationists to the next tri-county meeting, citizens' groups realized that they were being denied the opportunity to cooperate in planning. About this time Joe Browder of the Audubon Society and Gary Soucie of the Sierra Club briefed executives from major airlines on the environmental impact of the jetport. Both men were disappointed by the executives' lack of ecological awareness. Because effective regional planning was clearly impossible, conservationists were forced to demand relocation of the jetport in order to protect the park.

A visit to the Everglades in late March 1969 by Secretary of Interior Walter Hickel drew more national attention to the issue and, in effect, publicly committed him and his department to protect the park. Early in April, however, the Port Authority announced that a jetport would be built whether the conservationists and the public wanted it or not. The Everglades Coalition responded to this announcement with a six-page letter of protest to the secretary of transportation, and the letter also asked for a meeting with the secretary. The meeting on May 14 between senior officials of the departments of Transportation and Interior, the NPS, FAA, and representatives of the Everglades Coalition was one of many turning points that were favorable to conservationists. At the National Audubon Society's annual convention in late April, Senator Henry M. Jackson and Undersecretary of the Interior Russell

E. Train expressed concern for the preservation of the Everglades wilderness. Jackson called special hearings on the issue before the Senate Interior Committee, and Train's attitude seemed to rouse the Interior Department to advocate saving the park.

Despite such national attention, not all of the interested parties were aware that the jetport controversy had become a national political issue. The Jackson hearings, which stimulated massive publicity favoring the conservationists, were not attended by senior members of the Port Authority. During the summer of 1969, as a result of national publicity and the conservationists' efforts, the Department of Interior, the National Academy of Sciences, and a private group headed by former Secretary of Interior Stewart Udall began to investigate the environmental impact of the jetport. When the three studies were finally completed in December, they documented many contradictions and hazards in the jetport project.

Also in late 1969, Miami-area college and high school students applied the pressure of publicity to the airlines in an attempt to force them to withdraw support for the project. Guided by conservationists, particularly Joe Browder of the National Audubon Society, students distributed 10,000 "Move the Jetport, Save the Everglades" bumper stickers, and on one occasion they passed them out at major airports across the country. Their success was soon apparent; airlines adopted a low profile throughout the remainder of the controversy.

Another tactic Joe Browder used to protect the Everglades was to have the National Audubon Society file suit against drainage district proposals that were being readied by private developers on the fringes of the jetport site. NPS and the Interior Department intervened on behalf of the Audubon Society—a clear demonstration of the support the conservationists had gradually won.

Outcome

On January 6, 1970, a Jetport Pact was signed by the secretaries of interior and transportation, Governor Kirk of Florida, and Miami's Mayor Hall. A three-year agreement which could be renewed by mutual consent, the pact required the Port Authority to begin immediately to search for another jetport site. The existing one-runway facility could be used, but only for flight training exercises during the three years, and then only under rigorous environmental safeguards. President

Nixon called the decision to stop the jetport "an outstanding victory for conservation." But the issue was still not permanently resolved. The natural areas and water resources of the region are constantly threatened by expanding urban development and a growing need for air transportation, and policies for development inevitably conflict with policies to preserve wilderness. It is difficult to balance the goals of each while maintaining a sound ecology.

CASE IV   Protecting the Natural Character of Small Localities: Berkshire Hills, Massachusetts

The Berkshire Hills in western Massachusetts are one of the last remnants of rural landscape in the rapidly developing Boston-Washington corridor. The region has long been famous for its wide, rolling fields backed by wooded ridges, its unspoiled wetlands that date from the last glacial retreat, and its ecosystems that are the habitat of uncommon mammals, birds, and wildflowers. Some residents in the Berkshires who have become notably ecologically minded in recent years have helped form policies to protect unspoiled countryside. The kinds of "natural" areas they consider worthy of preserving vary considerably. Examples include small areas of forests, mountain slopes, wetlands areas such as shorelines, lakes, swamps, and wild rivers, and even historic farmsites. Some of the sites protect only a few acres, but they fit into the local view of unspoiled scenery and wilderness. Each year, however, road construction projects, leisure homesite developments, and shopping centers encroach on the dwindling open space and scenic areas.

Citizen opposition to the destruction of the scenic beauty of the Berkshire countryside was initially supported by local business interests. In 1967, Donald B. Miller, publisher of the award-winning newspaper, the *Berkshire Eagle,* together with prominent business leaders, conservationists, and the financial support of local industries, formed a private organization to facilitate efforts to preserve the environment of the region in the face of rapid development. This organization, known as the Berkshire Natural Resources Council (BNRC), has acted as the catalyst, liaison, and clearinghouse in all matters involving natural areas in the Berkshire Hills. The council has been such a dominant force in so many instances of environmental policy formation that the movement to preserve natural areas in the region is synonymous with the

BNRC. A summary of some of the BNRC's activities will identify the issues involved in open space preservation in the Berkshires, and an examination of the BNRC's role in a highway construction case will illustrate its effectiveness as an environmental advocate.

The BNRC has set up and supported citizens' groups to participate in a wide range of policy areas: the protection of wild rivers, the preservation of mountains, lakes, and historic sites, the restriction of road construction projects, and the establishment of land trusts to manage woodlands. In five years it has acquired, or assisted communities in acquiring, over 6,000 acres of open space and natural areas worth over a million dollars. The council helped obtain a $600,000 grant from the Ford Foundation for state conservation commissions. The BNRC has also created a subsidiary land trust, the Berkshire County Land Trust and Conservation Fund, which has been given fifteen parcels of land constituting over 1,500 acres of natural areas. As a legislative advocate, the BNRC has worked on bills such as the Conservation Restriction Act and the Wetlands Protection Act, and it wrote Massachusetts' Scenic Mountains Act.

The BNRC regards itself primarily as a service agency, and toward this end it has set up a host of small, single-purpose, ad hoc citizens' groups to serve as advocates for natural area protection. One of the most successful of these satellites was Save Scenic Monterey (SSM), a citizens' group opposed to the construction of a 7.3-mile, $6 million Route 23 bypass that would have adversely affected the swampland, wildlife, and forest of Monterey wilderness. The village of Monterey, with a population of only 610, found that maintaining its 7.3-mile stretch of old Route 23 was too expensive. The state agreed to assume responsibility for old Route 23, but only if it could widen the road from twenty-two to thirty-six feet in order to qualify for federal financial assistance. The state also offered Monterey County an alternative —a new bypass, which would also qualify for funds from the federal Highway Trust Fund. Each alternative, however, entailed severe environmental costs, and the new bypass route in particular threatened unique areas of landscape.

The Actors

In the case of the proposed relocation of Route 23, the BNRC-backed SSM took the dominant preservationist role. An ad hoc and loosely organized opponent of SSM was Save All Monterey (SAM). The key government agencies involved were state and local bodies. The state Department of Public Works and the Department of Natural Resources held primary jurisdiction in the case, but the commonwealth's Joint Legislative Committee on Transportation was also involved. Locally, members of the Board of Selectmen of Monterey, the planning board, the finance committee, and the conservation commissions were involved in decision making during the dispute over policy.

The Policy Process

Public concern over the proposed reconstruction and relocation of Route 23 first surfaced in February 1972. The state Department of Public Works (DPW) held a design hearing in Monterey during which an unofficial hand vote showed that opponents of the project outnumbered supporters seventy-two to forty-four. The Save Scenic Monterey group, on the advice of BNRC, was represented by an attorney at this meeting. The attorney forcefully attacked the DPW for being excessively tardy in contacting the state Department of Natural Resources for rights to 7 ½ acres of Swann State Forest for the proposed road. Three years had passed since the corridor hearing, and it had taken DPW until spring 1971 to initiate legal procedures for taking the land.

When the Joint Legislative Committee on Transportation conducted hearings on the land transfer bill in Boston on February 8, 1972, the SSM group arrived with forty organized protesters on a hired bus from Monterey. One member of the protest group, a professional songwriter, sang the "Ballad of Route 23" to the astonished but appreciative committee. The song eulogized old Route 23 and protested the destruction of Berkshire countryside. (Subsequently the song was recorded and became a hit throughout western Massachusetts.) The tactics of SSM were in part responsible for the committee's unanimous rejection of the land transfer bill. The state Department of Natural Resources declared at the hearing that it would neither approve nor oppose taking land for Route 23 until an environmental impact statement was completed. The citizens had convinced the committee that Berkshire people wanted to retain their environment in a natural state. That proponents of the project did not appear at the hearing was not simply an oversight on their part. The SSM had purposely kept as quiet as possible any news of the impending hearing and of their intended appearance.

As a result of town elections less than two weeks later, SSM forces gained control of both the Monterey Planning Board and the Board of Selectmen. The town of Monterey was so divided on the issue that both SSM and its opponents drove fleets of four-wheel drive vehicles through a snowstorm to bring 75 percent of the town's 370 voters to the polls. SSM had to contend with mounting opposition from the newly organized Save All Monterey Committee (SAM), but with the backing of BNRC, SSM clearly conveyed the views of the majority of Monterey residents to decision makers. Late in February, a joint house-senate Committee on Transportation turned back the DPW's request to use state forest land for Route 23. At this point DPW had to find an alternative route, but before a new route could be chosen an environmental impact statement had to be prepared. A Boston firm of consulting engineers was hired by DPW to prepare the impact study.

To insure that the citizen viewpoint was fully represented, BNRC and SSM decided to prepare their own impact study. BNRC provided SSM with funds to have two law students prepare the Citizens' Environmental Impact Statement. SSM began its task in June 1972, with input coming primarily from the two law students, a botanist, a biologist, a civil engineer, and resource persons at BNRC headquarters. Released in August 1972, the SSM environmental impact statement presented a cost-benefit analysis that showed the costs of the Route 23 bypass would exceed by three to four times the benefits. The SSM statement rejected the proposed bypass on ecological and economic grounds. In complying with the requirements of the National Environmental Policy Act with regard to alternative proposals, the statement recommended that DPW repair and widen the existing Route 23. SSM distributed its statement to every significant policy-making body and also to John Volpe, secretary of the U.S. Department of Transportation. Without highway trust funds, which Volpe controlled, the DPW could not construct the bypass. For this reason SSM focused its attention on the federal level at this time. The local citizens' groups also drew the attention of national media such as *Newsweek* and the *Christian Science Monitor* to the issues.

While waiting for the state's environmental impact report, due in October 1972, the citizens lobbied to win the favor of the governor, who had argued strongly for environmental protection and increased citizen participation in state policy making. The BNRC sponsored a meeting at Butternut Basin in late October to discuss natural areas preservation and the Route 23 issue. The guest of honor, Governor Francis W. Sargent, said he was happy to see citizen participation in decisions for the Berkshire environment, and said he would personally examine the results of hearings to be held later in November. The BNRC showed the governor slides of the area and presented him with maple syrup from a historic farm that lay in the path of the proposed bypass. The syrup was labeled "The Last Maple Syrup in Monterey." Just prior to this meeting, SSM had dramatically drawn attention to its cause at the Environmental Input Hearing that discussed the DPW environmental impact statement. The president of SSM asked the participants in the hearing to stand if they opposed the project. Of the 130 people present, 85 to 90 percent stood in opposition to the bypass. The details of this expression of opposition received widespread coverage in Berkshire Hills' newspapers.

Outcome

On February 17, 1973, the state Department of Public Works dropped its plans to relocate Route 23 on the grounds that the costs outweighed potential benefits. Although the DPW agreed with the SSM statement that the proposed bypass was uneconomical, it did not endorse the statement's conclusion that the feasible and prudent alternative was to resurface and widen old Route 23. Whether the state will assume responsibility for the old Monterey Village strip of road, as requested by the Monterey community, or upgrade it, as SSM suggests, remains an open question.

CASE V   Open Beachlands: Padre Island, Texas

By the mid-1950s, 93 percent of the Gulf and Atlantic coastlands of the United States were privately owned. Alarmed at the seemingly inexorable march of development, conservation-conscious Department of the Interior officials, some vote-conscious congressmen, conservation organizations, and individuals urged that remaining open beach areas be preserved for public use. The struggle to preserve Padre Island, the longest unspoiled island beach along the Atlantic and Gulf coasts and the longest barrier island in the world, has continued for more than two decades and still is not yet finally resolved.

Padre Island is a barrier-dune island extending 117 miles along the Texas coast from near Corpus Christi to Brazos Santiago Pass near Brownsville. The largest portion of the island remains, for the most part, untouched by development. The island's resources, chiefly public open space and wildlife, have become increasingly valuable as the population within a 300-mile radius has escalated to more than eight million. The white pelican uses Padre Island as a wintering place and nesting ground; the great blue heron, the rapidly disappearing brown pelican, and the last of the almost extinct whooping cranes winter in nearby sanctuaries provided by the National Audubon Society. The island, with its surrounding lesser islands built from material (spoil) dredged from navigable channels such as the Laguna Madre, is the natural habitat for the coyote, skunk, wild pig, kangaroo rat, panther, ground squirrel, badger, and a teeming fish population.

Padre Island has other valuable resources. Archaeological treasures dating back 500 to 1,000 years have been discovered on the island, giving scientists information about ancient Tonkawa Indian communities of the area. Geologists have used the island to study the movement of offshore sandbars, and other scientists have investigated the role that dune barriers play in the protection of the mainland from hurricanes. Oil fields and grazing lands have attracted development interests to the area. But the island's chief resource, its potential for tourist development, has been one of the major considerations in the conflict over natural area preservation. This semibarren expanse of beaches and coastal waters has been the focus of a series of policy conflicts that have involved all levels of government, private industry, dozens of conservation groups, labor groups, and thousands of individual citizens.

The role of citizens as preservationists in the course of the policy process has been outstanding. On numerous occasions, citizens' groups provided a major part of the impetus required to overcome obstacles in the path of preservation. Because conservationists originally wanted to protect the island *for* people, they at first pursued federal park status and later sought national seashore status for Padre Island. But as more people with more leisure time began using the island for vacations, the citizens' groups realized that Padre Island National Seashore had to be saved *from* people. If Padre Island was to provide beach recreation facilities and also be a unique wilderness and a wildlife sanctuary, then its wild and primitive aspects had to be protected. Since about 1968, conservationists have worked to include a portion of Padre Island in the National Wilderness Preservation System.

The Actors

At the federal level of government, the U.S. Department of the Interior, through its National Park Service (NPS), has played a leading role in policy formation since the 1950s. More recently, the Environmental Protection Agency has become involved through its studies on Padre Island. At both federal and state levels, legislators have participated in policy formation. Within Texas, the state Parks Board, the Land Commission, numerous chambers of commerce, county commissioners, the Coastal Bend Regional Planning Commission, and the state Highway Commission have had great influence on policy at various times. Real estate developers, the Padre Island Development Company, the Padre Island Land and Cattle Company, firms holding oil, mineral, and grazing leases, fishermen, summer homeowners on the island, and sportsmen have all participated in policy making during the twenty-year conflict.

The conservationists' position was represented in part by the Texas Conservation Council (TCC), a statewide organization interested in establishing parks, preserving natural areas, and protecting wildlife. Much credit should go to members of this organization, especially to its president, the late Armand Yramategui, and to board members Ann Spear and Laurence and Anella Dexter. Established in 1958, the Texas Conservation Council included the members of a group known as Texas Beaches Unlimited, which had fought successfully for the Texas Open Beaches Bill. Also, the council received considerable support from the Outdoor Nature Club of Houston, Texas Garden Clubs, the Corpus Christi Outdoor Club, the Alice Audubon Society and other Audubon chapters, and the Sportsman's Club of Texas. The *Houston Press* gave valuable support to the conservationists throughout the battle to establish the national seashore.

The Policy Process

The distinctive wilderness of Padre Island had been recognized before World War II, but the first step leading to a protective policy did not take place until 1955. The Seashore Recreation Survey of 1955, conducted by the National Park Service, called for public acquisition of ninety-eight miles of beachland between the developed northern and southern tips of the island. As far back as September 1956, the Outdoor Nature Club of Houston had resolved to encourage acquisition of the island for public benefits. At this time, Congress and some units of the federal administration in Washington, D.C. (particularly the Department of the Interior) were inclined to protect unspoiled shorelines. Texas newspapers increasingly urged the government to consider a park proposal. Conservationists publicly expressed their fear of a rush to close off private beaches in the south Texas area just as Florida and other states had closed their beaches. The public demand for action was recognized in 1958 by U.S. Senators Ralph Yarborough and Lyndon Johnson and by Congressmen Joe Kilgore and John Young. Senator Yarborough, in particular, wanted to keep beaches in the Southwest open to the public, and he emphasized that doing so would attract tourists and money to the area. The first legislative action in Texas for preservation came in April 1959, when Congressman Roger Daily submitted his Padre Island Park Bill.

Daily's bill emphasized open beaches as a tourist attraction that could stimulate economic growth for Texas. The purpose of the bill was to allow the state to acquire the island and then deed it to the NPS to operate a national park. The bill was well supported by state agencies and numerous citizens' groups such as the TCC, the Womens Guild of the Museum of Natural History, and the Texas Ornithological Society. Anella Dexter, a member of the board of directors of TCC, showed slides of the island to the house State Affairs Subcommittee at hearings on the bill. About the same time, Senator Yarborough introduced a bill in Congress to make it possible for Padre Island to be operated as a national park.

In June 1959, a group of south Texas legislators posed a threat to park and seashore plans by demanding that no more than a 30-mile strip in the center of the 117-mile island be designated as parkland. (Congressman Daily wanted to set aside 40 to 60 miles.) Another obstacle to the park was Governor Daniel's announcement that the state Parks Board could not handle the state project financially. Meanwhile, real estate development on Padre Beach at the southern tip of the island was booming. But a rumor that the Department of Interior was soon to have up to $15 million available for beach acquisition projects brightened prospects. Conservationists consequently pressured political representatives to establish either a national park or seashore.

The announcement of U.S. Senate interior subcommittee hearings in Corpus Christi in December 1959 on a Padre Island National Seashore aroused widespread interest. When the *New York Times,* President Eisenhower, and the *Christian Science Monitor* publicly commented in favor of a seashore plan, national attention was also focused on Padre Island. Senator Neuberger of Oregon included the Texas island in her omnibus bill which named several seashore areas such as Cape Cod, Indiana Dunes, and Oregon Dunes for shoreline protection. In Texas, the TCC elicited support for preservationists by collecting 12,300 signatures from 355 cities and towns on a petition favoring the seashore plan. Conservation groups contacted state legislators and congressmen; and delegations to the hearings were led by county judges, county commissioners, and sportsmen's clubs. The state Board of Parks transferred its December meeting from Austin to Corpus Christi so its members could attend the hearings. Participation at the hearings was organized by the Texas Conservation Council, which arranged for delegations from more than sixty Texas cities to speak in favor of the proposed national seashore.

The hearings raised a number of issues crucial to later policy developments for Padre Island. Although most of the 250 people who attended the first session of the hearings favored the national seashore plan, local support was not unanimous. Many local citizens had enjoyed access to the area for years, but they did not perceive that rapid population growth would threaten their access. The political influence wielded by private interests favoring a massive tourist business was a formidable obstacle to the efforts of seashore proponents. Also, some residents of local communities wanted to retain private land holdings on the island. Some states' rights proponents strongly objected to giving the federal government control of the island by giving the NPS jurisdiction over the proposed seashore.

The size of the area to be included in the seashore was a major issue at the hearings. Congressmen Kilgore and Young had introduced House bills which specified a smaller area for the seashore than Senator Yarborough's S. 4. The National Park Service announced for the first time that its survey of May 1958 recommended an eighty-eight-mile strip for recreational and wildlife preservation. Although most Texans now seemed to favor preservation, they disagreed on how big the reserve should be. Nor was there agreement as to whether Padre Island should be given status as parkland or seashore. The less restrictive seashore status seemed necessary because of existing leases on oil mineral rights on the island.

Between December 1959 and mid-1963, when President Kennedy authorized funds for the Padre Island National Seashore, the preservationists had to overcome numerous opponents. In May 1960, it was alleged that Senator Lyndon Johnson (who denied it later) and Representative Kilgore refused to agree to the eighty-eight-mile proposal of the NPS. They argued that the state of Texas had intended to give only fifty miles to the secretary of the interior when it passed consent legislation in June 1959 in favor of a federally controlled national seashore area. This dispute held up planning at a time when both the Department of Interior and President Kennedy, who had sent a special message to Congress advocating national seashore status, were recommending to Congress that Padre Island be reserved.

In October 1960, Willacy County officials asked the state Highway Commission to have a causeway constructed from Port Mansfield to the island, because businessmen and local government were attracted by the revenue prospects of another "gold coast." A few months later, in March 1961, the Valley Chamber of Commerce, Cameron County Parks, and other groups opposed the eighty-eight-mile park proposal because of the loss of taxable property. By this time, conservationists realized that the cost estimate for land acquisition had risen from $4 million in 1958 to $8 million, and that local delays were causing federal authorities to favor Cape Cod and Point Reyes as national seashore sites. The TCC contacted 7,000 Texans, urging them to write Lyndon Johnson to ask him to support the eighty-eight-mile proposal without waiting for further consent from the Texas legislature. In April 1961, Armand Yramategui, president of the TCC, testified on behalf of conservationists in Washington, D.C., at a Senate public lands subcommittee. Yramategui accused Congressmen Young and Kilgore of Texas of being unrepresentative of the majority of the public for advocating a bill asking only sixty-five miles for a seashore site. Presenting the Senate subcommittee with petitions bearing 5,486 names, Yramategui claimed that more than 100,000 Texans and people from 454 cities in 25 states had gone on record in favor of Senate Yarborough's bill which the Department of Interior had endorsed.

Other obstacles to preservation were still being raised. Congressmen Kilgore and Young called for a road down the length of the island for the "safety" of vacationers. This was just what real estate developers at both ends of the island wanted. But Secretary of Interior Stewart Udall refused to accept the road proposal, and at about the same time, the state granted NPS permission to plan an eighty-eight-mile preserve. Both events gave conservationists valuable support at this time, and they continued to muster more support. The TCC arranged for Judge Dancy of Cameron County to speak on radio urging preservation of Padre Island, and it coordinated public addresses to garden clubs, churches, and schools. In June 1961, a delegation of congressional and of federal and state administrative officials visited Corpus Christi and Padre Island. The TCC and other conservation organizations honored the visitors with a huge public reception, fish fry, and motorcade, all of which gave a sizable boost to the fight for the Padre Island National Seashore.

During the next eighteen months, the most serious threat to Padre Island came from a group of developers who wanted a Texas-style Miami Beach on the dune barrier. The developers' position seemed to be directed by land commissioner Jerry Sadler, who argued that a seashore would discriminate against school children by depriving the state of tax revenues. Sadler opposed transferring 100,000 acres of submerged land to the federal government. Conservationists were relieved when President Kennedy signed a bill designating 80.5 miles as a national seashore in late 1962. In January 1963, the Texas Conservation Council appropriately won a national award from the American Motors Company for its positive role in the issues of open beach policy in Texas and natural area preservation on Padre Island.

With legislation behind them, and with the help of the administrative expertise of the National Park Service, the preservationists worked confidently towards management of the Padre Island National Seashore. In the next few years, however, tourism and increased traffic across the causeway to Padre Island threatened the fragile ecological balance of the dune wilderness. In 1968, 360,052 visitors saw Padre Island, in 1971 the figure was 904,365, and by 1980, the Padre Island National Seashore was expected to receive up to a million visitors annually. The plans for a new causeway and highbridge increased the further threat to the wilderness aspects of the island.

The National Park Service and conservationists recognized the need to balance demands for recreation with wilderness preservation. The

TCC set out to study the possibility of wilderness zoning on Padre Island in 1968. TCC expressed its views on wilderness zoning through slide presentations and newspaper editorials. Through its liaison with Dr. Cottam, director of the Welder Wildlife Foundation at nearby Sinton, the TCC won a battle to have herds of grazing cattle removed from Padre Island. Dr. Cottam was also largely responsible for removing a private cabin from within the boundaries of the national seashore and for removing "squatters" from the spoil islands within the seashore. Dr. Cottam and TCC also convinced state and local officials that growth in the local economy need not depend on resort development. The example they gave to substantiate these economic claims was the Cape Hatteras National Seashore.

Outcome

The Wilderness Society and conservationists from many organizations generated support for the National Parks Master Plan and for wilderness designation for a substantial part of the Padre Island National Seashore at hearings in Texas in March 1972. With the question of oil leases unresolved, the TCC, the Lone Star Chapter of the Sierra Club, other conservationists, and the Coastal Bend Regional Planning Commission generally favored a modified wilderness concept or primitive status for the island. As a result of the NPS hearings, the general agreement was to "protect" the wilderness area, but no detailed agreement was defined. Some fishermen, beach sportsmen, spoil-islands homeowners, and the major developers continued to protest a wilderness classification. In September 1972, the Department of Interior declared that the Padre Island National Seashore was unsuitable for inclusion in the National Wilderness System. The Interior Department declared that it would continue to manage one-half of the national seashore reserve as a primitive area, and it would review the entire area for possible wilderness status when oil and gas leases expired.

CASE VI   Habitat Preservation: Lower Keys, Florida

Key deer, one of the smallest species of deer in the world, are found only in the Florida Keys. Adult key deer are no larger than a large dog; they are barely thirty inches tall, forty-five inches long and seldom weigh more than eighty pounds. The range of the deer is a small island

and water habitat barely fifty-one by seventeen miles. Big Pine Key and Howe Key Islands, south of the seven-mile Overseas Bridge on U.S. Highway 1, are principal parts of the deer's range. The subtropical range of the deer includes coral reefs and sandbars, salt-water marshes, and tropical vegetation—pine, mangrove, cactus, and scrub palmetto. The key deer's habitat is also the home of the raccoon, squirrel, the great white heron, and the roseate spoonbill. Millions of migratory birds of numerous species come to the key deer range from the north in winter and from the south in spring and summer.

The existence of the key deer was first recorded in Columbus' log of his fourth voyage to the New World. Until the 1920s, the deer were little disturbed by man, although fishermen occasionally killed some of the population, estimated at about 200 to 300, for meat. But the construction of the Overseas Highway cleared some of the land, and the remoteness of habitat alone no longer protected the deer. Residential and commercial development of the Keys and extensive fires dramatically reduced the deer habitat. As a consequence of habitat destruction and poorly patrolled and enforced Florida game laws, the population fell to about twenty-five deer in 1949.

The key deer was on the verge of extinction. Conservation groups, and some perceptive officials in government wildlife agencies, began campaigns to protect the deer in 1950. In contrast to other American species of wildlife, such as the heath hen, the key deer has responded to the eleventh hour effort to preserve it as a unique natural asset. Today the herd is estimated to be about 300.

The Actors

Both the federal government and the state of Florida have jurisdiction over wildlife populations and habitats in the lower Keys. The U.S. Department of Interior's Fish and Wildlife Service has been the most influential federal policy participant. James Silver, in particular, the southeastern regional director of the Fish and Wildlife Service, represented that agency. Florida's Game and Fresh Water Fish Commission was the principal representative of state policy.

Private groups most influential in policy formation were the North American Wildlife Foundation (NAWF), the Boone and Crockett Club (BCC), the National Wildlife Federation, the Wildlife Management Institute, and the National Audubon Society. The NAWF led the campaign to preserve the deer habitat and population. A nonprofit, tax-exempt organization, NAWF has worked since 1911 for the conservation, restoration, and improved management of wildlife and natural areas. In the case of key deer, as in many other cases, the NAWF cooperated with local, state, and federal agencies and other conservation organizations to promote preservation in the public interest. The R. E. and Ellen F. Crane Foundation, Philadelphia Conservationists Inc., the Wilderness Club of Philadelphia, and the Laurel Foundation gave significant financial support to the NAWF fund drive. The Honorable Charles E. Bennett, Jay N. "Ding" Darling, and Dr. C. R. Gutermuth have also received nationwide acclaim for their active role in preserving the wildlife refuge and natural area in public ownership.

The Policy Process

The first steps toward preserving key deer were initiated by the celebrated cartoonist Jay N. Darling, a member of the Boone and Crockett Club of New York and honorary president of the National Wildlife Federation (NWF) of Washington, D.C. Darling had witnessed the slaughter of deer by Cuban fishermen using fire and dogs to drive the animals into the water where they could be killed. A widely publicized cartoon produced by Darling for the NWF in about 1949 depicted the killing but did not raise enough public interest or funds to provide the necessary deer protection. At about that time, James Silver of the U.S. Fish and Wildlife Service's southeastern regional office in Atlanta tried to arouse public interest. Silver prepared a brochure advocating a sanctuary for the deer. Interest in the project was kindled by Florida groups and some national conservation organizations, and on March 2, 1950, Congressman Charles E. Bennett of Florida introduced a bill that proposed a Key Deer National Wildlife Refuge.

Concerned conservation groups, particularly the Boone and Crockett Club, the North American Wildlife Foundation, and the National Wildlife Federation tried to halt poaching of the deer as an interim measure. The BCC donated $5,000 to hire a game warden, who began patrols in the spring of 1951. The Florida Game and Fresh Water Fish Commission deputized the warden so that he had both state and federal enforcement authority. The National Wildlife Federation financed a similar protection program from June 1952 to June 1953. These early actions by conservationists helped the deer recover, although they were still far from protected and had no habitat or refuge area. Congressman Bennett's refuge bill, Senator Claude Pepper's companion refuge bill of 1952, and another bill proposed by Congressman William C. Lantoff in 1953 did not succeed.

A new step in policy took place in August 1953 when President Eisenhower signed the U.S. Department of Interior Appropriation Bill for 1954. This authorization provided for the leasing of 915 acres of privately owned land for key deer habitat land. Lessees could cancel the lease with ninety days' notice. The key deer had limited security. Although this effort to provide a safe range for the deer was a necessary supplement to the warden's protection service until mid-1953, the preservation of key deer still was uncertain.

In March 1954, the North American Wildlife Foundation authorized a definite action that would encourage public interest in the problem and cause the federal government to become active. The NAWF appropriated $10,000 to purchase the nucleus of a key deer refuge. Dr. C. R. Gutermuth, secretary of the NAWF, went to Florida and located a 17¼-acre water front lot on Big Pine Key which was suitable for a refuge headquarters for the U.S Fish and Wildlife Service. Gutermuth, the only active officer of the NAWF, contacted the owners of the site. The Crane Foundation, owners of significant tracts of land in the Lower Keys, donated the site to the NAWF, which subsequently transferred it to the government in 1955.

National interest in the program increased, and a new bill presented by Congressman Bennett was enacted in August 1957. The bill authorized acquisition of up to 1,000 acres of land by purchase, donation, or exchange by the Department of Interior for a key deer refuge. Up to $35,000 was authorized, but no funds were appropriated. The NAWF now realized that if the key deer were to be saved, the wildlife refuge would have to be financed privately.

Gutermuth, in behalf of the NAWF, began to intensify the program to raise private funds and secure land through donation. The Crane Foundation contributed $120,000 to the NAWF to purchase 500 of the 727 acres on Howe Key and 35 acres on Big Pine Key, provided the remainder of Howe Key could be purchased by the NAWF with funds from other sources. Additional funds were obtained from the Wilderness Club of Philadelphia, Philadelphia Conservationists Inc., the Laurel Foundation, and NAWF itself. In May 1961, the entire island was deeded to the federal government.

Outcome

In November 1963, Secretary of the Interior Stewart L. Udall dedicated the Key Deer National Wildlife Refuge. Donations of cash and land valued at $185,000 boosted the 6,200 acres of leased land to more than 7,000 acres within the refuge. Subsequently the Endangered Species Preservation Act of 1966 authorized the secretary of the interior to expand the refuge, and funds were appropriated in 1968 for this purpose. Recent ecological evidence recommended that a larger range was required for the deer habitat. The U.S. Fish and Wildlife Service has acquired almost 3,000 additional acres on Big Pine Key, Big Torch Key, and numerous surrounding outer keys. The federal government is also planning to build a visitor and interpretive center on Big Pine Key. The NAWF and other groups have continued to donate funds to the refuge by helping to support a series of key deer studies being carried out by scientists from Southern Illinois University.

Conclusion

The preceding cases reveal that the conception of what constitutes a natural area or species deserving protection often differs widely. There is, moreover, great diversity in the actual circumstances giving rise to natural area protection issues. These cases also demonstrate a positive correlation between the market system, economy, and the threatened status of many of the nation's public goods such as wildlife and natural areas (see Chapter 7, The Economy and Growth). The market mechanism does not allocate these public goods efficiently. In addition, the ethic of economic and industrial growth and the related increase in both the numbers and the mobility of the population have had serious implications for wildlife and natural areas. For instance, highways designed to connect areas of urban concentration threaten to bring permanent changes to the landscape. The escalating expansion of industrial processes and agricultural industries has placed unrelenting stress on the nation's lands, forests, drainage systems, and surrounding oceans. Scientists have warned of the irreversible impact that the accumulation of chemical pollutants may have on inland wildlife and ocean life.

The threat of economic development to the natural environment has been especially acute with respect to the nation's remaining free-flowing rivers. The aesthetic and scientific values of river systems, and of their wildlife, are difficult to quantify, and they have consequently received minimal attention in government policies. The Obed River case illustrates a turning point in the public's view of the values of river systems as wildlife habitats, as outdoor recreation areas, and as natural areas of scientific value. The Wild and Scenic Rivers Act of 1968 was intended to preserve some rivers of the United States in their natural, free-flowing condition and balance the policies of dam building with preservation. Although protecting wildlife and natural areas was considered in the course of policy formation, they were viewed as secondary benefits. The citizens' groups advocating protection of the Obed sought to preserve the natural and wilderness features of the rivers, but they also stressed wildlife and scenic values, and opposed excessive recreational use of the river area by visitors.

The Obed River case illustrates the problem that occurs when mission-oriented government agencies are out of touch with the changing needs of an ecologically conscious public. The Tennessee Valley Authority (TVA) (see Chapter 10, Institutional Behavior) frustrated the plans of citizen conservationists even after federal law placed the river in a special study classification for eventual preservation. The TVA also significantly influenced the outcome of a final federal task force report on the Obed. It appears that the U.S. Bureau of Outdoor Recreation (BOR) bowed to pressure from TVA and gave it jurisdiction over the future management of the Obed preservation area. Conservationists had fought hard to avoid this, and the BOR had assured the citizens' groups that their vigorous appeal would be respected in final decision.

The case of the New Jersey Great Swamp also shows some of the basic differences in protection afforded through different policies. The National Wildlife Refuge System which provided protection for the Great Swamp was designed to protect and perpetuate migratory birds and native and endangered wildlife. It also allows for recreation facilities if they do not conflict with wildlife objectives. Some forms of wildlife and certain ecological systems, however, can survive only in completely natural conditions, undisturbed by man. Therefore, in 1966, the eastern three-fifths of the refuge was designated as the Great Swamp National Refuge Wilderness Area. The Department of Interior and Congress, under the Wilderness Act of 1964, reviewed this roadless area within the refuge and gave it wilderness status, which assured that part of Great Swamp would always be preserved in a pristine state.

The key deer case in Florida showed that the creation of a wildlife refuge is not achieved simply by legislative action. Although citizens and conservation groups mobilized public opinion and finally got a number of legislators to propose protective legislation, the security of the refuge still was not assured. Legislation is not always adequate, or it is enacted too slowly, or it is not funded. Here again, as in the case of the Great Swamp, the North American Wildlife Foundation (NAWF) was forced to raise funds to acquire the necessary land. Because the game laws of Florida and the federal government were not being enforced, the Boone and Crockett Club and the NAWF took the initiative of funding a warden's position.

The case of the proposed jetport in the Everglades reveals the traditional neglect of ecological considerations in development projects. The adverse consequences for wildlife and wilderness were passed off as the price of progress. The Everglades case also illustrates the uncoordinated and conflicting nature of many government policies. Millions of dollars had been invested in establishing Everglades National Park. But at the same time, the U.S. Army Corps of Engineers' water management projects threatened the park's existence. The U.S. Department of Transportation and the Dade County Port Authority proposed a jetport that would adversely affect the entire ecological system of the Everglades, yet the National Park Service, at the same time, had responsibility to protect Everglades National Park, one of the key components of the Everglades ecosystem. The initial failure in this case was not the lack of government; it was a failure of government to coordinate policies and to clarify public objectives in relation to irreplaceable natural assets.

The Monterey, Massachusetts, highway project was an example of development and rural residential expansion that threatened to disfigure the landscape and natural areas of the region. Wildlife was also threatened because habitats were being destroyed. In this case, a regional citizens' body, the Berkshire Natural Resources Council, assisted a local group to protect its natural and historic environment. The BNRC realized that local and state governments had neither the finances nor the essential expertise to handle natural area preservation. The costs of land acquisition were beyond the scope of existing institutions, and the political power of organized development interests was too strong. Consequently, the BNRC set out to assist local government to enforce existing environmental statutes, and to advocate and draft new protective legislation. The council established a workable technique for public acquisition of natural areas and open space; it arranged state and federal funding for local government, hired engineers and consultants as advisers for local institutions, and helped prepare funding applications. The BNRC's trust fund activities added flexibility to cumbersome and inadequate local and state government operations.

The fight to preserve Padre Island, first as a national seashore and then as a wilderness area, revealed many of the issues that are common in confrontations over policy for natural areas and wildlife. First, local and state authorities wished to retain traditional tax revenue bases. Their hope for tax revenues from the growth of the tourist business led them to oppose preservation of Padre Island as a natural area with restrictive uses. Second, the conservationists, who were at first only a minority, tried to protect a public good in an economy based on private ownership of land. They argued that the wilderness and wildlife resources not only belonged to every Texan, they were the common property of all Americans. Third, the immediate costs of land acquisition were beyond local and state budgets; only federal budgets could meet these costs. But the defenders of local and states' rights objected strongly to federal control of the resources of Padre Island. Finally the development-oriented philosophy of many Texans was counter-ecological.

Citizen action in each of the cases treated in this chapter have revealed many innovative and carefully planned strategies. Many of the approaches and tactics used in the cases should be emphasized because they have significantly influenced policy formation. Realizing that scenic beauty, natural areas, and the value of wildlife cannot be precisely measured, citizens' groups have used experts to support their views. The Monterey citizens' group in the Berkshires prepared an environmental impact statement based on legal, scientific, and economic data. The river preservationists in Tennessee compiled detailed river survey reports to justify their arguments.

Citizens' groups have often employed unusual methods for achieving their goals. The Berkshire land trust plan and consultative support for government agencies proved to be successful arrangements for assisting public land acquisition. The private purchase and deeding tactics of the Great Swamp and key deer protectors were also innovative and successful. As an indirect outcome of the work of conservationists striving to protect the Everglades, the Everglades Jetport Pact was established, and this pact is a model arrangement for bringing together major parties with differing authority or interests. Through this mechanism, coordination and planning were centralized and given public visibility.

These cases of citizen involvement in policy making for natural areas and wildlife, and other cases like them, demonstrate that there is no general law or policy, either state or federal, that can be relied upon to protect the aesthetic quality of the environment. The value in natural areas is largely aesthetic, but a large number of Americans still give wildlife and natural areas a low priority in social goals. In recent years, however, an increasing amount of public participation and political response has developed. An increasing number of communities and citizen groups are striving to protect small pockets of wilderness and wildlife habitats.

Conflict over cases such as the Everglades, Padre Island, and Great Swamp attracted national attention. In each case, local citizen groups aroused public concern over impending environmental degradation, but the response of the nation in favor of preservation was a crucial factor in the final decision making. These cases illustrate that concern for the nonrenewable and rapidly dwindling remnants of wild and natural areas and wildlife extends beyond the confines of any single interest or region. Whether a case received limited recognition, such as the Berkshire Hills, or nationwide publicity, as did the Everglades, the contribution of citizen groups to policies for preservation of wildlife and natural areas is indispensable.

Readings

Brower, David Ross, ed. *Wildlands in Our Civilization.* San Francisco: Sierra Club, 1964.

Eveleth, P. "New Techniques to Preserve Areas of Scenic Attraction in Established Rural-Residential Communities: The Lake George Approach." *Syracuse Law Review* 18 (1966), p. 37.

Fawcett, Charles W. "Vanishing Wildlife and Federal Protective Efforts." *Ecology Law Quarterly,* 1 (Summer 1971), 520–560.

Gale, Joseph. "How The 'Great Swamp' of New Jersey Was Saved." *National Parks Magazine,* 191 (August 1963), 11–14.

Laird, John Edwin. *The Politics of Arrogance: A Case Study of the Controversy Over the Proposed Everglades Jetport, 1967–1970.* Miami: University of Florida Press, 1972.

Lucas, Robert C. "Wilderness Perception and Use: The Example of the Boundary Waters Canoe Area." *Natural Resources Journal,* 3 (January 1964), 394–411.

McCloskey, Michael. "The Wilderness Act of 1964: Its Background and Meaning." *Oregon Law Review,* 45 (1966), 288–321.

Mazzucco, Ronald J. "Federal and State Protection Against Commercial Exploitation of Endangered Wildlife." *Catholic Law,* 17 (Summer 1971), p. 241.

"Mineral King Valley: Who Shall Watch the Watchman?" *Rutgers Law Review,* 25 (Fall 1970), p. 102.

Nash, Roderick. *Wilderness and the American Mind.* New Haven: Yale University Press, 1967.

II

CRITICAL ASPECTS
OF MAN-ENVIRONMENT
RELATIONSHIPS

The chapters and cases in Part II are concerned with problems that arise in connection with the impact of certain critical aspects of human society upon its environment. Five aspects are considered: energy, economics, health, the quality of urban life, and the final chapter deals with institutional aspects of environmental policy and management. Emphasis in these chapters is less upon the actual environmental impact of human activities and more upon reciprocal or interactive relationships, because it is in the interactions between environmental and other values that choices must be made and that political conflicts frequently occur.

The probability of conflict is increased by the paradoxical circumstance that environmental relationships, fully comprehended, are necessarily holistic—they are never less than the aggregate of their complex parameters—whereas the means available for coping with their problematic aspects are almost always atomistic. For example, energy uses in human society interrelate with a very broad range of human affairs—environmental, economic, technological, physiological and demographic. But public policies in relation to energy sources, uses, and effects have failed historically to recognize or to take account of these interactive factors.

The several aspects of man-environment relationships included in this section are critical because the fulfillment of the essential human needs (to which these aspects relate) threatens environmental conditions upon which the continuing fulfillment of all human needs ultimately depends. Conflicts in the fulfillment of needs arise primarily because the method of meeting those needs, and the magnitude of their demands on the environment, are inconsistent with the carrying capacity or renewability of the environment. There are a limited number of ways in which such conflicts can be met. In brief, they are:

(1) To sacrifice one need for another;

(2) To compromise or accommodate conflicting needs; and

(3) To redefine needs to obtain a synthesis of values.

Many of the cases described in this volume arose because environmental values were being sacrificed, usually unnecessarily, to economic considerations. Conflicts ostensibly over energy, land use, recreation, or civil rights were often discovered to be basically economic in character. Nevertheless, the economic issues themselves are complicated and the critical questions are often:

(1) Whose economic interests are affected; and

(2) How do the economic interests concerned correspond to a public interest?

For example, the economic interests of homeowners may differ sharply from the economic interests of public utility corporations in siting power plants. Public interests are involved on both sides.

A major aspect of economic policy affecting environmental quality relates to the concept and implementation of policies for economic growth. The expectation of economic growth, and a belief in its necessity or inevitability, are implicit in a large number of legislative acts and administrative policies affecting the environment. The missions of the United States federal agencies with greatest impact upon the environment (for example, the Army Corps of Engineers, the Bureau of Reclamation, the Bureau of Land Management, the Forest Service, and the Tennessee Valley Authority, among others) have been strongly biased toward the promotion of economic objectives. Environmental considerations have only lately been introduced, largely through requirements in the National Environmental Policy Act. But the implicit assumptions of public officials regarding priorities among values and the reasonableness of public protest appear to have been rooted in a tradition that long antedates NEPA. The traditional assumption has been that the highest and best uses of the environment—with certain special exceptions—are those that maximize economic growth.

Our case studies, however, suggest that a more sophisticated understanding of economic values is spreading among the American people. Citizens have learned to dissect agency cost-benefit analyses, and have increasingly shown an informed skepticism regarding the claims of government-sponsored development and public works schemes. There has been a growth of demand for consideration of alternative means to the economic objectives of government and industry. Legitimate ends no longer seem to justify an indiscriminate choice of means.

The unnecessary sacrifice of ecological, aesthetic, or hygienic values to bureaucratic convenience or special-interest advantage at least is being challenged as never before in recent American history. Although it cannot be confidently stated that certain fundamental and relatively permanent changes are being introduced into the structure and practice of public planning and decision making, this clearly appears to be the present trend. Organized citizen action in public planning and decision making may create a fourth branch of government that, at least in the policy areas in which it proves practicable, will make self-government a functional reality rather than merely a symbolic representation.

6

Energy

Introduction

Environmental implications of the nation's rapidly escalating energy consumption are numerous. Stripmining for coal, oil shales, and tar sands could devastate millions of acres of landscape by the year 2000. The impact of strip mines, processing plants, and industrial wastes on surface and subterranean hydrological systems would be enormous. Weather could be influenced by massive heat dissipation due to energy production. The combustion of fossil fuels generates by-products such as carbon dioxide and water vapor, and adding substantial quantities of these elements to the atmosphere could lead to climatological changes. Enormous quantities of mercury and other chemical and solid wastes such as slag and ash are emitted each year from coal-fired plants. These emissions and wastes have widespread environmental repercussions. Oil spills from wells and tankers, or from leaking gas and oil

190

pipelines, are a risk incurred in transporting fuel. Moreover, enormous tonnages of air pollutants, thermal pollution of waterways and shorelines, and hundreds of millions of gallons of radioactive wastes have already been produced by energy extraction, processing, transportation, and usage.

In the next quarter century, given current growth projections, these problems and others related to them will multiply. The land alone required for electric power plant sites in 1990, assuming current 8 percent annual increases in electricity demand were to continue, would be roughly 6 percent of the land and water area of the United States. Human settlements, industries, highways, and railways occupy barely 4 percent of the area of the United States today. By 1990, estimates suggest that 500,000 miles of transmission lines may lace the nation, occupying roughly 10 million acres. Power plants also could require 30 percent of the nation's fresh water runoff for cooling purposes by the turn of the century if present energy demand projections are accurate.

Before examining the formation of energy policy, it is instructive to investigate the causes of the nation's thirst for energy. Energy is one of the fundamental factors of production in the economy. But the rate of increase in energy demand has far exceeded the growth in the gross national product (GNP). The nation's population growth is exceeded fivefold by the increase in electric energy consumption. Since World War II, America has continually substituted high-power consumptive products for lower-power consumptive goods: aluminum requires far more energy to process than steel, artificial fibers more than cotton. The throwaway economy (see Chapter 7, The Economy and Growth) has also meant substantial increases in energy consumption. Disposable bottles, cans, and paper containers require much more energy than returnable or reusable containers.

The shift in demand from fossil fuels to electric power, largely because of cleanliness and convenience, has stimulated the production of electricity. Moreover, the price of electric energy has been falling for decades, due to economies of scale as large utilities with huge markets have become more common. Decreasing block-rate pricing structures have been used by the utilities to encourage large industrial consumers. Under this arrangement, the price of power decreases as usage increases. Numerous government policies, illustrated by the Rural Electrification Act and the Tennessee Valley Authority, also encouraged the use of electric power. Demand for electricity has also been significantly stimulated by promotional advertising, as well as by the pricing activities of the utilities. In recent years, an estimated $300 million a year has been spent on advertising by the electric utility industry alone to encourage greater power consumption.

There is as yet no comprehensive national policy for energy in the United States. During the years 1973 and 1974, the Congress and the president grappled ineffectively with the basic energy issue. Major attention was focused on the immediate and short-term fuel shortages associated with the 1973 war in the Middle East and subsequent increases in the cost of crude oil obtained from the nations forming the Organization of Petroleum Exporting Countries (OPEC). But the 93d Congress passed two important laws that could assist in the formulation of a national policy and improve the effectiveness of comprehensive planning for the nation's uses of energy. They were the Federal Energy Administration Act of 1974 (PL 93–275) and the Energy Reorganization Act of 1974 (PL 93–438). The first bill gave statutory status to the principal executive agency for the administration of current policies for the conservation and allocation of energy supplies. Of possibly longer-range significance, the second act established the Energy Research and Development Administration (ERDA) to plan for the enlarged availability and efficient use of all forms of energy. This act abolished the Atomic Energy Commission (AEC), transferring its licensing and regulatory powers to a Nuclear Regulatory Commission and its research and development functions to ERDA. To help guide policy development, an Energy Resources Council was authorized and was established by executive order on October 16, 1974.

The Energy Reorganization Act contains the following general statement of policy which ties together energy and environmental quality needs:

> The Congress hereby declares that the general welfare and the common defense and security require effective action to develop and increase the efficiency and reliability of use of all energy sources to meet the needs of present and future generations, to increase the productivity of the national economy and strengthen its position in regard to international trade, to make the Nation self-sufficient in energy, to advance the goals of restoring, protecting and enhancing environmental quality, and to assure public health and safety.[1]

[1] Par. 10, p. 723 § 2 (a).

The Department of Interior and the Nuclear Regulatory Commission have the statutory power and duty to shape certain aspects of energy policy, but the Federal Power Commission (FPC) has been the principal energy regulatory agency. Established in 1920, the FPC has authority to issue permits and licenses for non-federal hydroelectric projects, to regulate rates in interstate transactions of electric power and natural gas, and to issue permits for operation and construction of interstate pipeline facilities. Broadly, the FPC was given planning authority to assure an abundant supply of electrical energy for the nation. The FPC was also vested with the responsibility for ongoing power planning. But in its power planning surveys, the FPC has merely endorsed energy industry task force reports. There is no evidence that the FPC has studied the effect of rate structures on energy use patterns. The FPC has played a passive role in licensing procedures and has objected to public input in decision making, attacking "environmentalist" objections to expansion of energy production and consumption. Utility company and state regulatory commission "benevolence" have customarily been accepted by the FPC as satisfactory regulation. The FPC has no control over most steam-generating plants and transmission lines, nor do many of the states. Consequently, private utilities often select plant sites and transmission line routes with relative freedom. State regulation of powerful interstate energy conglomerates is generally so weak that the best hope of policy reform on behalf of environmental quality may be to reorganize and reorient the FPC.

The energy crisis of 1973 ultimately drew attention to a long-term problem: the need for renewable and environmentally tolerable forms of energy—properties not characteristic of any major form of energy now in common use. The economic hardship and personal inconvenience brought on by the fuel shortages helped to sharpen the nation's perception of many of the energy-related issues overdue for consideration. But for a few months in 1973–1974, the daily activity of Americans was measured in terms of energy consumption. Energy consumption became the common denominator for measuring traditional economic, social, and ecological values. The nation faced a choice: either the supply of energy had to be increased or demand had to be decreased not only for the present, but for the future.

Increasing the supply of energy required serious consideration of the environmental impact of increased extraction, processing, use, and waste disposal problems. New technologies were years short of effective operation, and it seemed possible that traditional fuels could be exhausted before new technologies would be operating. Refinery and transportation capacities for oil were not adequate in the short-run, and might not be in the long-run, for coping with escalating demands. Foreign oil imports were subject to foreign policy changes, trade agreements, and national security agreements that were not secure, as the Middle East cut-off of oil in 1973 demonstrated. Consideration of the increased energy supply argument showed that fuel sources were finite, that anticipated demands appeared to be infinite, and that both short- and long-term planning was needed.

The decreased demand alternative posed critical questions of policy and value. Population stabilization seemed necessary if any approximation of present per capita energy consumption were to be maintained. Proponents of the concept of a steady-state economy received increased, although minority, credibility in economic circles. Planning for the manufacture of less energy-consumptive products would be a step toward waste reduction. The enormity of energy waste throughout the country was shocking to previously unaware citizens. Barely 42 percent of the nation's energy supply was used after losses through the processing, distribution, and utilization stages in the economy. Electric power plants convert only 40 percent of the heat they use, automobiles convert only 25 percent of the heat they use, and better building designs could save 25 percent of the fuel currently used for heating. Only 30 percent of the oil was being extracted from the ground in the United States before fields were abandoned. Research showed that enormous energy savings could be made through: (1) establishing mass transit systems and reducing the dependence on heavy, energy inefficient private automobiles (almost 30 percent of the energy consumed goes to transportation, especially automobile use); (2) improving architecture to eliminate energy wasted for heating, excessive lighting, and air conditioning; (3) freighting by train rather than road; (4) creating innovative community plans that would increase land-use efficiency; and (5) increasing reliance on communications technology to reduce travel.

Although many people appear either to be unaware of the implications of the long-term problem or to assume that the government will plan in the public interest, there have been American communities in which energy, its extraction, transmission, and generation were issues antedating concern over shortages. The effect of energy technologies on the quality of the human environment was arousing public concern long before shortages had become a cause for concern. Numerous communities throughout the nation since the early 1960s have faced the tradeoffs required by choosing between energy availability or quality of life. By the early 1970s, citizen groups nationwide were challenging existing energy policies, watchdogging and suing government agencies, and building up public awareness of the issues. Conservation of energy can lessen the impact of existing energy technologies upon the environment. But in an advanced industrial society there are limits beyond which the uses of energy cannot be reduced. Improved technologies for extraction, transmission, and uses of energy may offer the best hope of reducing the harmful impact of the energy system on the environment.

CASE I   Power Plant Siting: Bodega Head, California

Sonoma County's coastline was one of the last natural stretches of scenic seashore in California in the late 1950s. Bodega Harbor was one of the safest harbors on the 300 miles of black rock coast between San Francisco and Coos Bay, Oregon. Sonoma Coast State Park and the area around Bodega Bay provide sweeping vistas of sand beaches, cliffs, caves, and sea caverns. In the spring, wildflowers such as blue lupine, yellow lupine, and the California poppy bring color to the rugged coastline. Bounding Bodega Bay on the north is a magnificent granite promontory known as Bodega Head, a remnant of a former archipelago. The San Andreas (geological) Fault, which was the source of the famous 1906 San Francisco earthquake, cuts off Bodega Head from the mainland and passes through Bodega Bay east of Bodega Head.

The little fishing port of Bodega Harbor is forty miles north of San Francisco's Golden Gate Bridge. Commercial fishing had earned the coastal community roughly $1.5 million annually. As the coastal center of California's crab, salmon, and shrimp fleet, Bodega Harbor produced more than the San Francisco fishing fleet. Bodega Bay also lay within the heart of northern California's milk-producing region. The coastal area of Sonoma County remained a scenic treasure because it had escaped the commercialization and industrialization that had overtaken much of California.

Because of the geographic, engineering, and economic advantages of Bodega Bay, one of the nation's largest investor-owned power monopolies, the Pacific Gas and Electric Company (PGE) announced in 1958 that it planned to build a $63 million boiling-water nuclear reactor on Bodega Head. The facility would supply the additional electric power supposedly needed in the San Francisco Bay region. The world's largest reactor was planned for Bodega Head; with a 350,000 kilowatt capacity, the generator would supply two-thirds of San Francisco's daily power by 1965 if PGE's plan ran smoothly. Bodega Bay was an ideal site, according to economic and engineering calculations, because it provided access to large quantities of water for cooling condensers. Cold water from the bay could be pumped through the reactor (250,000 gallons a minute) and the warm water discharged into the ocean on the other side of the promontory.

The proposal to build a nuclear reactor on Bodega Head sparked one of the nation's earliest controversies over nuclear power plant siting. At first, a few local landowners and fishermen protested some of the incidental consequences such as transmission line rights-of-way and damage to fishing-fleet moorings. But within a short time, citizens formed effective groups to protest the use of Bodega Head for a nuclear reactor. The local, state, and federal government became enmeshed in the conflict. Due to the relentless pressure of citizens' groups, the PGE eventually withdrew its plan for the reactor at the site.

The Actors

At the federal level, the U.S. Army Corps of Engineers was a minor participant in the policy process. Because it had jurisdiction over navigable waterways, the Corps of Engineers held hearings at Bodega Bay prior to issuing a permit for a tidelands roadway. The National Park Service (NPS) lent some credibility to conservationists' claims that Bodega Bay and Hilton Head merited environmental protection. The NPS had reported on the scenic values of the open coastlands during a survey of potential national seashore preserves. The Department of Interior's role in offering the services of the U.S. Geological Survey (USGS) for geological consulting on the San Andreas Fault was crucial in the final policy outcome. The USGS subsequently warned against using Bodega Head as a nuclear site. The Atomic Energy Commission's (AEC) regulatory staff supported the USGS finding. The AEC report, it appears, finally persuaded PGE to abandon the site.

California's legislature, with its decision to hold public hearings, Governor Edmund G. Brown, and numerous state agencies all played

significant roles in decision making. The California Public Utilities
Commission (CPUC) was one of the principal administrative bodies in
the conflict. The CPUC decided that the evidence presented by PGE was
superior to that of the opponents. While the conservationists requested
reconvening the hearings, the CPUC was under continued appeal from
PGE not to do so. The state Division of Mines and Geology report on the
geological formations around Bodega Bay gave credibility to the conservationists at a point when most of the administrative reviews open
to the public had been exhausted. The state Division of Beaches and
Parks avoided its responsibility by acquiescing to the wishes of PGE.
After including Bodega Head in a master plan for park extensions, the
Division of Beaches and Parks played no role in opposing PGE throughout the conflict. Conservationists also accused the University of California of acquiescing to PGE since the reactor proposal preempted the
university's marine laboratory plans in Bodega Bay. To some critics of
the university, it appeared that millions of dollars of AEC nuclear research funding were more important than the public interest or the
university's commitment to an independent policy for scientific research generally.

The Sonoma County Board of Supervisors favored PGE; it blocked
all means of citizen involvement in decision making at the county
level. The Sonoma County Planning Commission was also development-oriented and ignored the public environmental interest. The
Santa Rosa Press-Democrat staunchly supported the developers and
PGE-oriented county agencies. A group of businessmen in the county
formed the Sonoma Committee to Develop Bodega Bay, but it seemed
to confine its work to lobbying efforts of minor significance.

PGE was by far the largest electric utility in California. PGE's generating capacity of over 6 million kilowatts included hydroelectric
plants, steam turbines, and geothermal and nuclear plants. The economic and political power of the PGE had been recognized in California
for decades. The power of eminent domain almost assured the success
of PGE's land acquisition and power plant extension proposals.

The Northern California Association to Preserve Bodega Bay and
Harbor (NCAPBH), the Sierra Club, and the Committee to Preserve
Bodega Head (CPBH) spearheaded the conservationists. The Santa Rosa
Philomath Club, Parents and Others for Pure Milk, the New America
Democrat Club, and the California Democrat Council were other cit-
izens' groups that supported the main conservation organizations at

points in the policy conflict. The *Cloverdale Reveille* and *Sebastapol Times* editorially supported the conservationists. These newspapers broadcast the arguments of the citizens' groups and continually called on county government to open up the decision-making process so that the issues could be debated democratically.

The Policy Process

The process of decision making in the Bodega Head case gradually showed the citizens/interveners that local and state government agencies were continually serving the interests of PGE. Avenues for citizen participation in decision making were blocked at the county level by a development-oriented Sonoma County administration. Through the years of conflict, citizens realized the necessity of sound organization, the advice of experts, the necessity of continual publicity to stir public awareness, and the need for litigation to render government agencies more accountable to the public.

Sonoma Coast State Park was to be extended in 1955 to include Bodega Bay. The state master plan of the Division of Beaches and Parks had appropriated $350,000 to purchase 947 acres of the area, including Bodega Head. The U.S. National Park Service had recommended that the area be preserved for its scenic and recreational values during the mid-1950s. The University of California had chosen a 320-acre Bodega Bay site for a marine research station in 1958. Due to delays in acquisition on the part of the Division of Beaches and Parks, Bodega Head was still mostly in private hands in 1958. During that year, PGE approached the Sonoma County Superior Court through eminent domain proceedings and asked the court to condemn 408 acres of Mrs. Rose Gaffney's ranch. Mrs. Gaffney objected to the PGE takeover and became one of the citizen leaders who fought PGE. At this stage in the policy conflict, public opinion in Sonoma County appeared to favor the PGE plan. Tax revenue increases for the county treasury and a stimulant to the local economy were generally welcomed.

But the local community was not in favor of towers and transmission lines from Bodega Head through the Bodega Bay area. PGE required a seventeen-mile, twin-circuit, 220-kilovolt transmission line crossing the Valley of the Moon and Sonoma Highway. The unfavorable visual impact on the bay was not welcomed by most local citizens, but the Sonoma County Planning Commission had already granted

PGE a permit for construction of the line. A group of landowners and ranchers filed suit in the Sonoma County Superior Court requesting a writ to cancel the permit, alleging that the planning commission had exceeded its jurisdiction and had not posted an announcement of required hearings in the affected territory. Superior Court Judge R. J. Sherwin overruled the plaintiffs and supported the planning commission in February 1959.

Among local residents, perceptions of the issues were clearly divided by late 1959 and early 1960. The county administration, in particular the Sonoma County Board of Supervisors, supported the proposed nuclear development. The board of supervisors felt the conservation-oriented public was protesting because it did not understand the situation. One of the supervisors, who believed that a tax revenue boost was the ultimate in progress for the community, commented, "A million dollars ought to affect anybody's thinking." The state Division of Beaches and Parks suddenly lost interest in Bodega Head at this time, and did not oppose PGE. Throughout the 1959–60 period, the board of supervisors received a great deal of mail protesting the choice of Bodega Head for a reactor site or for any development, including transmission lines. A small group of local citizens formed the Committee to Preserve Bodega Head (CPBH), and with the Santa Rosa Philomath Club announced opposition to the PGE generator project. Late in 1960, the Sierra Club wrote to California Governor Edmund G. Brown, to State Senator J. A. Rattigan, and to the chairman of the board of supervisors protesting PGE's method of dealing with the public. The Sierra Club protested the PGE occupancy of Bodega Head without offering the people of the state any alternatives, and PGE's partnership with the board of supervisors in bypassing public debate.

The willingness of Sonoma County officials to accommodate PGE was demonstrated again in February 1962. PGE wanted to build a 2.7-mile, 35-foot-wide road in Bodega Bay to provide access to the nuclear generating plant. The county and PGE wanted the road built in the tidelands, because purchasing the rights-of-way on the built-up shoreline would be far more expensive for PGE and would take much longer. The county was to receive the road in return for granting the right-of-way to PGE. Because the Army Corps of Engineers has control over navigable waterways, the county applied to the corps for permission for the tidelands route. Local fishermen were alarmed; they objected to the road because the land fills would destroy 25 of the best

700 acres of boat-mooring space. More than fifty local citizens attended the hearings conducted by the corps at Bodega Bay, and most of them protested the county administration's effort to expedite the permit.

Discordant in their pleas and ineffectively organized, citizens and conservationists were more frustrated than successful up to mid-1962. In that year, PGE had to submit an application to the California Public Utilities Commission (CPUC) to seek approval for its electric generating plant at Bodega Head. In March 1962, CPUC held three days of public hearings to discuss the application. The hearings were poorly attended, and leaders of the conservation movement realized the urgent need for an adequate organization to promote opposition to PGE. Consequently, David Pesonen, a scientist, Karl Kortum of the San Francisco Maritime Museum, and Joel Hedgepeth, director of the University of the Pacific's Dillon Beach Marine Laboratory (close to Bodega Bay), activated citizens' forces and established the Northern California Association to Preserve Bodega Head and Harbor (NCAPBH). Within weeks of the first CPUC hearings, NCAPBH and others had elicited almost 200 written protests to the CPUC calling for a reopening of hearings. The majority of the letters opposed PGE's plan.

The citizens were successful in convincing the CPUC to reconvene public hearings in May 1962. At the new hearings, the conservationists charged the PGE and University of California with collusion because the university had quietly agreed to PGE's plan and would not oppose the utility. But PGE received considerable support from the Sonoma County Board of Supervisors, labor groups, the state Chamber of Commerce, and the California Farm Bureau Federation. PGE was granted a provisional permit by the CPUC in early November 1962. About this time, it was estimated that 80 percent of Sonoma County opposed the nuclear plant proposal and the planned tidelands road to Bodega Head. The Sonoma Chapter of the NCAPBH circulated a petition of registered voters to force a recall election on one of the county supervisors who strongly favored PGE.

Evidence of the increased organizational effectiveness of the citizens' groups was provided by the November 10, 1962, Santa Rosa public meeting that brought many of the basic issues to the forefront. More than 300 attendants heard speakers—nuclear physicists, a gastroenterologist, Bodega Bay residents, fishermen, Joel Hedgepeth of the Dillon laboratory, and conservationists—raise these crucial issues: the effect of the reactor's cooling water on marine life; the danger of iodine 131 entering the food chain and milk supply; the difficulty of disposing of plutonium; the threat of nuclear explosion (the proposed plant was an experimental prototype 1,600 times larger than the ARCO plant in Idaho that had closed due to near-explosive malfunctions); the pollution threat to San Francisco, which was downwind of the reactor emissions plume; the hazards of a site less than one-half mile from the San Andreas Fault; and the persistent refusal of the Sonoma County government to hear pleas for public discussion of the issues.

The conditional permit granted to PGE by the CPUC was challenged in January 1963 by the 500-member NCAPBH. This citizens' group filed a petition with CPUC accusing PGE of violating the November 1962 permit. PGE had begun construction, and the petitioners alleged that approval by the Atomic Energy Commission (AEC) was required to validate the permit. At the local level, the NCAPBH and the CPBH continually tried to influence the board of supervisors to hold public hearings by stirring public awareness of the issues. Local media documented evidence of a spill of radioactive material at PGE's Vallecitos Laboratory in March 1960, where forty-eight people had been irradiated. Citizens were warned again that the Bodega Head plant would be experimental and could also be the site of future radiation spills. In March 1963, four property owners and the citizens' groups filed suit in the superior court in Santa Rosa challenging the legality of a use permit granted PGE by the board of supervisors in 1960. Public hearings had not been held, and the plaintiffs alleged the board of supervisors had violated its mandate. But in May 1963, Superior Court Judge Gibson struck down the appeal with a ruling that hearings would be inappropriate after three years had elapsed and $1.5 million had been spent by PGE.

Aware that the majority of Sonoma County did not want Bodega Head as the site for a nuclear reactor, citizens' groups tried persistently to force the board of supervisors to reconvene public hearings. Twelve county women presented the board of supervisors a petition bearing 1,637 names of people demanding hearings. Newspaper editorials in the *Sebastapol Times* and others criticized the secrecy of the PGE and the board of supervisors. Governor Edmund G. Brown received an appeal from the citizens' groups but declared the controversy was a county issue. To counteract publicity given to its opponents, PGE distributed pronuclear materials and spoke to groups such as the Sebastapol Lions Club and Sebastapol Rotary Club. The board of supervisors rezoned Bodega Bay in order to avoid further court action and to avoid convening hearings. From an unclassified status, Bodega Bay was rezoned "agricultural," a zone in which a public utility was permitted without having a use permit and without holding public hearings.

In the search for administrative remedies, the citizens' groups were forced to direct their appeal to state and federal agencies and officials because the county administration had continually ignored requests for public input in decision making. Due to a citizens' group request and national publicity about the San Andreas Fault, Secretary of Interior Stewart L. Udall had expressed grave concern and offered the services of the U.S. Geological Survey to consult on the geological conditions at Bodega Head. The NCAPBH circulated a petition and forwarded it to President John F. Kennedy, who was asked to encourage the AEC to accept Secretary Udall's offer to assist in appraising the hazards of the PGE plant. At the same time, the 70,000 member California Democratic Council urged the president to intervene in the dispute and terminate the PGE proposal. The NCAPBH filed a sixty-five-page memorandum of action with the CPUC, charging PGE with false testimony on at least three counts in the second CPUC hearings. Research by the citizens' group had shown that PGE's reactor would be closer to the San Andreas Fault than allowed by law. PGE had claimed the foundation of the reactor would be rock, but geologists had informed the conservationists that the base was a clay-like quartz-diorite. Finally, citizens alleged that PGE had failed to give the AEC the final reports of earthquake consultants, warning of serious hazards. The CPUC was asked to reconvene hearings and reconsider PGE's conditional permit.

From May 1963 onward, the publicity campaign of the conservationists established credibility and drew substantial political support. The *San Francisco Chronicle* expressed grave concern over the hazards to public health and safety of siting a reactor on the San Andreas Fault. In June 1963, a large public meeting and publicity campaign were organized on Doran Spit in Bodega Bay by PGE opponents. They released 1,500 helium-filled balloons tagged, "This balloon could represent a radioactive molecule of Strontium 90 or Iodine 131," to demonstrate that air currents flowed from Bodega Bay toward San Francisco. The California assembly declared it would hold public hearings before an interim committee to investigate the PGE plan. The 22,000-member Sierra Club intensified its participation in the conflict, especially by calling on the CPUC to reconvene hearings. But on July 10, 1963, CPUC an-

nounced its refusal to reconsider the PGE permit and told the citizens
to take future complaints to the AEC.

After mid-1963, the tide of political and administrative opinion began to turn in favor of the conservationists. William Bennett, the president of CPUC, dissented from the July 10 CPUC ruling on PGE's permit,
and became a staunch supporter of the conservationists. U.S. Senator
Clair Engle of California called on the AEC to hold public hearings
promptly. In August, Acting Governor Glenn M. Anderson called on
the AEC to veto PGE's applications, and for PGE to seek a more suitable
site. James B. Koenig, staff geologist in the state Division of Mines and
Geology, issued a report in August 1963 on the geological formations
at Bodega Head. This report included scientific evidence that suggested the San Andreas Fault was not a suitable site for a nuclear
generator. Soon after, the Democratic party made the Bodega Head
site a political campaign issue in California. By late 1963, a seismologist,
who consulted both for NCAPBH and the U.S. Geological Survey reported that Bodega Head was an unsafe site for PGE's proposed plant.

Outcome

With the announcement of two conflicting AEC reports on October
27, 1964, the conservationists were victorious. The AEC's Advisory
Committee on Reactor Safeguards, composed of thirteen atomic experts
who advise on safety with regard to reactor construction and operation, reported that PGE could build on Bodega Head "without undue
hazard to the health and safety of the public." In contrast, the AEC's
own regulatory staff declared that the site "is not suitable . . . at the
present state of knowledge." Early in November 1964, PGE withdrew its
application for a permit from the AEC. Only four days after the PGE
withdrawal, the Sonoma electorate voted in a new board of supervisors who were opposed to the PGE nuclear plan and Bodega Head
as the site. PGE left behind a $4 million hole, seventy feet deep on Bodega
Head. In 1970, the utility offered to sell its tract on the promontory to
Sonoma County for recreational purposes, but the county chose to
lease the land. In 1973, the California Parks and Recreation Department proposed to purchase Bodega Head in its park expansion program.

Subsequent to the Bodega Head dispute, and doubtlessly influenced
by its outcome, PGE withdrew all of its plans to site generating plants

along the Pacific coastline. The Bodega case was also a catalyst of public concern for maintaining and protecting public access to the ocean interface. Although the California referendum of November 7, 1972, on protection of the coastal zone was primarily a land-use proposition, influenced by considerations over and beyond energy policy, the threat to public access to the sea revealed in the Bodega incident may well have been a significant factor in obtaining the popular votes needed to adopt the referendum.

CASE II   Economics of Nuclear Energy: Eugene, Oregon

By the late 1960s, the Bonneville Power Administration (BPA) had prepared an ingenious plan to involve major Pacific Northwest electric utilities in a cooperative scheme to meet their long-range power needs. The best hydroelectric sites in the region had already been utilized. Plans for the further development and industrialization of the Northwest indicated the need to turn to nuclear energy to ensure future supplies of cheap power. Declaring publicly that it could not keep abreast of the projected growth in demand for energy, the BPA proposed a cooperative scheme—a hydrothermal program in which individual public and private utilities would participate. One of the public utilities willing to join the program was the Eugene Water and Electric Board (EWEB).

The EWEB is a municipal utility. In November 1968, 79 percent of the registered voters of the city of Eugene approved a bond authorization of $225 million allowing the EWEB to construct a nuclear reactor in the area. None of the other utilities in the Northwest were municipal entities like the EWEB and, in this sense, it is unique. No other community, either in the Northwest or in the nation, had the opportunity to vote on the decision to construct a nuclear reactor in its vicinity.

Soon after the November 1968 approval of the bond issue to build the reactor, orchard farmers and others who had direct financial interests in the proposed reactor site sought more information about the impact of the plant upon their livelihood. The EWEB was asked to conduct a public hearing to discuss the implications of the plan, but they refused. The city council of Eugene was then approached with a request for a hearing. The council offered to cosponsor a public meeting with the EWEB, but again the utility refused. Widespread interest in the nuclear plant proposal had been generated by early 1969. A group of local citizens established the Eugene Future Power Committee (EFPC) in an effort to organize orderly inquiry into the implications of the hydrothermal plan for the region and particularly for Eugene. By mid-1969, the citizens' group was convinced that Eugene did not need the proposed multimillion-dollar reactor. Very serious risks would have to be taken if the plant were constructed. The EFPC set out to educate the public on the issues, convinced that the utility-industry-AEC litany of power needs doubling every ten (or eight, or six) years should be challenged at every opportunity. In little more than a year, the EFPC convinced the city of Eugene to reverse the 1968 ballot vote of approval, and the reactor program was postponed four years.

The Actors

The policy dispute over Eugene's nuclear reactor was contained within the state and largely within neighboring counties. The governor, legislative task forces, and several Oregon State University scholars had some indirect influence over the decison making. The Eugene press was particularly influential.

The Bonneville Power Administration and pronuclear energy industries substantially supported the EWEB. Chambers of commerce, a labor council, and a businessmen's group called Citizens for the Orderly Development of Electricity, supported the EWEB electrification plans. National figures, such as AEC officials and Congressman Craig Hosmer of the Joint Committee on Atomic Energy, urged support of the plant on their visits to Oregon. The combined efforts of these people and groups were only narrowly defeated in the city of Eugene ballot initiative.

The Eugene Future Power Committee lead opposition to the reactor. Moral support was rendered by the Central Lane County League of Women Voters, which helped pass out petitions and get the delay amendment on the city ballot. The Oregon Environmental Council, the Pacific Northwest Chapter of the Sierra Club, the National Sierra Club, and the Democratic party of Lane County endorsed the EFPC postponement plan.

The Policy Process

By mid-1969, the people of Eugene were embroiled in debate over the advantages and disadvantages of the nuclear reactor proposal. The

EFPC and local newspapers, in particular the *Eugene Register-Guard*, were stimulating considerable argument about the issue. The EFPC had investigated scientific literature on nuclear energy and had examined the experiences of other communities nationwide who had faced similar decisions about future energy availability. Issues of radiation, safety hazards, air and water pollution, the suitability of the Willamette Valley as a site, and the land-use problems in a prime agricultural area were debated by the community. The particular objection of the EFPC was that there was no evidence to indicate that nuclear power was needed in the Northwest for another twenty years.

Although the EWEB had at first refused requests for public meetings to discuss the nuclear issue, it later conducted two. At public hearings on July 24 and 25, 1969, in the city council chambers, the principal advocates for a Eugene nuclear plant expressed their views to the public. Written statements from many of the 200 participants at the hearings were presented to the EWEB for consideration and reply. In the council chambers on September 9, 1969, a panel was convened to answer questions raised in the July hearings.

The panel tried to convince the public that what Eugene needed was a nuclear power plant, and that the need was urgent. The BPA representatives reported that they could not continue to supply power to electroprocessing industries such as aluminum, chemical, and pulp-paper in the Northwest with existing power technology and sources. The BPA defended its faith in atomic power and reemphasized its intention to go ahead with the hydrothermal plan that included twenty nuclear power plants in the Northwest at a cost of $10 billion. Dr. Morton Goldman of Nuclear Utilities Services (NUS), a consulting firm, said no proof existed of radiation damage to humans from the generation of atomic energy. Goldman asserted that the Atomic Energy Commission (AEC) and the nuclear industry had established sufficient inspection safeguards for public protection. Agricultural scientists from Oregon State University spoke enthusiastically of the benefits of warm water from nuclear plant cooling operations for irrigation. The participants in the meeting were told by the pronuclear panel that only by using nuclear technology could power supplies match the escalating demands by color television, air conditioning, and household appliances.

The EFPC and its supporters were concerned that the panel had not attempted to break down consumption to indicate the separate power needs of residential consumers, light industry, commerce, and heavy industry. After a thorough investigation of the BTA's Ten-Year Hydro-Thermal Program, the EFPC concluded that the BPA was trying to attract and hold heavy industrial consumers in the Northwest. Only by shifting some of the power-production load to smaller utilities such as the EWEB could the BPA maintain its development-stimulating objectives. The EFPC realized the nuclear industry was barely a decade old, and Eugene's plant was to be the largest anywhere in the world at that time. Because dealing with unknowns in nuclear technology was a considerable risk, the citizens' group stepped up its publicity program to draw attention to the issues. In particular, the EFPC called for more environmental considerations in policies for industrial promotion in the Northwest and for regional planning and regulations for power development.

As early as late 1968, the original activist citizens, who later formed the EFPC, considered a petition drive to organize opposition to the bond authorization for $225 million given to the EWEB. But most of 1969 was spent attending EWEB meetings and doing publicity work. The National Committee to Stop Environmental Pollution (NCSEP) in Washington, D.C., had been contacted by the EFPC for advice and information. The NCSEP was trying to initiate a limitation on the powers of the AEC, and in order to effect a national moratorium on nuclear power development, it was acting as a clearing house for opposition to nuclear plant construction throughout the United States. The NCSEP's weekly news bulletin, *Watch on the AEC,* was used by the EFPC for data and advice.

During 1969, the EFPC discovered valuable information about the Eugene community which helped to achieve their public education objectives. The main promotional effort for the nuclear plant was directed toward the supposed economic benefits of plant construction. The EFPC convincingly countered this argument with research reports from the Anthropology Department and Water Resources Research Institute of Oregon State University which concluded that nuclear plant construction activities generally resulted only in an economic boom-and-bust pattern. But in door-to-door petition campaigning, the EFPC discovered that the average citizen in the community was reluctant to give up the notion of nuclear plants as safe, clean, dependable, desirable, and necessary without some assurance that alternatives to nuclear energy were available and better. This psychological insight motivated the EFPC to stress continually that alternatives were available. Gradually, EFPC persuaded the community that nuclear power could present serious problems.

The EFPC diversified its approach to community education, and its program for stimulating public awareness of the implications of the EWEB plans proved effective. Flyers were distributed at public meetings, supermarkets, and by door-to-door campaigners. Special bulletins were drafted on coastal impacts of the planned Florence reactor (proposed for a site west of Eugene, on the coast), on the economic impacts of the Eugene plant, and on radioactive wastes. Three public panels were sponsored by the Oregon Educational Foundation, and TV spots, commercials, and press coverage were scheduled. The Central Lane County League of Women Voters endorsed the goals and strategies of the EFPC and encouraged it to adopt a nuclear postponement plan. This plan proposed a postponement of Eugene's nuclear plant until January 1, 1974, so that detailed evaluations of the costs and benefits of the plant could be undertaken. A petition form was drafted by the EFPC that called for Ballot Measure 52 to be voted on at the 1970 primary elections.

The EWEB continued with plans for Eugene's reactor in the face of controversy. Site studies had commenced, and the EWEB had called for quotations from contractors on the $225 million project. Endorsing the utility's plan were the Springfield Area Chamber of Commerce, the Lane County Labor Council, the Malheur County Court, the Oakridge Chamber of Commerce, the Siuslaw Port Commission, the Florence City Council, and the group of Eugene businessmen organized as the Citizens for the Orderly Development of Electricity (CODE). Opponents of the utility's plan received some support early in 1970 when the state Sanitary Authority, the Oregon House of Representatives' Task Force on Pollution, and the governor's nuclear coordinator recommended against placing nuclear plants in the Willamette Valley. Two plants proposed by the EWEB, one at Noti and another at Oakridge, would lie within the valley.

As the citizens' groups pressed on vigorously for the petition drive to accompany Ballot Measure 52, pronuclear forces threatened brownouts, loss of tax payments to the county, loss of a construction payroll, and loss of seventy jobs to operate Eugene's plant. In a precise and informative brochure circulated throughout the community, *Yes 52 X We Can Wait—We Should Wait*, the EFPC stressed many fundamental issues: insufficient environmental data on thermal and radioactive pollution; insufficient evidence to support the EWEB's claim of an urgently required mammoth power boost; and insufficient evidence to ensure nuclear reactors would be reliable and safe. The EFPC also claimed that the 1968 city vote to authorize the bond issue was made without sufficient data being presented to the public; that for the first ten years of its thirty-year existence, the Eugene plant would sell power only to other areas of the Northwest; that little research had been done to support the claim that nuclear power was more economical than fossil fuel power; that EWEB and BPA were promoting electricity to stimulate economic growth; and that while the utilities and industry viewed economic growth as a savior for mankind, most of the community believed that growth destroyed the quality of their lives. But in March 1970, in spite of the environmentalists' progress, resolution of the conflict seemed as remote as ever.

In the first months of 1970, the EFPC made the public fully aware of the EWEB plan that would be sanctioned if voters affirmed the bond authorization on May 26. The EWEB would be investing $69 million for a 30 percent share in the Portland General Electric's Trojan plant to be built on the Columbia River near Rainier. Besides this, the EWEB would be permitted to go ahead on the $225 million Eugene reactor. The EWEB had plans to sell a major part of the Trojan output, to which Eugene was entitled, and also to sell a major part of Eugene's power for ten years beyond completion of the reactor. The EFPC clearly demonstrated that the EWEB would receive enough power for Eugene until 1981 from the utility's 30 percent share of the Trojan plant. Pronuclear forces had spent $40,000 in lobbying and the conservationists $4,000 by about March 1970, but by that time the EFPC had gained 4,528 signatures of registered voters of Eugene. Through Oregon's initiative petition procedure, this assured that voters would be given an opportunity to vote again on a city charter amendment, Ballot Measure 52, on May 26, 1970.

In what may have been a last minute effort to distract the Eugene voters, pronuclear forces drew the attention of the public to the coastal reactor siting controversy in Florence. At a meeting of local interests in Florence, called by Mayor Stuart Johnson and the Siuslaw Port Commission, there was a general feeling in favor of the coastal site. Pronuclear forces hoped the favorable attitude in Florence would cause the Eugene voters to abandon the fears conservationists had stirred. But during April, the Eugene citizens' group received support from other quarters. The *Eugene Register-Guard* published an editorial endorsement of Ballot Measure 52, and University of Oregon scientists called for the postponement about this time. A fourteen-part series entitled "The Nuclear Dilemma," written by Gene Bryerton, was sponsored and printed (10,000 copies) by the *Eugene Register-Guard*. This was a sound, scientific study of the full implications of the nuclear energy proposals for the region. Late in April, at a board meeting of the EWEB, citizens made it very clear that the state had no nuclear laws or any laws to enforce regulations with regard to a nuclear energy program.

By a narrow margin, the environmentalists won the May 26 vote on Ballot Measure 52. The Eugene reactor program was lawfully postponed pending further research until January 1, 1974. Pronuclear forces promptly resorted to litigation in an effort to invalidate the May 26 initiative. On August 4, 1970, nuclear proponents filed a complaint in court to overturn the initiative, they repeated the process until the fifth attempt was dismissed by the court in September 1972.

The Oregon legislature established the Nuclear and Thermal Energy Council in 1971. This council was vested with responsibility to establish criteria for siting nuclear plants and for approving sites. The EFPC methodically "watchdogged" the formation of the council and the activities of the EWEB during the year. Both at EWEB meetings and in the local press, the citizens' group called for more environmental concern in EWEB policies and for the abolition of decreasing, block-rate pricing structures for electricity.

Outcome

In November 1972, citizen group activists were gratified to receive a court decision requiring the EWEB to reimburse funds used in campaigning for votes during the 1968 and 1970 initiatives. The court declared that the EWEB had published only pronuclear evidence and had not presented a balanced argument. The EFPC had expressed this same opinion publicly for many months. In cooperation with the League of Women Voters, a symposium for public awareness was conducted in January 1973. This same year, an EFPC member was elected by a narrow vote to the board of directors of the EWEB over an incumbent businessman commissioner. Later this same year, the member was chosen by Governor McCall as the only public member of the new Energy Study Committee established by the legislature.

CASE III   Offshore Energy Development: Penobscot Bay, Maine

The Penobscot Bay in Maine and its periphery make up a magnificent maritime natural area: a largely unspoiled land of wooded hills, granite shores, and an island-studded coastal sea. Summer homes dot resort islands such as Isleboro, North Haven, and Vinalhaven. A stronghold of individualistic Yankee farmers, lobster fishermen, and some resort owners, the Penobscot Bay area has distinctive historic and scenic value. An estimated 1,300 fishermen earn their livelihood from the beautiful bay. As the megalopolises of the northeastern United States rapidly spread, this natural area of the Maine coast becomes increasingly valuable.

Penobscot Bay has potential as a deep-water port, particularly off Sears Island, but the surrounding seas are made treacherous by protruding rocks and ledges, swift currents, strong winds, and, often, heavy fog. Extreme caution is required in navigation. Even so, the water off Sears Island would permit supertanker docking within hundreds of yards of the shoreline; supertankers and large container freighters cannot get within ten miles of the shores of New Jersey and Delaware where oil refineries have been established. The escalating demand for petroleum products on the east coast of the United States, and the demand for deep-water handling facilities and refineries for low-sulphur Middle East oil, have made Sears Island and other potential deep-water ports in Maine attractive plant sites for oil companies.

In the first week of January 1971, Maine Clean Fuels (MCF), a subsidiary of Fuel Desulphurization of New York, announced plans to construct a $150 million oil-desulphurization refinery and deep-water terminal on Sears Island at the head of Penobscot Bay. The refinery was to produce 200,000 barrels a day and occupy eighty acres of Sears Island. An offshore docking terminal, designed to receive oil-carrying supertankers drawing seventy feet of water, required a 4,800-foot pier and channel dredging for 6,000 feet, a little over a mile. Crude oil was to be piped from the receiving terminal to the refinery, where it would be converted into petroleum products. The petroleum products were to be shipped to various Atlantic coast ports in 90,000-barrel barges. An estimated 1,500 barge trips each year would pass through Penobscot Bay channels.

For many years Maine's economy had lagged behind the national growth average. In the opinion of some of Maine's business and civic leaders, who felt the fisherman-farmer economy of the coast needed a stimulant or supplement, the Sears Island refinery and terminal project was attractive because it offered 300–500 permanent new jobs and local tax benefits. A majority of the 1,800 residents of nearby Searsport welcomed the project. The state Department of Economic Development also welcomed the proposed project and spoke of plans to use the refinery and deep-water port as the base for a huge marine industrial complex.

The MCF refinery proposal was presented, however, at a time of great change in environmental policy in Maine. A phenomenal land-development boom in the state had aroused public awareness of the need for environmental planning. The coastal zone had become the focus of a great deal of legislative reform in Maine and in neighboring coastal states. The citizens of Tiverton in Rhode Island, Riverhead on Long Island, and South Portland in Maine were three of at least six coastal communities that had recently opposed refineries and super-tanker terminals. Conservationists, public officials, and politicians throughout Maine were fast becoming active in environmental management reforms in the late 1960s. The Sears Island refinery proposal was blocked by extremely effective citizens' groups in order to protect the environment and natural beauty of Maine.

The Actors

In favor of the oil refinery proposal, besides its promoter MCF, were a number of the nation's major oil companies and members of the energy industry. The Sears Island proposal was a test case of Maine's Site Location Law of 1970. If MCF could overwhelm the new law and the infant regulatory agency, the Maine Environmenal Improvement Commission (EIC), the oil conglomerates would improve their chances of being permitted to build ports at other coastal sites such as Eastport, close to the Canadian border.

The commissioner for the Maine Department of Economic Development (DED) had hopes of building other concerns onto the Sears refinery installation—manufacturing plants, dry-cargo terminals, container docking facilities, and a major shipyard. The commissioner declared that Sears Island would be developed regardless of what environmentalists thought and regardless of what the general public wished. Searsport selectmen were in favor of the refinery proposal, "if it didn't affect the environment." The owner of 1,000 acres on Sears Island, Bangor and Aroostock Railroad, welcomed a stimulant to its sagging freight business.

Maine's Governor Kenneth Curtis was open-minded on the issue, because he wished to abide by the decision of the EIC. But he had previously opposed a similar refinery proposal at South Portland. The news media had a significant impact on policy as the majority of the regional newspapers gave editorial opposition to the refinery project. The *Republican Journal* of Belfast, the *Bucksport Free Press,* the *Island Advantages* of Stonington, the *Ellsworth American,* and the *Maine Times* all strongly opposed the MCF plan.

The spearhead of public opposition to MCF's refinery proposal was the Coastal Resources Action Committee (CRAC). Formed in December 1968, the CRAC group hired a professional lobbyist to represent conservation interests in the state. The group drafted, amended, and supported legislation advantageous to Maine's environment. Within two years of CRAC's formation, the state legislature had passed twelve major pieces of environmental legislation, including the 1970 Site Location Law, for which CRAC was credited as being the author and major contributor. Without the Site Location Law and CRAC's competent organization of expert witnesses for the March 1971 public hearings on the MCF application, the Sears Island refinery would have become a reality. The Maine Natural Resources Council, the state Audubon Society, the Maine Biologists' Association, the Sierra Club, a group known as Pollutorsport, the Conservation Law Foundation, and other conservation groups supported CRAC.

The Policy Process

The citizens' groups, town planning boards, and environmentalists of Maine's coast were not opposed in principle to economic development in the state. The consensus of the government, the members of the legislature, and the public was that Maine needed a broadening of its economic base. For generations, towns and cities had been controlled by individual local governments, each seeking to maximize its tax base and caring minimally for social and environmental problems. An estimated 85 percent of Maine's towns and cities had refused by the mid-1960s to enact even minimal zoning laws to control land-use development. But the phenomenal land boom and the aggressive drive of the oil industry to obtain coastal refinery sites during the early 1970s alarmed many people. Shoreline zoning and oil conveyance laws, land-use regulation laws, and the Site Location Law of 1970 were quickly enacted at the state level, because in the vast wildlands of the state there were few local governments, and elsewhere many organized communities were unable to deal effectively with the issue.

The opponents of oil terminals and refineries on Maine's coast had very little time to react and few avenues of approach to use in their efforts to block the oil industry's proposals. To stop the MCF proposal for Sears Island, citizens' groups considered either attempting to force the oil company to fully comply with some aspects of the state zoning and land-use laws or resorting to litigation. Since MCF would have to seek the approval of the U.S. Army Corps of Engineers for pier construction and channelization, citizens' groups also considered using the corps' involvement as grounds for insisting on compliance with the National Environmental Policy Act of 1969. They chose, however, to rely on the Site Location Law of 1970 and to give the new law its first test.

The Site Location Law focuses on major industrial projects. Commercial, residential, and industrial developments involving more than twenty acres are required to obtain permits from the EIC. The law empowers the EIC to place conditions upon the use of sites by developers to ensure the environment is protected. The EIC is also empowered by the law to deny sites if the effect on the environment is seriously damaging. The EIC is an independent commission whose ten members represent various interests: manufacturers, conservationists, municipal officials, air pollution experts, and the public. The law declares that EIC decisions are to be based on four criteria: financial capacity, including the ability to meet state air and water pollution standards; traffic movement; no adverse effect on the natural environment; and soil conditions.

Barely seven months elapsed between MCF's announcement of the refinery proposal in January 1971 and the EIC decision to deny the application for a permit. But the policy process was marked by conflict and an amazing amount of activity from all interest groups. On January 26, 1971, the Stonington-Deer Isle planning boards and selectmen sponsored a Penobscot Bay communities' public meeting entitled "Why Oil?" Of the 250 people who attended, only one, Commissioner Keefe of the DED, voted in favor of the oil refinery. Public sentiment about the issue began to arise beyond Penobscot Bay, and in response to this public concern, State Senator J. Sewall proposed a resolution in the legislature calling for all state agencies to cease activities that would result in the expansion of oil industry developments on the coast of Maine.

Senator Sewall called for the cessation of activities until the court's decision on a suit filed by ten oil firms that challenged Maine's Oil Conveyance Law of 1970. The Oil Conveyance Law had established new standards for oil conveyance and imposed a levy on barrels of oil landed in Maine. Revenues from the levy would be placed in a liability fund for the expense of oil spill emergencies.

The Sewall resolution was overwhelmingly approved in the state legislature by a vote of 28–1 in the senate and 116–27 in the house. While not legally binding, the resolution was an indicator of legislative feeling in February 1971. Conservationists hoped that this legislative action would curtail the attitude favoring industrial development expressed by Commissioner Keefe of the DED. But Keefe commented publicly that he would ignore the legislature resolution and the environmentalists as well, declaring he was bound by state statute to encourage industrial development. A *Maine Times* editorial called for the state legislature to refuse to appropriate Keefe's salary. In mid-February, Maine Community Betterment and the Rockport-Lincolnville-Camden Chamber of Commerce sponsored a public meeting in the Camden Opera House to discuss the oil refinery proposal. The coastal residents who attended voted against oil development in Penobscot Bay.

Substantial opposition was building up against the MCF proposal even before the firm's application for a permit was submitted to the EIC. The Maine Natural Resources Council announced its opposition to the expansion of petroleum complexes anywhere in Maine. Senator Edmund S. Muskie, U.S. Senator from Maine, voiced his disapproval of the oil refinery proposal. The Sierra Club joined the oil refinery opponents by mid-February. The state legislature became active again with the introduction of Senator Richard N. Berry's bill that would impose a moratorium on all coastal oil developments until the Oil Conveyance Law suit had been decided. Despite this evidence of mounting opposition and the fact that EIC was inexperienced, understaffed, and underfunded, the commission had to remain the citizens' main line of defense for Maine's environment after MCF had submitted its application to the EIC.

By late February 1971, CRAC had made significant organizational moves to coordinate the environmental forces. In particular CRAC hoped to influence the passage of Senator Berry's moratorium bill before the March 23 hearings in Searsport to be sponsored by the EIC. No hearings would be needed if the moratorium was enacted. CRAC coordinated the activities of a number of citizens' groups. Funding assistance for CRAC came from the Conservation Law Foundation (in New York), which was acting as a conduit for tax deductible contributions. A steering committee was established by CRAC to collect factual evidence to present as testimony at the Searsport hearings. It located expert witnesses in geology, marine biology, land valuation, navigation, oil handling, refinery operation, and, of course, competent attorneys. The CRAC strategy was to prepare the evidence which would have to be presented in order for the EIC, under the Site Location Law, to have a sound basis for rejecting the Sears Island proposal. Expert witnesses were recruited from Massachusetts, New York, and Rhode Island, and arrangements were made for their travel to Searsport.

The Bangor and Aroostock Railroad urged its employees to press politicians to favor the oil refinery proposal. From the data expressed in MCF's application to the EIC, it seemed clear that the railway company could earn from $4 to $6 million annual revenue in freight business. A group of coastal businessmen called Full Use of Our Environment was formed to lobby in favor of the oil refinery. But barely a week before the EIC hearings, there was more evidence of mounting public opposition. A citizens' group, known as Pollutorsport, had collected more than 10,000 signatures on a petition against the Sears Island refinery. Fifteen coastal communities had passed town meeting resolutions opposing the refinery, as had the Hancock County Planning Commission (by a vote of sixteen to one) against oil developments in Searsport. The EIC had received more than 1,000 letters of protest. CRAC and the local press publicized the statement of a former Camden marine pilot that there was no acceptable deep-water approach to Sears Island east or west of Penobscot Bay for 200,000-gallon super-tankers. The marine pilot predicted that MCF would actually be creating four times the amount of traffic predicted for the tankers, because the channels could accommodate tankers no larger than 50,000 gallons. This traffic, and that of the barges, would sweep lobster pots away from their beds.

The first days of EIC hearings in Searsport were allotted to MCF and refinery supporters. MCF argued that the refinery would help meet the rapidly rising demand for energy in Maine and New England. The refinery fuel would be low in sulphur and enable Maine to better combat air pollution. The promoters stressed the value of the economic stimulus to the region and the 500 jobs the development would create. But CRAC

and the news media publicized crucial factual omissions at the conclusion of the first two days of hearings. MCF had been unable to produce facts for almost every major aspect of their proposal: there were
no conclusive financial details; no facts on dredging; no evidence of soil
tests on Sears Island; no tests of Penobscot Bay's current flow; no plans
for landscaping the refinery; and no evidence of consultation with the
U.S. Army Corps of Engineers regarding piers and dredging channels.
Conservationists were surprised MCF had prepared so inefficiently for
its application.

The answer probably lies in the applicant's confidence that the
infant commission would approve the project. But evidence also suggests that MCF was not an established oil company, in the sense of the
domestic firms of Texas and the nation's western oil conglomerates.
As an oil promoter, MCF was actually hoping to bind together the
strengths of some. of the nation's established oil firms to make the
refinery a reality. Former Secretary of the Interior Stewart L. Udall had
given MCF an oil import allocation in January 1969, in hopes that low-
sulphur oil from the Middle East would ease the nation's air pollution
crisis. It seems, too, that Udall wished to break the oil-import wall
that President Johnson had helped maintain to favor Texas and domestic oil firms.

When the CRAC lead witnesses presented their arguments in the
latter days of the EIC hearings in Searsport, they were well prepared.
The environmentalists clearly demonstrated a number of inconsis-
tencies, evasions, and inaccuracies in MCF's application report. The
opponents to the project argued that MCF's plans for containing oil spills
would often fail. The firm's statements about fresh water needs for
the refinery were contradictory. Inaccuracies in statements about
settling lagoons for the treatment of polluted water were pointed out by
CRAC witnesses. MCF's claim that the Sears Island refinery would be odor-
less were rebutted. An oil spill on March 16, 1971, at the U.S. Air Force
tank-farm at Searsport was claimed by a marine scientist to have ruined
up to $1.3 million in clams. Scientists testifying for CRAC argued that the
impacts of oil pollution, dredging, and barge traffic would soon destroy
the lobster industry in Penobscot Bay. While awaiting the EIC decision,
CRAC submitted to the EIC a 23,315-signature petition protesting the
refinery proposal.

The EIC denied MCF's permit application on July 21, 1971. In EIC's
view, the developers had failed to demonstrate the technical capacity

to handle a major oil spill. Furthermore, the cost estimates varied unreasonably between $5 million and $30 million for the project; and MCF had no estimate of the turning-circle channels required by the tankers. It appeared also that MCF's sole asset was an import quota permit of 100,000 barrels per day. Oil companies anxious to establish facilities on the northeast coast would have had to build the refinery, and it seemed that MCF was not capable of doing so itself.

Outcome

Although the request was denied due to the combined efforts of citizens' groups, the pressure for development of Maine's coast by the energy industry continues to test the state's coastal protection legislation and the strength of environmental activists. In August 1971, MCF filed a notice of appeal against the EIC decision with the Maine Supreme Court. At about the same time, the Pittston Company had released a proposal for a $350 million refinery further north of Eastport. The natural advantages of the Maine coast for deep-water ports are so appealing to the oil industry that land-use conflicts seem certain to recur.

CASE IV Priorities for the Scenic Hudson: The Storm King Mountain Project

The most intense concentration of people and urban areas in the United States is in the New York-New Jersey megalopolis. With a population density of more than 800 people per square mile, New Jersey has twice the population density of India. In the quarter century beyond 1960, the New York metropolitan area is expected to envelop as much undeveloped land as it has so far occupied since the purchase of Manhattan from the Indians almost 350 years ago. This concentration of people, industries, transportation, and communications systems requires an enormous supply of energy. Electrical energy demands alone exceed the national increase of 8 percent per annum. The energy industry, particularly electric utilities, have barely been able to keep abreast of demand, and when they occasionally failed to supply the full demand in peak summer periods in recent years, power brownouts have followed.

One of the nation's biggest electric and gas utilities, Consolidated Edison Company of New York City (Con Ed), serves the densely populated areas of New York City's five boroughs and a part of Westchester County. Con Ed operates a system of a dozen or more generating plants, a number of which are fossil fueled. These generating facilities have been found to contribute almost 40 percent of the total emissions of nitrogen oxides in New York City. Nitrogen oxides, a component of smog, are injurious to the respiratory system. At Indian Point near the Hudson River, Con Ed has a complex of nuclear electric generating plants that have been the focus of increasing protest and public scrutiny in recent years.

In 1960, Con Ed began to plan for the construction of a hydro-electric generating plant forty miles up the Hudson River from New York City. The site for the hydroelectric project was a magnificent gorge that had been described as comparable to parts of the Rhine in Germany. Striking in scenic grandeur and rich in pioneering history, the Hudson River Gorge is relatively narrow and flanked on both sides at the proposed plant site by 1,000-foot granite cliffs. Storm King Mountain occupies the west bank, Breakneck Ridge the east. This stretch of the Hudson is largely unspoiled and one of the few remaining natural waterways in the northeastern states.

Con Ed's project was to incorporate newly designed reversible-turbine technology. Storm King was proposed as the site for a hydro-electric pumped-storage facility—a device for pumping water which would then be energized by the return flow of the water, once motors were reversed. A storage reservoir was proposed that would, in effect, hold liquid energy. When peak power supplies were needed, the reservoir-storage release would assist. During off hours, the turbines would pump water from the Hudson up into the reservoir in readiness for emergencies.

The Storm King project, to cost $150 million, would generate 2 billion kilowatts of electricity with a possible capacity of 3 billion kilowatts. Eight reversible turbines at the base of Storm King would pump water through a tunnel forty feet in diameter for two miles through the mountain, elevating the Hudson River water 1,100 feet to a mountain valley reservoir. The valley was primarily within the domain of the village of Cornwall, and was partly owned by Harvard University through its interests in Black Rock Forest. Five dams and dikes would create a basin of 12 billion gallons with a water-surface area of 240 acres. The powerhouse would be roughly 80 percent submerged in the mountainside, and the first 1.6 miles of transmission lines would be submerged under the river. Upon resurfacing, transmission lines would traverse 9.2 miles of Putnam County, across the Appalachian Trail, and stretch a total of 45 miles to New York City. The lines would occupy a 250-foot right-of-way on towers 125 feet high. Rockblasts from the foot of Storm King Mountain were to be used to create a 57-acre waterfront park for Cornwall.

The Federal Power Commission (FPC) was expected to issue the required license for the project, and Con Ed hoped to have the turbines in operation in 1968. The FPC granted Con Ed the license in March 1965, and soon after, another utility, the Central Hudson Gas and Electric Corporation, announced plans to build a similar plant on the west bank of the Hudson Gorge at Breakneck Ridge. But as early as 1963, more than thirty national, state, and local conservation groups, landowners from Putnam and Westchester counties, historians, fishermen, and sportsmen joined in support of the newly formed Scenic Hudson Preservation Conference to oppose the Storm King project. The ensuing conflict, with Con Ed and the FPC as protagonists against the conservationists, has lasted more than a decade and a half without final resolution. Storm King has drawn national attention, involved federal, state, and local governments, the courts, industry, and public interveners. It has become one of the nation's most famous cases of conflict over conservation policies, illustrating the problems of institutional accountability and of coherence in the nation's policies for energy and the environment.

The Actors

The Federal Power Commission is the agency with both the power and the responsibility to resolve many of the environmental problems associated with electric power. The responsibilities and authority of the FPC relating to electric energy derive principally from the Federal Power Act of 1920 and the Flood Control Act of 1938. But during the half century the commission has been operating, the FPC's planning and licensing procedures have come to protect the practices the commission should regulate. (See Chapter 10, Institutional Behavior.) The Storm King case reveals the power and the duty the FPC has to shape electrical energy policy. The case also illustrates how difficult it is for public interveners to participate in or modify policy dominated by the FPC. The commission adopted a passive role in the reconciliation of competing policy options, but it was clearly more accommodating to the utility than to conservationists.

The Environmental Protection Agency (EPA), the U.S. Army Corps of Engineers, and the U.S. Department of Interior's Fish and Wildlife Service were other federal agencies that became involved in policy making for Storm King. As the result of a suit filed by conservationists late in 1973, Con Ed was instructed by the court not to begin riverfront construction until the utility obtained a permit from the Army Corps of Engineers. The court affirmed that a permit would be needed under the Federal Water Pollution Control Act. Under Section 404 of this act, power to grant or reject a permit rests with the administrator of the EPA as well. The U.S. Department of Interior, through the Fish and Wildlife Coordination Act, recommended stipulations in its report to the FPC. Three ichthyologists from the Department of Interior refuted Con Ed's ichthyological consultant during FPC hearings. The FPC, in most cases, incorporates the department's recommendations in licenses for power projects.

At the state level there were a number of participants in policy formation. In general, the state of New York was business-oriented and welcomed the possibility of new power-utilizing industries that could be attracted to the state. The tax revenues generated by Storm King were eagerly anticipated by the state government; and early in the 1960s, Governor Rockefeller publicly announced his support. Late in 1968, however, the city of New York intervened in the proceedings, claiming Con Ed's newly modified plant design was a threat to the tunnel that carried the city's water supply, and opposed the project. Subsequently, the commissioner of the New York State Department of Environmental Conservation declared that the tunnel would not affect the city's water supply. State Senator R. Watson Pomeroy set up hearings in November 1964, to further discuss the project that had become a political issue by this time. Congressman Richard Ottinger of New York, the Democratic candidate for the U.S. Senate, arranged hearings also. Following these developments, the Rockefeller family bought the land that the Breakneck power plant was to be built on and turned it over to the state of New York as a park.

Participants in policy, at the local level, were also numerous. The town of Cornwall supported Con Ed because its tax revenues would triple to $150 million, new jobs would be created, the town would receive water facilities at no cost, and a new community swimming pool and a waterfront park were to be established by Con Ed. Con Ed was able to establish alliances in Westchester County in the early 1960s by increasing noticeably its charitable contributions. Building-trade and electrical-workers unions sided with Con Ed at the promise of lucrative contracts and jobs. Communities like Cortlandt, Putnam Valley, and Yorktown, which were to carry the burden of transmission lines, at first opposed Con Ed's plan, despite the offer of revenue incentives. But changes in the proposed route caused these three communities, after 1965, to alter their challenges. Finally, Harvard University announced in 1973 that it did not intend to sell the 300 acres of its 3,400-acre tract of Black Rock Forest required by Con Ed.

The conservationists were organized by the Scenic Hudson Preservation Conference (SHPC) established in November 1963. With a membership that grew to 18,000 and with the support of at least thirty conservation organizations, SHPC has led the opposition against the FPC and Con Ed for almost a decade and a half. The moral and financial support given to SHPC by many other local, state, and national conservation organizations warrants their identification: National Audubon Society, Adirondack Mountain Club, Citizens Committee on Natural Resources, Federation of Garden Clubs, Garden Clubs of America, National Trust for Historic Preservation, Nature Conservancy, New York-New Jersey Trail Conference, Park Association of New York City, Sierra Club, Izaak Walton League, the Wilderness Society, National Parks and Conservation Association, Hudson River Conservation Society, and the Taconic Foundation. With the assistance of a public relations firm, national mailing and donation campaigns, an enormously effective public education program, the support of philanthropic private foundations, and the guidance of excellent attorneys and directors, the SHPC has won concessions from the FPC. The project has been stalled successfully because of litigation and legislative action initiated through SHPC's activities.

The Hudson River Fishermen's Association (HRFA), formed late in 1964, has continually publicized the Indian Point nuclear plant's fish kills and has opposed the Storm King plant. The HRFA has filed a number of suits on its own behalf and has received the support of the Natural Resources Defense Council (NRDC) in protesting the environmental consequences of the growth in Con Ed's energy system.

The Policy Process

Con Ed was hoping to have the Storm King plant operational by 1968. To do so required knowledge of siting, design, and engineering details by the late 1950s. Between this time and the public announcement of the project in September 1962, Con Ed spent a great deal of effort obtaining governmental and political support for its proposal. The original Cornwall town water reserve would be drowned by the Storm King elevated reservoir. Through Con Ed's efforts, legislation was passed permitting Cornwall to dispose of its reservoir, and the town attorney received $133,000 for assisting Con Ed with administrative and legal procedures. At the time Con Ed applied for a license from the FPC in 1963, alternative energy sources to meet projected demands for 1968 were not readily available. Unless the FPC granted the license to Con Ed, New York City would be threatened with power brownouts. Because the FPC had planning authority for assuring an abundant supply of electric energy, and given that the FPC had only once in forty-five years denied a power project permit on aesthetic grounds, Con Ed's license was almost assured.

The application by the utility for a license was filed in March 1963. Public notice was given in the *Federal Register* and in a small rural weekly newspaper in Goshen, New York, many miles from the project site. Indirectly, the FPC's annual report of 1962 brought more unfavorable publicity to the issue than public announcements. A New York attorney and conservationist, L. O. Rothschild, was shocked by the aesthetic and environmental implications of the project as described in his copy of the annual report. Rothschild challenged the value of the Storm King proposal in an article published in the *New York Times* early in 1963. Soon after, the *Times* editorially protested the environmental implications of the project. With FPC hearings due late in 1963, Rothschild and six others met to form the SHPC as an organization to represent the views of conservationists, and immediately hired an attorney, former Commissioner D. C. Doty, to represent the citizens' group in forthcoming hearings. In a short time, the National Audubon Society, the Sierra Club, thirty conservation groups, and 13,000 members of the SHPC joined in opposition to the project.

SHPC petitioned to intervene in the FPC hearings, but Con Ed opposed allowing the conservationists to participate. SHPC's legal representative, D. C. Doty, was not permitted to present technical testimony.

The conservationists had not had sufficient time, expertise, or money to mount a full-scale challenge to the well-organized utility. In June 1964, the FPC hearing examiner approved Con Ed's license. This approval, however, was only an initial decision; the final order would be required from the FPC's five commissioners. Yorktown petitioned the FPC to reopen hearings on the Con Ed application in August 1964, but the results were not encouraging. While SHPC was trying to arrange financial support from foundations, Con Ed's president was encouraging the same organizations to deny assistance to the utility's opponents. In an effort to maximize the efficiency of its operations, SHPC engaged a public relations firm (Selvage, Lee and Howard) to help promote an educational campaign. With the assistance of the firm, SHPC obtained the support of State Senator R. Watson Pomeroy, who arranged hearings on the Storm King issue beginning in November 1964.

It was as a result of these hearings, when fishermen provided information on the danger that the Storm King project held for Hudson River, that the Hudson River Fishermen's Association (HRFA) was established. The HRFA immediately campaigned to publicize the Indian Point nuclear power plant's fish kills and to publicize further threats to fishing posed by the Storm King hydroelectric project. Doty, the attorney for SHPC, was permitted to argue for the conservationists before the FPC late in 1964, and he also petitioned to reopen hearings in January 1965. But on March 9, 1965, the full commission gave the final order of approval for Con Ed's license.

At this point in the policy process, the conservationists had no alternative but litigation. Without the financial support of the Taconic Foundation to finance a suit appealing the FPC decision, the Storm King project might well have begun. On October 8, 1965, in the U.S. Court of Appeals, Second Circuit, arguments were heard in the suit against the FPC filed by SHPC and the towns of Cortlandt, Putnam Valley, and Yorktown. Plaintiffs challenged the FPC license and the commission's refusal to reopen proceedings or to accept additional evidence on basic issues. In its ruling of December 29, 1965, the court agreed with the conservationists. The court did not revoke Con Ed's license, but remanded the case to the FPC for further hearings, with specific instructions on how to deal with the issues. The conservationists and communities had won a moral victory.

The court found that the FPC had neglected many of its responsibilities. The commission had failed to consider crucial issues such as cost, public convenience, and reasonable alternatives. The FPC was criticized in the court's ruling for its passive role in defending the public interest. The court also ruled that the commission could not act as an umpire, blindly calling balls and strikes for the adversaries before it. Public interest must be protected by the commission, according to the court. The FPC incurred further criticism for narrowly interpreting its mandate, for refusing to accept evidence on fish kills, for blindly accepting Con Ed's arguments and data, and for dismissing SHPC's views on the grounds that the conservationists were not an aggrieved party. The FPC was ordered to consider natural beauty in the new hearings. Con Ed appealed the decision to the U.S. Supreme Court, but in May 1966, the Supreme Court upheld the position of the lower court by refusing to hear the case.

The Storm King case had become a well-publicized political issue by 1966. The case was back in the hands of the FPC for further administrative action. Both SHPC and Con Ed prepared for the forthcoming FPC hearings by organizing data and testimony, and by publicizing their views as widely as possible. Con Ed hoped that its proposals to place the power plant underground and to alter certain transmission line routes would satisfy its opponents. But the conservationists were emphasizing many more fundamental issues and value questions than just aesthetic beauty. In particular, the issues of generating alternatives and protection of fish resources were emphasized by the conservationists. The publicity generated by SHPC and the HRFA on these issues between 1966 and 1968 won the citizens' groups considerable public support and credibility.

A gas turbine alternative to Storm King had been suggested by SHPC in the first hearings before the FPC. The conservationists argued that gas turbines could supply New York City's needs as well as the Storm King generators while reducing air pollution and causing less damage to natural resources. The utility produced "expert testimony" to prove that the SHPC proposal was inefficient and inappropriate. Refusing to accept the opinion of Con Ed and the FPC, the SHPC acquired extensive technical information on the gas turbine alternative. The alternative was purposely publicized by the conservationists in court actions, before legislative bodies, and in the press. The SHPC informed the public that gas turbines were cheaper than the Storm King proposal, readily available, and that Con Ed should use them. Under public pressure,

Con Ed installed a gas turbine in 1967. The utility soon announced that gas turbines could provide 2 million kilowatts of nonpolluting peak power. Estimates indicated this could be achieved at less cost than the Storm King project. The conservationists again seemed correct. Con Ed's adoption of the new technology prevented power breakdowns through 1967–68.

The HRFA was later proven correct in its argument that the river area around the proposed plant played a crucial role in marine ecology. The anadromous fish resources of the Hudson River were of great ecological and economic value. The fishermen had been denied the opportunity to testify in the first FPC hearings. As the result of relentless pressure on state legislators, independent investigations of the fish problem were conducted and widely publicized. After the second official FPC hearings, from November 1966 to May 1967, the proceedings were reopened for the Connecticut Board of Fisheries to intervene. The fishermen, their attorneys, and expert witnesses raised serious doubts about the claims of Con Ed's consulting ichthyologist.

Ewing G. Simpson, the FPC hearing examiner, recommended issuing the Storm King license in August 1968, in spite of the growing public support for the conservationists. In November, the FPC reopened the case for further hearings on New York City's complaint that the project endangered the Catskill Aqueduct, which carried 40 percent of the city's water, but the next month Simpson renewed his recommendation to license Storm King. After determined prompting from the conservationists, the FPC heard additional arguments in May 1970, and commission members took the unusual step of visiting the site on July 20. But on August 20, 1970, the FPC issued a 116-page decision licensing the Con Ed project.

The conservationists had no alternative other than to seek judicial review of the FPC decision. The National Resources Defense Council represented SHPC, the Izaak Walton League, the National Audubon Society, and the National Parks and Conservation Association in a suit against the FPC. The plaintiffs alleged lack of compliance with the 1965 court remand, absence of substantial evidence to support the FPC decision, and failure to comply with statutory mandates. In a two to one decision the court ruled in favor of the FPC and against SHPC and NRDC, with a strong dissent from Judge Oakes. On June 19, 1972, the conservationists' attempt for a Supreme Court retrial was refused by the Court. In a lower court decision in New York State, involving SHPC against the commissioner of the Department of Environmental Conservation, the conservationists lost in April 1973.

Conservationists continued the legal attacks in the New York federal district court. Plaintiffs in the case—the SHPC, HRFA, and the Atlantic Chapter of the Sierra Club—argued that Con Ed must obtain permits from the Army Corps of Engineers under the Federal Water Pollution Control Act for riverfront excavation activities. The court affirmed that a permit would be needed and prohibited Con Ed from dredging and filling. Hearings must be held before a permit is granted, and citizens' groups will again coordinate expert testimony for these hearings.

Outcome

The Storm King issue is still not resolved. Conservationists have expanded the doctrine of standing-to-sue, terminated the Breakneck Ridge plant, and improved the design of the Storm King project. The FPC has been forced to consider environmental factors in decision making, but the agency is still largely unaccountable to the public.

CASE V   Energy in America's Last Frontier: The Trans-Alaska Pipeline

All but 1 percent of Alaska's 375 million acres are in a natural state. Alaska contains the greatest variety of unspoiled scenic grandeur, wildlife habitats, and wildlife populations in North America, and to many Americans, it should remain that way. Conservationists speak for a significant portion of the nation's people who view Alaska's resources and untrammeled wild areas as the common property of all Americans. They argue that Alaska should be preserved for future generations. Development should take place only after comprehensive and detailed land-use planning to ensure maximum protection of the environment.

But there is a second view on policy for Alaska's future. With its rich oil, gas, and copper reserves, its flowing water, and its untapped mineral potential, Alaska is seen by industrial concerns as America's last great frontier for economic development. This view is shared by many Alaskans, mainly for economic reasons. The declining economic input from military bases and the over-exploited salmon fishing industry, together with the increasing costs of government infrastructure, have seriously strained the state's economy. To ease the strain, most of Alaska's 300,000 inhabitants have advocated developing the state's resources. Economically and politically powerful industrial corporations also have encouraged development, and the state government has traditionally sought stimulants for the economy. (See Chapter 7, The Economy and Growth.)

The debate over land-use policy in Alaska has focused, since the mid-1960s, on two issues: land claims of native Alaskans and proposals for the Alaska pipeline, which followed the oil strike in Prudhoe Bay in 1968. The first issue began when Alaska was made a state in 1959. The federal government, which owned 95 percent of the land in Alaska, entitled the state to select for itself 104 million acres from unreserved public lands. As the state was selecting lands pursuant to federal grants, the natives of Alaska—Alaskan Indians, Eskimos, and Aleuts—counterclaimed. Through groups such as the Arctic Slope Native Association, the Northwest Native Association, and the Alaska Federation of Natives, the indigenous peoples submitted claims by 1967 to 370 of Alaska's 375 million acres. In an effort to protect Alaskan lands until these native claims could be decided, Secretary of Interior Stewart L. Udall imposed a freeze on all public lands which halted all private development, state selection of land, and federal withdrawals. The state of Alaska opposed the land freeze and so did the oil industry, which recognized that the native-claims issue had to be resolved before it could proceed with development plans. Together they pressured Congress to enact the Alaska Native Claims Settlement Act of 1971. It was hoped this act would end the freeze, reconcile the land-ownership conflict, and allow oil developments to progress.

The second issue affecting land-use policy in Alaska has been the 1968 oil discoveries near Prudhoe Bay on the north slope of the Brooks Range in the Arctic Circle. Conservative estimates predicted the Prudhoe field held 10 billion barrels of crude oil; other estimates suggested a reserve of 70–80 billion barrels, which would make the Prudhoe field the second or third largest field in the world. In July 1968, prior to any public consideration of Alaska oil policy, the Trans-Alaska Pipeline System (TAPS) group was formed by Atlantic Richfield and other oil companies to plan development of the field. In February 1969, TAPS (then composed of eight oil companies) announced plans to construct a 764-mile pipeline, four feet in diameter, to carry oil from Prudhoe Bay to waiting tankers at the port of Valdez on the Pacific coast of

Alaska. The pipeline, which would accommodate two million barrels of oil a day, was routed across 641 miles of federal land. TAPS applied to the U.S. Bureau of Land Management on June 10, 1969, for land-use permits required for crossing federal land.

To many Alaskans the benefits to be derived from the proposed oil-field developments appeared bountiful. Alaska's state treasury would receive production taxes and royalties, an estimated $238 to $370 million a year between about 1980 and 2000, and Alaskan natives would receive $500 million of the state's royalties. The United States could look forward to a potentially more favorable balance of payments. Since increased domestic crude-oil production would reduce the need for imported oil, dollar outflow was expected to be reduced $700 million annually by 1980. Less reliance on foreign supplies also supported security arguments in favor of the pipeline. With the delivery of Alaskan oil, domestic production would meet an estimated 47 percent of the U.S. demand for oil, an increase in independence of roughly 8 percent.

The oil industry expected enormous profits, which explains their haste to market Alaskan oil. The oil could be delivered to the east coast relatively cheaply, and it could be delivered to Japan for less than Kuwait oil. While eager to exploit the resources, the oil industry was equally eager, so it appears, to exploit certain institutional arrangements. The developers were determined to use the trans-Alaska pipeline route despite the possibility of using trans-Canada routes, one of which was known to be economically and environmentally preferable to the trans-Alaska route. A study of alternative routes and markets for Alaskan oil concludes that the trans-Alaska plan is more profitable to oil companies than other routes only "under certain interesting schemes for the ultimate delivery of oil."[2] The oil conglomerates avoided negotiations with Canada because they had more to gain with the trans-Alaska plan. Moreover, the Nixon administration and the Department of Interior did not thoroughly investigate alternatives with the Canadians, and it now appears they served the interests of the oil industry rather than the nation.

Generally, the benefits of exploiting Alaskan oil appeared attractive for Alaskans and Alaskan natives, for the country as a whole, and

[2] Charles J. Cicchetti, *Alaskan Oil: Alternative Routes and Markets* (Baltimore: The Johns Hopkins University Press, 1972), p. 142.

especially for the oil conglomerates. But counter-arguments pointed out questionable features of the proposed benefits. To the nation, the development of Alaska's unique natural resources was not a significant benefit. Economic stimulation of Alaska could be accomplished by less environmentally expensive means. Increasing domestic oil production to save up to about $1 billion annually on revenue outflow would not significantly improve our balance of payments. Alaskan oil could partly alleviate the energy crisis by raising the domestic oil supply by 8 percent; but when energy conservation measures could reduce the consumption of oil far more than 8 percent, the gain is small. Conservationists argued that the size of the Alaska pipeline project (estimated cost $3.5 billion) and the lack of information about the fragile Alaska environment prevented an accurate analysis of the pipeline's full costs and benefits. There was little doubt that the construction and operation of the pipeline involved numerous risks that could result in environmental degradation, though how much damage and the costs of that damage, economic and environmental, were both unpredictable.

The risks that entailed serious environmental costs were terrain disruption and permafrost degradation. Permafrost is frozen earth predominantly covered with a thin layer of moss and arctic shrubs. This tundra vegetation acts as an insulator during the summer months, regulating the flow of heat into the frozen permafrost. Without the cover, the permafrost thaws, leading to massive erosion and destruction of fragile vegetation. Oil spills along the pipeline could contaminate any of the eighty streams crossed by the pipeline, seriously affect the tundra around the pipeline, or have serious impacts on fisheries in Prince William Sound and perhaps the Canadian coast. The southern 400 miles of the pipeline would cross areas of high seismic action, increasing the possibility of an oil spill. The extraction of tens of millions of cubic yards of construction materials from surrounding lands and streams could lead to some permafrost degradation and stream siltation. Big game animals, such as caribou, may have their migratory habits interrupted by a surface pipeline. Finally, the subsistence life-style of native Alaskans would probably be affected by industrialization, resultant pollution, and particularly by the accelerated changes caused by an increase in the white population.

Issues such as these, and the enormous number of participants in policy formation for the Alaska pipeline, were the ingredients of a complex policy conflict. Environmentalists in Alaska, such as the Alaska

Conservation Society, were joined by groups of fishermen, some groups of Alaskan natives, and some of the major conservation organizations in the nation in an effort to protect Alaska. The conservationists held development back for almost three years through litigation. But the pressure of the energy crisis in 1973, the haste of oil developers and the state of Alaska, and the Supreme Court's decision not to rule caused the final decision-making authority to be remanded to Congress. Even though exploitation of Alaskan oil could not alleviate the oil shortage in the short run, Congress stampeded into action in an effort to counteract what appeared a formidable threat to the nation's economic stability. Oil-development interests appeared to have more access and influence in high government circles than any other interest groups. In Congress, the developers prevailed and the pipeline was exempted from court challenges under the National Environmental Policy Act.

The Actors

The Department of Interior, with its broad authority over the public lands, was a central participant in policy. Within the department, both the Bureau of Indian Affairs, with its responsibilities for Indians, and the Bureau of Land Management (BLM) had significant roles to play in decision making. The BLM, which manages 60 percent of federal public lands and administers the laws pertaining to these lands, is responsible for mineral leasing on public lands such as those in Alaska. State Department officials also advocated the trans-Alaska route in the interest of haste and national security.

The Alyeska Pipeline Company (Alyeska), formerly TAPS, wielded enormous influence in Alaska and in Washington, D.C. Alyeska even offered to pay the Interior Department's environmental impact statement costs ($2.7 million) if a permit was granted. The AFL–CIO, United Automobile Workers, National Oil Jobbers Council, and the Seafarers International Union of North America lobbied extensively for the Alaska pipeline. The state of Alaska was anxious to hasten the construction of the pipeline. The governor, and most of the Alaskan congressional delegation, campaigned strongly for the pipeline in the state and in Washington, D.C. Even U.S. Senator Henry M. Jackson of Washington wanted construction on the pipeline to start, although he opposed the move to bypass the National Environmental Policy Act (NEPA). At the beginning of the controversy the secretary of the interior was Walter J. Hickel, a former Alaskan construction expert and developer. Ironically, Governor Hickel lost favor with the Nixon administration before the pipeline became an issue, in part for his zeal for environmental protection generally.

Environmentalists were led mainly by the Wilderness Society, the Environmental Defense Fund (EDF), and the Friends of the Earth (FOE). The Alaskan natives' land claims influenced the evolution of policy for the pipeline. The Alaskan Federation of Natives, the North Slope Native Association, and the Northwest Native Association were the principal native representatives. The Cordova District Fisheries Union objected to the use of Prince William Sound as an oil terminal and filed suit against the secretaries of agriculture and interior.

The Policy Process

When plans for the Alaskan pipeline were announced in February 1969, Secretary of Interior Walter Hickel formed a task force to study the problems posed by the project. The North Slope Task Force, a government-wide group including numerous agencies, submitted a report to the president in September 1969. In December, TAPS submitted an application (amended from its June application) to the BLM asking for a 54-foot primary right-of-way for the pipeline. TAPS also submitted two separate applications for special land-use permits. One permit requested extra access and construction space of 11 feet on one side of the pipeline right-of-way and 55 feet on the other. The second application requested a 200-foot width for a haul road and pipeline construction surface from Livengood to Prudhoe Bay.

The Center for Law and Social Policy, on behalf of its clients, the Wilderness Society, the Environmental Defense Fund, and Friends of the Earth, filed a complaint for declaratory and injunctive relief against the secretary of interior. The conservationists declared that Secretary Hickel intended to issue special land-use permits to TAPS, and that another permit for rights-of-way would violate the width restrictions of Section 28 of the Mineral Leasing Act of 1920. Plaintiffs argued that the Interior Department could not use special-use permits to extend the width limitation (twenty-five feet on either side of the pipe) imposed by the Mineral Leasing Act. On April 23, 1970, Judge Hart issued a preliminary injunction against issuance of the permits and rights-of-way.

The court also ruled that the Interior Department, the defendant, had not fully complied with the National Environmental Policy Act. Conservationists had been aware that the inadequate ten-page impact statement contained no environmental analysis and had been filed only in response to litigation. The department had filed an impact statement for the haul road only and not for the pipeline. Judge Hart ruled that these two aspects of the same project could not be separated. The preliminary injunction was thereby made effective against the entire project, not just the haul road. Conservationists were at first successful in halting construction of the pipeline, but it would be two years before the Department of Interior was ready to comply with NEPA.

While Congress was still considering the Alaska natives' land claims, the state of Alaska claimed and took title to tracts of land under the land selection provision of the Alaska Statehood Act. Part of the claim was the area around Prudhoe Bay. This action and others led to an immediate protest from Alaska's natives. When Secretary Hickel modified the land freeze, previously ordered by Secretary Udall, to allow developers of the pipeline and haul roads onto land claimed by the natives, the natives filed suit. In this suit (*Allakaket* v. *Hickel*), the natives sought an injunction against the issuance of a haul road permit on land they were claiming in the bill pending before Congress. In April 1970, Judge Hart granted a preliminary injunction against authorization of the haul road permits. Meanwhile, Rogers Morton replaced Secretary Hickel.

Throughout 1971, the policy process involved complicated issues and an increasing intensity of conflict. The Interior Department issued a draft of an environmental impact statement in January and held hearings on it in Anchorage, Alaska, and Washington, D.C. The draft was widely criticized as inadequate for meaningful evaluation of the pipeline project. The U.S. Army Corps of Engineers, in particular, was highly critical of the draft statement. National conservation organizations launched a major effort to obtain public hearings on the forthcoming final impact statement. President Nixon and Secretary of Interior Rogers Morton were inundated with letters and wires during the year requesting at least sixty days for analysis and public comment after the final environmental impact statement was made public.

In the meantime, citizens' groups generated a great deal of public comment on an alternative pipeline route through Canada. A proposed trans-Canada pipeline would pass through the Mackenzie Valley to

Edmonton, Canada, from which two limbs would branch—one to Chicago and the other to the West Coast. This route would have the advantages of avoiding active seismic areas and eliminating the need for shipping oil down the coast. Moreover, a natural gas pipeline was probably going to be built across Canada from Prudhoe Bay in the near future. But the trans-Canada route would cross more permafrost and rivers, cost much more, and take perhaps three years longer to complete. It would, however, avoid the costs and hazards of transport by sea. In the U.S. House of Representatives, Congressman Les Aspin (D-Wisconsin) and nineteen other members introduced a joint resolution that would halt the Alaska pipeline until a comprehensive study of the Canadian alternative could be made.

Major developments in pipeline litigation took place during 1971. The state of Alaska and the Alyeska Pipeline Company (formerly TAPS) both were allowed to intervene in *Wilderness Society* v. *Hickel*. The state had sold oil leases to the oil firms and was supporting the project. The Honorable David Anderson, British Columbian member of Canada's House of Commons, and the 150,000-member Canadian Wildlife Federation asked for permission to intervene in *Wilderness Society* v. *Hickel*. The interveners opposed the coastal tanker proposals that threatened oil spills along the Canadian coast. In a related issue, the Cordova District Fisheries Union, which represented 450 members, opposed the use of Valdez on Prince William Sound as the pipeline terminus. A delegation of the union members visited major cities in the lower forty-eight states to publicize the protest. The union filed suit in the U.S. District Court in Washington, D.C., against the secretary of agriculture and the secretary of interior. Plaintiffs requested an injunction and asserted that the U.S. Forest Service permit for terminal facilities at Valdez exceeded the maximum acreage limit (eighty acres) allowed by such a permit.

Meanwhile, Alyeska and the state of Alaska took further steps to hasten the development of oil reserves. Their activities affected Mineral Leasing Act issues. In March 1971, Alyeska filed an application for rights-of-way for twenty-six communications sites. In July, the state of Alaska applied to the BLM for a highway right-of-way across public lands for a road running from Prudhoe Bay to Livengood which Alyeska had contracted to build. The state also applied for leases of public lands for construction of three airports along the pipeline route and for free-use permits for gravel to facilitate construction of the airports and highway. William A. Egan, governor of Alaska, planned to ask the Alaska legislature to approve financing a state takeover of the pipeline project. Alyeska would build the pipeline as an agent of the state. This plan would maximize the state's financial return from north slope oil. In Anchorage on September 26, where he was to meet Japan's Emperor Hirohito, President Nixon announced that his administration was committed to the development of Arctic resources.

Three months later, in December 1971, Congress passed the Alaska Native Claims Settlement Act. Congress awarded Alaskan natives $1 billion for their regional development corporations and 40 million acres of land to be selected from 112 million withdrawn by the secretary of interior. Secretary Morton also withdrew 4.5 million acres for a utility corridor for the oil pipeline. The secretary was also ordered under the act to withdraw for study up to 80 million acres of lands suitable for inclusion in the national system of parks, forests, wildlife refuges, and wild and scenic rivers. With passage of the act, the land freeze was ended and the land ownership conflict in Alaska was supposedly at an end.

The long-awaited final environmental impact statement from the Department of Interior was issued on March 20, 1972. The report was six volumes long with three more volumes of supplemental analysis; it cost $12.7 million and required 175 man-years of work. Secretary Morton ignored voluminous objections from conservationists who requested public hearings on the final impact statement. The secretary allowed just forty-five days for the public to prepare comment on the 3,550-page statement. The Wilderness Society, the Friends of the Earth, and the EDF, at Secretary Morton's invitation, submitted on May 4 a 1,300-page analysis of the scientific, engineering, economic, and national security aspects of the proposed pipeline. In retrospect, his invitation for comments seems insincere. Just seven days after receiving them—hardly enough time for a thorough review—Secretary Morton decided to issue the necessary permits as soon as the courts would allow. The environmentalists' four-volume analysis represented the findings of seventy-five engineers, scientists, and other experts who had analyzed the government's environmental impact statement. Their report criticized the government's impact statement for five main reasons: (1) it had accepted and included the value premises of the oil companies sponsoring the project; (2) project controls were vague and meaningless; (3) alternatives had not been adequately considered, particularly the combined oil and gas pipeline through Canada; (4) the Department of Interior's data on economic and national security aspects were inadequate; and (5) insufficient information existed for the Interior Department to rule on the pipeline applications. Secretary Morton had stressed the need to hasten the delivery of oil to the lower forty-eight states, and Undersecretary of Interior Pecora announced that any further hearings or public discussion of the issue would be a "circus."

Attorneys for the Wilderness Society, FOE, and EDF immediately filed a motion in the U.S. District Court in Washington, D.C., against Secretary Morton, asking, in effect, for a permanent injunction against issuance of a trans-Alaska pipeline permit. On August 15, 1972, Judge Hart in an oral opinion held that the Interior Department had complied with the National Environmental Policy Act and the Mineral Leasing Act. He dissolved the preliminary injunction, denied a permanent injunction, and dismissed the complaints. Conservationists again filed suit (Wilderness Society v. Morton) questioning the lawfulness of Morton's May 11 decision. Plaintiffs argued that the department was violating Section 28 of the Mineral Leasing Act and Section 102 of the NEPA as well, because the final environmental impact statement was inadequate. On February 9, 1973, the court ruled that the secretary of interior lacked authority to grant special land-use permits, and the granting of the permits had violated both Section 28 of the Mineral Leasing Act and applicable Bureau of Land Management regulations. Judge J. Skelly Wright ruled that the project must be enjoined until Congress changed the Mineral Leasing Act to allow a wider right-of-way. The proponents of the pipeline project took the decision to the Supreme Court, but the Supreme Court refused to consider it.

Up to this stage in the policy process, attempts at conflict resolution had been conducted between the executive branch and the courts. From this stage on, the issues were argued primarily in Congress and the debate lasted several months. Early in the conflict, U.S. Senators Gravel and Stevens of Alaska announced they would press for amendments to the Mineral Leasing Act to allow issuance of the permits. The Nixon administration and the oil interests pressed for the trans-Alaska pipeline as the quickest way of supplying oil to the lower forty-eight states. The AFL-CIO and the state of Alaska also pressed for approval of the project, and the United Automobile Workers and National Oil Jobbers Council lobbied for the pipeline. The Seafarers International Union of North America, hoping for a stimulus to shipping construction, opposed the trans-Canada alternative. The Department of State favored the trans-Alaska pipeline and stressed to Congress that the Canadian position on a trans-Canada route was not favorable; this, of course, was the policy position of the Nixon administration.

At this crucial point in congressional debate, the State Department misrepresented the position of the Canadian government. The Canadians supposedly were insisting on majority ownership of a pipeline through their country. This was not true. The Interior Department did not have direct communications with the Canadians. There was never any clear knowledge of Canada's policies with regard to formal approval, financing, and control of a proposed trans-Canada pipeline. Environmentalists within Canada reminded their government of the dangers of both pipeline projects. It appeared that Canadian officials were receptive to a trans-Canada proposal, but were given little opportunity to participate in decision making.

Conservationists were marshalling congressional support for legislation that would defer approval of the pipeline, so that studies of the trans-Canada alternative could be conducted. The chairman of the Council on Environmental Quality, the administrator of the Environmental Protection Agency, and the energy policy coordinator of the Office of Science and Technology asserted that the Canadian route should be studied. U.S. Senators Mondale, Bayh, and Haskell and Congressmen Anderson, Udall, and Saylor advocated the study of a trans-Canada route. Environmentalists were successful in getting the media to focus on NEPA and the Alaska oil issues once it was clear an amendment to NEPA was imminent. The *New York Times, Washington Post,* and *Boston Globe* printed editorials against the amendment to override NEPA. But the gas and oil shortage facing the nation altered the balance of power in Congress; the pleadings of environmentalists were no match for the political persuasion generated by an impending energy crisis.

Outcome

While the opponents of the Alaskan pipeline had concentrated on building up the credibility of the Canadian alternative, interests favoring the pipeline had pressured for the success of S. 1081 and H.R. 9081. Each bill exempted the pipeline from court challenges under NEPA. The issues had finally been decided, not on environmental grounds, but on the country's alleged need for oil and gas. The energy crisis and what were described as the needs of national security were considered top priority. The president signed a compromise bill into law in mid-November 1973. Construction work began again on the Alaska pipeline in the summer of 1974.

CASE VI   Pricing Policies and Energy Demand: Connecticut's Public Utilities Commission

The state of Connecticut's two largest utilities are the Connecticut Light and Power Company (CLPC) and the Hartford Electric Light Company (HELCO). Both utilities were parts of the Northeast Utilities Company, which expected sales of electric energy to continue to increase at an annual rate of 8 percent, as they had in recent years. HELCO had announced it had set a goal for increasing sales sixfold in the twenty years from 1970 to 1990. CLPC and HELCO each had had two rate increases within two years of 1972, applied for a third that year, and expected to continually increase rates as the costs of expansion increased beyond revenues.

Connecticut's Public Utilities Commission (CPUC) has the authority to grant or deny rate increases for the utilities. In February 1972, CLPC sought an increase in operating revenues of $25.75 million, and on July 28, the CPUC granted an increase of $14.5 million. Rates for electricity consumption increased accordingly, and the state's consumers would carry the burden. Soon after the rate increase decision by the CPUC, Hilda Swaney et al. (Low-Income Interveners) and the city of Hartford appealed the CPUC's actions in separate legal suits. The interveners alleged that the block-rate pricing structures used by the utilities, and condoned by CPUC, were discriminatory toward low-income earners and stimulated excessive energy consumption.

The issues and legal arguments raised by the city of Hartford and the Low-Income Interveners were essentially the same as those raised by a second group of interveners in a suit against the CPUC over HELCO's application. It is the HELCO case we focus on in this case study. HELCO applied to the CPUC in February 1972 for an increase in operating revenues of $10.89 million and was granted $6.33 million in July. Expenditure plans for the period 1972–77 for generating plants, transmission lines, and construction were claimed by HELCO to be over $500 million. To finance this expansion program HELCO had to borrow 75 percent of the capital. Financiers advised HELCO that earnings of 8½ percent to

8 ¾ percent on its rate base would probably be needed in order to bor-
row capital at reasonable interest rates. The CPUC's approval of a $6.33
million increase in operating revenues produced an 8 ¼ percent rate of
return on the rate base.

The citizens' groups opposed the spiraling pattern of rate increases
that discriminated against the smaller consumer. Diminishing, block-
rate pricing structures encouraged large consumers of energy because
prices fell as consumption increased. Environmental considerations,
however, demanded that prices should increase with consumption to
deter extravagant demand. The public interveners recommended alternative pricing structures that were more in harmony with policies for
energy conservation, resources scarcity, and protection of the environment. Environmentalists argued that HELCO's goal of a sixfold increase
in energy sales would lead to a similar multiplication of generating
plants, of pollution, and of the depletion rate of energy reserves. Because the heat-conversion efficiency of fossil-fuel plants is roughly 33
percent, reducing electricity consumption by one unit means a threefold
reduction in fuel demand. The citizen groups fought to reform pricing
structures on the grounds that yesterday's pricing ideals no longer suit
today's environmental, social, and economic concerns.

The Actors

HELCO's plan to increase electricity sales and stimulate demand
through traditional means of pricing, promotion, and advertising was
the fundamental cause of the policy dispute. Energy shortages and the
escalating costs of generating and distributing electricity invalidate the
traditional claim made by utilities such as HELCO that increased sales
benefit the public.

The CPUC was a conservative regulatory agency, trying to defend
traditional regulatory and pricing patterns. Taking a passive role in the
regulatory process, the CPUC made little or no effort to weigh the evidence of the interveners in the public hearings. Since the late 1960s,
many utility commissions in other states had reformed or considered
reforming traditional pricing and advertising policies.

The citizens' groups in the HELCO-CPUC case were represented by
attorneys from the National Resources Defense Council (NRDC), a
nationally known group of public-interest attorneys and scientists. The
local groups who challenged the validity of the CPUC order were the

Berkshire-Litchfield Environmental Conservancy Council (BLECC) and the Connecticut Citizen Action Group (CCAG).

The Policy Process

Policy for establishing increases in utility rates had traditionally been decided by the utilities and the CPUC. Utilities generally strive for maximum plant expansion—so that even when their ability to cope with supply is limited, they stimulate demand for electricity. This is in contrast to nonregulated industries which, when faced with demand in excess of supply, usually increase prices and ease promotional activity. Regulatory commissions such as CPUC generally evaluate the reasonableness of rate proposals put to them in applications from utilities. In order to fully understand the claims of the interveners in the HELCO case, it would be helpful to understand fundamental features of utility behavior and the criteria used by the CPUC to arrive at its determination.

HELCO had cogent reasons for maximizing demand for its product and planning to grow sixfold by 1990. HELCO's profits were determined by multiplying its rate base (capital investment of $362.415 million) times the rate of return. The CPUC verified the rate base and determined the rate of return, generally within the nationally accepted range which was normally 6–8 percent. Profits for HELCO could be increased by two methods. If the rate base remained constant, which meant no new capital investment (plant building), an increased rate of return approved by the CPUC would increase profits. An alternate means of increasing profits would be to expand the rate base (by plant expansion) while holding the rate of return constant. HELCO planned both to expand its rate base and to apply for an increase to 8.58 percent in the rate of return. In order to maximize rate-base extension, HELCO stimulated demand for electricity through advertising, promotion, and decreasing price structures. Increased expenses due to promotion and advertising had no effect on HELCO's profits, because such expenses were absorbed by or deductible from operating revenues and were ultimately carried by the public. According to HELCO, its claim for an increased rate of return and its plan for expanding facilities were justified because of greater demand from its service area. The CPUC traditionally accepted this rationale. The CPUC determined a rate increase of $6.330 million would produce a "reasonable" rate of return of 8.25 percent.

Upon receiving HELCO's application on February 25, 1972, the

CPUC announced dates for public hearings. BLECC, CCAG, the city of Hartford, and others petitioned to intervene, and the CPUC permitted them to participate. Seventeen days of public hearings were held between May 25 and July 14, 1972. During the hearings, HELCO's representatives remained noticeably silent, even though the burden of showing that the rate increase was just and reasonable lay with the applicant. Throughout the hearings, the citizens/interveners concentrated on giving testimony on environmental issues and on the implications of decreasing block-rate pricing structures.

The citizens' groups arranged for experts to present their testimony. In particular, three prominent scientists testified for the environmentalists that traditional rate structures were unfair to low-income earners, unjustified, environmentally harmful, and encouraged wasting already depleted energy resources. More specifically, the scientists pinpointed the harmful ecological consequences of fossil-fuel generation and transmission practices. Polluting emissions from fossil-fuel plants in Connecticut accounted for 55–80 percent of the sulphur dioxide, 20–35 percent of the particulates, and 20–40 percent of the nitrogen oxide emissions in the air. Human health is endangered by each of these emissions. Also, since fossil-fuel plants require enormous quantities of water for cooling purposes, they are responsible for increasing the thermal pollution of waterways. One of the scientists pointed out that HELCO planned to broaden the nuclear-generating component of its generating grid, even though one of its existing plants had already been involved in an accident which released radioactive material into the environment. The participants at the hearing were warned of the possible genetic and carcinogenic (cancer-producing) effects of long-term, low-level radiation exposure. HELCO's sixfold expansion plans also called for making irreversible commitments of limited land resources to single-purpose use. The citizens stressed the adverse environmental effects at each of the extraction, processing, transportation, and waste disposal stages of electric energy production.

The environmentalists also focused on the lack of cost justification for traditional block-rate pricing structures during the hearings. It was HELCO's duty to show the nature of its application was just and reasonable, but the utility omitted any evidence of cost justification. BLECC had an electrical engineer and an economist argue the interveners' position. In testimony, these experts demonstrated that the cost of supplying electricity was increasing for HELCO. At the same time, the decreasing rate structure (costs per unit diminish with greater consumption) meant less revenue per kilowatt-hour as the consumption of electricity increased. This situation resulted in the attrition of earnings and necessitated HELCO's continual rate increase applications. In other words, HELCO was continually seeking rate increases because its profits were dropping. As the price advances instituted by HELCO usually increased the cost to each consumer classification by an equal percentage, the status quo allegedly was maintained.

The expert witnesses for the environmentalists showed that HELCO's policies resulted in discrimination against low-volume consumers in favor of high-volume consumers. The utility's price structures acted as a stimulus to growth in electricity consumption, with adverse consequences for the environment and the so-called energy crisis. HELCO's representatives admitted in cross examination that they had little or no information on cost data for electricity production, and did not intend to perform a cost of service study as a foundation for justifying rate increases by costs. The lack of evidence to justify HELCO's rate structure appeared to be of little consequence to the regulatory commission (CPUC).

By a vote of two to one, the CPUC granted HELCO the $6.330 million rate increase. The CPUC's opinion was a mere two-page editorial, rather than a rational opinion based on the record. Conservationists claimed the CPUC had not resolved any of the central issues raised in the hearings: attrition of earnings, energy conservation, pollution, inequitable treatment of customers, or the promotion of costly and scarce energy. The CPUC was alleged to have avoided duties imposed by Connecticut's Environmental Protection Act of 1971, the state's Public Utilities Act, and its Administrative Procedure Act. It was obvious also that the CPUC had not kept abreast of trends in many other states which had moved to eliminate quantity discounts and to cut back on advertising. The citizens' groups were forced to resort to litigation, their only remaining avenue for resolving the issues and requiring CPUC to carry out its legal responsibilities.

In August 1972, the National Resources Defense Council, on behalf of the citizens' groups, sued the regulatory commission (CPUC) on the grounds that the structure of rate increases discriminated against the smaller consumer of electricity and ultimately encouraged energy use. The plaintiffs alleged also that increased energy use was harmful to the environment. The case was one of the nation's first court challenges to the structure of utility rates. The court was asked to resolve the legal questions arising from CPUC's refusal to base decisions on the record, despite explicit orders to consider energy conservation, cost justification, and pollution.

More specifically, the plaintiffs' claim was based on the following fundamentals of law. Connecticut's Environmental Protection Act of 1971 required that all agencies must consider environmental impact in their actions in any proceeding where adverse environmental impact has been alleged. Presuming that the proper allocation of costs was its main responsibility, the CPUC erroneously concluded that it could not consider the environment in rate-setting procedures. The CPUC also violated the Connecticut Public Utilities Act by failing to deal with the cost-allocation issue. HELCO had the burden of responsibility to show that the rate structure was justified. HELCO did not do so, nor did the CPUC order the utility to do so, and it approved the discriminatory rate structure on the basis of tradition. Finally, under the state's Administrative Procedure Act, CPUC was obliged to make decisions based on rulings on all issues raised by citizens' groups, and it did not clearly establish a basis for its decision except for tradition. The CPUC erroneously placed the burden of proof on interveners rather than on the applicant, HELCO.

Outcome

The court, however, ruled against the interveners in June 1974. Ruling that the plaintiffs' arguments at the public hearings had been "interesting and maybe appealing," but not persuasive, the court considered the basis for the CPUC decision "logical and rational," and declared that HELCO's evidence supported the decision of the defendant, CPUC. During earlier hearings, plaintiffs had demonstrated the format of a flat-rate structure, one that would be based on a single price per unit of electricity used, regardless of quantity. The citizens' groups, BLECC and CCAG, claimed the flat-rate structure would decrease energy consumption, thereby contributing to the conservation of diminishing reserves and aiding in the protection of the environment. CPUC had concluded that the proposal would result in the "repeal of the industrial revolution." On this issue, the court ruled that the plaintiffs failed to present evidence of any feasible and prudent alternative. The plaintiffs also called for further hearings, but the court concluded more hearings would be useless. The defendant, CPUC, was exonerated from each claim of abuse of discretion registered by the plaintiffs.

Conclusion

At every stage of energy production and use, some measure of environmental degradation, however small, inevitably occurs. To understand the various and complicated interrelationships between energy production and use, resource usage and environmental protection, a systems approach is necessary. The need to develop the increasingly scarce energy resources of the nation as a total system—extraction, production, conversion, transportation, and residuals—has been recognized, but much of the work required to establish a systems approach has yet to be carried out. Objectively considered, short-range and long-range goals for demand and supply do not yet exist, nor do the means for reconciling competing views of optimum resource management and use. The cases reviewed in this chapter illustrate different aspects of citizen involvement in the formation of policies that attempt to establish a balance between expansion of the nation's energy system and environmental protection. After examining some of the broad implications of the energy-environment problem, we will comment on each of the cases.

We have described many of the environmental consequences of uncontrolled expansion in the nation's energy system. The ways separate communities, some local governments, and states have grappled with the issues have also been illustrated. But the problem is a nationwide one, requiring leadership on the part of the federal government. There is a fundamental necessity to correlate policies and management for energy and for the environment. At least four basic aspects of policy must be considered in any plan to deal effectively with energy-environment problems.

First, there is a need to reduce the exponential or geometric growth rate of energy consumption. Programs to conserve energy and reduce waste are essential. Second, the trend toward energy-intensive industrial activities, such as fertilizer manufacturing and aluminum production, requires immediate review. With 30 percent of the nation's energy consumption in transportation, reconsideration of the role of automobiles and the extension of mass transit systems in urban areas is required. Third, institutional reforms to clarify public responsibility and reduce the fragmented governmental structure that traditionally has had authority in energy and natural resource administration are urgently needed. Even at the height of the energy shortages in 1973–74 when governmental organization was a principal item of political and governmental discussion, the establishment of new or reorganized agencies was slow. Numerous interest groups, congressional committees, existing bureaucracies, advisory bodies, and the White House were all debating the most desirable forms restructuring should take. Finally, there is a need to open decision-making processes to public participation. Government agencies and the energy conglomerates do not have all the experts. The effects of future management of the nation's energy resources and the environment will be so pervasive that the public's interest must be protected, and allowing public participation in decision making is one way to help protect this right.

Protection of the public interest requires a consideration of one fundamental issue: Is continual growth in the demand and supply of energy, at exponential rates, in the public interest? Citizen groups in the cases considered in this chapter faced this basic issue, but the question for the nation as a whole cannot be answered on a case-by-case basis. The problem requires examining a larger question: the role of growth in the nation's future. Policy makers need to consider the interrelated concerns of future power demand and supply, alternative sources of energy, and the preservation of natural resources. Perhaps the public interest may best be served by modifying national priorities in accordance with the wishes of an informed public. Since the 1960s, the nation has altered some of its priorities by formulating legislation for environmental protection, but there is little doubt that policies for environmental protection will clash increasingly with demands for energy development.

It is not clear whether energy or the environment will take ultimate priority during the mid-1970s, or whether each issue will be resolved through some form of compromise legislation. Congressional committees, the White House, the Federal Energy Administration, the EPA, and energy and resource agencies such as the Nuclear Regulatory Commission and the Department of Interior are each pursuing different policy priorities. Energy interests, the Interior Department, and the White House are urging oil-shale development and pilot programs, vastly increased leasing of outer continental shelf lands for oil and gas exploration, and the deregulation of natural gas. At the same time, environmentalists are gathering increasing political support for legislation on land-use planning, regulations for strip mining, and restrictions on extension of federal authority in deep-water port development. Legislation for increasing energy conservation by recycling is also supported by environmentalists.

At the state level, there is ample evidence of new legislation emphasizing land-use planning, more comprehensive environmental management, and the need to calculate the full costs and benefits of further energy-related development. People in a number of regions of the nation, such as the coal lands of the Southwest and the Northern Plains and the coasts of Delaware and Maine object to assuming the environmental costs for energy-hungry urban centers hundreds of miles away. This situation could be the forerunner of future interregional conflict. Let us now examine some of the significant implications of the individual case studies.

The Alaska pipeline case demonstrates a classic confrontation between an industrial society with 45 percent of its fuel supply based on oil and the forces for environmental protection. The pipeline project presents large environmental risks, is the world's largest free-enterprise investment at over $3 billion, and involves debatable benefits and a dubious rationale. The Alaska treasury stands to earn over $250 million a year, the oil companies will gross about $7 million a day at full capacity, and the domestic oil production-consumption ratio will be increased slightly. National security supposedly is enhanced to some unquantifiable degree by reliance on a little more domestic oil production, but the vulnerabilities of sea transport and transshipment generally have been played down.

The Sears Island, Maine, case demonstrates the nature of development pressures generated by the growth in oil consumption in the nation. Maine has about ten potential deep-water ports suitable for supertanker facilities and associated oil refineries. Foreign oil carried in economically efficient supertankers must be landed close to markets on the East Coast. More energy facilities such as refineries, terminals, and monobuoys (offshore pipeline connections for tankers) are needed if America's use of foreign oil continues. Floating installations have been planned because onshore sites are becoming scarce. Environmental opposition to building coastal energy facilities is based on the fear of damage to marine ecosystems, wildlife habitats and populations, the threat to fishing industries, and the diminishing of beach access, open space, and aesthetic grandeur. The Sears Island case illustrated the nature of complex land-use and sea-use decision making.

The Storm King controversy was one of the nation's most important administrative law cases in recent decades. The landmark decision on the first major suit in the case conferred standing on the environmental groups and set a precedent for later litigation in environmental law. But neither the environmentalists, Con Ed, nor power consumers in New York finally won the case; after more than a decade, the dispute is still not completely reconciled. Environmentalists have been gratified to the extent that the Hudson Gorge is still undeveloped, but continued litigation is required to prevent the Con Ed proposal. The public still has little or no opportunity to participate in planning through the administrative channels of the Federal Power Commission. The Storm King case reveals the increasing energy demands of the nation's urban areas and some of the environmental consequences of energy production. The case also demonstrates the inadequacy of fragmented regulation of power development in the United States.

Bodega Head was the site of one of the first of many citizen challenges to a major power installation. The local community was not prepared to assume the risks posed by safety hazards associated with a nuclear reactor near a geological fault line. The residents of Bodega Bay were also determined to preserve the scenic quality and tranquility of rapidly diminishing coastal open space. The conflict was symbolic of the larger land-use question facing every part of the nation. There was no planning agency in California or at the federal level that had the responsibility to correlate programs for siting energy facilities while protecting natural areas and open space. Californians have attempted, through mechanisms such as the California Coastal Zone Conservation Commission and a proposed voter initiative on a nuclear power moratorium for the state, to regulate energy-environment problems during the early 1970s.

Eugene's Future Power Committee's efforts to postpone the construction of a nuclear power plant were in some ways unique, but they addressed a problem common to many communities. Without thorough and scientific studies of the full economic, ecological, and social consequences of constructing and operating nuclear power plants, utility companies press communities into accepting them. Citizens are generally unaware of the implications of such decisions, and few citizens analyze the developers' rationale for projects that are advertised as vital to economic progress. Eugene discovered that power facility proposals were almost exclusively intended to serve industrial expansion; regional industrial expansion was given priority over community needs. The plight of Eugene paralleled the problems of communities in the Southwest and Great Plains which must bear the costs of energy extraction, development, and environmental degradation while the energy is being consumed in distant markets that have rejected polluting energy facilities within their own surroundings.

In the case of the citizens' groups versus the Connecticut Public Utility Commission, the petitioners, challenging the validity of the commission's order allowing HELCO to maintain decreasing rate structures and promotional sales activities, were aware of the inadequacy of yesterday's regulatory ideals. These ideals do not suit today's social and environmental circumstances or concerns. Connecticut's regulatory commission is one of a majority of state utility commissions that are maintaining traditional practices. In contrast, about twenty regulatory commissions have taken steps to eliminate or reduce quantity discounts in the interest of energy conservation. Many commissions have also acted against advertising and sales promotion by refusing to allow these costs to be included as expense items. The attorneys general in Massachusetts and North Carolina have testified before state commissions, disapproving quantity discount practices.

In the future, the relationship between policies for energy development and environmental management may be greatly influenced by the federal administration's "Project Independence," the goal of which is to become independent of foreign energy supplies, particularly Arab oil, by the 1980s. Using more domestic coal is one alternative, but tripling of coal production and harnessing coal gasification technology by 1985 have serious implications for the strippable, low-sulphur coal reserves in the West. The energy industry appears determined to develop the coal reserves of the Great Plains and to phase out the deep mines of Appalachia and the East. Already strip-mine productivity is at least three times the productivity of deep mines. But the higher water content and lower BTU rating of western coal over eastern coal means more of it must be burned to provide equivalent heat. Proposals to transport the power by slurry pipelines, overhead electric transmission lines, and by rail to midwest and eastern markets have economic, social, and environmental implications of enormous magnitude. Moreover, the allocation of scarce water supplies in semiarid areas of the West presents difficult economic and political issues if water is diverted from present uses to energy production. What has become known as the "East-West dispute" is being argued in state legislatures and in Congress.

Proposals to gradually convert the nation's energy base to nuclear power (60 percent of total power by 1990) also have profound economic, social, and environmental implications. The federal government, the nuclear energy industry, and environmentalists are continually involved in debate and litigation in efforts to influence policy. (See Chapter 7, The Economy and Growth.) It appears that at local, state, and federal levels environmental protection groups are gathering political support for their challenge to the liquid-metal fast-breeder reactor (LMFBR) program, which proposes that at least 1,000 nuclear reactors be in operation by the year 2000. The consequences of this proposal for safety, land use, the disposal of radioactive residuals, and thermal pollution are enormous. Public awareness of the issues and extensive participation in decision making are essential to maintain institutional accountability and to protect the public interest in these policy matters.

Readings

Caldwell, Lynton K. "Energy and the Environment: The Bases of Public Policy." *The Annals of the Academy of Political and Social Sciences,* 410 (November 1973), 127–138.
———. "The Energy Crisis and Environmental Law: Paradox of Conflict and Reinforcement." *New York Forum,* 20 (Number 4, 1975).
Fletcher, Katherine and Malcolm F. Baldwin, eds. *A Scientific and Policy Review of the Prototype Oil Shale Leasing Program: Final Environmental Impact Statement of the U.S. Department of the Interior.* Washington, D.C.: The Institute of Ecology, 1973.
Garvey, Gerald. *Energy, Ecology, Economy: A Framework for Environmental Policy.* New York: W. W. Norton, 1972.
Miller, G. Tyler. *Energy and Environment: Four Energy Crises.* Belmont, California: Wadsworth Publishing, 1975.
Nelkin, Dorothy. *Nuclear Power and Its Critics: The Cayuga Lake Controversy.* Ithaca: Cornell University Press, 1971.
Noone, James A. "Energy Issues Threaten Recent Environmental Gains." *National Journal Reports,* 6 (March 2, 1974), 305–308.
Permar, David, II. "A Legal Solution to the Electric Power Crisis: Controlling Demand Through Regulation of Advertising, Promotion, and Rate Structure." *Environmental Affairs,* 1 (November 1971), 670–693.
Scheffer, Walter F., ed. *Energy Impacts on Public Policy and Administration.* Norman: University of Oklahoma Press, 1974.
Steinhart, Carol and John. *Energy: Source, Use, and Policy in Human Affairs.* North Scituate, Massachusetts: Duxbury Press, 1974.
Yannacone, Victor John, Jr. *Energy Crisis: Danger and Opportunity.* New York: West Publishing, 1974.

7

The Economy and Growth

Introduction

Unfettered growth of the economy, an increasing population, more intensive use of technology, and accelerated use of energy and other resources have produced some unwanted side effects. The awesome costs of environmental degradation and repair face the nation like a mammoth unpaid public debt. Paradoxically, the quality of life in the United States has decreased as material prosperity has grown. More than 100 million tons of fly ash, carbon monoxide, and poisonous particulates are spewed into the air each year. By 1990, the amount of sunlight reaching the earth could be dangerously reduced by air pollution, and that situation might seriously modify the planet's climate. Physicians advise thousands of patients a year to leave urban areas because of health hazards caused by air pollution. Chemical wastes from industry and agriculture have all but ruined Lake Erie and many of the nation's waterways, and they leave marine life in coastal zones critically affected. Mammoth recycling programs are desperately needed to cope with the 4.3 billion tons of solid waste produced by the economic system each year.

Landscapes are being increasingly degraded as a result of mineral extraction, hydroelectric projects, stream channelization, highway projects, airport projects, and the spread of urban areas. Open space, free-flowing rivers, and wildlife habitats have been destroyed by sprawling human settlements and industrial development. Industrialization and wasteful energy consumption have rapidly depleted known supplies of fossil fuels, copper, iron, chromium, silver, and nickel. These symptoms and others point to a basic weakness in the economic system: unplanned, excessive growth is destructive.

The economy has been enormously productive and destructive at the same time. Economic history offers some explanation of the paradox. Individual material prosperity was the primary goal of American frontiersmen, and the means to this end was to exploit the economic potential of natural resources. Moreover, from the time of land grants and timber franchises, government policies fostered development of the nation's natural resources. But the United States was by no means unique in this attitude. Economic theories popular in the western world have promoted private ownership of resources, recommended the profit motive as an assurance of business efficiency and innovation, and justified the market-pricing mechanism as the most efficient means of regulating the supply and demand for goods and services. More recently, the economic theories of John Maynard Keynes have been a dominant force behind an ethic of growth-mania. Some economists have assumed that the aggregate wants of the population are infinite and should be served by making aggregate production infinite. The total economic pie (GNP) was to be made bigger so that everyone could have more of it. This materialistic view has been significantly advanced by a corporate business culture. The business-value bias of such groups as chambers of commerce may have played a more dominant role in urging limitless economic growth than have economists. But economic growth is also a firm principle in most socialist theories.

The belief that resources were unlimited and that exploitive behavior was acceptable underlay what Kenneth Boulding termed a "cowboy economy." Many continue to believe that maximizing consumption and production (GNP) is the ultimate measure of success for the economy. This attitude has shaped numerous government policies which have the specific goal of enhancing economic growth. Government promotion of maximum employment, production, and purchasing power are goals expressed in the Employment Act of 1946. Other goals such as an adequate rate of growth, support of price levels, and a favorable balance of payments are also considered vital to the national economy. The government provides subsidies to industry that encourage growth: for example, depletion allowances, capital-gains shelters, direct grants, and low-interest government bank loans. Government agencies promote hydroelectric projects and the private use of nuclear energy; and highway projects have been subsidized by roughly $4 billion annually through the Highway Trust Fund.

The economy of the pioneer and the economy of unlimited and indiscriminate growth characteristically have been evaluated by means of principles and analytical techniques that do not measure the full costs and consequences of economic programs. An obsession with GNP growth excludes consideration of the costs of enormous waste production and the finite supply of resources: using the GNP as the common measure of growth is misleading. The GNP is used to measure the output of the economy and is not a suitable mechanism for measuring economic well-being. The cost of cleaning air, purifying streams, collecting solid wastes, building freeways to relieve congestion, and paving over open space for airports are all calculated in the GNP, along with the production of wheat and steel.

Large capital investments (for example, in dam projects) have required foregoing present consumption in favor of estimated future gains. For such projects, an interest rate or discount rate was struck to calculate a cost-benefit ratio. While cost-benefit analysis is a valuable means of assessing a project's desirability, too often artificially low discount rates have been approved by the government in order to justify projects that might otherwise be abandoned. Moreover, there have been many difficulties in calculating a ratio of total costs to total benefits. Traditionally, "intangibles" such as public health, the beauty of the landscape, or wildlife values that are not easily quantifiable were given little or no attention in cost-benefit analyses.

Because public goods such as unique natural areas were not adequately allocated by the price mechanism, many such "priceless" resources have been overexploited. "Free goods" such as air and water were not quantifiable either, and they often became receptacles for disposal of wastes. Poisoning the air with contaminants and rendering rivers biological deserts were considered "externalities," or secondary effects, of economic progress, and were given little weight in cost calculations. New accounting techniques are required in economics to include environmental costs. Even a simple, two-column, "full benefits" and "full costs" system that considered environmental, social, and economic criteria would open issues to public scrutiny and question.

Many economic policies and practices of the government reduce the full production costs of industrial activities and encourage resource depletion. The government has interfered with the price mechanism in some industries to the detriment of efficient resource use. For instance, most public utility commissions keep energy prices artificially low for big users by pricing structures that encourage inefficient use. Electricity consumption has been rising by 8 percent annually, but there have been almost no increases in the price for twenty years.

Many other industries also enjoy government-regulated, fixed-price structures that prevent competitive pricing, even though competitive pricing would help reduce excess capacity in many of the nation's leading industrial sectors. Tax subsidies, in the form of resource depletion allowances, stimulate the exploitation of oil, timber, coal, and other natural materials. Industries have also been allowed to discharge wastes and produce thermal pollution almost cost free.

Neither the price mechanism nor the government can control the efficient use of resources while exponential growth proceeds uncontrolled. The rate of growth of the nation's economy compounds problems because it is a "compounding" rate. The fixed percentage increase rate is analogous to the compound interest of a bank account. The GNP compounds at a rate of 4 to 5 percent annually, doubling every twenty years. Short periods of doubling time are a special feature of exponential growth.

Economists are divided among themselves as to what the ultimate goals of the American economy should be. The "cowboy economy" emphasizes maximizing production and consumption. A new breed of economists, however, believing in what Kenneth Boulding calls a "spaceman economy," is rapidly growing in numbers. Their view is that since all resources are limited, resource utilization and pollution should also be limited; the economy must be maintained in harmony with, not at the expense of, the ecological system. These economists measure the total stock of human and nonhuman resources and propose what they call a steady-state economy. Their revolutionary concept argues the necessity of maintaining a constant stock of capital and production and a constant stock of people. A steady-state economy would maintain lower rates of production and consumption in harmony with environmental limitations. In such an economic system, ecologists would advise economists on rates of pollution and resource depletion that are tolerable in a finite ecosystem.

Economic planners are faced with a dilemma. Growth must be continued for some reasons but reduced for others. For example, to keep the unemployment rate from exceeding 6 percent (the 1971 level), the economy must accommodate more entrants to the labor force each year, until at least 1985, than it ever accommodated in any year of the nation's history. Economists differ on the ability of the economy to realize the high rate of growth necessary to accomplish this employment goal. If current living patterns continue, the energy-generating capacity of the economy must continue to grow at a high rate for at least a decade to supply the anticipated demand for electricity. The increasing costs of pollution control, mass transportation systems, and huge investment programs to develop new energy technologies require billions of dollars that can be generated, in the short run, only through economic growth. But on the other hand, the need to stop the degradation of the environment and enhance the quality of life requires that the exponential growth rate of the economy be reduced.

The public is aware of many of the symptoms of stress brought about by uncontrolled exponential growth. The symptoms of conflict between fundamental economic and environmental policies are obvious, but few of the causes are understood. There is little consensus on what should be done to alleviate the problem. It is not yet clear whether the public is ready to pay the higher taxes needed to clean up past ecological degradation or to accept the reordered priorities of a steady-state economy. But there is ample evidence to show that the traditional counter-ecological trend of the economy is being confronted with a growing trend of critical sentiment.

An increasing proportion of the public is now questioning the traditional compulsion toward indiscriminate growth, and is protesting the environmental deterioration caused by unguided growth. More and more people realize that deleterious consequences of rampant growth may outweigh its benefits. For example, citizens are objecting to the environmentally damaging placement of new power plants even at a time when energy supply is at a critical point. There are numerous instances of citizens protesting the wasteful principles of built-in obsolescence and throwaway convenience. Protests against the manufacture of certain chemicals, insecticides, herbicides, and detergents have challenged the traditional prodevelopment bias of the economy. Witness the conflicts over mining rights, oil drilling and pipelines, supersonic transport, the expansion of highway systems, dams, ship canals, and urbanization generally. Some citizens are attempting to limit the influx of population and to control economic growth in their communities. Others are challenging the economic concept of land as a commodity, while still others are pointing out the weaknesses in conventional economic tools of measurement such as cost-benefit analysis. The environmental movement seems to be contributing to a new concept of growth that is organic and renewing—not indefinitely expansive and hypertrophic.[1]

CASE I   Technology: The Supersonic Transport

One important way to strengthen the economic capabilities of a nation is to improve the technical efficiency of its industrial processes. Since the technological capability of an economy depends upon its stock of machines and technical knowledge, the research and development of new technologies is an expensive but vital function. One industry in which the United States has led the world with technological sophistication is the aerospace industry; and our superior aerospace technology has been a cornerstone of national economic growth. American aerospace technology has put men on the moon, created the world's most luxurious airline system, provided millions of jobs, and generated billions of dollars in foreign exchange from sales of equipment overseas. In the early 1960s, the aerospace industry intended the next great advance in aviation technology to be the supersonic transport airplane (SST).

An airplane traveling faster than sound is called supersonic. The SST, planned by the Boeing Company and associated manufacturers, was to carry almost 300 passengers at an altitude of 64,000 feet and a cruising speed of 1,800 mph. Air-traveling time would have been cut in half. Construction of prototype designs and preparation of inventions

[1] See Lynton K. Caldwell, "Environmental Policy in a Hypertrophic Society," in *Natural Resources Journal*, 11 (July, 1971), pp. 417–426; and M. Mesarovic and E. Pestel, *Mankind at the Turning Point: The Second Report to the Club of Rome.* New York: E. P. Dutton/Reader's Digest Press, 1974.

of spare parts for a final model was estimated to cost $4 billion. Both aerospace manfacturers and airline companies anticipated handsome profits, and at least 200,000 new jobs would be created throughout the nation. The project would provide a "multiplying" and "rippling" effect throughout the economy that would stimulate more material prosperity. President Kennedy embraced the plan to "get America moving again." In competition with the European Concorde SST and the Soviet T4–144 SST, the U.S. SST would prevent losses up to $11 billion if U.S. airlines were to buy foreign supersonics. Gains in the balance of payments and national prestige were eagerly sought by the White House and the Congress.

At first, most Americans, including three presidents, welcomed the new advance in aerospace technology and the promises of progress and increased material prosperity. The SST project would be a symbol of challenge to Nikita Krushchev's vow that the Soviet economic system would "bury" America. But a number of scientists, economists, ecologists, and groups of citizens, after studying the economics of the SST and its impact on the quality of life, began to question its advisability. On a transcontinental flight from New York to California sonic booms would disturb an area fifty miles wide for more than 2,000 miles. Energetic shockwaves would strike buildings, people, and all life throughout the 100,000 square mile area affected by the sonic boom; and some ecologists feared the adverse impact on wildlife and also on commercially valuable species of animals and fish. Some scientists thought that an age of supersonic airplanes might have long-term effects on the stratosphere which could produce climatological changes because massive water vapor accumulations, due to fuel combustion, would alter the balance of atmospheric gases. Toxic pollutants from fuel burning would also increase air pollution near airports. Citizens began to question the estimated $60 million-per-plane price tag and the unconvincing projection figures that were being used to justify the project economically.

The controversy surrounding the SST program highlighted the aircraft noise pollution issue that had been considered, but consistently rejected, in Congress for more than a decade. Excessive noise is injurious to human health; evidence to this effect was massive but not widely known. Noise pollution from transcontinental jet flights and particularly on the flight paths in spreading urban areas had already been a source of public protest and had developed into a national political issue. The SST program threatened to exacerbate the problem. Through the period of the SST policy conflict, a significant portion of the American people was made aware of the costs in the quality of life that would have to be paid for the material benefits of economic growth. The SST program was eventually rejected.

The Actors

Presidents Kennedy, Johnson, and Nixon and their administrations all supported the SST program. Secretary Volpe of the Department of Transportation (DOT) and high ranking officers of his department urged members of Congress to support the SST. The Federal Aviation Administration (FAA) and its former head, General William F. McKee, pressured the White House to support the project. DOT and the FAA were perhaps the staunchest promoters, together with the aerospace industry, of the SST project and were powerful policy participants. The Air Line Pilots Association (ALPA), Air Transport Association (ATA), the Association of Machinists and Aerospace Workers, the AFL-CIO, manufacturers, and subcontractors pressed for the completion of the SST program. A promotional organization, the National Committee for the American SST, was established by promoters to "sell" the project to the nation. Leaders of both political parties and U.S. Senators Warren G. Magnuson and Henry M. Jackson of Washington, the state that had the most to gain from Boeing contract expenditures, favored the SST and wielded significant political influence in the Congress.

U.S. Senator William Proxmire of Wisconsin and Congressman Sidney Yates of Illinois were strong opponents of the SST. Many other congressmen championed efforts to have the Congress pass legislation controlling the sonic boom and noise pollution effects of the SST project. Of concern to congressmen opposed to the SST were its unfavorable environmental implications (noise pollution, annoyance factor, possible stratospheric damage), its shaky economic justification, and the heavy dependence of industry on government funding of the program. A number of groups rejected the argument that the nation must accept the sonic boom as a price of progress: the National Aircraft Noise Abatement Council, the National Academy of Sciences, the National Academy of Surgeons, the American Speech and Hearing Association, the Wilderness Society, the New York City Council, and the City Council of Santa Barbara, California.

The leading citizens' groups opposing the SST were the Sierra Club, the Citizens' League Against the Sonic Boom (CLASB), and the Coalition Against the SST. Formed by William A. Shurchiff in March 1967, the CLASB became a dominant force in the policy process. By disseminating scientific information throughout the nation, by using expert witnesses at congressional hearings, and by maintaining contact with the media, CLASB directed nationwide attention to the SST issues. Major federations of scientists and environmentalists joined CLASB within two years of its foundation. The joint forces working through CLASB and the Coalition Against the SST had such a significant impact on Congress' final decision that Senator Proxmire credited environmental activists with the victory.

The Policy Process

The controversy over the SST lasted a little more than a decade, although the conflict over noise pollution from aircraft and related noise abatement questions preceded the SST issue. The duration of the conflict can be roughly separated into two phases. The first phase (1959–68) was characterized by a general national commitment to the economic progress that the SST allegedly would generate. During the second phase (1968–71), citizens became involved in public decision making and questioned the conventional assumptions regarding economic growth and progress. Popular views about the benefits and costs to society of the economic growth inherent in the so-called advances in aerospace technology changed dramatically between 1967 and 1969.

The government first became interested in developing a commercial SST early in 1960. The FAA's Bureau of Flight Standards established a Supersonic Transport Group to study the air worthiness and the operations and maintenance aspects of the SST. In a report to the FAA in early 1961 this group recommended continuing government and industry research on the SST. By late 1962, the FAA's Supersonic Transport Advisory Group strongly urged the federal government to share with industry the costs of developing a commercial SST.

During this period (1960–62) Congress had been exploring the need for an SST. Aerospace superiority was not only prestigious, it was also a significant factor in the balance of payments of the national economy. In August 1961, Congress appropriated $11 million for the first year of a two-year exploratory research program. In January 1963, President Kennedy created a cabinet-level coordinating committee for the SST program. Short-term research contracts were given to Boeing and Lockheed. In mid-1963, Pan American Airlines made a public announcement that stimulated the federal government to make a formal commitment to the commercial SST program. Pan American announced that it was going to purchase six foreign-made Concorde SSTs. In June 1963, fearful of the adverse effects such a purchase would have on the nation's balance of payments, President Kennedy called for the commencement of a domestic SST design and construction program that he described as "essential to a strong and forward-looking nation." In November Congress voted $60 million for SST design research.

Now committed to an SST, the federal government embarked on a contract with industry. The government was to subsidize development of the commercial SST and also to share royalties on sales under certain conditions. Initially, 75 percent of development costs were to be met by the government and the balance by industry. By July 1965, no satisfactory design had been proposed, and President Johnson ordered another eighteen months of design competition. SST promoters hoped the government would eventually inject $1.1 billion into preliminary development—90 percent—and that industry would pay 10 percent. Beyond the stage of prototypes and preliminaries, another $3.3 billion would be needed to produce an operating SST. It was obvious that manufacturers and airlines wanted government to assume the enormous financial risks of the project.

The second phase of policy with regard to the SST began about the time CLASB was formed in March 1967. The group made rigorous studies of research in supersonic transports, carried out by Bo Lundberg of the Aeronautical Research Institute of Sweden. Lundberg's research revealed a wealth of information about the economic, engineering, ecological, and social impacts of SSTs. CLASB also analysed information published in government reports on sonic boom tests carried out over St. Louis, Oklahoma City, Chicago, and in California between 1961 and 1968. These tests, which used supersonic military planes smaller than the proposed SST, revealed scientific measurements of sonic booms, the extent of and cost of damages, and the extent of damage suits claimed by the public. The estimates of prospective population disturbance and damage to buildings were enormous. In May 1967, Senator William Proxmire, the leading senatorial opponent of the SST, wrote a congratulatory letter to CLASB members thanking them for the research data he had been sent. In September of 1967, the Sierra Club announced its opposition to supersonic flights over land. Soon the Environmental Defense Fund, the Massachusetts Audubon Society, the Friends of the Earth, the National Audubon Society, and other environmental groups also actively opposed the threat of SST's sonic booms. The CLASB worked in close cooperation with these groups, providing them with technical information. Many of the most important reports, articles, and news releases written or collected by the CLASB were reprinted and distributed widely—to 200 leading newspapers, to fifty leading columnists, to fifty TV and radio stations, to congressmen, and to key government agencies. In some instances, sixty FFA officials and twenty Boeing officials received CLASB literature. Early in 1969, the director of CLASB spoke to the president's Ad Hoc SST Review Committee. Over 100,000 copies of a source book, *SST and Sonic Boom Handbook,* edited by CLASB founder William Shurcliff, were sold or distributed free in the United States and Europe.

Aircraft noise from jet traffic had been an issue of growing public concern for some time. Between 1960 and 1968 almost one hundred bills directed at aircraft noise abatement had been introduced in the Congress. As demands for expensive appropriation increases for the SST program mounted in Congress, so did demands for congressional resolution of the noise pollution issue. In the summer of 1968, environmentalists, some members of Congress, many city and county officials, civic groups, and other critics of the SST were pleased to see passage of the Aircraft Noise Abatement Act (H.R. 3400). The new act placed President Johnson's administration in a dilemma. The FAA had already committed hundreds of millions of dollars to SST development, but the new noise abatement legislation directed the government to consider the abatement of excessive aircraft noise.

Before and after the passage of the act, the FAA was approached many times by citizens' groups and congressmen appealing to the agency to impose a ban on SST flight over land. The FAA appeared to ignore the Aircraft Noise Abatement Act, and chose to ignore local bans on sonic booms established in Santa Barbara, California, and Dearborn, Michigan, in 1967. CLASB continued to monitor the actions of the FAA and Department of Transportation and to broadcast news of current developments at every opportunity.

A number of government studies and reports on the economic, social, and environmental impacts of the SST had significant influence on the debate during 1968–69. Secretary of Interior Stewart Udall had appointed a team of scientists to study the effects of noise and the sonic boom on man. Although their report found that many contentions about the sonic boom were based on emotion, prejudice, and scanty evidence, it also warned that the political, psychological, and socio- logical reaction of the American people to the sonic boom could force curtailment of overland SST flights. In his first month in office, President Nixon directed the Department of Transportation to investigate all aspects of the SST program. But this step appeared to be equivalent to using a fox to guard the chicken coop. A 1968 Senate appropriation of $142 million, voted by a majority of fifty-four to nineteen, was one of the last victories for the SST proponents.

Subsequently, the president appointed an interdepartmental Ad Hoc SST Review Committee which reported its findings in March 1969. The report was withheld from the public for more than six months, and was at last released on October 31. The committee report was funda- mentally critical of the SST program, and President Nixon ignored the conclusions of this report in September 1969, when he urged that the SST program should continue. The committee report gave ammunition to the overwhelming public doubt and mounting opposition to the program.

Panels of the review committee disputed the argument that the bal- ance of payments would be favorable, and they were dismayed by un- verifiable economic judgments and differing opinions of economic experts. The committee viewed the prospective damages to the environ- ment as serious, and panelists questioned whether Americans would ever accept sonic booms as a part of "progress." The committee criti- cized the FAA for playing a dual role as promoter of the SST and guard- ian of aviation safety. Dr. Lee DuBridge, director of the Office of Sci- ence and Technology, deplored the government subsidy of the SST, which he felt was neither commercially attractive nor publicly accepted. Undersecretary of Interior Russell Train was alarmed by the lack of positive justification for the SST and by the threat of further environ- mental deterioration. Assistant Secretary of Labor Arnold Welser claimed that the uncertainty of economic benefits from the SST gave no economic grounds for developing the project further.

By early 1970, the major opponents of the SST, such as Friends of the Earth, the Sierra Club, and CLASB, were joined by a large segment of the press in questioning the logic of the program. By the summer of 1970, serious concern was being widely expressed about the estimates of atmospheric pollution from the exhaust of the sst. Many senators opposed the project, and they supported citizens and ecologists in December 1970 with a fifty-two to forty-one vote against further funding. Widespread publicity showed nationwide doubts about the feasibility and desirability of the program.

To counter the tide of protest, sst backers organized a promotional group in January 1971 known as the National Committee for an American sst. By distributing bumper stickers and arranging an extensive newspaper and magazine advertising campaign, the promotional group tried to sell the sst to the American public. sst backers urged subcontractors to the aerospace manufacturers to put pressure on receptive state politicians.

Outcome

But in March 1971, after almost ten years of supporting the sst with government funds, the House of Representatives voted 215 to 204 against further appropriations. After having committed $864 million to the sst, the government discontinued financing the project. At this point, the sst was still two years and $436 million away from the completion of its prototype. In the early months of 1971, Capitol Hill had been engulfed in mail on the sst. Senator Proxmire, the arch congressional opponent of the sst, credited the persistent economic and ecological arguments of citizens' groups as the major cause of defeat of the supersonic transport program.

CASE II   Subsidized Growth: Rampart Dam, Alaska

Alaska, the largest state in the union, is populated by less than a half million people. In 1960, the average population density for the United States was 60 people per square mile; Alaska's was only 0.4 people per square mile. More than half of the working people in the state were military personnel or civilian state or federal employees— all paid from public funds. Alaska's economy has long been dependent on the expenditure of public funds, and its rate of growth has always lagged behind the rates of the lower forty-eight states. Remoteness from national markets and high labor costs have deterred industrial development. Over much of Alaska, harsh climatic conditions and a comparatively high cost of living with relatively few cultural amenities have deterred population expansion through immigration.

Consequently, the potential annual yield from a forest harvest of three billion board-feet and the abundant natural gas, copper, and oil resources have been developed very slowly. Fish and wildlife resources traditionally have provided a major part of the economic base of the state, but they have not held the key to rapid economic expansion. The tourist and recreational resources of the state have been utilized very slowly. Most Alaskans, and a considerable number of federal agencies, have striven to release the economic potential of the state for decades. Prior to the trans-Alaska pipeline proposal, the boldest plan to stimulate the development of Alaska, was the Rampart Dam project, which came from the U.S. Army Corps of Engineers in 1960.

Rampart Dam was to be constructed on the Yukon River. A wall, 530 feet high and 4,700 feet long, would hold back a water surface area of 10,000 square miles. Larger than Lake Erie, it would have become the largest artificial lake in the world. The project would have cost up to $2.8 billion. Following completion of the dam, waters would continue to rise for at least twenty years until the dam was filled. Designed to produce 34.2 billion kilowatt-hours of hydroelectricity annually (almost three times the capacity of Grand Coulee Dam), Rampart Dam would have generated fifty times the amount of energy required by the state of Alaska in 1960.

The ecological costs of the dam would have been extremely high. More than 400 miles of the mainstream Yukon, 12,000 miles of tributaries, and 36,000 lakes and ponds in the Yukon Flats would have been flooded. Spawning areas for anadromous fish would have been destroyed, and the habitats for waterfowl, moose, bear, and fur-bearing animals would have been inundated. The dam would have negated a thirty-year national endeavor in waterfowl preservation in the Yukon Flats, which are the annual breeding grounds for at least two million ducks, geese, and cranes from all the major North American flyways. Subsistence fishing by local inhabitants and the pelt-harvesting industry would also have been seriously damaged, and the ancestral homes and hunting grounds of the Venetie and Chalkytsik Indians would have been covered by the impounded waters.

Alaska's most distinctive resources are spectacularly beautiful open spaces, wildlife, and natural areas, yet these resources have historically commanded a low priority in comparison with the potential economic returns from timber, minerals, and cheap electric power. Although some Alaskans were eager to protect and preserve their magnificent natural resources, other Alaskans demanded immediate material prosperity, which was assumed to follow industrialization. But in Alaska, industrialization required a greatly increased labor force, larger consumer markets within the state, and access to the markets of the nation. A catalyst for economic growth was sought, and developers at the state and federal level saw hydroelectric power as the answer. It was thought that construction of the Rampart Dam would provide the state's economy with a necessary boost. The project, therefore, could have served a major part of its economic purpose even if the dam had been destroyed the day after its completion.

In the view of certain Alaskans, as well as critics in the lower forty-eight states, the dam proposal was extremely unsound and unwise. Numerous conservation groups and some forward-thinking personnel in government agencies raised fundamental value questions about objectives, costs, and benefits of the project.

The Actors

The Army Corps of Engineers, which had developed the project, was naturally one of its staunchest promoters. The Department of Interior had principal jurisdiction over the project, but it shared some responsibilities with the Department of the Army in evaluating the power market and natural resources aspects of the Rampart Dam project. On the authority of the Fish and Wildlife Coordination Act of 1934, the U.S. Fish and Wildlife Service prepared reports on the project's impact on wildlife. A number of consultants' economic reports on Alaska's development also had a significant impact on the final policy outcome. The most influential of these reports came from the Battelle Memorial Institute, Arthur D. Little, Incorporated, of Massachusetts, the Resources Development Corporation of New York, and the University of Michigan.

The governor of Alaska, the mayors of the principal cities in the state, and U.S. Senator Ernest Gruening were leaders of a majority of state, governmental and political proponents of the project. Yukon Power for America (YPA), a nonprofit public relations and lobbying organization, established solely to press for political support for Rampart Dam, spearheaded a powerful band of supporters.

The primary state conservation group urging a full examination of the economic, social, and ecological impact of the project was the Alaska Conservation Society (ACS). The diligent work of ACS, and of national conservation organizations within the Natural Resources Council of America, in publicizing the inadequacy of the scientific and economic justifications for the project probably had the most significant influence on the Department of Interior's final decision not to propose Rampart Dam to Congress.

The Policy Process

The Army Corps of Engineers first suggested the Rampart Dam proposal in College, Alaska, in 1959. Arguing that almost unlimited electric power could be generated in Alaska, the corps held that power-intensive, electro-process industries would be willing to locate in the state. Industries such as aluminum processing would find that importing necessary materials to Alaska was economically feasible because cheap power would offset transportation costs. Excess power could be transmitted 2,000 miles to the rapidly industrializing Pacific Northwest. Construction alone would bring $60 million to the state annually, and the population was expected to double many times in a few years.

From 1960 on, the proponents of "growth at any cost" were in conflict with the proponents of "planned growth." The latter, inaccurately tagged as "duck lovers" and "selfish conservationists," stressed the need to analyse all aspects of the Rampart project before making final decisions. The policy process was dominated by the actions of these two blocks of participants. Since the final decision on Rampart Dam rested with the Department of Interior, both groups worked incessantly to gain credibility and enough public support to influence policy. In the meantime, the Department of Interior coordinated numerous feasibility studies. Through the years, the strategies of the two major policy participants, the conservationists and the developers, highlighted the course of events.

The Alaska Conservation Society was formed in February 1960, specifically to monitor economic growth. As population and consequent economic development increased in Alaska, the ACS anticipated conflicts about the best way to use many areas. The ACS wished to present an alternative to the values of immediate financial gain. In May 1961, the ACS published a critical analysis of the ramifications of Rampart Dam. The analysis posed fundamental value questions about the nature and alternatives of progress for the state that were to underlie all future ACS statements about the project.

How much should Alaska grow and in what directions? Should we continue to dedicate ourselves to the increase in number and nearness of our neighbors and the rate at which we exchange money? Can we decide on a point of diminishing returns, beyond which the addition of a thousand people only divides the economic pie into more pieces, and where each population increase means the sacrifice of some personal liberty or inward ease? What should we emphasize as our basis of prosperity?[2]

The ACS strongly questioned the rationale for building Rampart Dam and the feasibility of industrial proposals. It recommended economic expansion based on wisely managed natural resources and tourism. The ACS's regularly published *News Bulletin* and other periodic news releases were mailed to every legislator, government agency, and citizens' group of political significance. The critical task of publicizing information on Rampart policy development was ably carried out by the ACS. The second strategy of the group was to call for a wait-and-see approach from all decision makers. Until the scientific analyses, expected to be provided by the Corps of Engineers and the consultants, were made available, the ACS argued, promotion of the project was premature and inappropriate.

By late 1960, most members of the Alaskan legislature supported the Rampart project. Then, in early 1961, the Arthur D. Little report on the industrial possibilities for Alaska came as a dowsing of icewater to Rampart supporters. The Little report declared the Rampart plan unrealistic. In response, the Army Corps of Engineers, in consultation with Rampart promoters, immediately commissioned the Development and Resources Corporation of New York to compile a report dealing specifically with the market for Rampart power. The report was just what the promoters sought, recommending prompt commencement of the project.

The local and state governments and chambers of commerce in Alaska supported the Rampart plan with hysterical fervor. In September 1963, the first joint meeting of the city councils of Anchorage and Fairbanks formed a promotional group for Rampart Dam known as Yukon Power for America, Incorporated (YPA). A month later, the Anchorage City Council appropriated $10,000 to fund YPA in order to sell the concept of Rampart Dam to Congress and the nation. In January 1964, H.B. 243 was introduced in the Alaska legislature. It proposed that

[2] Alaska Conservation Society. *News Bulletin,* 2 (May 1961), p. 16.

$12,000 be appropriated to run an animated display and to distribute literature on the dam project at the New York World's Fair in 1964–65. Rampart Dam promoters saw this as one more way of selling the project to the nation.

Opposition to the project, however, was not dormant. An October 1963 meeting of Yukon Flats communities declared opposition to the project. A survey conducted by the *Tundra Times* in November 1963 confirmed that villagers above and below the dam site opposed the project. Throughout 1963, the ACS kept a flood of news releases and editorials in circulation, and in February 1964, an ACS press release was submitted to the state legislature for consideration. The press release clearly demonstrated that available data showed the costs of the project outweighed its benefits. The legislature was criticized for using public funds to support the Rampart promoters through YPA. The citizens' group also raised critical questions that had not been faced in detail in previous studies: the climatic changes due to Rampart Dam should be investigated; damage payments to residents must be included in costs; and without extensive mitigational projects, wildlife resources would be irreparably damaged. The protesters also pointed out that it was impossible to estimate marketing feasibility for power demands fifteen to twenty years away. An editorial by the vice-president of ACS, appearing in its *News Bulletin* of December 1964, clearly demonstrated, on the basis of scholarly research, that the prodam thesis of competitive power from Rampart Dam was not valid.

The U.S. Fish and Wildlife Service's report on the fish and wildlife resources that would be affected by Rampart Dam was published in April 1964. The report implied that the dam's influence on wild animals and fish, their habitat, and on the people who depended on them for sustenance or enjoyment was so disastrous that the project should not be commenced. This report was strongly criticized by Senator Gruening and the governor of Alaska, and the YPA immediately planned to prepare an analysis to contradict it. Soon after, ACS published data that showed the transmission of excess high voltage power to the Pacific Northwest was not feasible.

In July 1964, at the instigation of the Boone and Crockett Club of New York City, the Natural Resources Council of America (NRCA), together with some of the nation's most prestigious and influential conservation organizations, took a positive role in the policy process. The NRCA's member organizations funded a research group from the

University of Michigan to investigate both the ecological and economic consequences of Rampart Dam. Released early in 1966, the Michigan study used scientific evidence to support the view that the dam should not be authorized. It described the Rampart project as the most expensive gamble ever suggested in hydroelectric development, with little evidence to indicate a high probability of success. The Michigan report spelled doom for this ill-conceived scheme.

The final phase of the policy conflict began with the publication of the Department of Interior's field report on the project in January 1965. The promoters of Rampart Dam received no encouragement from the field report, which revealed that potential mineral deposits in Alaska had been exaggerated, that low-cost power would not lead to resource development, and that power rates would not even be as cheap as originally proposed. The secretary of interior assigned a task force to evaluate the field report and public reactions to it. In the meantime, Alaska House Bill 242, the Yukon Valley Authority Bill, had been introduced by dam promoters. This bill would have removed control of the dam site and valley from the people of Alaska and created an authority to raise $1.5 billion in revenue bonds to carry out the entire project. The bill created a storm of protest from the Alaskan public and did not survive in the legislature.

Outcome

Early in 1966, H.B. 464 to establish the Rampart Dam Development Commission to promote the project passed the Alaska House of Representatives. But studies subsequent to the Department of Interior's field report continued to prove that the costs would be enormous and the benefits limited. The secretary of interior agreed that Alaska's economy should be developed, but he closed the Rampart Dam case on June 15, 1967. The secretary was convinced that the project was not the most desirable means of accomplishing the objective.

CASE III   Nuclear Economy: Breeder Reactors

The rapidly increasing costs of fossil fuels have resulted in a trend in both government and industry toward developing nuclear energy. Nuclear technology is considered the only means of keeping pace with the growth of the national demand for energy. The former Atomic

Energy Commission (AEC) projected that supplies of low-cost uranium fuel will be exhausted by 1990. Consequently "breeder" reactors have been favored as the nuclear generator of the future. The breeder reactor converts uranium into fissionable material, producing more fissionable nuclear fuel than it consumes. By using breeder reactors, the nation's nuclear energy resources could be extended for centuries. The most common breeder to be developed since research on them began in 1945 is the liquid metal fast breeder reactor (LMFBR). The AEC planned to produce more than one-fourth of the nation's electric energy by plutonium-breeding LMFBRs by the year 2000.

In 1971 President Nixon raised the LMFBR to top priority in the national energy program. America is now ready to move ahead on a $6.4 billion nuclear breeder reactor program. The first demonstration plant is planned to be ready in 1980. Proponents of the program argue that breeders will operate more efficiently than conventional light water reactors.

There is certainly a desire in the nation for prosperity, for which a plentiful supply of safe, low-cost, and environmentally sound energy is mandatory. But there is no unanimous support for the trend toward a nuclear-based economy. If LMFBRs take the dominant role planned for them by the AEC and electrical industry proponents, the nation may well have a plutonium economy.

Scientists, economists, and numerous environmental groups have been challenging for more than a decade the trend towards a nuclear economy. They have raised many questions, still unanswered, about the economic feasibility, the desirability, and even the necessity of making nuclear energy the foundation of the economy of the future. Throughout the country, numerous instances exist of conflicts between the AEC (now NRC) and environmentalists over problems such as thermal pollution and the siting of nuclear power plants. But public reaction to government policies in support of the breeder reactor program has intensified during the 1970s. Citizens have turned from fighting individual nuclear reactor plants to questioning the impact of the entire breeder technology on American society.

The Actors

Three main interests dominated nuclear power policy for almost a quarter century: Congress' Joint Committee on Atomic Energy (JCAE), the Atomic Energy Commission, and the nuclear reactor manufacturers and electric utility industry. The JCAE and AEC, created by the Atomic Energy Act of 1946, continually reviewed the atomic energy program. The public has played an insignificant role in policy formation for most of the twenty-five years since passage of the act.

Congress relied heavily on JCAE advice, and its unique nature gave it extraordinary powers. The JCAE was the only congressional committee which acted as both a legislative committee (drawing up bills), and a conference committee (acting on differences between Senate and House versions of similar bills). The JCAE and the AEC had the dominant role in all nuclear energy legislation. Because the AEC was required to keep the JCAE continually informed, the two worked closely together. The role of the JCAE in relation to the AEC has generally been that of apologist and advocate rather than impartial supervisor and defender of the public interest, broadly construed. Both the JCAE and AEC were accused of zealously promoting nuclear power as their primary goal, because they gave public safety only secondary considerations. Neither the JCAE or AEC seemed to represent fully the public interest.

Principal defenders of the public interest in the suit against the AEC's breeder program were two environmental groups: the Scientists' Institute for Public Information (SIPI), a nationally known group that intervenes in environmental policy formation on behalf of the public, and the Natural Resources Defense Council (NRDC), which participates in numerous areas of environmental policy. NRDC's staff of lawyers and scientists combine scientific research, public education, and litigation in order to improve the quality of the environment. NRDC has an outstanding record of monitoring the work of key federal agencies and intervening in policy formation on behalf of environmental groups.

The Policy Process

Although it was SIPI and NRDC that brought suit against the AEC in 1971 in an effort to force the commission to produce an environmental impact statement on the breeder technology, there were many other earlier attempts by citizens to influence nuclear policy. A review of some of these attempts to influence policy will help illustrate more clearly the evolution of strategies used by the public in recent years.

Since the 1960s, numerous citizens' groups have intervened in proceedings and testified at hearings conducted by the AEC at the construction and licensing stages of plant development. Individuals and conservation groups have often sought to ascertain and publicize the position on the nuclear economy held by political representatives and government officials. Dozens of antinuclear groups have organized extensive public education programs on the benefits and costs of nuclear power. There have also been a number of counter-suits aimed at blocking the siting and construction of nuclear plants. These strategies have had limited success. (See Chapter 8, Environmental Health.)

During the 1970s citizens have attempted to participate in atomic energy decision making by many different means. Each new strategy testifies to the growing concern of the public about the advisability of government- and industry-backed policies accelerating the breeder program. There have been numerous attempts to establish a national moratorium on the nuclear program. Senator Mike Gravel of Alaska proposed a bill calling for an instant stop to the entire program until health and safety problems were greatly reduced. In November 1973, Congressman Hamilton Fish of New York introduced H.R. 11079 which called for suspending AEC construction licenses for one year so that the National Academy of Sciences could study nuclear safety. California Congressman Jerome R. Waldie's H.R. 13716, introduced in 1974, called for a five-year moratorium on nuclear plant construction and licensing. His bill also proposed that the U.S. Office of Technology Assessment should investigate nuclear hazards during the moratorium period. The JCAE's disposition toward nuclear promotion, however, meant that a moratorium proposal had little chance of success.

Another attempt to influence policy was the effort to secure a moratorium in California. A coalition of environmental groups, Californians for Safe Nuclear Energy, proposed that a Safe Nuclear Energy initiative be placed on the state's November ballot in 1974. Although it did not ban plant construction or operation, the initiative proposed that utilities prove the nuclear energy system to be safe. If they could not prove it, they would have to cease operation. The coalition was confident it could collect the 325,000 signatures necessary to place the issue on the ballot.

The National Interveners (NI) is a coalition of 108 antinuclear groups that has been operating since 1972. By giving advice to environmental groups on effective citizen participation in AEC hearings, the NI has had considerable influence throughout the nation. A group in New Jersey, the Task Force Against Nuclear Pollution (TFANP), has obtained almost 60,000 signatures from all parts of the country on petitions opposing nuclear power. The TFANP sorts signatures by congressional districts, updates the tallies monthly, and mails them to legislators to inform them of their constituents' concern.

The Natural Resources Defense Council filed suit in 1971 on behalf of the SIPI to compel the AEC to prepare and circulate an environmental impact statement on the LMFBR. The AEC had failed to prepare and circulate the statement required by Section 102 (2) (C) of the National Environmental Policy Act. The SIPI's statement of claim raised most of the serious problems inherent in the LMFBR program for which scientists and economists have not found satisfactory solutions. SIPI pointed out that plutonium 239 was to be the main fuel for LMFBRs, yet plutonium is one of the most toxic and explosive substances known to man. Only a few kilograms destroyed Nagasaki in 1945. According to AEC plans, hundreds of thousands of kilograms of plutonium would be in circulation throughout the country by the year 2000. SIPI also pointed out that LMFBRs would produce tens of millions of gallons of radioactive waste products in the next twenty years if AEC plans continued—wastes that are extremely hazardous. Exposure to small quantities of radioactive substances such as strontium 90 and iodine 131 can cause death, disease, and genetic mutations. The SIPI drew attention to explosion hazards in the reactor core from "criticality" (explosion) incidents in handling, shipping, or processing fuel or from earthquakes. Thermal pollution due to waste heat discharges from reactors was also a major concern. Besides describing the environmental impact of the AEC's LMFBR program, SIPI drew attention to many questionable assumptions that underlay the AEC's position on alternative technologies.

On June 12, 1973, the U.S. Court of Appeals for the District of Columbia ruled that the AEC must file an environmental impact statement. In response to the ruling, the AEC issued a statement of intention to prepare such a document, but it also reaffirmed its intention to continue work on the breeder program in the meantime. A little later in 1973, environmentalists failed in their attempt to get an injunction against the demonstration program pending completion of the AEC's statement.

Outcome

Environmentalists have continued their opposition to the AEC's (and now ERDA's) eagerness to make breeder reactors the nation's main source of energy. Cost-benefit analysis is a new line of attack. Dr. Thomas B. Cochran, who is associated with NRDC, has argued that the costs of breeder technology will outweigh its benefits. He has questioned a number of assumptions in areas of uncertainty, and is convinced that it is impossible to demonstrate the economic advantage of breeder reactors. A number of other studies by economists and energy experts support Cochran's conclusions. Some estimates show that the capital required to convert the U.S. energy system to one based on nuclear technology would possibly produce an undesirable strain on capital resources. The capital requirement to build enough reactors to supply one-fourth of U.S. energy needs in the year 2000 (based on the government's demand projections) would be about $200 billion. In 1974, the value of all the U.S. electric utility plants was near $95 billion, but the accumulation of this capital took place over many years.

The increasing public interest in decision making with regard to breeder reactors has been a significant political challenge to the entire nuclear energy program. The breeder program, although strongly supported by the Nixon and Ford administrations and by a majority in the House of Representatives, has encountered serious opposition in the Senate. And a growing number of scientific and broadly representative citizens' groups have asked for further study before the federal administration's commitment to build a pilot breeder plant on the Clinch River in Tennessee is implemented. The issue of a plutonium economy has come before the National Council of Churches, which has asked for the considered judgment of scientists regarding the risks involved. The breeder reactor issue obviously involves questions of safety, health, and national security. But underlying the controversy is a fundamental division between the adversaries over the question of economic and technological growth. Persons committed to the idea of generalized growth in the economy see the breeder as the only presently feasible answer to anticipated energy demands. But anti-expansionist advocates, who favor a stabilized population and economy, argue that a massive increase in available energy will not be needed if growth is controlled and directed toward purposes with low-energy demand. Thus, the controlling factor in the breeder reactor dispute may be the outcome of the public debate on growth policy, and that is not presently foreseeable.

CASE IV   Restricting Throwaways: Bowie, Maryland

The city of Bowie, the second largest city in Maryland, is a suburban bedroom community near Washington, D.C., and Baltimore. It is also a major manufacturing center for cans and bottles. Located in Bowie, the Sparrows Point plant of the Bethlehem Steel Company is the nation's second largest producer of tin-free steel plate used by the container industry. Yet despite the city's close association with the container industry, some of the city's conservation-minded citizens, early in 1970, took a bold step to try to curb the litter caused by throwaway beverage containers.

Bowie citizens raised the broad issue that the production of throw-away containers, by squandering energy and depleting natural resources, was economically wasteful. A number of perceptive local citizens, led by Ellis L. Yochelson and supported by hundreds of local high school students, set out to ban the use of throwaway beverage containers in the city. As an incorporated community, Bowie had the power to pass its own laws and plan for its environment. Yochelson's primary goal was to have the city council pass an ordinance to control sales of one-way containers which increased the city's solid waste burden. The resultant Bowie ordinance was the first in the country, but by late 1971, 36 similar bills were before Congress, 235 bills before legislatures in more than forty states, and innumerable ordinances proposed in towns and cities throughout the nation. The number of bills introduced at all levels of government continues to increase each year, and several states have already passed legislation to regulate throwaways.

The Actors

Authority for decision making in Bowie rests with the city council. The city charter provides that the mayor, city manager, city attorney, and councilors share most of the authority over policy making. The mayor is a member of the city council and does not have veto power. Bowie officials were responsive to a rapidly growing local demand for a new ordinance to ban throwaway beverage containers.

Ellis L. Yochelson, a paleontologist, had been disturbed by bottle and can litter for more than a decade. Before 1970, he had been teaching geology and hydrology, and as a scientist interested in sedimentary rocks, he learned from extensive field work that bottles were degrading the landscape. He once satirically predicted that the beer bottle would become the index fossil of the future. His research into the bottle problem alerted him to the larger problem of solid waste in a throwaway economy. Yochelson and some active high school teachers and students generated most of the political pressure for the ordinance.

National conservation groups were not involved in the policy process until April 1971, when the Natural Resources Defense Council appeared first as *amicus curiae* and later as attorney for the city of Bowie. For the most part, local citizens acted independently of national citizens' action groups. An educational organization, formed originally by wooden crate manufacturers of America, called the Crusade for Cleaner Environment, provided basic data on the throwaway issue, encouraging proponents of the Bowie ordinance. Because the crate manufacturers' livelihood had been seriously reduced by throwaways, they advocated a return to refillable beverage containers. Local Jaycees, various parent-teacher associations, citizens' associations, and other organizations supported the drive for a cleaner environment. The strongest opposition to the Bowie ordinance came from merchants' associations, liquor dealers, Bethlehem Steel, and the container manufacturers who forecast economic loss and unemployment if a ban on nonreturnables was imposed.

The Policy Process

The policy process for Bowie's bottle ordinance had three stages of development. The first stage involved Yochelson's decision to fight the solid waste problem and his method of approach. Educating the community (largely through stories and letters in local weekly papers) and building political support for his objective were the main activities during the first stage of policy formation. The second stage began after Bowie passed a city ordinance prohibiting the sale of throwaway containers in the community. Further study by Yochelson and advice from environmentalists in Oregon indicated that requiring a deposit would probably be as effective as a ban. So the city council replaced the original ordinance with a deposit law in February 1971. The final stage in policy formation involved court suits challenging the validity of the second ordinance. Since the ordinance did not receive a judicial hearing until March 1974, enforcement of the law was delayed for three years.

Throwaway containers became an issue in Bowie when Ellis Yochelson was requested to speak on "Earth Day and the Environment" at a local high school in the spring of 1970. With more than a ten-year interest in the solid waste problem, Yochelson decided to address the high school audience on the environmental and economic implications of throwaway beverage containers. In preparing his "Earth Day" talk, Yochelson considered two questions: first, what could be said in a short time that students could readily grasp, and second, with facts in hand, what could they do to resolve the problem? Yochelson duplicated petition forms and proposed to the 400–500 students that the city ban the sale of throwaway beverage containers.

The enthusiasm of the students and a number of teachers resulted in more than 2,000 names on the petitions within a matter of days. Students organized litter cleanups in neighborhood streets and conducted numerous surveys at local supermarkets. These surveys revealed that 76 percent of the city's residents wished to stop the use of throwaway beverage containers. Next, Yochelson and student organizers addressed the mayor of Bowie and the city council, urging them to ban throwaways. The tactic generated extensive press coverage and a congratulatory commendation from the mayor. The small group of citizens and students kept in constant contact with the city manager and the city attorney; Yochelson personally called on each city councilor in private and received favorable responses.

Early in June 1970, the city attorney drafted a law banning the sale of soft drinks and beer in nonreturnable cans and bottles. This law, City Ordinance 70–6, was discussed in two hearings (as required by the city charter), the first in June and the second in July. The first hearing received little attention in the community or from those opposed to the ban. Between the two hearings, however, high school assemblies generated more enthusiasm, and students continued activities designed to draw favorable publicity to the litter problem. At a three-hour hearing in July, a conflict emerged between the forces favoring the ban—the general community, students, and Jaycees—and those opposing it, led by representatives of merchants' associations, Bethlehem Steel, United Brewers Association, and soft drink associations. Following the second hearing, however, the mayor and council unanimously passed the ban on nonreturnable cans and bottles.

The Bowie ordinance drew national press and television publicity. During the next six months, the mayor and city manager recorded 6,000 inquiries wanting details and copies of the bill. (The city's Xerox copying bill doubled.) Richard Chambers of Oregon, who had been struggling since 1969 to have a bottle bill passed in that state, contacted Yochelson and provided valuable information on citizens' experiences with litter legislation in Oregon and in British Columbia, Canada. Chambers and Yochelson discussed the difficulty of implementing the ban expressed in the Bowie ordinance, and agreed that a less restrictive measure would be more effective. (In spite of this, citizens of Oberlin, Ohio, passed a bill which not only bans throwaways, but makes their possession within the city limits illegal. This law has been upheld in court.)

In February 1971, following new hearings, the city council unanimously repealed Bowie's ban on throwaway cans and bottles and passed a revised version, City Ordinance 71–4. The first ordinance banned throwaway containers for certain kinds of beverages; the revised version said that the containers could be of any material so long as it was returnable. The deposit was intended to insure that the community would not be burdened with unreturned containers or the cost of their disposal.

With the new ordinance's effective date set for April 11, 1971, activity relaxed. Yochelson was requested to assist with similar laws for mandatory deposits in adjacent Howard County, Maryland, and also at the state level. The Bowie group was successful in assisting the passing of the Howard County bill requiring a five-cent deposit, although the county bill subsequently came under litigation.

In February 1971, the Washington, D.C. Soft Drink Association and local liquor dealers filed two suits against the city of Bowie and its deposit ordinance. In March, the city attorney of Bowie decided to waive enforcement of the law until it had been tested in court. At this point, Yochelson persuaded the Natural Resources Defense Council, a public-interest law group, to plead Bowie's case. Early in 1972, a declaratory judgment by the judge of the county circuit court upheld the right of the city to pass such a law. This declaratory judgment was later rescinded upon appeal. In March 1974, after numerous legal maneuvers, the suit came before the county circuit court which upheld the Bowie ordinance. This ruling has been appealed again by liquor dealers and soft drink manufacturers.

Outcome

The Bowie case has indirectly influenced the policy process throughout the country. Partly as a result of the publicity given Bowie, litter and the solid waste problem have become major issues of environmental and economic policy at all levels of government. High school students in Baltimore, influenced by Bowie students at a conference, approached U.S. Senator Charles Mathias. He introduced S. 1377 in the 92nd Congress, giving the issue its first effective federal legislative publicity in March 1972. This bill, in turn, laid the groundwork for S. 2062, which attracted major attention in March 1974. The citizens of Bowie demanded more regulation to cut down on the amount of waste material and refuse, for there is no such thing as a "disposable" container. As one of the first attempts to set new policies challenging the extravagance of the throwaway economy, Bowie's experience has set a precedent for legislation in other communities and other states.

CASE V   Private Property and Public Goods: Big Thicket, Texas

The Indians called the area "Big Woods." Biologists and zoologists have called it the "biological crossroads of North America" and the most richly substructured region on earth. With 100 soil types and sixty inches of rainfall annually, the Big Thicket contains climatic zones resembling those found in the semitropics, southwestern deserts, the deep South, and New England. This intermesh of soil and climate zones supports eight major plant communities: upland, savannah, beech-magnolia, baygall, palmetto (bald cypress) hardwood, bog, streambank, and floodplain forest. Big Thicket harbors at least thirty varieties of orchids and thirty varieties of ferns, as well as four of the five known insect-eating plants in the United States. The hills, lowlands, ponds, and vegetation are the habitat of rapidly disappearing alligators, panthers, the Texas redwolf, and bears. Big Thicket is the home of rare herons, the golden eagle, and perhaps the last of the ivory-billed woodpeckers. The probable extinction of the ivory-bill symbolizes what has been lost and what must soon be preserved if the ecological survival of Big Thicket is to be assured. Of the original 3.5 million acres of Big Thicket, only 300,000 acres remain today.

The extraordinary biological diversity of Big Thicket underlies the claim that the area is of national significance. Big Thicket is one of the last great wilderness areas—a public good representing a value that may be defined as belonging to people generally. But for centuries, the profit-motivated economy has placed little value on this area as a unique and irreplaceable resource. Because it was considered a resource of limited productive value in a goods-producing economy, its exploitation aroused little public interest. Since the public was long unaware of its values, Big Thicket was not a subject of protective regulation. Pine forests were the most profitable natural resource to develop, so until the 1960s, Big Thicket's value to a business-oriented society was primarily as a source of lumber and wood pulp. Lumber companies have dominated exploitation of Big Thicket since the 1870s, and today six private companies own most of the Big Thicket land. The enormous ecological costs of stream dredging, clearcutting forests, bulldozing, and polluting the land with herbicides and pesticides were passed off as "externalities." Neither economists, business firms, nor the government included the full costs of destroying this irreplaceable ecosystem in their business accounting. The profit-oriented economy was not concerned about the devastation of the Big Thicket. Its environmental qualities may have properly been described as "public goods," but the land itself was privately owned.

When the Republic of Texas became a part of the United States, the new state retained jurisdiction over its own public lands. Thus there never were federal lands to set aside for conservation purposes. During the 1960s some Texans became concerned that so little of the natural environment of the state received federal protection. They urged conservationists to step up their long fought battle to preserve Big Thicket. Conservationists nationwide called for analyzing the total costs and benefits of preserving Big Thicket, and asked that the full costs be calculated of allowing lumbermen and real estate developers to use the area for short-term profit. Since the 1920s, lumbermen had resisted proposals to reserve Big Thicket as a parkland, but by 1968, public pressure had caused the timber industries to consider a compromise. Representing the timbermen, the Texas Forestry Association began to agree to some preservation.

Two key issues concerning the area are still unsolved. How much of Big Thicket should be preserved? Should the economics of local employment be subordinated to a new economics of national concern that pits short-term profits against long-term preservation? The history of citizens' involvement in policy making for Big Thicket helps illustrate these issues and others that involve reconciling economic and ecological values.

The Actors

The private interests which have dominated policy in Big Thicket have been oil-drilling companies, real estate developers (with names such as Hoop'n Holler Estates), and the lumber firms. The third largest landholder in Texas, Eastex, Inc., a subsidiary of Time, Inc., is the largest private owner. Santa Fe Industries and International Paper are other major absentee landholders. The U.S. Department of Interior's National Park Service has been the main actor at the federal level of government. A number of congressmen and senators have played critical roles in Big Thicket policy formation. Conservationists have been significant participants in decison making and in generating public pressure on legislators and administrative officials. They have also played the dominant role in making the local and national public aware of Big Thicket's unique natural resources. The leading citizens' groups have been the Big Thicket Coordinating Committee, the Big Thicket Association, the Texas Committee on Natural Resources, the Lone Star Chapter of the Sierra Club, the National Audubon Society, the Nature Conservancy, and the Texas Environmental Coalition. Over forty citizens' groups supported the Big Thicket Coordinating Committee, which represented the conservationists after 1968.

The Policy Process

The earliest attempts to establish legislative protection for Big Thicket were made by conservationists who had gradually become aware that effective change in policy could only come from the federal level. At the local level, the massive political power wielded by oil and timber companies thwarted preservationists' plans. These firms had been receiving special consideration in the courts and local tax offices for decades. The first coordinated conservation organization was the East Texas Big Thicket Association (ETBTA), formed in 1927. With the support of a biological survey report in 1936 from the Texas Academy of Science, the ETBTA proposed a national area of 430,000 acres at Big Thicket. Scientists located a million acres of virgin forest at this time. The Great Depression and World War II interrupted the ETBTA proposal and others that followed it. After the war, timber interests and the lack of governmental and political concern in Texas and Washington, D.C., smothered preservationists' proposals. In 1964, the Big Thicket Association (BTA) was launched to preserve portions of Texas wilderness and the Big Thicket, and to build a museum in Saratoga in which to preserve the heritage of the region.

The railroads, introduced for logging in 1876, had doomed the wilderness. In less than a century, only one-tenth of the original area remained in a natural state, and it has been readily acknowledged in the last decade that time is running out for Big Thicket. Rumors of "the Feds" taking over Big Thicket as a park were widespread by the 1960s, however, and local citizens feared the loss of industry, jobs, and the onset of economic disaster. The new conservation group, BTA, was organized in a more sophisticated manner than its predecessors. Sophistication, tenacity, and organization kept the BTA functioning in the face of increased opposition.

Conservationists gained support for their cause in 1965 after U.S. Senator Ralph Yarborough was taken on a tour of Big Thicket by members of several groups, including the BTA. In 1966, Yarborough submitted S. 3929 to create a 75,000-acre Big Thicket National Park, a move strongly commended by naturalists, explorers' clubs, garden groups, Rotarians, Texas Audubon members, and oil, chemical, and atomic workers. Unfortunately, Yarborough's bill was left idle in the Senate Committee on Interior and Insular Affairs for nearly five years. But during late 1965 and again in 1966, the National Park Service (NPS) made reconnaissance surveys of the area and sabotaged the conservationists' objectives by recommending that 35,500 acres in nine separate units be preserved. This plan was later referred to as the "string of pearls" national monument proposal.

Lumbermen had helped in the NPS 1966 survey and were happy with the proposed Big Thicket National Monument, but conservationists were not at all satisfied because the isolated patches of wilderness would soon be surrounded by tourist facilities, roads, and hot dog stands. Conservationists were so concerned about the continuity of the vital water table linking the "pearls" that they proposed establishing a national riverways. To counter the campaign of public relations introduced by the timber companies at this time and to halt the ruthless tree cutting in areas between the "pearls," the citizens' groups stepped up publicity. Workshops of scientists, professional people, and representatives from numerous conservation groups drafted resolutions, discussed the scenic riverways proposals, and kept in close communication with politicians and government officials. The Lone Star Chapter of the Sierra Club proposed an alternative plan for a 100,000-acre greenbelt concept. In an effort to express their preferences, conservationists coordinated a meeting in Silsbee, Texas, in December 1968, which NPS representatives and Senator Yarborough attended. The Big

Thicket Association later showed aerial photographs of clearcutting in Big Thicket to contradict forestry specialists who said that the area was unchanged from its 1935 condition.

The National Park Service issued another study team report in 1968 which added some areas and streamways, including 48,000 acres in easements, to earlier proposals. By this time, Senator Yarborough had increased the acreage of his Senate proposal to 100,000. Conservationists exerted as much influence as possible at this time to attract national media attention and to rally national conservation groups. To strengthen its political power and coordinate the vast network of citizens, the Big Thicket Coordinating Committee was formed of representatives from twenty-three conservation groups. While the conservationists united and faced the legislative stalemate, the timber interests, rice farmers, oil drillers, and real estate developers accelerated the denuding of Big Thicket.

The first real steps towards creating a national park came in 1970. Senate hearings, held on June 12 in Beaumont, Texas, on Yarborough's bill were significant because they emphasized the economics of parklands in the Big Thicket. Yarborough clearly showed that only 3.3 percent of the acreage of affected counties would be invested, and that travel to national parks in America in 1967 resulted in $952 million in taxes for the federal government and made up $4.5 billion in personal income. Lumber companies in the Big Thicket had consistently ignored these facts. The Texas Forestry Association, the lumber industries' public relations front, was sharply cross-examined by Yarborough. The hearings generated a great deal of favorable publicity for preservationists. In his final days in the Senate, in December 1970, Yarborough saw his bill passed, although it had been amended to read an area of "100,000 acres or less."

The citizens' groups, under the guidance of the Big Thicket Coordinating Committee, had worked most effectively during 1970. In March, the BTCC and Sierra Club had extensive discussions with the Texas Parks and Wildlife Commission in an endeavor to convince that agency of the local tax revenue potential in a parkland proposal. In a follow-up, the Sierra Club strongly urged the state Parks and Wildlife Commission to act as a supplement to federal authority in the event a Big Thicket National Park was created. Up to this time, the Parks and Wildlife Commission had proposed nothing for Big Thicket, but it was interested in earning revenue. In September, the Big Thicket Association and ten other conservation groups sponsored the first annual Big Thicket Nature Pilgrimage. Over 2,000 people attended the field trips, movies, picnics, and Big Thicket up-date sessions on recent legislation provided by forty leading conservationists and scientists. Supreme Court Justice William O. Douglas had been taken on a tour of the area in 1970, and his visit attracted national media attention to the positive efforts of the preservationists. The Wilderness Society commended the citizens' work during the year and alerted national members of its organization to the Big Thicket issues.

On December 13, 1970, the Big Thicket Coordinating Committee proposed the establishment of a 300,000-acre national area. It was to be administered by the National Park Service and would remove only 2.6 percent of Texas' 11.5 million acres of commercial timber land from exploitation. The detailed proposal showed that tourism drew $1.5 billion to Texas annually, whereas timber products were worth only $50 million. The Big Thicket conservationists convincingly showed that a 300,000-acre national area could generate $142 million annually while the timber industry in Big Thicket was earning a mere $13 million.

Yarborough's bill had not been matched with legislation in the House in time for passage in 1970 and had died. Without uniting the Texas congressional delegation behind one measure, the state politicians introduced a flood of bills for a Big Thicket National Park in 1971: H.R. 3618 introduced by Congressman Eckhardt, set aside 191,000 acres and was comprehensive enough ecologically to be endorsed by the BTCC; Congressmen Pickle, Patman, and Brooks introduced bills reserving 100,000 acres; Senator Lloyd Bentsen reintroduced the Yarborough bill but amended it to read "not less than 100,000 acres"; and Senator John Tower's bill called for 81,000 acres. The Eckhardt bill, as proposed, would do little harm to the lumber companies, it was argued, because for the most part, only swampy lowlands were to be surrendered to the national park.

Early in February 1972, the BTA generated publicity and fueled the enthusiasm of its members by organizing a naturalist-guided houseboat tour of some Big Thicket waterways. The Lone Star Chapter of the Sierra Club encouraged its members to telephone and write letters to congressional committeemen endorsing Eckhardt's new proposal for a 100,000-acre Big Thicket National Biological Reserve. In June, at the Parks and Recreation subcommittee hearings on a group of Big Thicket bills, Edward Fritz (of the Texas Committee on Natural Resources) and others presented detailed economic and scientific testimonies to support park proposals. Fritz showed that the average annual tax loss per county would be only $8,000 when the Big Thicket National Park was established. While the citizens' groups' economic analysis positively favored the local economy, it also stressed an environmental corridors concept for Big Thicket. During 1973, the BTA and BTCC contacted Time, Inc. and Eastex, Inc. directly to appeal for extensions of moratoriums on timber cutting and to invite representatives of the firms to the annual Big Thicket Nature Pilgrimage. Favorable editorial coverage of BTCC statements continued to show how the local economy would profit by a Big Thicket preservation.

Conservationists fought desperately during 1973 to stop the increased clearcutting and bulldozing in some unique biological reserve units of Big Thicket that were to be preserved by proposed bills. In desperation, the Big Thicket Coordinating Committee agreed to a compromise that limited the preserve to 100,000 acres on the advice of the National Park Service that 100,000 acres was all that was politically feasible. By October 1973, conservationists were advised to settle for 84,000 acres. Conservationists were anxious to expedite congressional action. Several hundred scientists from thirty states petitioned the government to preserve at least 200,000 acres in Big Thicket Biological Reserve. Many schoolchildren organized to support preservation of Big Thicket and to boycott publications of Time, Inc.

In December 1973, the House of Representatives passed compromise legislation creating an 84,500-acre national reserve at Big Thicket. This bill represented two compromises, one between Texas congressmen Eckhardt and Wilson and another between conservationists and local lumber and residential interests. Since passage of the House legislation, antipreservationists in surrounding counties have worked feverishly to generate political opposition in the Senate to the biological reserve. Local county residents opposing the preserve lobbied through an organization called "Save Our Homes and Land." The BTCC, on the other hand, vigorously protested the omission of a unique area of arid, sandy land from the preserve.

Outcome

In December 1973, the Senate passed a bill for a Big Thicket area of "not more than 100,000 acres." There the matter stands. A House-

Senate conference committee has yet to be formed to reconcile the differences between the two bills, and the fight to preserve Big Thicket is still going on after almost half a century.

The Big Thicket Coordinating Committee and over fifty affiliated citizens' groups have contributed rigorous scientific and economic evidence to support an economic study of the area being conducted by Lamar University in Beaumont, Texas. The fight for Big Thicket is a reminder that public goods and unique aspects of the environment have been excluded from traditional economic calculations. The new planning for Big Thicket reveals how slowly people accept the need for restraining economic growth or reorienting it in relation to irreplaceable ecological values. The citizens' research into the consequences of uncontrolled economic and industrial growth in the Big Thicket area has revealed the enormous unpaid debt incurred by exploiters of the region: the rivers, air, and soil are polluted; forests and water supplies are depleted; open space has been crossed with roads, pipelines, and power lines; and the natural chains of flora and fauna have, in some instances, been irreparably disrupted. These secondary costs are the "externalities" that the economic system has ignored. The citizens' research has clearly shown that a Big Thicket National Biological Reserve would supplement the local economy, not ruin it; employment and enterprise would increase, not stagnate. The unique biological heritage could be preserved and still be compatible with an economically sustained forest industry.

CASE VI   Cost-Benefit Analysis: Allerton Park, Illinois

Robert Allerton Park is a 1,500-acre black-soil woodland in the Sangamon River Valley in central Illinois. In 1946 Robert Allerton, the descendant of a wealthy property owner, donated a 1,500-acre tract of land to the University of Illinois. Allerton intended that the land be held in the public trust as an educational and research center, a public park, a wildlife and plant reserve, and as an example of landscape gardening. He donated an extra 3,775 acres of nearby farmland to provide permanent income for the maintenance of Allerton Park. The park's uplands and lowlands include trails, natural gardens, and wildlife; it is the habitat for thousands of insect species, eight species of birds, twenty-eight species of mammals, and hundreds of species of vascular plants and fungi. Continuous ecological and animal research has been undertaken in the park's ecosystems for more than forty years. In 1970, 1,000 acres of Allerton Park was declared a National Natural Landmark by the U.S. Department of Interior.

The integrity of the Sangamon Valley, including the park, was threatened in 1962 when the U.S. Army Corps of Engineers' proposal to construct Oakley Dam was authorized by Congress. The $29 million cost of the forty-nine foot high dam was approved for purposes of water supply, flood control, and recreation. In 1966, the corps decided to raise the height of the dam and to spend $64 million to include sewage dilution or low-flow augmentation as project objectives. The increased dam height meant that 650 acres of Allerton Park would be permanently inundated by backwaters, and another 200 acres would be flooded periodically. The corps also announced its intention to channelize 100 miles of downstream waterway at a cost of $18 million. In 1969, the corps announced it would increase the dam height again to meet Illinois' new water quality standards. Now, the monetary cost of the project was set at $75 million and the ecological costs had risen enormously, too.

In 1967, citizens had realized that the revised Oakley Dam project was threatening Allerton Park. A group of concerned citizens formed the Committee on Allerton Park (CAP) to oppose the corps. Many members of CAP knew of the corp's record of insensitivity to ecological and aesthetic values. Prepared to meet the corps on a scientific and professional level, CAP drew into its membership economists, biologists, botanists, zoologists, engineers, and lawyers. The CAP group analyzed the rationale and economic justifications of the Oakley Dam proponents and the corps, and in the process, CAP completed an exhaustive critique of some of the economic techniques used by the federal government. Cost-benefit analysis was the corps' main technique for economic accounting. The Committee for Allerton Park exposed the weakness of the cost-benefit technique, as well as numerous errors the corps made in applying it. CAP showed that the revised Oakley Dam project was impossible to justify economically.

The Actors

Participants in the policy process for the Oakley Dam project came from federal, state, and local government, from numerous sectors of private industry, and from almost every part of the community. The

Army Corps of Engineers led the proponents of the project. The U.S. Department of Interior's Federal Water Pollution Control Administration (FWPCA) helped the corps in planning the project. The CAP discovered that FWPCA used inaccurate data to support the corps' sewerage dilution objective. The Illinois Division of Waterways, many state politicians, and officials of the city of Decatur supported the project. Chambers of commerce and prodam interests helped establish the Sangamon Valley Association to promote the project. The University of Illinois was silent about the Oakley Dam's threat to Allerton Park until public protest forced the university to take a stand. The University of Illinois had been accused earlier of failing to protect another of its unique biological areas (Volo Bog) from developers. The university was torn between the demand from the public to protect Allerton Park and the possibility of budget reductions brought about in retaliation by prodam forces in the state legislature.

Opponents of the Oakley Dam project also came from every level of government and most sectors of the community. The Department of Interior's National Park Service strongly opposed allowing backwaters to enter Allerton Park. In December 1970, the corps' own Environmental Advisory Board recommended that the corps reappraise and reconsider environmental values in project planning. The Illinois Nature Preserves Commission and the University of Illinois Committee on Natural Areas both opposed the revised Oakley Dam proposals. Groups of citizens and farmers throughout the state, such as the Friends Creek Valley Association and the Sangamon Valley Watershed Preservation Association, voiced stiff opposition to the Oakley Dam. The Sangamon River Improvement Association, ten county governments, and national conservation organizations such as the Environmental Defense Fund disapproved of the project. Eighteen hundred Illinois organizations took antidam stands. But leading the antidam movement was the Committee for Allerton Park. Through its scientific data and its widely communicated publications and advocacy, the CAP was a dominant force in decision making for Allerton Park.

The Policy Process

The Sangamon River drained flat agricultural lands and had been subject to extensive flooding for decades. Lake Decatur had been constructed in 1922 in the hope of regulating floods and stabilizing Decatur's water supply, but some of the worst floods ever recorded in the area occurred in 1926 and again in 1943. The Army Corps of Engineers proposed Oakley Dam and fifteen other projects on the Sangamon and Illinois Rivers in 1947. Although the corps insisted these projects were necessary and economically feasible, conservationists and farmers defeated them. But severe droughts in 1953 and 1954 and the results of a 1956 siltation survey, showing that Lake Decatur had lost 30 percent of its original storage capacity, resulted in new plans to dam parts of the Sangamon River system. But in 1959, Decatur voters defeated a referendum to build another dam to supply city water. That same year, however, the Water Advisory Committee of the Decatur City Council recommended active contact with the corps on the Oakley Dam project.

The history of these first proposals for damming the Sangamon and its tributaries reveals the conflicting views about further flood control and water supply projects. A common view was that dams, which were destined to silt up, brought doubtful gains to central Illinois. Even so, the power of prodam forces was significant. In 1962 the Oakley Dam was authorized by Congress. The process of decision making for the Oakley Dam project had its roots in a conflict that had continued for decades. The determination of the Army Corps of Engineers was one of the dominant forces in the policy process after 1962. In 1966, the fourth siltation survey of Lake Decatur in thirty years showed that 35 percent of the storage capacity had been lost. The corps reacted by increasing the height of the proposed Oakley Dam by fifteen feet, enlarging the capacity of the impoundment, and increasing costs to $64 million. According to this revised plan, almost 700 acres of Allerton Park would have been permanently flooded, yet this revision of dimensions was planned without public or congressional hearings. The corps' actions caused the protectors of Allerton Park to organize the CAP in 1967, thereby adding another forceful participant to the policy process.

The Oakley Dam controversy had not been resolved eight years after the Committee on Allerton Park had been formed. Numerous project revisions and studies, the election and defeat of politicians, and the filing of lawsuits did not solve the problems. The policy process evolved through activity and conflict in three main areas. These areas are separated here for purposes of emphasis; they actually developed in an interdependent fashion.

The first area of policy formation considered by all the major participants was a search for alternatives to the project. The CAP proposed several alternative construction plans that included full protection of Allerton Park. With the support of a 20,000-name petition in 1967 and an 80,000-name petition in 1968, CAP was able to influence Illinois congressmen to ask the corps to reconsider its proposal. In 1968, the University of Illinois' Harza Report spelled out six alternatives to the original Oakley Dam project. Each alternative was less expensive than the corps', achieved the same goals, and protected Allerton Park. The public pressure for alternatives seemed to stir the corps to further considerations.

Early in 1969 the corps released twelve project alternatives, all of which included one or more dams. Another proposed extension to the height of the dam would cause extensive periodic flooding of the park and increase the cost to $75 million. The University of Illinois and Committee on Allerton Park rejected all the corps' alternatives. The Illinois Division of Waterways proposed a "Waterways Alternative" that the University of Illinois, the state, and the city of Decatur formally agreed to on May 29, 1969. The "Waterways Alternative" reduced some of the unfavorable features of the corps' proposal and included several desirable aspects such as a greenbelt recreation area below the proposed dam site. CAP agreed to accept this alternative if the corps would adopt it.

But the corps did not respond until early the next year. In May 1970, the state and the corps proposed a "modified project," far more detrimental to the watershed of the Sangamon and to Allerton Park than the May 1969 agreement. The corps did not follow the guidelines for planning a project set out in *Environmental Guidelines for the Civil Works Program of the Corps of Engineers*. Although the corps was obliged to consider nonstructural alternatives to the project, all of its proposals included one or more dams. The corps was now determined to build two dams, and it was repeatedly revising construction dimensions that meant substantial cost increases and additional water storage. The corps announced that the 1962 project dimensions were no longer economically feasible. CAP's economic analysis revealed that the corps wanted to increase the water storage capacity of Oakley Dam simply to create a move favorable cost-benefit ratio.

The controversy over cost-benefit analysis was the second area of concentration in the policy process. The CAP realized that the corps had to arive at a benefit-to-cost ratio of greater than one in order to meet congressional requirements for funding. Throughout 1969 and 1970,

CAP's economists and scientific personnel analyzed the corps' economic data. The conclusions CAP reached were continually publicized and used as data to support alternative specifications. The Army Corps of Engineers was frequently informed of the CAP cost-benefit findings, but instead of conferring with the CAP, the corps and its supporters launched expensive public relations and propaganda programs aimed at undercutting public respect for the conservationists.

Cost-benefit ratios calculated by the conservationists destroyed the economic justification for Oakley Dam. Underground water supplies from the Mahomet Valley aquifer were shown to be less costly and of better quality than the water expected from the Oakley reservoir. Moreover, the low-flow augmentation proposed by the corps to improve water quality and recreation was shown to provide little more than mudflats—at an extra cost of over $5 million. But CAP concluded that the corps needed this part of its proposal to improve the economic analysis. The CAP also showed conclusively that many of the corps' claims of recreational benefits from the Oakley Dam were spurious. This was a crucial finding, because the Oakley project's claimed benefits were primarily recreational; flood control was the second largest benefit claimed for the Oakley Dam. The CAP revealed that the dam would inundate three times as much land as it would protect. Less costly flood control alternatives existed, but the corps ignored them. CAP demonstrated that most of the benefits claimed for Oakley Dam by the corps and its supporters could be achieved by treating the upper Sangamon watershed for erosion control, developing a greenbelt, and using water from aquifers for the city of Decatur.

The benefit-to-cost ratios calculated by the corps were riddled with errors. An original ratio of 1:15 meant that an annual average of $1.15 in benefits would be returned for each dollar in costs. Correcting an error in the corps' calculation of the interest rate for the costs of an alternative water supply reduced the ratio to 1:05. Including the greenbelt in flood reduction benefits was also an error on the part of the corps. Correcting this mistake brought the ratio down to 1:0.97, and made the benefits now less than the costs. The corps had used the 1962 interest rate of 3.25 percent in its calculations. Refiguring the ratio at the current interest rate of 5.125 percent, CAP further lowered the ratio to 1:0.69. By correcting errors in claims for recreation and water quality and by including aquifer water as the least costly alternative, the conservationists reduced the ratio to 1:0.49. The CAP could have reduced the ratio even further if it had quantified the costs of certain depleted resources, the economic hardship to farmers and some local counties, and the new roads and bridges that would be needed once the dam was built.

Conservationists had demonstrated that the Oakley Dam project was not economically sound. But political forces in local and state government and the corps itself were determined to begin the project. The conservationists were then forced to enter the third area of action—litigation in the courts. In January 1971, CAP, the Environmental Defense Fund, the Piatt County Board of Supervisors, scientists, landowners, and others filed suit to enjoin construction of the Oakley Dam. Defendants in the case were the secretary of the army and the chief of engineers of the corps. The plaintiffs alleged nine complaints under the National Environmental Policy Act of 1969, the Water Resources Planning Act of 1965, other federal laws, and the Fifth, Ninth, and Fourteenth Amendments to the U.S. Constitution. The suit charged the corps with planning deficiencies, inadequate consideration of the values of natural areas, and lack of consideration of alternatives. Plaintiffs also alleged that the corps' benefit-to-cost ratios were exaggerated, and that the revised project was so different from the 1962 plan that new statutory authorization was necessary. An amended complaint pointed out that the corps had not obtained the necessary legal agreement from the state of Illinois and therefore could not begin construction.

A number of other suits were filed during 1972. Farmers of the Sangamon Valley Watershed Preservation Association sued to prevent retiring Governor Ogilvie from signing recreation and water supply contracts with the corps. The Friends Creek Valley Association sued the city of Decatur and Macon County for using tax revenues to support a prodam public relations organization.

Outcome

Despite so much protest, Governor Walker gave conditional approval to the project in 1973, but the corps delayed beginning construction. CAP continued to monitor the activities of politicians and public officials, and to alert conservationists to current developments. Rather than reviewing the CAP alternatives and cost-benefit calculations, the corps hired consultants to study the opposition to the proposed dam.

A major step toward victory for the antidam forces came in January 1975 with a resolution by the Board of Trustees of the University of Illinois to the effect that the Oakley Dam was not in the interest of the university, that a potential threat to Allerton Park remained, and that there should be no further appropriations for the project by state or federal governments.

What now appears to have been the decisive defeat of the project began with the publication of a report by the General Accounting Office on the economic and environmental aspects of the Oakley Dam. In March 1974, U.S. Senator Charles Percy of Illinois requested the GAO study and, after a year of analysis and consultation with the corps, Decatur city officials, and CAP, the GAO reported that the cost-benefit ratio was an unacceptable 1:0.91.

Publication of the GAO report was followed by withdrawal of support for the project by Illinois Senators Percy and Adlai Stevenson III, and by the failure to request funds for the project by Governor Walker and Congressman Madigan. At a meeting of the principal actors in May 1975, Colonel Miller of the corps' Chicago district office announced that increased construction costs and lowered benefit calculations indicated that the project would be placed on an inactive list.

Thus the project was defeated but not wholly demolished. The telling argument against Oakley Dam proved to be economic, even on the basis of an unrealistic 3.5 percent interest rate. However, until the project is deauthorized by the Congress, it may be reactivated. In this instance, an ad hoc citizens' organization, well-led and persevering, appears to have converted or defeated the prodam authorities, but the report of the GAO was a critical factor in the outcome.

Conclusion

Economists have developed the concepts of cost-benefit ratio and opportunity or alternative cost in an effort to more scientifically explain, and more rationally operate, the economy. The concept of the GNP, the common measure of the total productivity of the economic system, was an appropriate measure of achievement in an economy based on Keynesian doctrines of more for more, full employment, and maximum productivity. Market-pricing mechanisms have been used as a basis for the allocation of resources and as the cornerstone of methods to achieve some equilibrium between demand and supply of commodities. The nation was reasonably satisfied with these fundamental objectives, and the means economists applied to achieve them, until a correlation between economic growth and environmental degradation was recognized during the 1960s. It appeared the more economic growth society had, the less environmental quality it had. Inadequate accounting concepts were part of the problem.

Economic growth is not always what people think it is. The Gross National Product (GNP) is misleading, because "goods" and "bads" are both included in the tally, with little or no distinction between the two. Market prices are not completely rational and efficient because, in many instances, prices do not reflect full social benefits and costs. Growth and the GNP are based on these prices and costs. Cost-benefit ratios have customarily given little or no weight to the aesthetic and intangible values that have become increasingly important aspects of the quality of life. Society needs to discard invalid applications of cost-benefit analysis, but retain and improve the instrument itself. The economic system has almost ignored the unintended consequences of economic growth such as externalities, the loss of public goods, and potential ecological degradation. An increasing proportion of the public—and the academic economic community—are calling for more public debate of the problems posed by growth.

More people are beginning to reconsider the implications for the environmental quality of life of unguided, undifferentiated growth. The actions of citizen groups such as those described in this chapter testify to increasing public inquiry on fundamental questions: Can growth be maintained? If growth is to continue, what will the societal costs be in relation to resources, the quality of life, and the environment? Why grow at all? Do the benefits warrant the costs? Is it possible to slow growth rates? What are the implications of proposals for a steady-state economy with a slower growth rate? Economists usually arrive at conflicting answers to these questions, and few economists agree on the finer details of the problems and their solution. But a closer examination of the nature of growth gives some insight into the complexity of the issues, and may throw light on some approaches to wiser economic-environmental policies.

Economic growth—essentially a growth of production and consumption—is a result of a combination of factors: government policies that stimulate expansion; the work ethic of the culture, particularly since the industrial revolution; population size; a growth in output per man-hour; and a combination of knowledge, the stock of capital, and advances in technology. It is generally agreed that the public would not favor passing up the advantages of automation for scythes. It seems probable that growth, in some sense, will continue, although not necessarily material growth at exponential rates. An examination of trends in growth since World War II suggests that redirection of economic growth is a fundamental necessity for environmental quality and social well-being.

It appears that the major factors in environmental degradation are not population growth or the growth of affluence. Both factors are significant, but in interaction with other causes rather than as isolated phenomena. Of greater concern are some forms and methods of production and consumption that society has become accustomed to. Environmental degradation has increasingly followed from new technologies. Many current productive activities have a more intensive environmental impact than do the productive activities being displaced. Detergents that are nonbiodegradable and require intensive energy processes, synthetic fibers, nonreturnable containers and throwaway home conveniences, plastics, cement used for the highways replacing rail systems, chemicals, and aluminum have all been sources of per capita consumption increase of enormous magnitude. Most of the manufacturing processes for such goods are energy-intensive, escalating the depletion of fuel resources and resulting in waste heat, thermal pollution, and numerous forms of environmental degradation. These and other counter-ecological trends in the economy are urgently in need of investigation. Technological transformations and new programs of resource and energy management, based on ecological principles, are required to harmonize economic and environmental policies.

The Rampart Dam case illustrates the differences in perception from the local to the national level. Many Alaskans were willing to destroy the natural environment and resources for immediate monetary gain, but almost every conservation organization in the United States raised the basic question of priorities: should short-term economic benefits be pursued in preference to wisely managed, long-term benefits? The loss of wildlife, the loss of the traditional life-styles of fishing and hunting, and the destruction of pristine wilderness were considered by Rampart Dam promoters as part of the price of progress. Local representatives of business and labor were more willing to accept these losses than were a minority of local conservationists and the nation at large, to whom the unique wild areas of Alaska had become all the more valuable because of the rapid destruction of the nation's other natural areas. Unregulated pursuit of economic expansion would have led to the displacement of a self-sustaining, distinctive ecological base of the Alaskan economy by a short-term, physically and ecologically vulnerable, man-managed system, the costs of which would have been borne by Amercans far beyond the frontiers of Alaska.

The case of the supersonic transport was used to illustrate three main points. The first is the leading role that scientific and technological progress play in the growth and productivity of the economy. Second, the economic justification for many technological projects can be refuted, even before complex environmental consequences can be ascertained. Finally, the rejection of the SST by the American people was a turning point in public attitudes toward uncontrolled economic growth and technological expansion.

The SST program was a direct extension of the technologies and engineering inventions generated by the world's most sophisticated aerospace industry. The American economy's productivity had been enhanced for decades by the aerospace industry and supporting industries such as airlines, military aviation suppliers, and associated subcontractors. The technological transfer (or spin-off) from advances made in aerospace engineering probably had significant impact on the expansion of productivity in numerous sectors of the economy. Some economic growth experts, particularly Professor Robert Solow, believe that more than half of the increase in productivity of the American economy is attributable to technological change. To their way of thinking, advances in science and engineering, through programs such as the SST, are vital to an economy seeking growth.

To its promoters both in government and industry, the SST program was a necessary and normal increment in economic stimulation and growth. But citizens' groups warned the nation that predictions of economic benefits were unreliable. There were few firm buyers for the plane, the national and international airplane markets were saturated, and the project appeared to be a tremendously high financial risk. Added to the economic risks were the serious ecological consequences of the SST that the nation refused to accept as a price for progress: noise disturbance to wildlife, disruption of domestic tranquility, possible adverse stratospheric changes, and increased toxic pollution in the vicinity of airports. Cancellation of the SST was one of the nation's first and most dramatic expressions of an attitude that questioned traditional preferences for growth.

Big Thicket is an example of irreplaceable resources rapidly being destroyed by an economic system incapable of allocating them efficiently. The case of Big Thicket illustrates fundamental weaknesses in the pricing and marketing of resources. The problems of preserving this natural area of southeast Texas are typical of the problems of organizing market mechanisms for public goods. The nation is in urgent need of policies and mechanisms that will protect and provide public goods such as Big Thicket. Irreplaceable resources such as Big Thicket also have what economists call an option value. Conservationists and much of the public wish to refrain from actions which have irreversible consequences on Big Thicket such as clearcutting, oil production, and stream channelization. Their goal is to retain an option for future use of the area. Retaining this option means retaining it for all Americans. This jointness of supply and product indivisibility cannot be handled by the traditional economic mechanisms for pricing and marketing. The private owners of Big Thicket are encouraged by the free market to pursue logging, real estate development, and oil exploration because this is the way to achieve the highest net earnings from resources over the short term. The market does not allocate the resources of Big Thicket in favor of the overall returns to society.

The Oakley Dam case was used to illustrate the challenge by citizens to the misuse of cost-benefit analysis for decision making. Cost-benefit analysis had been the most hallowed mechanism for economic decision making for decades. In fact, until the 1960s a national consensus on economic growth had led to the acceptance of cost-benefit analysis as a technique for social problem solving. Although essentially a technical choice mechanism, this method was used to supply inputs of information to help make decisions that, in many cases, were basically political. The damming of a valley changes the basic characteristics of the area forever; future generations would have to live with the consequences of decisions made decades earlier. Cost-benefit analysis provided only a partial answer to questions of equity in such instances. During the later 1960s, the American public began to seek quality as well as quantity in economic development. The Oakley Dam case symbolized a weakening of the former growth consensus, and a consequent dissatisfaction with cost-benefit analysis for making social choices.

The citizens of Bowie, Maryland, reacted to one of the symptoms of a weakness in the national economic system. In protesting the pollution caused by nonreturnable containers and the waste of natural resources inherent in throwaway packaging, the citizens took the first step toward dealing with the crucial problem of a materials balance. Materials in the production process are converted to goods and services which, in turn, end up as many forms of solid waste. Our economy has developed on the principle of maximum production to meet unlimited demands. This principle admits of little concern for conservation of limited resources, for recycling resources, or for the social costs of the by-products of production. The materials-balance concept, however, is like an accounting mechanism for the economy. The flow of resources and materials must be treated as a closed-loop system. Citizens' groups across the nation are protesting the concepts of "built-in obsolescence," "convenience" or "throwaway" life-styles, and the enormous solid waste problem. Communities such as Bowie are touching on the symptoms of a breakdown in an economy not geared to operate a materials-balance system.

In protesting the Nuclear Breeder Reactor Program, the Natural Resources Defense Council (NRDC) and the Scientists' Institute for Public Information (SIP) articulated the public's growing concern about the existing policy for a nuclear economy. The public has increasingly demonstrated its wish for quality along with quantity in economic progress. The information used by the Atomic Energy Commission (AEC) and the energy utilities in projecting future energy demands and the availability of key resources such as uranium has not been adequate for the rational prediction of either. Moreover, the clear and present environmental hazards posed by the breeder reactor are far more convincing. With a diminishing consensus for "business as usual" in the economy, the public may not be willing to rush into a spectacularly costly, high technology gamble. Citizens' groups are raising the larger question of long-range planning that is necessary in the economy. The free-enterprise, high-profit, market economy is not suitable for allocating priorities where there is no margin for policy error.

As mentioned previously, the pricing system helps allocate scarce resources. Also, there are instances of badly adjusted mechanisms in the economy that stimulate excessive consumption. This situation is especially notable in the electrical energy industry, where artificially low pricing encourages consumption, economic growth, and consequent environmental degradation. Pricing structures that do not reflect the full cost of electric power production and use in effect subsidize excessive and wasteful uses of energy, because artificially low prices for electricity do not encourage energy conservation. Yet many state public service commissions and the Federal Power Commission have authorized promotional pricing structures that subsidize industrial users by requiring residential consumers to pay more. Large industrial consumers may pay ⅓ as much for electricity as do small consumers.

Citizens' groups fighting block-rate pricing systems have revealed that regulatory bodies are using old policies in an era of new problems (see Chapter 6, Energy, Case VI). Diminishing block-rate structures were acceptable decades ago to encourage economic growth when generating costs were dropping as markets expanded. Yet electricity has consistently been sold too cheaply because producers have not been required to pay the costs of environmental degradation. Today, citizens are more aware of the environmental impact of the nation's largest industry, the electric utility industry: landscape degradation due to transmission lines and damming, crop and property damages due to sulfur dioxide and nitrogen oxide emissions, thermal pollution, strip mines, oil slicks, and millions of acres occupied by generating installations. In an effort to have pricing act as a control on demand, the citizens have proposed a number of more rational and realistic rate structures. Citizens' groups have also pointed out that regulatory agencies are more concerned with assuring an abundant supply of electric energy and serving industry than they are with protecting the environment and serving the public interest.

Readings

Brooks, Paul. "The Plot to Drown Alaska." *The Atlantic Monthly*, 215 (May 1965), 53–59.

Chen, Kan, Karl F. Lagler, et al. *Growth Policy: Population, Environment, and Beyond*. Ann Arbor: University of Michigan Press, 1974.

Daly, Herman E., ed. *Toward a Steady-State Economy*. San Francisco: W. H. Freeman, 1973.

Dorfman, Robert and Nancy S., eds. *Economics of the Environment*. New York: W. W. Norton, 1972.

Findley, Roger. "The Planning of a Corps of Engineers Reservoir Project: Law, Economics and Politics." *Ecology Law Quarterly*, 3 (Winter 1973), 1–106.

Gunter, A. Y. *The Big Thicket: A Challenge for Conservation*. New York: Viking Press, 1972.

Meadows, Donella H. and Dennis L., et al. *The Limits to Growth*. New York: Universe Books, 1972.

Mesarovic, Mihajlo E. and Eduard Pestel. *Mankind at the Turning Point: Organic or Cancerous Growth?* New York: E. P. Dutton, 1974.

Schurr, Sam H., ed. *Energy, Economic Growth and the Environment*. Baltimore: The Johns Hopkins University Press, 1972.

Watt, Kenneth E. F. *The Titanic Effect*. New York: E. P. Dutton, 1974.

8

Environmental Health

Introduction

Man's degradation of the environment, whether intentional or not, poses a serious threat to human health. The fact that a continually rising economic standard of living in the United States has been accompanied by a decline in environmental quality has resulted in perhaps the most difficult dilemma confronting the nation today. Technology, which made possible the rise in our economic standard of living and helped solve many threats to health, has also created a host of new problems which endanger our well-being. Among these are air pollution, water pollution, harmful noise levels, new types of occupational hazards, unsafe food additives and pesticides, radiation from nuclear power sources, and many others. As our understanding of environmental health problems has increased so have the policy conflicts involved in most of these issues. These conflicts are particularly difficult to resolve because the impact of many environmental health problems is so extensive. Housing, for example, has psychological and socio-logical repercussions, as well as physiological ones.

The significance of environmental health problems can be appreci-ated if one considers how high medical costs have risen in the United States. Health care has become one of the largest consumers of man-power in the nation. Expenditures for health account for a sizable por-tion of the Gross National Product. A projection by the Department of Health, Education and Welfare estimates that national health ex-penditures will rise from $67 billion in 1970 to between $155.7 and $189.2 billion per year by 1980, or 8 to 9.8 percent of the GNP. Dr. Paul Kotin, director of the National Institute of Environmental Health Sci-ences, has calculated that the total environment-related health costs of the American people amount to $35 billion a year. Of this amount, he estimates that $10 billion is spent each year for treating people with health disorders and disabling handicaps caused by environmental factors, and that the remaining $25 billion represents the amount lost in wages and services due to environmentally caused diseases. The cost of treating Americans for cancer alone will account for 4 to 5 per-cent of the nation's entire health budget in 1975, according to one fed-eral estimate.

In spite of these rising expenditures, health standards in the United States in the past two decades have deteriorated drastically in some cases. Dr. Jean Mayer, nutritition adviser to President Nixon, pointed out that the average life expectancy of twenty-year-old men is higher in thirty-six foreign countries than it is in the United States. In twenty-one nations, the life expectancy of twenty-year-old women also surpasses that of American women. Infant mortality rates are another indication of a decline in American health standards; rates in the United States are higher than those in twelve other countries.

There is no question that the increase of pollution, in all its forms, is directly related to the decline of health in America. According to Dr. Luther Terry, former surgeon general of the United States, much of the speculation and controversy about whether or not pollution causes disease is irrelevant to the significance of pollution as a health hazard. Moreover, environmental problems other than pollution also contribute to health problems. For example, the deteriorating aesthetic quality of urban environments may have a significant impact on mental health. Hunger, noise, ignorance, and poverty also directly affect health, yet many of these critical factors have been neglected in the formulation of environmental policy.

A brief review of environmental health issues illustrates the difficulties of formulating adequate environmental health policies. In the past, elected officials as well as private citizens have been preoccupied with two crucial areas of health-related policy—the quality of water and of air. Federal involvement in water quality control did not begin until 1948 (see Chapter 4), and air quality problems were not subject to federal action until 1955 (see Chapter 6). The weaknesses of federal policies controlling air and water quality have been discussed in other chapters, yet the health problems created by deteriorating water supplies and air pollution have been afforded at least a certain amount of attention from decision makers. This has not always been the case with some of the other equally serious threats to health. It is important, therefore, to review some of these major problem areas of environmental health.

Noise: In the present day urban environment, noise is pervasive, constant, and enervating. It is estimated that sixteen million people in the United States suffer from some hearing loss directly caused by exposure to excessive sound. By far, the largest noise maker in cities is industrial machinery, half of which, it is estimated, generates potentially harmful noise levels. According to the Environmental Protection Agency, between six and as many as seventeen million workers are exposed to potentially harmful industrial noise. The general public, however, is also exposed to a deafening variety of sounds. A test of college freshmen in 1969 revealed that a shocking 61 percent failed to hear high frequencies. In addition to affecting hearing, excessive noise can alter endocrine, cardiovascular, and neurological functions and cause biochemical changes in an individual. These alterations may be manifested in irritability, increased susceptibility to infection, gastrointestinal malfunctions, high blood pressure, and heart disease.

In spite of increasing scientific evidence about the dangers of noise, no federal standards regulated major sources of noise other than airplanes until the fall of 1972. The Federal Noise Control Act, signed on October 28, 1972, authorized the Environmental Protection Agency to establish limits on noise produced by interstate trucks, buses, trains, and construction equipment. However, the Federal Aviation Administration still retains jurisdiction over all civilian air traffic, which is the most acute single source of noise. This split jurisdiction over noise control is a subject of controversy. Several cities have passed noise control ordinances more comprehensive than federal legislation, but at both levels, enforcing the regulations remains the key problem.

Occupational hazards: Industrial workers suffer from a variety of hazards associated with certain occupations. Many of these hazards are created by airborne pollutants such as asbestos (which causes silicosis), coal particulates (which cause miner's pneumoconiosis), metal particulates, chemical fumes, pesticides, enzymes from detergents, and many others. People working with uranium or at nuclear power plants may be exposed to excessive radiation. Recent studies also indicate that the people working in these high risk jobs may expose their families to the same hazards. Asbestos workers, in particular, have been found to carry the fibers home in their hair and clothing, spreading cases of fatal lung cancers and lung abnormalities to their spouses and children. Other not so hazardous influences affect the health of America's workers. Light may create environmental hazards if it is insufficient, too bright, inconstant, or glaring. Similarly, temperature extremes may present health hazards. Aside from chemical and physical threats to their health, workers are also affected by various psychological and sociological factors such as attitudes toward the work, the potential for upward mobility, interpersonal tensions, crowding, or isolation.

In 1970, Congress passed the Occupational Safety and Health Act, which required the secretary of labor to establish safety standards with the assistance of the National Institute for Occupational Safety and Health (NIOSH). The implementation of the act, however, was assigned to both the Department of Labor and the Department of Health, Education, and Welfare. This act followed closely the passage of the 1969 Federal Coal Mine Health and Safety Act. No standards, however, exist to protect the mental health of workers, even though studies have shown that adequate lighting, agreeable surroundings, proper temperature, and good interpersonal relationships will affect workers in offices as well as in factories.

Food additives and pesticides: There are about 3,000 food additives in use today in the United States, an average of three pounds per person per year. While some additives markedly diminish spoilage of certain foods (an advantage to both the consumer and industry), many are now being used to supplement foods which have little or no nutritional value whatsoever. Furthermore, while some additives may be "safe," others have not been adequately tested. Until 1958, the Food and Drug Administration had little control over the chemicals added to food, and only about thirty-five chemicals have ever been removed from use in the history of federal control. Food additives with no significant nutritional value create a particular problem in areas of poverty where people do not understand or cannot afford a properly balanced diet. But the problem also exists among middle-class Americans whose diets have become increasingly unbalanced in the last few decades by excessive use of heavily advertised, over-processed, synthetic foods and beverages.

Other unnatural agents found in foods include hormones, antibiotics, pesticide residues, waxes, and shellacs. Pesticides, in particular, are a source of concern since many foods such as shellfish contain concentrations of certain toxicants as much as 200 times the level normally found in the environment. Pesticides can interfere with the functioning of the central nervous system, and under certain conditions they can be lethal. Pesticide spraying is regulated by the Department of Agriculture, but controlling pesticide residues in food is under the jurisdiction of the Food and Drug Administration (FDA). Specific residue tolerances are set by the FDA for food crops entering interstate commerce.

Radiation: A certain amount of radiation is present in the environment from natural sources. Unnatural sources of radiation, however, are increasing to the point where they may directly affect health. In the home, color television sets and microwave ovens present potential health hazards. Standards for radiation emissions were set for new ovens and televisions in 1969, when the hazard was discovered, but earlier models have no protective devices and new ones may still emit dangerous levels of radiation. Excessive radiation is also sometimes received from faulty x-ray machines.

These sources of hazardous radiation, however, appear relatively insignificant in comparison with the potential health hazards presented by the development of nuclear power. Many informed persons, concerned about nuclear radiation hazards, believe that the current standards of exposure set by the Federal Radiation Council are too high to be safe, and feel that most nuclear power generators are located too close to populated areas. The problems connected with nuclear power policy have been particularly complex, since the agency responsible for protecting public safety and setting radiation standards at specific facilities, the Atomic Energy Commission, was (until 1975) also responsible for developing nuclear power. One of the weak spots in the AEC's supposed protection of the public's health, for example, was the fact that the AEC had no policy protecting the public from the hazards of radioactive wastes being transported through populated areas.

Noise, occupational hazards, additives and pesticides, and radiation are only a few of the main problems relating to environmental health. Other important environmental problem areas include disposal of solid waste, aesthetics, open space, recreation, and, of course, air and water quality. Unfortunately, citizens have not always recognized these problems as problems in environmental policy in the broader quality-of-life sense. However, as the following cases demonstrate, policy issues affecting environmental health have begun to attract increased public participation in the past few years.

CASE I   Occupational Health: Black Lung Disease

Pneumoconiosis, or black lung disease, is a debilitating respiratory affliction caused by breathing coal dust; it poses a critical health problem in one of the nation's most important industries. In the United States today there are approximately 150,000 active coal miners, and in the past twenty years, over one million miners have been exposed to a daily dose of coal dust. It is commonly estimated that at least 125,000 active and former miners now have black lung disease. The disease is irreversible. A 1965 Public Health Service report estimated that one out of every ten active miners in the Appalachian soft coal mining area, and one out of every five former miners, had x-ray evidence of the disease.

According to government statistics, the death of 4,000 men every year has been attributable to black lung. In spite of these statistics, only three states provided workmen's compensation before 1969 for black lung victims, and of these three, only Pennsylvania had actually paid any claims. States have been reluctant to compensate miners because the medical community in the United States and various government agencies have refused to recognize coal dust as the cause of pneumoconiosis, even though the disease had been identified in Britain in 1942 and had become compensable there the following year. This case study will examine the tactics used by coal miners to publicize and gain compensation for a serious environmental health problem.

The Actors

Historically, the Bureau of Mines (BOM) in the Department of Interior has been the government agency most responsible for the health and safety of coal miners. This bureau was established in 1911 at the specific request of the United Mine Workers of America. The first Federal Coal Mine Safety Act, however, was not passed until 1941. Until then the BOM had no right to enter coal mines, and even after passage of the act, it had only limited inspection and enforcement authority. In no instance prior to 1969 did federal legislation place appropriate emphasis on the health hazards associated with coal mining.

Another federal agency responsible for coal workers' health was the Public Health Service of the Department of Health, Education, and Welfare (HEW). In general, this agency tended to consider occupational health problems outside their concern. It was not until 1963 that the Public Health Service attempted to ascertain how widespread the incidence of black lung disease was among coal miners. The twenty-six states where coal is mined in the United States also neglected the miners' plight by not providing compensation for disabled coal miners or measures to prevent the disease.

Three doctors in West Virginia, the principal coal-producing state in the nation, were the chief instigators of the miners' fight for black lung benefits. They headed a group called the West Virginia Physicians for Miners' Health and Safety and were instrumental in organizing the West Virginia Black Lung Assocation, which played the key role in the activities leading up to the passage of the 1969 Federal Coal Mine Health and Safety Act.

The Policy Process

On November 20, 1968, Consolidation Coal Company's mine No. 9 at Farmington, West Virginia, blew up. The explosion killed seventy-eight miners and focused the attention of citizens and legislators across the nation on the plight of mine workers. This explosion was not unusual; it was just more dramatic than most mining tragedies. But it did force officials to recognize the hazards of working in coal mines; within three weeks after the explosion, Secretary of the Interior Stewart Udall summoned a national coal safety conference. The explosion also added weight to the arguments of the three West Virginia doctors trying to organize miners to fight for better conditions in the mines. The three doctors, led by Dr. I. E. Buff, a Charleston cardiologist, conducted a six-month campaign during the fall and winter of 1968 to win compensation for black lung victims in West Virginia.

On January 26, 1969, more than 3,000 coal miners met in Charleston at the first statewide meeting of the West Virginia Black Lung Association. The highlight of the meeting was an attack prepared by Ralph Nader on the negligence and duplicity of W. A. Boyle, president of the United Mine Workers of America (UMW). Nader's speech was delivered by Congressman Ken Hechler of West Virginia who vigorously supported the miners' cause. The outcome of the meeting was a demand that the state legislature grant compensation to victims of black lung disease. The miners also insisted that mine owners make radical changes in their underground operations to remove particles of coal dust, the cause of black lung disease.

On February 11, several weeks after this meeting, hundreds of West Virginia miners jammed the galleries of the state house in Charleston to voice their demands at a hearing on health programs conducted by a joint meeting of the senate and house judiciary committees. The marathon, six-hour hearing was the direct result of the health campaign led by Dr. Buff. Proponents of the legislation to curb black lung disease assembled a formidable array of medical experts to testify. Among them was Dr. Jethro Gough, a Welsh pathologist and a leading international authority on pneumoconiosis. He was flown in from England at the expense of the West Virginia physicians' group. Outside the chamber, protesters sang songs and carried a black coffin symbolizing death in the mines.

When no action was taken on the legislation, a group of miners, led by members of the West Virginia Black Lung Association, began leaving the mining pits in a wildcat strike on February 18. One week later, more than 30,000 coal miners were on strike. The strike was not supported by the UMW, but more than two-thirds of the state's 44,000 coal miners participated, effectively shutting down West Virginia's coal industry. By February 26, the state's house Judiciary Committee approved the black lung compensation measure, putting the burden of proof on the state instead of the claimant. On March 10, the bill was signed and miners returned to work.

Meanwhile, on February 27, congressional hearings on health and safety standards in coal mining opened in Washington, D.C. Mine owners, represented by the National Coal Association, which had been opposed to the West Virginia legislation, offered to pay the costs of safety measures. The president of UMW, W. A. Boyle, testified and threatened a nationwide coal strike if reforms were not forthcoming.

Finally, on March 3, President Nixon submitted a bill to Congress designed to reduce deaths from coal mine accidents and to protect miners from black lung disease. It was similar to a bill offered by President Johnson in 1968, but the Nixon measure was stronger in that it specified dust levels and authorized mine shutdowns for violators. On May 27, the chairman of the Senate labor subcommittee, Harrison Williams of New Jersey, who had been in charge of the hearings on health and safety, offered Congress an even stronger bill limiting respirable dust levels to the three milligrams per cubic meter of air recommended by the Public Health Service.

While Congress was considering the legislation, the miners continued to threaten a nationwide strike if it was not passed. Pressure in Ohio forced Governor Rhodes to sign a black lung compensation bill for the state on August 27. Finally, the national bill was passed by both the Senate and the House in October and approved in early December.

On December 30, 1969, President Nixon signed the Federal Coal Mine Health and Safety Act. For the first time, federal law recognized an occupational disease and provided federal funds to pay some remuneration to its victims. The battle had only begun, however, because many miners and miners' widows who could not prove the incidence of black lung disease according to the rules of the 1969 act were ineligible for the benefits. After another legislative battle, the Black Lung Benefits Act was passed in 1972. This act provides for compensation even if an x-ray does not show black lung. Many miners, however, have been unable to collect their compensation because of expensive legal and medical services which the claimant must pay for. At least one state, Kentucky, has remedied this situation by providing these services free to black lung victims. Other benefits not now available, such as treatment, rehabilitation, and social services, will also be a part of the program established in 1975. The new program is being funded by the Appalachian Regional Commission and NIOSH, both federal agencies.

Outcome

Legislation alone will not eliminate black lung disease; efforts to eliminate the disease must also include education of the miners. The United Mine Workers' field service office has set up clinics throughout the Appalachian areas to teach miners how to protect themselves against coal dust. The organization also has other educational, health-oriented programs to help reduce the incidence of the disease. Encouraging news from the Bureau of Mines is that an estimated 94 to 95 percent of the mine areas they have tested now have a dust level of two milligrams or less per cubic meter of air. This figure, however, is disputed by UMW's Dr. Lorin Kerr, a nationally known expert on black lung, who believes that the BOM estimate is erroneous by 15 percent or more. If the Ford administration, in the hopes of spurring coal production, continues to support the passage of weakening amendments to the 1969 act, even this limited progress toward protecting the health and safety of the nation's coal miners may be wiped out.

CASE II   Noise Control: New York City

New York City has the dubious distinction of being one of the noisiest cities in the world. In 1972, the city's Bureau of Noise Abatement estimated that background noise in midtown New York frequently reached eighty-five decibels (dba) during the work week—a level that not only interferes with conversation but also provokes adverse physical reactions, such as constriction of the small arteries and quickening of the pulse and respiration rate. New York City has had a noise code since 1936 outlawing "unnecessary noise," but it was rarely enforced because the police were reluctant to issue summonses. And like noise ordinances in most American cities, the one in New York failed to include many of the major sources of noise. In 1972, however, a combination of citizens' and governmental action effectively altered the city's noise regulations, creating what is thought to be the nation's strictest noise control legislation.

The Actors

A leading actor in the 1950s in New York City's battle against noise was Mayor Robert Wagner. During a visit to Paris, France, in 1956, Mayor Wagner was impressed by that city's effective ban on horn honking. Consequently, following his return to New York he established the Committee for a Quiet City. After four years of study, its funds exhausted, the committee ended its existence with a vigorous campaign against horn honking. This campaign was only temporarily effective.

In the 1960s, a resident of New York named Alex Baron took up the struggle to alleviate the noise problem. In an effort to lower the noise level on upper Sixth Avenue, where he lived, Baron became an expert on noise. In May 1966, he attended and addressed the fourth International Congress for Noise Abatement in West Germany. There he discovered noise-reduced air compressors and jackhammers, as well as quieter garbage trucks. Returning home, Baron persuaded a group of scientists and citizens to found the Citizens for a Quieter City, Inc. (CQC). This group, which began operating in January 1967, was a prime initiator of the noise legislation and noise abatement program in New York. At the governmental level, New York's Mayor John Lindsay and several councilmen became active supporters of the effort to reduce noise.

The Policy Process

The Citizens for a Quieter City began its educational program in 1967 by preparing and distributing literature on noise abatement. Members presented papers before professional societies and sent representatives to meetings related to noise control. They also encouraged Mayor Lindsay to authorize a task force on noise control, which he did in 1967. In 1969, following the task force recommendations, the Bureau of Noise Abatement was established within the city's Environmental Protection Administration (EPA). The bureau, endorsed by the CQC, was the first office of its kind in the nation; no similar bureau existed at that time on the municipal, state, or federal level.

While the task force was conducting its study, CQC continued to press for a variety of reforms. The group was responsible for an improvement in the noise insulation provision of the city's new building code, adopted in November 1968. They also initiated a quiet garbage truck project and inspired the development of a quiet metal garbage can.

By 1971, however, it had become evident that the Bureau of Noise Abatement, established two years earlier, was severely limited in its ability to implement a noise abatement program. Consequently, on June 8, 1971, Mayor Lindsay proposed a Noise Control Code. The proposed code set limits for the first time on many of the major sources of urban noise and included a means to enforce the code. At the first public hearing on the code held September 9, 1971, public reaction was mixed. Many people felt the code did not go far enough, while representatives of the construction industry argued that the code was much too strict.

To help educate the public to the necessity for a noise code, the Citizens for a Quieter City opened a storefront named Project Quiet City on November 14, 1971. This pilot program in noise abatement was financed by the Ford Foundation. The opening-day ceremonies began with a parade led by the 1972 Vanguard electric car—a silent, two-passenger vehicle, costing $2,286, with a range of forty to sixty miles on one electric charge. Other ceremonies included a demonstration of quieter construction equipment. The CQC remained active through 1972; a "Quiet Week" proposed by the CQC was authorized by Mayor Lindsay on May 7, 1972.

On June 28 of the same year, the mayor's noise control legislation was approved unanimously by the city council's Committee on Environmental Protection. This legislation covered everything from automobile horns to factory noises. During the next few months, while the council considered the legislation, the construction industry conducted a massive campaign to pressure councilmen to defeat the legislation. However, by a vote of thirty-one to five, the city council adopted the noise control code on September 12, 1972. On October 4, Mayor Lindsay signed the new code, although he proposed an amendment to allow emergency night construction to continue. Penalties for violation of the code may go as high as a $25,000 fine and one year in prison.

To enforce the code, city inspectors from the Department of Air Resources (where the Bureau of Noise Abatement is located) may issue notices to violators. Each inspector must take an intensive five-day course to learn how to operate the technical equipment used to monitor noise. Violators of the code are brought before the Environmental Control Board, an administrative tribunal composed of the administrator and three departmental commissioners of the New York City EPA, the commissioner of building, and four citizens, three of whom must be experts in air, water, and noise pollution control. Violation notices may also be issued by city police, but these cases must appear in criminal court.

Outcome

The noise code of New York City has met with moderate success. The Air Resources Board has only twenty-three inspectors, and it really needs police cooperation to be more effective. In 1972, a total of 3,604 notices of noise ordinance violation were issued in the city, and in one month alone (June), 416 notices were issued on horn honking. However, the number of notices dropped to 32 in July, 1 in August, and none in September. According to the Air Resources Board, the decrease in the number of tickets issued was due to administrative neglect rather than to citizens' compliance.

One major effort to abate noise appears to be particularly effective —the 1974 requirement that all motor vehicles in the city be equipped with a city/country horn. The city horn is less intense than the standard horn, and even the country horn required for New York City is limited to seventy-five dba. The city/country horn was on a manual selector in 1974, but in 1975, the horn became automatic, regulated by the speed of the vehicle so that at lower speeds the noise of the horn is reduced. Use of the horn is prohibited except in cases of emergency. Further efforts to lower noise levels will depend largely on education campaigns and citizens' participation if the 1972 code is to become completely effective.

CASE III   Pesticides Regulation: People for Environmental Progress

Forest fires are a serious problem in southern California, particularly during the late summer. In order to reduce the threat of fires, the U.S. Forest Service has been spraying phenoxy herbicides in California's national forests. The main phenoxies being used are (2,4–D), (2,4,5–T), and (2,4–DP). These herbicides are fat-soluble, a characteristic they share with DDT. Phenoxy herbicides also contain dioxin, a highly toxic, fat-soluble, persistent contaminant that accumulates in body tissue. The lethal dosage of dioxin is about one-third the size of a grain of sugar; in smaller doses it is alleged to cause cancer, brain injury, and genetic damage.

When news of an intended spraying of 30,000 acres of forest in California reached a California nonprofit corporation, People for Environmental Progress, (PEP), in the summer of 1973, the group decided to prevent the spraying on the grounds that it would be a health hazard. This case is particularly interesting since the average age of PEP members is thirteen.

The Actors

PEP, incorporated in 1971, has approximately 600 members in southern California. The case of PEP against the U.S. Forest Service and the Department of Agriculture, the two agencies with jurisdiction in the case, was supported by the city of Los Angeles.

The Policy Process

PEP challenged the spraying of herbicides in California's national forests in early summer 1973, primarily as a threat to "the lives and health of those today, as well as children yet unborn." PEP gathered scientific data from experts to buttress its charges and filed complaints with the Forest Service. When the service failed to act on the complaints, PEP decided to bring suit in June 1973 in district court against the Department of Agriculture and the Forest Service, both of which claimed their programs were necessary to help prevent forest fires.

PEP's evidence, presented to the court to secure a preliminary injunction against spraying, was based on alleged violations of two federal acts—the Federal Insecticide, Fungicide, and Rodenticide Act of 1972 (FIFRA) and the National Environmental Policy Act (NEPA). FIFRA requires that no registered herbicide be used in a manner inconsistent with its labeling. The labels of the phenoxy herbicides intended for use in the California forests require protection of water supplies, avoidance of watershed areas, protection of nontarget foliage, and prevention of poisonous drift. PEP obtained evidence from forestry records and other sources which showed that no emulsifier was used in some sprayings (resulting in drift), that spraying had occurred close to and around waterways, and that herbicides had been found within waterways, according to an analysis by the Forestry Service. The alleged violation of NEPA, according to PEP's suit, was that the two federal departments failed to prepare and publicize adequate project plans with respect to several project areas and had not prepared proper environmental impact statements.

PEP also challenged the Forest Service's contention that the spraying would reduce fire hazards. Some of the spray is mixed with diesel oil as an emulsifier, yet diesel oil is flammable. The sprayed areas, once ignited, would also release poisonous fumes which would carry for miles. To further support its claims, PEP sought and received valuable support from various members of the scientific community. The group filed affidavits from, among others, Dr. Jaqueline Verrett of the Food and Drug Administration and Dr. Samuel Epstein, a cancer expert from the Case Western Reserve University.

On September 17, 1973, the city of Los Angeles filed suit to intervene as a plaintiff in PEP's suit. Several hundred acres of the Angeles National Forest, where herbicides are regularly used, are within the city of Los Angeles. A year earlier, the Los Angeles City Council had adopted a resolution demanding that the Forest Service post the areas which were sprayed and announce in a public notice the fact that the chemicals were dangerous. Since this resolution was ignored by the Forest Service, the new Los Angeles district attorney decided to intervene in PEP's case. His decision was based on the fact that Los Angeles city firemen are committed by a legal agreement to help fight fires in the Angeles National Forest. The city of Los Angeles contended that its firemen had been directly endangered by the spraying and that a number of firemen's deaths from smoke inhalation could be directly attributed to the spraying of chemicals and their toxic residue.

Outcome

Following the city of Los Angeles' intervention, a preliminary injunction motion against spraying was denied. A pretrial conference for a permanent injunction was set for April 15, 1974, and the trial for sometime in May 1974. This date was later postponed. PEP hoped that a precedent would be set against the use of phenoxy herbicides on the grounds of an imminent health hazard. But the case was not tried. Instead a compromise settlement was reached among the parties concerned—PEP, the Forest Service, and the city of Los Angeles.

Under a stipulation before the United States District Court for the Central District of California, the Forest Service declared that it did not presently plan to use (2,4,5–T) or any brushland management in or near the Angeles National Forest. But should it propose it do so at some future date, the Forest Service would give notice to the city of Los Angeles at least 60 days in advance, and would post warnings to the public in areas subject to any herbicide treatment. In effect, PEP achieved its objective without actually winning its case.

CASE IV   Drug Policy and Public Health: Food Additives

Food and drug policy has attracted very little citizens' participation in spite of growing concern among informed people about the safety of some of the chemicals consumed daily by millions of Americans. A noted authority on food additives, Michael Jacobson, has succinctly summed up the controversy over additives in his book *Eater's Digest:*

> Food additives can save consumers time, raise corporate profits, create new products and improve old ones, and make foods more nutritious. On the other hand, many additives have not been adequately tested, some persons may be sensitive to certain additives, many factory-made foods made with additives are devoid of nutrients, and some chemicals may be used solely for cosmetic, deceptive, or irrational purposes.[1]

The value of food additives and their effects on health have largely been ignored by the general public. Most people either are unaware of the quality of chemicals they consume, or lack the expertise to comprehend and interpret the significance of additives listed on packages or bottles. The prevailing assumption of consumers is that any food additive allowed by the government must be safe. The number of cases of citizens challenging the safety of specific additives or the general policy has been few, but recently several groups have begun to influence policy on food additives.

The Actors

Three citizens' groups have been especially prominent in recent efforts to influence food additives policy—the Environmental Defense Fund, the Center for Science in the Public Interest, and the Natural Resources Defense Council. These groups have concentrated their efforts in legal actions. Other consumer groups, such as Consumers Union and Consumer Action Now (CAN), have also tried actively to educate the public about the dangers of certain food additives and questionable practices in the food industry.

The government agency responsible for protecting the health of the consumer by controlling drugs and food additives is the Food and

---

[1] Michael Jacobson, *Eater's Digest: The Consumer's Factbook of Food Additives,* (Garden City, New York: Doubleday, 1972), p. 20.

Drug Administration (FDA). Until 1958, when the Food Additives Amendment was passed, the FDA was, for all practical purposes, powerless. It did not have even the authority to ban the use of chemicals of questionable safety or those not adequately tested. The Food Additives Amendment of 1958 requires the manufacturer to provide the FDA with data which establishes the safety of the additive.

The Policy Process

There are a number of critical problems with food additives policy. First of all, tests submitted to the FDA from the manufacturer tend to prove the safety of the new additive, since the additive presumably will benefit the manufacturer in some way. The FDA does some testing on its own, but the agency lacks both the staff and the time to test thoroughly all the additives. Under the law, if the tests are not completed within 180 days, the new product (after initial approval by the FDA) is automatically approved for market. The public then has 60 days to object. Not only is the public usually incapable of judging the safety of a product, but also, until recently, the consumer could not even examine the data on which the supposed safety of the food additive was based.

Second, the manufacturers' tests are performed on animals. As numerous studies have shown, species vary greatly in their sensitivities to certain chemicals. In the case of the now-famous drug thalidomide, for example, women are at least 30 to 200 times as sensitive as rabbits, mice, rats, hamsters, or dogs—the usual experimental animals. This drug was never officially approved in the United States, but the disastrous effects of the drug on pregnant women in Europe are well known.

Another weakness of the food additives policy concerns labeling. Food processors are not required to indicate on the label of their products that a poisonous pesticide was used in the production of food. Nor are "standardized" foods such as bread required to list all their ingredients on their labels. In any case, the standards are usually set to suit the industry rather than the general public.

The most effective method for citizens to ban the use of specific additives has been through legal suits or petitions. Three recent examples of this approach concern DEP (diethyl pyrocarbonate), DES (diethylstilbestrol), and asbestos.

DEP is a preservative used in white wine, beer, and other beverages. In 1971, Swedish scientific research found that DEP reacts with traces of ammonia in the beverages to produce urathan, a known carcinogen. Any known carcinogen is prohibited from use by the Delaney Amendment to the Food, Drug, and Cosmetic Act. On January 20, 1972, the Environmental Defense Fund petitioned the FDA to prohibit the use of DEP. On February 11, 1972, the FDA banned the preservative.

DES, a synthetic hormone used to fatten livestock, was shown to cause cancer in laboratory animals. After further scientific tests revealed that DES remained in meat intended for human consumption, EDF and the Natural Resources Defense Council filed suit on October 28, 1971, requesting that the FDA prohibit the use of DES. On August 2, 1972, the FDA ruled that DES could no longer be added to cattle and sheep feed, but still allowed stockmen to use it in ear implants. When further tests showed that DES was present in the meat of animals 120 days after ear implantations, the FDA issued a total ban on April 20, 1973. A legal quirk has now reopened the issue, but DES is not expected to come into use again. Unfortunately its effects cannot be removed by law. Since 1945 the drug had been given to thousands of pregnant women to prevent miscarriage, and by 1971 a direct correlation had been found between DES and a high rate of susceptibility to an often fatal form of vaginal cancer in the daughters of these women (*Newsweek*, January 26, 1976, 65–66).

Asbestos, a known carcinogen, contaminates food on some occasions when asbestos filters are used in the preparation of foods and drugs or with the addition of talc to foods, drugs, and cosmetics. Although the FDA has known for several years of practical alternatives to asbestos, no action was taken against its use. On June 27, 1973, the Center for Science in the Public Interest and EDF petitioned the FDA requesting the immediate promulgation of regulations to prohibit adulteration of food and drugs with asbestos. In response to the petition, the FDA proposed regulations for asbestos levels in food, drugs, and cosmetics. EDF submitted comments on the FDA proposal in December 1973 and is awaiting the results.

Outcome

Although citizen action can, in some cases, lead to prohibiting the use of certain chemicals in food production, government agencies should, by law, assume the active responsibility for protecting the public's health. Since the FDA is underfunded to do thorough analyses on every substance, every effort should also be made by the FDA to quickly act upon evidence supplied by citizens and scientific organizations regarding potential health hazards from specific substances. Unfortunately, the FDA and other agencies charged with protecting the public from health hazards seem to be oblivious of the serious threat posed by the ever increasing number of chemicals being used in the United States. The slowness of the governmental machinery in suspending the use of the pesticides aldrin and dieldrin is a good example. Even though scientific evidence had found that dieldrin causes cancer in mice in dosages as low as 0.1 parts per million, the lowest dosage ever tested in an animal species, EPA did not move to restrict sales of these pesticides until October 1974, nearly four years after EDF had petitioned for a ban on these chemicals. Shell Chemical Company has now appealed the suspension order in a federal court. Meanwhile, the toxic substances control act of 1973 languishes in a congressional conference committee, bitterly opposed by industry. This act would require manufacturers to establish the safety of new chemicals before they are released —a wise step toward protecting the public.

CASE V Questionable Drinking Water: Reserve Mining Company, Lake Superior

Lake Superior is the largest freshwater lake in the world.[2] It has almost 3,000 miles of shoreline, most of which is still in a wilderness state. The major urban intrusion on the lakeshore is the city of Duluth, Minnesota, which became an important port when the St. Lawrence Seaway was opened in 1959. Among the industries located on Lake Superior is the Reserve Mining Co. of Silver Bay, located about sixty miles north of Duluth. Reserve Mining Co., a joint subsidiary of Armco and Republic Steel Companies, mines a low-grade ore called taconite. Since 1950, Reserve has been dumping 67,000 tons of taconite "tailings" daily into Lake Superior. These tailings became the subject of controversy in 1969, when they were believed harmful to the lake, and again in 1973, when it was discovered that 40 percent of the tailings

---

[2] Lake Superior, 350 miles long and 160 miles wide, has a greater surface area than any other lake in the world. Lake Baikal, in Russia, has more water volume.

were composed of cumingtonite, an asbestos-like fiber. The existence of cumingtonite in the drinking water of Duluth and several smaller north shore communities constitutes a potential health hazard, and this discovery has greatly influenced the controversy over the Reserve Mining Company. In this case, the federal and state agencies have cooperated with environmental groups in an attempt to halt Reserve's waste disposal method.

The Actors

The original permit which allowed Reserve to deposit wastes in Lake Superior was authorized in 1947 by the Army Corps of Engineers. The controversy over the dumping of tailings arose in 1967, when the corps and the Department of Interior agreed that all dumping permits should be reviewed with environmental considerations in mind. The corps asked for the Department of Interior's help in reviewing the Reserve Mining Company's permit, and Secretary of Interior Stewart Udall assigned a task force of five Interior Department agencies to investigate and make a recommendation concerning Reserve's dumping practices. The department's regional director, Charles Stoddard, was put in charge.

During the summer of 1968, the "Taconite Study Group" made its investigation, and on December 31, 1968, Stoddard sent his findings to the corps, to Reserve Mining, to Minnesota officials, and to the appropriate agencies in Washington. The report concluded that taconite tailings were probably accelerating eutrophication of the lake and recommended that the company be given a maximum of three years to find another disposal site. The report, as might be expected, was strongly attacked by Reserve. The Department of the Interior, for unknown reasons, then tried to suppress the report and refused to acknowledge it as an official report. Because of the controversy, however, Stewart Udall did decide to hold a Federal Enforcement Conference in Duluth in May 1969.

Several citizens' and environmental organizations participated in the conference: the Sierra Club, the United Northern Sportsmen, the Save Lake Superior Association, the Izaak Walton League, the Environmental Defense Fund, and Clean Air-Clean Water. These groups had been trying to arouse public sentiment about Lake Superior but had had little success until the findings of the Stoddard report. Some of these groups eventually became interveners in the two legal cases involving Reserve, and were active in pressuring the government to file suit against the company.

Interestingly, the states bordering Lake Superior did not join the enforcement conference until 1971, when the newly elected Democratic governors of Minnesota and Wisconsin decided to participate. Their Republican predecessors had refused to participate officially in the call for the conference. After the Minnesota and Wisconsin governors joined the conference, the governor of Michigan agreed to follow suit. Later, however, all three states—Minnesota, Wisconsin, and Michigan —joined as interveners in the federal government's suit against Reserve. The Minnesota Pollution Control Agency unwillingly had become involved in 1969, however, when Reserve Mining filed suit against them in the Lake County District Court.

The key actor in the controversy, of course, was the Reserve Mining Company. Since the original permit hearings in 1947, Reserve had consistently attempted either to undermine policy procedures of government agencies or to ignore government decisions altogether. Aligned with Reserve were the residents of the town of Silver Bay and several other smaller communities in the Silver Bay area who counted on the company's 3,000 jobs.

The Policy Process

The case of Reserve Mining versus the Minnesota Pollution Control Agency was basically an appeal by Reserve regarding the validity of certain portions of the federal-state water quality standards of Minnesota as they applied to the company. Reserve also wanted to postpone the permit hearings ordered by a Hennepin County judge in a suit brought by the Sierra Club and the Minnesota Committee for Environmental Information during the fall of 1969. Reserve won an injunction in April 1970 to halt the permit hearings until after the decision on its appeal.

The Lake County trial began in June 1970 and continued until December. Both sides flew in witnesses from all over the country. On December 15, 1970, Judge Eckman ruled that the antidegradation of water quality clause in the Minnesota legislation was not applicable or enforceable against Reserve, and that the effluent standard of the state was unreasonable, arbitrary, and invalid as applied to Reserve. However, he also ordered Reserve to alter its discharge method and to contain taconite tailings in the Great Trough, the deepest part of the lake, where Reserve Mining had claimed all its wastes were deposited. The judge set a deadline of May 15, 1971, for Reserve to submit its plans to the Minnesota Pollution Control Agency.

On January 14, 1971, the second meeting of the second session of the Federal Enforcement Conference began, and the next day Reserve proposed to add thickeners and a settling agent to the tailings to keep them in the Great Trough. In March, however, the technical committee of the conference decided this solution was unacceptable. When the company failed to present an alternate plan, the Federal Environmental Protection Agency (EPA) administrator, William Ruckelshaus, issued a 180-day notice to Reserve on April 28, 1971, under the Federal Water Pollution Control Act.

Reserve did not meet its 180-day deadline, and so on February 17, 1972, the U.S. Justice Department, at the request of EPA, filed suit against the Reserve Mining Company. Several environmental groups that had attempted to call attention to the pollution problem during the April 1971 to February 1972 period and had pressured the federal government to file suit against Reserve became interveners in the case. These groups included the Minnesota Environmental Law Institute (created for the trial), the Northern Environmental Council, the Save Lake Superior Association, the Michigan Student Environmental Conference, and the Environmental Defense Fund. On Reserve's side were eleven other groups, including local units of government and commercial and civic groups such as the Silver Bay Chamber of Commerce.

The government's case against Reserve originally was based almost entirely on the allegation that discharging tailings caused pollution in violation of federal water quality laws. But before the trial began, a report from a University of Wisconsin professor in June 1973 alleged contamination of the water supplies in several Lake Superior communities due to the presence of large amounts of asbestos-like fibers. The EPA considered the danger significant enough to recommend that children under six should not drink tap water until tests to determine the effects of the asbestos-like fibers on human health were completed. At the same time, Federal District Judge Lord ruled that the issue of airborne abestos-type fibers was also to be considered in the Reserve case.

The discovery of cumingtonite in water drawn from Lake Superior really affected the position of the case for the plaintiffs. The media, which had made a tremendous effort to play up the danger of pollution to Lake Superior, now had a cause célèbre to write about; articles publicizing the potential health hazard of asbestos in the water supply were readily consumed by a concerned public. Only in Silver Bay, where patrons of the local taverns jokingly ordered "bourbon and asbestos," did the seriousness of the health problem fail to arouse the public.

The trial against Reserve continued until March 9, 1974, when the judge ordered a recess until the three independent studies on the cumingtonite health hazard were completed. On March 20, 1974, Judge Lord held a public hearing in Duluth in which he expressed his concern about the danger of the asbestos-type fibers in the water supplies and his hope that Reserve would soon present alternative disposal sites on land as had been ordered previously. On April 20, when Reserve failed to produce any plan at all, Judge Lord ordered the company to shut down its plant. While the judge was aware that closing the plant would severely disrupt the area's economy, he said, "The court must consider the people downstream from the discharge. Under no circumstances will the court allow the people of Duluth to be continuously and indefinitely exposed to a known human carcinogen in order that the people in Silver Bay can continue working at their jobs." On April 22, however, three federal appeals court judges granted a temporary stay to permit Reserve to resume operations. As a result of this decision, the longest environmental trial in U.S. history returned to the courts.

Outcome

On June 4, 1974, the same panel of the appeals court found that there was insufficient evidence to support Judge Lord's finding that an immediate health hazard existed. The decison virtually insured that Reserve could continue to discharge carcinogenic tailings into the lake while it converted its system to on-land disposal, a process officials estimated would take from three to five years. The three states involved in the proceedings, as well as a number of environmental groups, again filed suit to stop the discharges but the appellate court ruled, in March 1975, that even though the discharges are a threat to health, Reserve could continue to dump the tailings into Lake Superior since the company had to be given "reasonable" time to convert to on-land disposal. Minnesota, Wisconsin, and Michigan along with the environmental groups then requested the Supreme Court to step into the controversy by setting a two-year deadline for Reserve to end its pollution. The

Court rejected that request in April 1975, although the matter is expected to come before the Court later so the justices can decide whether to give the case a full-scale review. Although critics feared that Reserve would continue to postpone the switch to an on-land disposal site as long as possible, the company's resistance appeared to be weakening under the pressure of public action, court rulings, and, perhaps, a corporate recognition that the ultimate cost of non-compliance would be higher than the cost of a prompt change in disposal methods.

Nevertheless, the controversy continues in the press. On May 25 and June 29, 1975, letters in the *New York Times* carried on the debate. On the earlier date, U.S. Senators Nelson, Hart, and Percy cited "substantial medical evidence that drinking Lake Superior water containing asbestos fibers creates a health risk." In the latter issue, M. R. Banovetz, executive vice president of Reserve Mining denied this allegation and declared that the company had proposed a $252 million on-land tailings disposal plan and that the public hearings on a state permit for this plan had only begun on June 23. And so the final outcome of the case remains in doubt.

Meanwhile the United States Court of Appeals for the Eighth Circuit removed Judge Lord from further jurisdiction in the case on grounds of bias against the company. After the Court had rejected his plea to retain jurisdiction, he declared: "I have done my best to provide for the maximum protection of the public health consistent with due process to all concerned. As of today I can do no more."[3]

CASE VI   Nuclear Radiation: The Davis-Besse Reactor, Ohio

There are currently 36 nuclear power plants operating in the United States and another 146 are under construction or on order. By the end of the century, more than 1,000 will be in service, producing millions of gallons of high level radioactive waste that will have to be handled, transported, and reprocessed every year. To date, radioactive wastes have been handled with amazing success, although some radioactive wastes do escape into the environment. In the past, escaped radiation has been kept under the safety limit set by the Federal Radiation Council, but this limit (.5 REM of radiation per person per year) has increasingly been criticized by scientists as being too high. Researchers work-

[3] *New York Times,* January 8, 1976.

ing for the former Atomic Energy Commission estimated that if the entire population were exposed to radiation at the level deemed safe, the cancer and leukemia death rate would increase by 10 percent annually and the rate of genetic changes would increase by 5 to 50 percent. Even though this estimate is controversial, most scientists now agree that even the slightest amount of radiation is hazardous to health.

The threat of increased radiation in the environment, the possibility of a major accident at a nuclear plant, or the possibility of an accident while radioactive wastes are being transported has generated a great deal of citizen concern. A typical struggle of citizens attempting to influence nuclear power policy occurred in Ohio, near Port Clinton on Lake Erie, in early 1970. Citizens attempted to halt construction of the 870-megawatt Davis-Besse nuclear power plant on the grounds that it was a threat to public health.

The Actors

The federal agency responsible for licensing nuclear power facilities has been the Atomic Energy Commission (AEC). By law, applications for a license are discussed in hearings held in the area where the proposed plant is to be built. The public, along with state and local authorities, can attend these hearings. Theoretically, any member of the public with legitimate concerns may participate in the proceedings. The Environmental Protection Agency (EPA) also plays a role in nuclear power policy: it examines all AEC proposals and reviews the required environmental impact statements to determine if human health and the environment would be adequately protected from radiation and other factors. In the Davis-Besse case, however, the AEC had not yet complied with this provision of the NEPA.

The state of Ohio also had jurisdiction in the Davis-Besse case because the 1970 Water Quality Act required that every applicant for a federal license or permit for construction or operation of facilities which may result in discharges into navigable waters must obtain a state permit certifying that the discharges would not violate the water quality standards of the state.

The major citizens' groups intervening in the Davis-Besse case were the Coalition for Safe Nuclear Power (later Safe Electric Power) and a student group from Bowling Green State University called LIFE. The coalition, formed in early 1970, consisted of about nine groups; its sole purpose was to fight the Davis-Besse plant.

The Policy Process

The construction hearings for the proposed Davis-Besse plant were scheduled to begin on November 23, 1970. Prior to the hearing, the AEC granted a variance to the applicants, Toledo Edison Co. and Cleveland Illuminating Co., to allow them to start construction at their own risk. This was a general practice of the AEC, but one of the interveners objected to it before the permit was granted. Nevertheless, construction continued—even through the hearings, which took place off and on from November 1970 to February 1971.

The Coalition for Safe Nuclear Power was not granted intervener status until December 9, 1970, after the hearings had already begun. The coalition had little time to prepare its case, but it presented a list of about forty issues it wanted to discuss. These included radiation standards, emergency plans and procedures in case of an accident, transportation of radioactive wastes from the plant, and the actual safety of the proposed site, which was close to the population centers of Detroit, Toledo, and Cleveland. The AEC's rules about what could be discussed at construction hearings eliminated approximately three-fourths of these issues from consideration. Some of the remaining issues raised by the interveners were granted consideration, but that allowance was granted only to LIFE, not to the coalition. The wording of the coalition's contentions was considered unacceptable to the AEC hearing board.

On March 23, 1971, the AEC ruled that construction on the Davis-Besse plant could proceed. The interveners filed an appeal with the AEC for a stay of construction pending the environmental hearing required by NEPA. When this request was turned down, the coalition then filed an appeal with the U.S. district court on May 21, 1971. The appeal was based on the fact that the AEC had not fulfilled the requirements of NEPA. On October 21, the court ruled that the AEC had to hold another hearing, and the ruling specified what the AEC should consider at the hearing. The record of the hearing was then to be returned to the district court.

In the interim, the Ohio Water Pollution Control Board had held its hearing on the Davis-Besse nuclear plant on July 28. The board ruled that radioactive waste was not included in the state's nondegradation clause governing water quality and granted the required permit.

After further delays, the AEC finally scheduled a hearing for May 2, 1972, to determine if construction of the Davis-Besse power plant should be suspended pending the full hearing to consider the NEPA requirements. Although the interveners had prepared their case and were ready to present witnesses, the AEC hearing board decided to limit the hearing only to the environmental effects of construction between May and December of that year. This decision, in violation of the court order, prevented the coalition from presenting its witnesses. On the day the AEC was to turn the record of the hearing back over to the district court, they filed a request for an extension of time to hold an additional hearing of issues "not allowed" at the May hearing. This second hearing was held on July 7, but this time the coalition could not produce the witnesses that had been available in May. On July 9, the hearing board ruled that construction of the Davis-Besse plant should not be suspended. The interveners filed their exceptions to the ruling, but it was affirmed by the AEC appeals board.

When the AEC turned the record of the hearings back to the district court, as ordered, the court was in summer recess. When the court reconvened, the AEC promised to hold the full environmental hearing "as soon as possible." This hearing was scheduled for May 22, 1973, when the power plant was about half finished. The hearing board required all testimony of the interveners be submitted in written form prior to the hearing. The principal witness for the coalition was Ernest Sternglass, director of radiological physics at the University of Pittsburgh School of Medicine. Sternglass based his testimony on two research studies drawn from radiation monitoring reports in the vicinity of two small nuclear reactors—one on the Ohio River and another at Plum Brook, about twenty-five miles from the Davis-Besse site. The studies showed radiation levels in soil, water, and milk to be very much higher than would be expected from the reported releases of the reactors. The monitoring studies used by Sternglass had been undertaken by the Ohio EPA, and another set was obtained from Bio-Test Laboratories.

Outcome

Despite Sternglass's testimony and other issues raised by the interveners, the AEC hearing board ruled that the requirements of NEPA had been met and that construction of the Davis-Besse plant could be completed. The coalition had spent close to $10,000, raised through contributions, to prevent the construction of the plant. They estimated that they would have needed approximately $100,000 to wage a successful battle against the AEC.

Conclusion

The shortcomings of our environmental health policies derive largely from perceptual, legal, and institutional inadequacies. While these inadequacies are encountered in almost all of the policy areas considered in this book, they are especially troublesome in the area of environmental health. For this reason, it is useful to consider the effects of these inadequacies on policy formulation in the cases included in this chapter. Two key perceptual problems inhibit the formulation of satisfactory environmental health policies.

The first is the general tendency of both decision makers and citizens to think in terms of specific health problems rather than to consider the larger environmental framework of health relationships. Man's health today depends essentially upon the interaction of two ecological universes: the internal environment of man (the bio-social organism) and the external multi-environments in which he exists. Recognition of this interaction is the first step in formulating good health policies. The failure to consider the intricacies of this interaction results in contradictory and even hazardous policies. Such policy failures were seen in California when the national forest in Los Angeles was sprayed with herbicides, with little thought given to the spread of the chemicals in the food-chain or even to the safety of the fire fighters. Or again, when an asbestos-like fiber was dumped into Lake Superior on the false assumption that the wastes would undoubtedly settle in the deepest part of the lake without affecting the lake's ecosystem or the drinking water of the lake communities.

Understandably, policy makers are reluctant to make decisions on health-related problems when even expert opinion is divided on the subject. The practice of the courts recently has been to insist upon demonstrable proof of a health hazard. The courts' insistence upon demonstration of cause-and-effect proof in the area of environmental health has seriously limited the citizen's ability to challenge practices dangerous to his well-being. Such proof is available in clinical medicine, but (as almost all of the case studies illustrated) it is rarely available in the field of environmental medicine. Faced with such scientific uncertainties, regulatory agencies have been in a quandary to decide what are acceptable standards. Dr. John Finklea, director of the National Environmental Research Center in North Carolina (the principal EPA health laboratory) has outlined some of the problems facing the courts and health agencies which influence perceptions of environmental health issues:

1. There is usually insufficient information regarding the exposure to environmental agents because health-related environmental monitoring has been underdeveloped and because of wide variations in human reactions to the same agents.
2. The links between exposure and disease are complex. For example, the effects of infrequent short-term peak exposures may well differ markedly from the effects of long-term exposures or frequently repeated short-term exposures over a long time. Furthermore, a single environmental agent may contribute to a number of different disorders and a single disorder may result from a combination of agents.
3. Environmental health studies are limited by deficiencies in vital records and imperfections in assessment of death and illnesses. A research data base which draws on the results of studies in occupational as well as clinical settings is usually lacking.

The second critical perceptual problem, which is directly related to the first, is the fact that much of the public and many decision makers simply do not know that certain environmental problems even exist. As indicated earlier, citizen activity in health problems has primarily been concentrated upon water and air pollution issues. Most citizens do not give a second thought to the safety of food additives, nuclear power plants, x-ray machines, or pesticides. Especially in urban areas, problems of noise, housing, light, and so on are usually considered normal aspects of city life.

The lack of public participation in policy decisions relating to mental and social well-being has highly significant sociological and political implications. Various studies have shown that a citizen's awareness of his exposure to health-endangering environmental situations is directly related to social patterns and, in a large percentage of cases, to economic status. What this means in geographic and socioeconomic terms is that the urban poor, who live where many health problems are critical, are most likely to suffer the full effects of their unhealthy environment. (See Chapter 9, The Quality of Urban Life.)

More important, however, is a fact brought out by most of the case studies in this book: while poor people living in often deplorable environments in the inner city are more than aware of their plight, they are not usually among the ranks of citizens active on environmental policy issues. The reason is simple. Efforts to affect or generate policy require, above all, time, money, and information—commodities which are scarce in economically, or educationally, impoverished areas. The result is that poor people tend to have limited access to policy channels.

A second group with an inordinate proportion of health problems are workers in certain hazardous occupations, for example, coal miners. What is atypical in their case, however, is that coal miners have been able to influence policy on their own behalf. Yet, as the black lung case study brought out, incitement to strike for black lung compensation came first from the efforts of local physicians; it did not occur naturally among the workers. While some workers are increasingly aware of the hazards they face daily in their jobs, most workers, like the urban poor, do not yet perceive the extent of the threat posed by their working environment. Once again, ignorance results in limited concern for and influence on, the policy process.

The question of access to policy-making channels reveals some of the particular legal and institutional problems that citizens face in attempting to affect environmental health policy. Until very recently, many areas of environmental health policy were left to state and local agencies. As the New York City case on noise illustrates, local agencies often have vague standards or no enforcement authority to implement their policies. On every level of government, political organization and practices have failed to keep up with technological innovation and the concomitant problems of a growing population.

The establishment of the Environmental Protection Agency (EPA) in 1970 was a major step toward consolidating areas of policy which had formerly been divided among several agencies. The EPA administers laws that regulate the use of pesticides, control the disposal of solid wastes, and establish general standards for radiation emission, noise, and protection of food and drinking water. Yet the case studies indicate that a number of key areas in environmental health policy remain under the jurisdiction of other agencies—for example, the Food and Drug Administration (FDA), the Nuclear Regulatory Commission (NRC), and the Energy Research and Development Agency (ERDA). Moreover, the establishment of the EPA has not had much influence to date on most environmental health policy issues. Enforcement is usually the decisive test on policy, yet most enforcement actions brought by EPA, as the case studies illustrate, involve cases of water pollution, such as the Lake Superior-Reserve Mining case.

This controversy occasioned one of two recent court cases which may indicate the major problem with the authority used by EPA to enforce standards. In the Reserve Mining case and in another case involving the EPA's regulations phasing out the lead content of gasoline (see Chapter 4, Air Quality and Climate Modification), the court ruled in each case that EPA had not furnished definite proof that the asbestos or lead had caused demonstrable illness in a substantial part of the population. In both cases, EPA relied on what it believed to be the preponderance of scientific data suggesting adverse health effects. The affected industries produced their own scientific studies to indicate the opposite. The court agreed with the industries. In both cases, there was suspicion, even among the dissenting judges, that the majority opinion reflected concern for economic considerations rather than health-related ones.

The National Environmental Protection Act (NEPA) has met with equal difficulties in actual enforcement. Two examples of citizen action using the NEPA were examined in this chapter. In the Davis-Besse nuclear power plant case, the NEPA failed to influence the final decision, and the ultimate outcome of the PEP case against forest spraying is, as yet, uncertain. While NEPA has been effective in some cases, federal, state, and local action in the area of environmental health has, for the most part, failed to protect the public welfare. One of the most shocking examples of this failure was the disclosure in the spring of 1975 of the preliminary findings of EPS's water pollution tests which showed that at least one suspected carcinogen was in the public water supply of all seventy-nine cities surveyed. At that time, the agency said that there was no reason to suspect different findings for the rest of the nation's public water sources. Considering that the nation did not have a drinking-water supply law until December 1974, the state of the public water supplies is understandable, perhaps, but not excusable.

Because of the inability of government agencies to act, or the ineptitude of government enforcement efforts, the agencies have consequently often become an adversary to the public in environmental health policy issues. This happened in the black lung case, the food additives cases, the PEP case (at the federal agency level), and the Davis-Besse power plant controversy. Several of the case studies also illustrate the fact that many government decisions relating to environmental health are made in response to a crisis, not as an expression of policy.

A third institutional and legal problem affecting environmental health policy concerns the powers of specific agencies such as the AEC (now part of ERDA) and the FDA. These agencies have been able to determine "officially" what is safe for the public in their respective jurisdictions—nuclear power and food and drug policy. Confrontation with these agencies has usually entailed two problems: first, the public has usually lacked the expertise to challenge the agencies' assertions and, second, citizens have had little opportunity for meaningful participation in the policy process of either agency. In AEC hearings, for example, the commission's own rules strictly regulated what topics would be considered and who would be allowed to intervene. If an agency was able to refuse to consider critical health safety issues because it did not approve of the language used by the citizen interveners, the chances for influential citizen participation were obviously minimal. The AEC was successfully challenged by citizen groups on occasion, but such cases were the exception rather than the rule (see Chapter 6, Energy, the Eugene nuclear power case in 1970, and Chapter 7, The Economy and Growth, the LMFBRs and the Scientists' Institute for Public Information in 1973). Now that the AEC has been substantially incorporated into ERDA, perhaps the citizen will have a better chance of influencing critical health-related energy policies.

The extent of institutional and legal obstacles confronting concerned citizens in the area of environmental health policy is shown by the fact that, in most of the examples cited in this chapter, citizens had to take their cases to court. Protest and confrontation tactics were used in two cases (black lung and New York noise control), but these confrontations were followed by legal action in the form of new legislation. While a variety of tactics have been effective in air and water pollution (see Chapter 4, Air Quality and Weather Modification, and Chapter 3, Inland Waters), environmental health conflicts usually end up as legal suits. The two main difficulties with suing are that it costs a tremendous amount of money and usually drags on over several years. For example, the Davis-Besse group spent nearly $10,000, PEP has spent more than $2,000, and so on. These are considerable sums when one considers that they are raised by donations and do not include the many hours of volunteer help and donated legal services. The Lake Superior citizens' groups openly admit that they probably would not have had the financial strength to carry out the court battle with Reserve Mining Company if the federal government had not joined their side.

Even if the citizens do win their cases, legislation is not sufficient to ensure that the public health really will be protected, as all of the case studies show. Nor is legislation a substitute for comprehensive, long-range policies. The fundamental concern about environmental degradation should be, but usually is not, its threat to health and life. Attempting to treat the symptoms with a few halfhearted efforts to control the causes of certain health problems is not the answer. We cannot, for instance, successfully improve inadequate housing until we confront the more basic problems of poverty and its concomitant life-styles. The interrelationship of environmental health problems makes it essential to overcome these difficulties at the perceptual, legal, and institutional levels. To do this, we must educate the public and become involved in policy decisions so vital to our well-being.

Readings

Baron, Robert Alex. *The Tyranny of Noise*. New York: St. Martin's Press, 1970.

Dansereau, Pierre. *Challenge for Survival: Land, Air, and Water for Man in Megalopolis*. New York: Columbia University Press, 1970.

Duhl, Leonard J. "Environmental Health: Politics, Planning, and Money." *American Journal of Public Health*, 58 (February 1968), 232–237.

Fishbein, Gershon. "The Future of Environmental Health at the Federal Level." *American Journal of Public Health*, 58 (March 1968), 441–445.

Frederickson, H. G. and Howard Magnas. "Comparing Attitudes Toward Water Pollution in Syracuse." In *Politics, Policy and Natural Resources*, edited by Dennis L. Thompson. New York: Free Press, 1972.

Hanlon, John J. "An Ecological View of Public Health." *American Journal of Public Health*, 59 (January 1969), 4–11.

Kupchik, George. "Environmental Health in the Ghetto." *American Journal of Public Health*, 59 (February 1969), 220–225.

Lee, Douglas H. K. *Environmental Factors in Respiratory Disease*. New York: Academic Press, 1972.

Sargent, Frederick, II. "Man-Environment Problems for Public Health." *American Journal of Public Health*, 62 (May 1972), 628–633.

United States Environmental Protection Agency. Office of Public Affairs. *Health Effects of Environmental Pollution*. Washington, D.C.: U.S. EPA, 1973.

World Health Organization. *Health Hazards of the Human Environment*. Geneva: World Health Organization, 1972.

9

Quality of Urban Life

Introduction

Although urban communities have existed for at least 5,500 years, it was not until the nineteenth century that they became the immediate environment for a significant fraction of the population of any nation. In the United States, the population was transformed from a predominantly rural one (60 percent in 1900) to a predominantly urban one (70 percent in 1970) in only seventy years.

By 1974, however, the trend toward urban living, which began in the first decade of the twentieth century in America, has suddenly reversed direction. For the first time (except for a brief period during the 1930s), the movement back to small cities and towns in the United States has overtaken the growth in metropolitan areas. Evidence of this dramatic turnabout emerged in a study conducted for the Census

332

Bureau for the period 1970 to 1973. The study found that the most significant population growth during the three-year period occurred in counties not adjacent to metropolitan areas; the growth of these counties cannot, therefore, be attributed merely to the expansion of a neighboring big city or its suburbs.

This remarkable demographic change has been attributed to two broad developments: (1) growing disenchantment with metropolitan areas, which are beset with high crime rates, pollution, and other problems; and (2) the increasing availability of jobs in rural areas and small cities—even those far removed from the big metropolises.

Both of these trends indicate critical issues affecting the quality of urban life in America today. Some of the consequences of the incredibly rapid urban growth of the 1960s such as urban sprawl, increased solid waste, housing and health problems, inadequate transportation systems, and loss of open space have reached crisis proportions in many American cities. The crisis has become particularly acute because many of the problems affecting the quality of life in American cities are regional, and even national, in nature, but the resolution of these problems has often been left to underfunded and generally reluctant local governments. Even though technical solutions may be available to meet metropolitan requirements, policy-making bodies in the metropolitan areas have been unable to cope politically with these issues.

The necessity of establishing more efficient and effective institutions to meet the problems of the urban environment is essential if, for example, the deleterious consequences of unplanned urban growth are to be overcome. The encroachment of urban areas on agricultural land has been severe, yet few areas have policies dealing with the protection of neighboring farm lands. Each year for the past decade, 350,000 acres of farmland have been devoured by urban development. Another 1.9 million acres of rural land have been lost each year to highways, airports, and flood control projects. Generally, this farmland has been superior to the new cropland that has replaced it. Not only has such expansion taken good farmland out of production and reduced open space around urban areas, but it has also created a visible disunity in many metropolitan communities. Most of the development around urban centers has, in fact, been segmental. The social importance of this condition of scatteration and random clutter should not be overlooked. As the noted urban specialist Kevin Lynch has pointed out, "When the parts of the city lack visible relation to one another, their incoherence can contribute to a sense of alienation—of being lost in an environment with which one cannot carry on any sort of dialogue."[1]

How, then, should decision makers cope with the question of urban growth? Is there an ideal size for a city? And what type of planning would ensure an optimum size and character? How can cities already beyond their optimum size develop a methodology to meet the needs of their residents? Certain communities have attempted to determine their growth to protect the quality of life, but public opinion, both local and national, is quite divided on the issue. Efforts to control population growth in already established cities have not been very successful for a number of reasons. (See the Boulder case study in this chapter and the Petaluma case in Chapter 1, Land Use.)

One method of ensuring an appropriate level of population in an urban community, however, is the development of "new towns." New towns are planned communities, usually built by private developers in the United States. Two of the most famous examples are Reston, Virginia, only twenty-five miles from Washington, D.C., and Columbia, Maryland, midway between Washington and Baltimore. The former was developed for a population of 75,000, while the latter has a goal of 100,000. A major problem with such communities is that they have tended to exclude many low income families. Furthermore, there is very little existing legislation to guide the development of new towns, and the problems of incorporation and the provision of adequate public services are not insignificant. Most important, perhaps, are the difficulties of ensuring citizen participation and establishing an institutional framework which cannot easily be subverted by the developer.

Planned communities can avoid many of the problems of already established urban areas such as poor housing, lack of open space, and inadequate transportation systems. This is no consolation, however, to those living in what is termed "the central cities." Because of the general movement of whites to the suburbs in the past two decades, the poor and certain ethnic minorities have become the predominant residents in many of America's largest cities. According to a report in 1968 of the National Commission on Urban Problems, by 1985, 70 percent of metropolitan whites will be living in the suburbs and 75 percent of metropolitan nonwhites in the central city. The concomitant economic

---

[1] Kevin Lynch, "The City as Environment," *Scientific American* (September 1965), 209–214.

pattern of the poor in the cities and the wealthy in the suburbs does not apply uniformly to all metropolitan areas; there are numerous suburbs that are relatively poor in their tax base, and there are heavy concentrations of taxable assets in central cities. Nevertheless, the revenue imbalances among the political units of most large urban areas are extremely pronounced.

Local governments increasingly face a crisis: the people now living in the central cities tend to require more government services than other sectors of society, but the loss of the middle and upper income families, as well as industries and retail firms, from these areas has meant that the central cities are usually unable to raise sufficient tax revenue for the services required. "Required services," however, is a euphemism cloaking the more serious social problems which are equally as critical as the physical problems of the central cities.

Evidence indicates, for example, that poor housing plays an important role in the development of mental illness. Overcrowding, poor lighting, noise, and unsanitary conditions have an obvious impact upon residents (see Chapter 8, Environmental Health), but it is often difficult to establish a causal connection between specific evidence of poor housing and the deplorable social conditions that frequently are associated with it. These include poor health, economic deprivation, improper nutrition, family instability, and poor quality community services. Such conditions are especially prevalent in the deteriorating sections of larger cities, where today nearly two-thirds of all nonwhite families in the central cities are estimated to live in neighborhoods marked by substandard housing and general urban blight.

Another serious policy problem which afflicts the central cities as well as the surrounding areas is the lack of open space and recreational areas. This need is often disregarded in urban communities, by both citizen and decision maker alike, with significant consequences for the quality of urban life. Unfortunately, the open space that remains in most cities is often a conglomeration of unrelated areas. Some communities have adopted various types of greenbelt plans to help preserve a planned pattern of open space in and around rapidly expanding urban areas. Atlanta, Houston, Raleigh, and San Antonio have all had some success with such policies. The Willamette riverfront in Oregon is also being developed as a greenbelt area through the crowded Willamette Valley (see Chapter 3, Inland Waters). Greenbelts, of course, serve as additional recreational space, but the real problem in the central cities is not just the need for more recreational space, but the need for more functional space—for example, neighborhood centers where local residents can meet to discuss their goals and plans or merely get to know one another. However, since residents in the central cities often lack both the access to necessary policy channels and the knowledge and skill to use those that are available, community participation in planning and developing public facilities and open space is usually nonexistent.

No discussion of the quality of urban life in America, however brief, can neglect the problem of transportation. There is no question that past and present transportation policies have greatly affected the urban and nonurban environments in the United States. In particular, our national and state transportation policies have directly encouraged the trend toward dependence on the automobile as the major form of transportation. Today, this dependence is having serious consequences, diminishing both our fuel reserves and the ability of the atmosphere to absorb all the added pollutants.

Only six American cities currently have any significant form of public transportation besides buses: New York, Chicago, Philadelphia, Boston, Cleveland, and San Francisco. One hopes Washington, D.C.'s rapid transit system will be completed in the nineteen seventies. With very few exceptions, larger U.S. urban areas are now served by public transit authorities which were established to bail out private carriers. Only three states (New York, Pennsylvania, and Massachusetts) provide any significant financial support for urban transit systems, and only a few states have a statewide administrative agency responsible for public transit. Yet the state highway agencies are generally responsible for the planning, construction, and operation of urban freeway systems. Since highways are perhaps the major factor in determining the specific directions of metropolitan development, the lack of state cooperation in public transit development has greatly limited the policy choices of the local communities.

Inadequate transportation systems, lack of open space, urban sprawl, and all the consequences associated with the inordinate growth of the cities (increased solid waste, destruction of historic sites, water pollution, air pollution, noise, etc.) are all acting to decrease the quality of urban life in America. Unfortunately, the brunt of many urban problems has fallen on the poor and on minority groups, as indicated above, and these are the citizens with the least access to policy channels and to the means necessary to conduct an effective struggle on their own behalf. Although many of these problems appear almost insurmountable, citizens' efforts to confront some of the issues offer a small sign of hope for the future.

CASE I   Quality versus Size: Boulder, Colorado

In 1960, the city of Boulder was a small college town located in the natural basin of Boulder Valley, Colorado. Foothills of the Rocky Mountains bordered the western edge of the city and mesas bordered two other sides. Though only twenty-three miles from Denver, the city was valued for its open space and natural beauty. In one decade, however, the population in Boulder jumped from 58,000 in 1960 to 70,000 in 1970; most of this increase was due to immigration.

Boulder is not an average American city. Not only are there obvious physical constraints on its growth (the mountains and a shortage of water), but the residents of Boulder are uncommonly aware that the growth of their city can be controlled, or at least significantly affected, as a matter of public policy. This awareness has been the major stimulus to Boulder's efforts to limit its population.

The Actors

Boulder's attempts to control the size of its population have been guided by a combination of the city council and citizen initiative. Since the 1950s, the city council has been actively concerned with the growth issue. The city planning commission has played a somewhat secondary role in the various controversies over the years.

A number of citizens' groups have supported growth studies or sponsored legislative initiatives that have appeared on the Boulder ballot. These include the League of Women Voters, PLAN Boulder, People United to Restore the Environment (PURE), and Zero Population Growth (ZPG). Both PURE and ZPG played key roles in the 1971 proposed referendum to limit the population of Boulder to 100,000.

The federal Department of Housing and Urban Development (HUD) subsequently became involved in the Boulder growth issue when the city asked HUD to provide two-thirds of the funding for a growth study commission set up in 1972.

The Policy Process

Some important growth policy decisions made prior to the 1971 referendum must be examined in order to understand the attitudes of the local population and the impact of these attitudes on the decision-making process in Boulder. In 1958, the city passed a "blue line" regulation which established a perimeter surrounding the city beyond which no water service would be supplied. This measure was welcomed by the citizens as a means to protect the foothills' scenic landscape from being urbanized. In 1968, the city adopted a greenbelt program to protect open space around the city's edge. The program included the eventual purchase of some 2,740 acres, and the principal source of funding (approved by the voters in 1967) was a sales tax. In the past decade, Boulder has also adopted a fifty-five-foot building-height limit to prevent population congestion and has attempted to discourage urban expansion by charging a high price for water and sewer hookups. In December 1970, both the city and county of Boulder adopted a Boulder Valley Comprehensive Plan, which controls land use in a fifty-eight square mile area in and around Boulder.

By 1971, it became obvious to city residents that in spite of their efforts to protect the character of Boulder, the city was rapidly changing due to pressures for development. In a survey conducted by PURE to test the opinion of the citizens, 70 percent of the respondents wanted the city to restrict growth while only 4 percent favored encouraging growth. Furthermore, 79 percent felt that continued growth would have undesirable effects on their way of life and 86 percent indicated they did not expect a stabilized population would adversely affect their way of life. Based on the results of this opinion poll and on a cost-benefit analysis of past growth done by ZPG, PURE and ZPG decided to sponsor jointly an initiative on the municipal ballot in 1971, seeking "to stabilize the ultimate population of the city of Boulder near one hundred thousand." The city council, however, became concerned about the potential impact of such a move and offered its own initiative:

> The city government, working with the county government, shall take all steps necessary to hold the rate of growth in Boulder Valley to a level substantially below that experienced in the 1960's and shall insure that the growth that does take place shall provide living qualities in keeping with the policies found in the Boulder Valley Comprehensive Plan.

After a heated campaign, the council measure was affirmed by the electorate (70 percent in favor) while the ZPG initiative was defeated by 60 percent. In response to the decision, the city council formed a citizens' study commission to perform a $100,000, one-year growth analysis study of 375 square miles in and around Boulder. The council obtained a HUD grant to research the issue. The citizens' advisory group performed its duties apart from the town's planning staff, and the commission's ten-volume final report, finished in late 1973, contained very detailed recommendations for local and state policies pertaining to growth. The county commissioners have implemented one of the report's recommendations by forming a consortium of cities in Boulder County, with one representative from each city council or town board. The state legislature has yet to act upon any of the recommendations.

Outcome

Boulder's interim growth plan, however, suffered a serious setback in the spring of 1974 when a developer filed suit against the city for refusing his request for water and sewer hookups. The court ruled that the city was acting as a public utility by regulating public services and, therefore, was not allowed to choose its customers. The case has been appealed to the state supreme court, but the lower court's decision does not appear promising for the city's efforts to control its growth.

Meanwhile, Boulder has sought a new and more positive approach to the problem of urban sprawl. Under a new Growth Management System (GMS), the city hopes to concentrate growth in the downtown area by increasing height and density allowances while restricting developments at the suburban fringes. City Manager Archie Twitchell has described this novel approach as "revolutionary."

CASE II   Solid Waste Disposal: Louisville, Kentucky

Disposing of solid waste is one of the major problems confronting urban decision makers. While many new methods are now becoming available for the treatment and disposal of solid waste, the new technology is often very expensive. The city of Louisville, Kentucky, has traditionally incinerated its solid wastes. Although effective, incineration has been a major contributor to air pollution and may not be the best method of disposing of some materials which might be put back into productive use through recycling. The polluting effects of incineration were not generally recognized in Louisville until the incinerator received seventy-four citations from the city and county air pollution control inspectors between April 1965 and April 1969. Louisville's approach to solving the incineration problem illustrates the difficulties confronting both the citizen and decision maker in attacking the more fundamental issues of solid waste disposal in urban areas.

The Actors

The Louisville and Jefferson County Air Pollution Board was the official government agency responsible for controlling emissions from the incinerator. Jurisdiction over the city's solid wastes, however, was in the hands of the Department of Sanitation. By citing the incinerator for violations, the city was, in essence, fining itself for failing to observe the air quality legislation passed by the city and county in 1970. The city, consequently, had no other choice but to issue the incinerator a series of variances until a plan of action could be drawn up to halt the pollution.

Mayor Frank Burke became a powerful figure in the efforts to cope with the city's solid waste problem. His office decided to sponsor a bond proposal which would finance an immediate solution to the air pollution problem. An impressive number of citizens' groups supported the mayor's proposal. These included the League of Women Voters, Action for Clean Air, Inc., Strategies for Environmental Control, the Louisville Audubon Society, numerous unions, and the Louisville Chamber of Commerce. The incinerator bond proposal was also vigorously supported by the media. There was, in fact, little organized opposition to the bond issue.

The Policy Process

In June 1971, Mayor Burke appointed a six-member advisory committee to study the incineration problem. After considering both the corrective measures needed at the incinerator and alternative methods of waste disposal, the committee reported that the best solution available at that time was to install air pollution abatement equipment at the incinerator. The recommendation was based on economics: pollution control equipment would cost only a third of what a new incinerator or a new waste disposal method would cost. The committee hoped that in another fifteen years—the projected life of the existing incinerator—a better method of solid waste disposal would be feasible. In the meantime, Mayor Burke promised the key groups concerned with the problem (in particular, the League of Women Voters) that he would appoint a citizens' group to study a regional waste disposal solution for the Louisville area.

As a result of the advisory committee's findings, the city administration decided to support a $3.2 million bond proposal which would bring the city's aging incinerator into compliance with the clean air laws. The bond issue required no new taxes, a large factor in its favor. Nevertheless, passage of any bond issue is difficult in most cities, and in this case the incinerator bond was on the ballot with another bond issue for floodwall and drainage improvements which did require a property tax increase. The incinerator bond proponents were concerned that the voters might confuse the two issues and reject the incinerator bond. The problem was critical because a two-thirds majority was needed to pass the bond.

In order to publicize both the necessity of the incinerator bond and the fact that no tax increase was required, the mayor's office employed the Godfrey Communications Company, a Louisville public relations firm. Private citizens' groups also helped to win public endorsement by running a tremendous campaign in favor of the bond. The League of Women Voters printed and distributed flyers and brochures concentrating on the effects of pollution in the city. They also sponsored a tour of the local landfill and incinerator for forty key individuals, including the mayor, to point out the complexity of the solid waste problem.

Other groups volunteered for door-to-door canvassing, and a special effort was made to arouse residents of the Manly and Jackson areas of the city where, according to a study by a Louisville graduate student, air pollution from the incinerator was most concentrated. All of these efforts were combined with tremendous support from the press, TV, and radio.

Outcome

The efforts by the city officials and citizens' groups in publicizing the bond issue proved to be effective on election day, November 7,

1972, when the voters passed the incinerator bond issue by a margin of about 68 percent. The solid waste study committee was then established, as promised by Mayor Burke. But a new mayor, elected the following year, appointed another committee to study local rather than regional solid waste disposal processes. This conflicting assignment of two committees has somewhat hindered the efforts of the original committee which still hopes to convince the new mayor that a regional solid waste disposal program is necessary.

CASE III   Housing and Lead Poisoning: New York City

Delapidated housing is a critical problem in many urban areas. The impact of poor housing upon its inhabitants is both physical and psychological, although the exact extent of damage wrought by inadequate housing is not known. One of the most severe physical effects often resulting from poor housing is lead poisoning. This is a condition which occurs when young children consistently consume quantities of lead-based paint or plaster. Excessive absorption of lead may cause hyperactivity, mental retardation, kidney disorders, or even death. It is estimated that some 250,000 to 400,000 American children between the ages of one and six have absorbed damaging amounts of lead from paint.

In New York City, Health Department officials have estimated that anywhere from 6,000 to 30,000 children have a level of lead in their blood above the level certain to cause damage. This case study describes the efforts of citizens, initially led by four members of the Scientists Committee for Public Information (SCPI), to combat the problem of lead poisoning and (less overtly) poor housing in New York City.

The Actors

Four key members of SCPI—Glenn Paulson, Edmund Rothschild, Evelyn Mauss, and Joel Buxbaum—formed a special subcommittee of SCPI in February 1968 to review the problem of lead poisoning and to plan a program of action. Their efforts were later augmented by a radical-liberal community organizer, Paul DuBrul, who formed the Citizens to End Lead Poisoning (CELP). This citizens' group included residents of Brooklyn slums and other poverty neighborhoods, representatives of health groups in other parts of the city, and a few SCPI members. CELP was supported by various politicians, including Mayor Lindsay, and by the media.

Like other American cities, New York had banned (in 1959) the use of lead-based paint for interior walls, but the provisions of the city code had never been enforced. The major city agency in charge of the lead poisoning problem was the Health Department; a second key agency, the Housing and Development Administration, theoretically operated in conjunction with the Health Department to enforce standards and relocate families from homes painted with lead-based paint. But these agencies appeared to be ill-equipped to cope with the situation.

The Policy Process

The four SCPI members' initial investigation of the lead poisoning problem in New York City disclosed that the root of the problem was dilapidated housing and that the ultimate solution was to repair old tenements. Although it had the authority to require landlords to repair apartments in which a child contracted lead poisoning, the department did not exercise its authority. Even if it did, the fines were too low to discourage offenders. The SCPI members also discovered in their investigations that it was impossible to test thousands of children in potentially affected areas, due to insufficient funds and personnel in the Health Department. The core SCPI group decided to run a testing experiment of their own in the summer of 1968 with the volunteer help of medical school students.

During the initial investigation period, Glenn Paulson had made contact with Paul DuBrul, who had a vast network of acquaintances he tapped for SCPI. He put Paulson in touch with the media, local politicians, and community organizations, and also helped the group design strategies to involve city government in the problem. The first attempts SCPI made to arrange appointments with the commissioners of health and the Housing and Development Administration failed. A few meetings were arranged with lesser officials in the department who, even if interested in the problem, saw little hope of preventing lead poisoning because of the impossibility of repairing all the old housing.

DuBrul and the SCPI group decided to try another strategy to get the city government to act. DuBrul's plan centered on involving the poverty neighborhoods. He formed a new group with primarily community members, and in August 1968, Citizens to End Lead Poisoning (CELP) came to life. CELP's program had three tasks: case detection, to be conducted by residents of the affected areas through existing antipoverty programs, neighborhood health centers, etc.; aggressive code enforcement, to be accomplished by community pressure against responsible agencies; and community organization, to be primarily an educational effort.

Before the formation of CELP, the commissioner of the Health Department had formed a task force to study the city's lead poisoning problem and to assess the department's efforts to solve it. The personnel assigned to the task force, however, were ineffective for a variety of reasons, not the least of which was bureaucratic red tape. What official services there were for detecting and treating lead poisoning were allocated to no fewer than four agencies within the Health Department. Cooperation between the Health Department and the housing authority was nonexistent. From August 1968 to the fall of 1969, for example, the housing authority requested opinions from the Health Department on 200 applications from families, alleging that the hazard of lead poisoning to their apartments should give them priority for placement in public housing. These requests were left unanswered for more than a year. Other signs of the Health Department's ineptitude were seen in the fact that approval of a warning poster about lead poisoning took nine months and that a pamphlet about lead poisoning was practically useless because it was written in very technical medical language meaningless to the layman.

Activating the bureaucratic wheels which had hindered the progress of CELP became somewhat easier in the spring of 1969. Following a six-month effort by Glenn Paulson, SCPI (along with the Health Department), the Public Health Association, the Health Research Council, and the Scientists' Institute for Public Information jointly sponsored a two-day conference on lead poisoning at Rockefeller University in March 1969. The conference served a number of functions. The conferees emphasized that without correcting poor housing conditions, no long-range solution to lead poisoning was possible. The conference also helped improve the status of the activists in the eyes of the city's medical establishment. And finally, a continuing committee on lead poisoning was formed at the close of the conference. This committee included Dr. Bernard Davidson, head of the Health Department's laboratories.

Further progress in the Health Department's growing awareness of the lead poisoning problem occurred when Dr. Mary McLaughlin became commissioner in July 1969. Three months later she announced a "stepped-up attack on lead poisoning." The Health Department's new tack coincided with a growing concern about the lead poisoning issue among local politicians and the media. The first politicians to raise the issue were two candidates for New York City offices: Carter Burden and Robert Abrams. Burden proved to be one of the most effective and concerned members of the group working against lead poisoning. His counterpart in the media was Jack Newfield, a widely read political writer and an editor of the *Village Voice*. Newfield not only wrote articles about the efforts of SCPI and CELP, but also appeared on television and encouraged other writers to publicize the seriousness of lead poisoning and poor housing. Many city officials later pointed to Newfield's articles as the catalyst of political pressure from a few thousand upper middle-class liberal voters. Pressure from this group called the lead poisoning issue to Mayor Lindsay's attention.

Mayor Lindsay appointed a new health services administrator who decided to demonstrate his abilities by taking up the lead poisoning cause. The new administrator, Gordon Chase, managed to overcome the Health Department's resistance to new programs and procedures. In the spring of 1970, Chase established a new Bureau of Lead Poisoning Control with Dr. Vincent Guinee as head. Among other achievements, Guinee arranged for the television station with the largest children's audience in the city to broadcast frequent public-interest announcements about lead poisoning and information on where to get children tested. Chase, Guinee, and Dr. McLaughlin held regular meetings with DuBrul, Paulson, and Carter Burden, among others, to continue receiving advice from the activists.

The goals of the Health Department's new program included not only the identification and treatment of poisoned children, but also the prevention of poisoning and repoisoning. To do this, the problem of housing also had to be attacked. The Housing and Development Administration, however, did not treat the problem with the same concern as the newly aroused Health Department. Since much of the Health Department's follow-up program depended upon the housing administration's Emergency Repair Program, the lack of full support from the administration really meant the failure of the Health Department's efforts as well. Yet, the housing administration was understandably discouraged with its task. A housing administration report found that only 60 percent of the apartments repaired by them met health code qualifications—and many of these apartments were almost as dangerous after repairs as before. Even if all the repairs could bring the apartments up to standard, the costs of repairing all the leaded apartments in poverty neighborhoods would be astronomical. One housing official summarized the hopeless situation by asking, "Is it really better to spend your money to de-lead 100,000 apartments than to build 10,000 new ones? It is a zero-sum game."[2]

Outcome

By 1971, much of the public pressure on the lead poisoning issue had dropped off, and most of the key activists had moved on to other problems. Even though a considerable amount of progress was made in combatting lead poisoning during the period of strong public involvement, the fundamental problem of dilapidated housing was largely untouched. And to the many poor people still living in such housing throughout the United States, lead poisoning remains a serious problem.

CASE IV   Urban Transportation: San Diego, California

In the early 1960s, the city of San Diego, California, faced a serious public transportation problem. For many years, transit service had been provided by a privately owned company, but gradually service deteriorated, patronage dropped steadily, and the system faced a fiscal crisis similar to that experienced by public transit nationally. In January 1963, the owners finally indicated that they could not continue operation much longer and suggested public ownership. Such a move was not guaranteed to ensure the stable financial operation of the transit system, as the experience of many other cities has shown. The San Diego experience, however, has become one of the most successful examples of a publicly operated transit system in a major metropolitan area.

The Actors

The city council was responsible for planning an alternative to the privately owned transportation system and for presenting it to the public. San Diego is a charter city (home rule) and is particularly

2 Quoted from Diana Gordon, *City Limits: Barriers to Change in Urban Governments* (New York: Charterhouse, 1973), p. 61.

adamant about maintaining jurisdiction over public services. Thus, even though the state of California adopted a bill at about the time of the San Diego crisis which would have allowed the metropolitan area of San Diego to form a transit district, this alternative was not considered acceptable to the majority of the local residents.

Citizens were active in San Diego primarily as voters, although a few key individuals like Harry Scheidle, chairman of the task force appointed by the city council, had a tremendous impact on influencing city opinion on the proposed alternative to the private system. Groups such as the League of Women Voters and the Committee to Support Proposition B also were important in ensuring the passage of the proposition. There was no organized opposition from either citizens' or business groups.

The Policy Process

In order to study the transportation situation in San Diego, a Special Transit Task Force was established by the city council with several prominent local citizens serving as members. During 1964 and 1965, the task force made extensive studies of the prevailing transportation conditions in the San Diego region. On February 1, 1966, it issued a final report to the San Diego City Council recommending acquisition of the transit system through a nonprofit corporation. Based on this recommendation, a charter amendment was submitted to the electorate authorizing acquisition of the privately owned system. The system was to be financed by a special transit tax (not to exceed ten cents on each $100 of assessed valuation of real and personal property).

Even though there was no organized opposition to the proposition, legislation which raises property taxes is never certain of approval. In many cities referenda to support public transit have been defeated. In San Francisco, one of two U.S. cities which has won voter approval of bonds to support rapid transit, the proposal to set up the Bay Area Rapid Transit District was passed by a very narrow margin. In San Diego, however, the choice was clear: either purchase the system or forego public transportation. Harry Scheidle and other concerned citizens, along with the League of Women Voters and the Committee to Support Proposition B, worked hard to publicize this choice. In June 1966 the San Diego voters approved the amendment to the city charter.

On July 1, 1966, the nonprofit San Diego Transit Corporation was formed, and the San Diego City Council appointed five prominent businessmen as its board of directors to establish policy on service rates, fares, and other administrative matters. On January 19, 1967, the city council passed and adopted an operating agreement between the city and the transit corporation which established the conditions under which the system would be operated. A few months later, the five directors formed the San Diego Transit Leasing Corporation for the purpose of borrowing $3 million to create local matching funds for a federal grant to purchase the system and 100 new buses.

Application for a federal grant was made possible under the 1964 Urban Mass Transportation Act, which authorized federal aid limited to two-thirds of the cost of transit improvement projects. San Diego was given a federal grant of $4 million, which allowed the city to purchase the transit system. The nonprofit corporation, however, was not organized as a part of the city government.

The corporation began operation on July 1, 1967. Initially, the city gave the corporation an operating agreement for only five years, because the success of the venture was highly uncertain. Public acquisition did not reverse the trend of declining ridership in the San Diego area, however, so the corporation's directors and management began a vigorous effort to rekindle public interest in riding buses. The corporation purchased new equipment and facilities with the aid of the federal money, and it established new rates. Ridership, however, still remained fairly constant, except for a marked increase in senior citizens and student riders, whose rate was a flat twenty-five cents with no additional zone charge.

The increase in ridership among senior citizens and students, coupled with new state legislation authorizing operating support for transit systems, led the transit management to recommend a twenty-five cent fare and no zone charge for all passengers in 1972. The corporate directors accepted the management's recommendation, and on September 1, 1972, the reduced fare went into effect. By February 1974 ridership was up 102 percent over February 1972. Although the lower fare was largely responsible for the increased public support of the transit system, changing public attitudes toward the environment and the shortages and increased costs of gasoline for automobiles have also been instrumental in the success of San Diego's system. The San Diego Transit Corporation has capitalized on changing attitudes and circumstances by stressing in its promotional campaigns that buses reduce air pollution and traffic congestion and conserve energy.

For the 1974–75 fiscal year, the San Diego Transit Corporation adopted an even more extensive "Action Plan" designed to make bus travel more competitive with auto travel. The plan involved adding six new express routes, eight new local routes, and increasing service on many other routes. This plan entailed increased expenditure, which has been supplied mostly through federal grant money.

Outcome

San Diego Transit Corporation now provides service within the city of San Diego, six urban municipalities, and unincorporated portions of San Diego. The system encompasses a 308 square mile area and serves a population of approximately 1.4 million people. The city's position is that urban areas must rely more and more on mass transportation if they are to meet America's energy, environmental, traffic, and economic problems.

CASE V   Historic Preservation: Vieux Carré, New Orleans, Louisiana

There are few cities in the United States with greater charm or character than New Orleans. Originally part of the French Empire, the city still reflects much of the French concept of city planning and architecture. The focal point of the city is the old French Quarter—the Vieux Carré. The heart of the 258-acre Vieux Carré is Jackson Square, site of the transfer of Louisiana from France to the United States in 1803, and considered one of the most historically important urban areas in the United States.

Following World War II, Robert Moses, the great freeway builder from New York (see Chapter 4, Air Quality and Weather Modification), was invited to New Orleans to update the city's chaotic transportation system. Moses prepared an arterial plan for the Louisiana Highway Department in 1946 which advocated the construction of an elevated riverfront expressway through the Vieux Carré. Moses' original elevated freeway concept was altered in the 1960s by the Louisiana Highway Department in order to comply with federal interstate highway standards. The proposed six-lane, 108-foot wide, 40-foot high elevated highway was to pass along the Vieux Carré riverfront in front of Jackson Square. The "Second Battle of New Orleans" was fought to stop the construction of this freeway.[3]

The Actors

On October 12, 1964, Congressman Hale Boggs of New Orleans announced that the Federal Bureau of Public Roads had decided to include the 3.5-mile Vieux Carré Riverfront Expressway in the Federal Interstate Highway System. Including the expressway in the interstate system made it eligible for 90 percent funding from the federal government, with state and local governments funding the remaining 10 percent. Because the project became a federal highway project, the Department of Transportation played the key role in the fate of the New Orleans expressway.

Proponents of the expressway included the state Highway Department, the New Orleans City Planning Commission, and the mayor of New Orleans. The principal private proponent was a group of downtown businessmen who had formed the Central Area Committee (CAC) of the chamber of commerce in 1957. CAC's position was that better automobile access to the downtown area was necessary for continued growth and development of the central area. Most of the local newspapers also supported the position of CAC.

The numerous opponents of the expressway included both the local and national chapters of the American Institute of Architects, the National Trust for Historic Preservation, the Vieux Carré Property Owners' Association, the Louisiana Landowners' Association, the Louisiana Council for the Vieux Carré, and a citywide coalition of organizations called the Crescent Council of Civic Associations. Three key individuals in the struggle to stop the expressway were Mrs. Martha Robinson, a preservationist, Mark Lowrey, an architect, and Harriet Kane, an author and preservationist. Their only local news media support was offered by the *Vieux Carré Courier,* a small newspaper which, nevertheless, was very influential in efforts to halt the freeway.

[3] A summary of the events in this case study was kindly provided in an unpublished study by Richard D. Baumbach, Jr. and William E. Borah, *The Second Battle of New Orleans: History of the Vieux Carré Riverfront Expressway.*

The Policy Process

After the New Orleans expressway became eligible for federal funding, a pilot project on historic preservation, funded by the U.S. Department of Housing and Urban Development (HUD), was completed on Vieux Carré in 1966. This study concluded that the proposed elevated structure would "create a visual and physical intrusion strongly alien to the traditional scale and character of the Vieux Carré. As a major visual distraction, the expressway will have a severely deleterious impact on Jackson Square's physical and environmental unity." Opponents of the expressway tried to impress this study on the mayor and businessmen of the city, but to no avail. The preservationists pointed out that the Vieux Carré still had its original street pattern and that 7 of the 14 buildings of national significance in the French Quarter would either be directly or indirectly affected because of their proximity to the proposed project. Many of the other 186 structures judged to be of major architectural-historical significance in the Vieux Carré would also be indirectly affected by the elevated highway.

The Central Area Committee (CAC) of the chamber of commerce, however, was convinced that the central city would decline and gradually deteriorate without a new expressway. CAC successfully persuaded other segments of the city's power structure that the expressway was necessary. With the help of the city's two large daily newspapers, the project was sold to the mayor and a majority of the city council; and with the city administration behind the freeway, public officials on all levels of state government generally supported the facility. Reflecting the apparent will of locally elected public officials, the Louisiana congressional delegation in Washington also supported the elevated freeway.

Highway proponents believed the Vieux Carré expressway would not only help revitalize the central area of New Orleans, but also would reduce traffic congestion in the French Quarter. This assumption was challenged by freeway opponents, who maintained that the freeway symbolized a deficiency in the transportation planning process that had produced it and illustrated a definite insensitivity to human values and needs. In spite of their sincere efforts, however, the freeway opponents lost the battle at the local level. On June 16, 1966, in a five to two vote, the New Orleans City Council rejected a resolution to undertake a six-month impartial and comprehensive study of alternatives to the proposed riverfront expressway.

With no hope left for influencing local decision makers, the preservationists decided to embark upon a national campaign to save Jackson Square and the Vieux Carré. A massive letter-writing effort was mounted to coordinate the New Orleans struggle with antifreeway struggles in other cities. Hand bills, fact sheets, memoranda, pictures, maps, and leaflets dramatizing the potential damage the elevated structure would have on the French Quarter were sent to newspapers and magazines all over the country. Local chapters of national organizations such as the American Institute of Architects mobilized support to bring pressure on their national membership to join the battle to save the Vieux Carré. Within a short time, the results of the national campaign became evident. The *Washington Post, Chicago Daily News, New York Times,* and *Boston Herald* all wrote articles on the French Quarter freeway. *Time, Newsweek, Life, Business Week, Architectural Forum,* and many other magazines with a wide audience helped make the New Orleans expressway a national issue.

In addition to the national publicity campaign, highway opponents filed suit in New Orleans, alleging that the proposed elevated freeway violated the state constitution and city ordinances created to protect the "quaint and distinctive character" of the historic Vieux Carré. Another group of concerned New Orleans citizens retained Louis F. Oberdorfer, a Washington lawyer and former assistant attorney general in the Kennedy administration, to initiate legal action if necessary. In April 1967, Oberdorfer made a presentation to Lowell Bridwell, federal highway administrator in the recently created Department of Transportation. Oberdorfer pointed out that Arthur D. Little, Inc., a nationally recognized research firm, had evaluated the transportation planning process in New Orleans and concluded that it had been neither "comprehensive [nor] continuous," as required by federal law. Moreover, Oberdorfer told Bridwell that the Little report indicated that there had never been a comprehensive study of alternatives, as required by Section 4 (f) of the recently enacted Department of Transportation Act. Oberdorfer argued that final approval of the New Orleans project should be withheld until the secretary of transportation determined that all federal requirements had been satisfied.

Bridwell was impressed by Oberdorfer's arguments, and, despite resistance by the local planning agencies, he was finally able to get an agreement to put the freeway at grade level in front of Jackson Square. The remainder of the expressway was to be elevated, however, and the freeway opponents continued to object to what they called a "Russian compromise." Bridwell gave official approval to the new plan on January 17, 1969, just three days before the Nixon administration came into office.

Bridwell's approval was withdrawn by Nixon administration officials when expressway opponents pointed out that the approval violated a prior agreement between the federal government and the preservationists' lawyers. The approval also ignored section 106 of the National Historic Preservation Act of 1966, which required that the President's Advisory Council on Historic Preservation comment on the project prior to final federal approval. The riverfront expressway proposal was consequently submitted to the Advisory Council on Historic Preservation, which included seven cabinet officers and ten other prominent American citizens.

On March 3, 1968, the advisory council reviewed the evidence, made an on-site examination, and concluded that even a partially elevated expressway "would have a serious adverse effect upon that quality of the District (Vieux Carré) which had been described as the 'tout ensemble,' a quality of high importance." The advisory council recommended a comprehensive study of all alternatives to the expressway. This recommendation was considered a major victory for the anti-freeway forces.

Outcome

In spite of a massive counter-offensive by the highway proponents, on July 9, 1969, Secretary of Transportation John Volpe cancelled the Vieux Carré Riverfront Expressway, stating that the project "would have seriously impaired the historic quality of New Orleans' famed French Quarter." The twelve-year battle was over, marking the first time that any segment of the 42,500-mile interstate system had been rejected for purely environmental reasons.

CASE VI   Recreation versus Development: Seward Street Mini-Park, San Francisco, California

The city of San Francisco is famous for its many hills. It is also a city where open space is at a premium because of the local geography:

located on a peninsula, San Francisco is very compact. One of the city's hills became the site of a ten-year battle to preserve open space on a block-long, weedy, uphill vacant lot. The lot was located in upper Eureka Valley, an area of mixed ethnic backgrounds, socio-economic status, and life styles. It was off one of the city's smallest streets, one-block long Seward Street, which is only twenty feet wide at its widest point. The battle began in 1963, when the neighborhood received word that developers planned to put an eighty-five unit apartment complex on the site. The residents believed such an apartment complex would destroy the family-oriented character of the neighborhood, and their sentiment touched off a struggle which has become one of the finest examples of community action to preserve open space in urban areas.

The Actors

Two groups of developers were involved in the Seward Street mini-park controversy. The initial group sold out quickly when confronted by citizen protest and financial difficulties, but the second group, Spartan Development Corporation, persevered until 1971, when they lost their building permit.

A number of city agencies had jurisidiction over the zoning of Seward Street and the eventual approval of the site as a mini-park. These were the city Planning Commission, which established the original zoning of the neighborhood as "family residence" (R–2) in April 1959 and, unknown to the residents, changed the zoning to "high density" (R–3) a month later at the request of one property owner in the neighborhood. The board of permit appeals became involved in the zoning struggle, as well as the board of supervisors. Later, when the mini-park idea was proposed, the city Parks and Recreation Department played the key role in determining the fate of the vacant lot.

Citizens' efforts were spearheaded by the Eureka Valley Promotion Association, led by Bert Schwarzschild, a neighborhood resident and electronic engineer. Schwarzschild found key people willing to commit themselves to the idea of a mini-park on Seward Street: local artist Ruth Asawa, League of Women Voters activist Audrey Rodgers, several landscape architects, two engineers, a city planner, and several politicians including State Assemblyman Willie Brown, State Senator Milton Marks, and City Attorney Caspar Weinberger (who later became the secretary of the Department of Health, Education and Welfare in the Nixon administration).

The Policy Process

In November 1959, only six months after the Planning Commission's private decision to rezone Seward Street, the first three-unit apartment building went up on the property of the owner who had secured the zoning change. Less than a year later, another six-unit apartment building was constructed by the same owner. Residents were concerned but not alarmed until news of the proposed construction of an eighty-five-unit structure reached them. So in early January 1963, three Seward Street neighborhood residents applied to rezone the disputed area back to its former R–2 status. Two months later, a petition by 103 of the 152 known property owners in the area was submitted to the Planning Commission in support of rezoning the area.

The signature-gathering process for the petition had given rise to the first Seward Street block party, where neighborhood residents met together for the first time and expressed their mutual concerns. In spite of their efforts, however, the commission turned down the residents' rezoning request in May 1963. The issue had been debated at several hearings of the Planning Commission and focused considerable public attention on the plight of tiny Seward Street. The neighborhood leaders, still pursuing their goal, decided to confront Mayor John Shelley with their problem in March 1964. Meanwhile, the Spartan Development Corporation had reduced the number of projected units from eighty-five to sixty-nine as required by the commission. The week after the Seward Street group's meeting with Mayor Shelley, the board of supervisors met to reconsider R–3 zoning in the city generally. The board decided to rezone the adjacent slope of the hill on Seward Street to R–2 but declined to rezone Spartan's property to R–2.

The neighbors waited until Spartan received its building permits, and in early March 1965, the neighbors passed the hat among themselves to raise the forty dollars necessary to appeal the four permits. Less than a week before the board of permit appeals hearing, the Seward Street residents, as a second part of their strategy, staged a test run of hook-and-ladder fire fighting equipment to see if it could move in tiny Seward Street. As the residents suspected, it could not, and the story appeared with photographs in all of the San Francisco newspapers. When the five members of the board of permit appeals met on March 25, 1965, they convened at the site of the proposed apartment building. The story was again covered by the media. In spite of the evidence of fire prevention difficulties, increased traffic congestion, and community opposition, the board decided to uphold the developer's right to erect the sixty-nine-unit building.

The Seward Street residents were not easily discouraged, however, and when bulldozers showed up later that year, the residents chased them off the site, creating another favorable newspaper story. The residents then appealed to the city, charging that the builder had not made a "continuous and diligent" construction effort, and the city decided to revoke Spartan's building permit. On March 6, 1966, the second Seward Street block party was held to celebrate the victory over the development company. The San Francisco Board of Supervisors added to the neighborhood's satisfaction by sending residents a unanimous resolution congratulating them on their victory.

The "Battle of Seward Street" was only half over, however. In the spring of 1969, the neighborhood learned that the city intended to develop a mini-park in Eureka Valley, but not at the Seward Street site. The Seward Street Neighborhood Task Force submitted a proposal to the mayor's office, outlining their reasons for supporting the Seward Street mini-park. The group's proposal stated:

> We have a unique idea: a neighborhood mini-park which will be the vehicle for developing and nourishing a healthy, involved and cohesive community. A neighborhood becomes "community" when people develop a sense of mutual trust. We believe that a self-help project where the neighbors plan, develop, and maintain their own park could achieve the above.

A year later, after much correspondence, officials from the city Parks and Recreation Department finally came to inspect the site and begrudgingly expressed their approval of a Seward Street mini-park.

The Seward Street neighborhood, believing victory was at hand, celebrated at its third Seward Street block party on May 24, 1970. The party raised $600. The park site was "dedicated" by the Eureka Valley Promotion Association. The following month, the mini-park committee held a "Design a Park" contest for local children in an all-day carnival held at the park site. At the same time, over 200 families in the immediate neighborhood signed a petition and statement of support for the proposed park.

It became apparent in early 1971, however, that the Parks and Recreation commissioners did not really favor the Seward Street site after all. The commissioners had met privately in April and rejected the proposal on the grounds that the Seward Street land was too expensive to buy and develop. The fact that the commissioners had made a behind-closed-doors decision created a stir in the local press, and the Seward Street neighborhood took the issue to Mayor Joseph Alioto, who then called on the parks commission to reconsider the matter. The commission agreed, and on May 13, 1971, this time with full press and TV coverage, the commission gave qualified approval to the park plans. The citizens' group's leader, Bert Schwarzschild, attributed the Seward Street neighborhood's success to group solidarity and press coverage. According to Schwarzschild: "I've learned that decision makers are most vulnerable to public exposure, and I have to admit that I've learned to use it very well. The press helped us a lot in getting over the top."

Outcome

From the summer of 1971 to the fall of 1972, the final plans for the park were worked out between the city and the Eureka Valley Promotion Association. The mini-park cost the city $37,000 for the lot and $42,000 to build the park. The basic design of the park had been conceived by the children in the "Design a Park" contest, with a forty-foot double slide as the highlight. On May 21, 1973, with all the fanfare that might be expected from a neighborhood which had fought for ten years to save a tiny bit of open space, the Seward Street mini-park was officially dedicated by the city of San Francisco.

Conclusion

The problems of urban areas discussed in this chapter emanate from a maze of political, technical, geographic, social, and ecological inter-relationships which together determine the quality of life in American cities. Many of the policy issues discussed throughout this book have, in fact, been problems stemming from what some have called "the urban crisis" in America. This chapter has concentrated on several specific concerns of urban policy which will be most critical in determining the fate of the nation's metropolitan regions: growth, solid waste, housing, transportation, and the preservation of open space and historic character in American cities. The six case studies delineate five sets of circumstances that have proved critical in the resolution of environmental policy issues:

1. The difficulty for both the citizen and decision maker to comprehend and act on fundamental policy issues with consideration for their interrelations and consequences;

2. The erosion of competence and responsibility at the local level of government in dealing with problems of the urban environment;

3. The failure of federal and state programs to meet the needs of metropolitan areas;

4. The effectiveness and perseverance of intelligently organized citizens' groups in overcoming the indifference and intransigence of local and state officials on environmental issues;

5. The critical role of volunteer civic leaders in confronting or persuading decision makers in government and business.

In all but one of the case studies (Boulder), the fundamental policy issue was avoided by treating a symptom rather than the basic problem. In Louisville, air pollution rather than the disposal of solid waste became the issue. In New York, lead poisoning became the focus of action rather than dilapidated housing. In New Orleans, businessmen and city officials were most concerned with the decline of the central city, while the more basic issues of the nature of urban transportation and the diminishing of America's cultural heritage were left in the background. This is not to say that the problems of air pollution, lead poisoning, and the decline of the central cities are not extremely important, but rather that lasting solutions to these problems will come only with more effective policies for dealing with basic issues: solid waste management (in areas where solid waste incineration is a major cause of air pollution), improved housing, and more balanced transportation systems.

Focusing public and official attention on the more basic policy issues of a controversy is no easy task, nor does such attention necessarily guarantee the development of solutions. Although citizen activists in these cases were, for the most part, aware of the basic issues they were confronting, the general public was not especially interested or receptive to the position of the core groups, except in the case of Boulder. Yet, in order to win official recognition of, and support for, their goals, the citizen activists in all but the San Diego case found it necessary first to gain the support of the public. Because the public tended to be apathetic about issues such as solid waste disposal, housing (usually a problem of the poor), and historic preservation, the tactics of the activists in Louisville, New York, and New Orleans were to avoid fundamental issues and stress the apparent problem—the symptom—which was likely to gain public attention and concern. While such tactics proved more or less effective in the short run, public and official interest in the more apparent problem waned in all cases with the lessening of pressure from citizen activists and the fundamental issues were left unresolved.

Even though this pattern tends to be typical of similar cases throughout the United States, there have been a few instances where a broader perspective on the same types of policy issues has been employed. In the Bedford-Stuyvesant area of New York City, two corporations founded in 1967 have imaginatively and successfully attacked the problem of poor housing in the sprawling 563 square block area that constitutes New York's largest black community. The key to the corporations' success has been involving local residents in the rehabilitation of their own community.

Another good example of effectively channeled community involvement in fundamental issues confronting urban areas was the controversy over the proposed Inner Belt-Southwest Expressway in Boston. Initially, antifreeway forces hoped only to halt the construction of the highway, but they eventually generated enough interest in the problem of regional transportation to gain the attention of the governor. The governor decided to appoint a task force in 1968 to study the Boston area's particular transportation needs. As a result of the first task force study, Governor Sargent decided to reverse the past transportation policies of the state of Massachusetts from building highways to considering all possible alternatives and their effects. Additional task forces have since been formed to continue the reorientation of the state's policy.

In disposing of solid waste, a few metropolitan regions have begun to see the problem from a regional perspective. The Association of Bay Area Governments (ABAG) in San Francisco has adopted a twofold plan to create a multijurisdictional solid waste management system with emphasis on resource recovery. The project has to be approved by the federal EPA and will require $3 million, with federal, state, and local governments contributing equal shares.

While perception of local and regional issues varies considerably from city to city, no metropolitan community's problems in the areas of solid waste, transportation, water pollution, or open space will be resolved satisfactorily until the problem of growth is confronted. This area of policy, however, is beset with legal, political, economic, and emotional entanglements. The Boulder case study, while not typical in the amount of community concern shown for the growth issue, is exemplary of the types of problems facing decision makers who attempt to limit population growth in their communities. Other cities which have tried to come to terms with the problem in their areas have also met with considerable difficulties. Both Petaluma, California (see Chapter 1, Land Use) and Boca Raton, Florida, have had their efforts to limit growth challenged in court. Petaluma experienced conflicting decisions in the courts, while the outcome of the suit against the city of Boca Raton is uncertain. The city of Ramapo, New York, which adopted a plan that regulates the timing of developments over the next eighteen years, has been more successful. The plan was upheld in the New York State Supreme Court in November 1972.

These initial attempts by communities throughout the United States to develop policies to control growth, however, reveal the inability of many local governments to cope with problems brought on by a rapidly expanding population. In many regions across the country, the available public services and means of protection are no longer adequate to meet demands. Ensuring sufficient water supplies, for example, is a serious problem in the majority of urban areas. Yet, arriving at a consensus on a growth limitation policy is practically impossible in most metropolitan areas, where each local government jealously guards its jurisdictional powers (as in San Diego, for example).

With local governments often unwilling or unable to meet metropolitan needs, the federal and state governments have taken increasing responsibility for metropolitan welfare. A typical example of the state role in urban affairs was seen in the New Orleans case study, where the state highway agency was actively supporting the construction of an interstate highway through the Jackson Square area. (See also the Overton Park case, Chapter 1, Land Use.) State approval and funding for urban highway systems has tremendously influenced the direction of metropolitan growth, yet the state highway agency is usually the only state agency with operating responsibilities in urban areas. For example, states usually authorize urban renewal legislation for their cities, but nothing in the state legislation provides guidance for the character, pace, and direction of the slum clearance efforts. It is also illogical for states to authorize the revitalization of the central cities on the one hand and to encourage the flight away from the cities on the other hand, by constructing more freeways and failing to control development on the urban periphery. For the most part, states have exercised little or no control over such important areas of environmental policy as land use, extension of local government units, public transportation, or historic site preservation. But there are indications that this situation is beginning to change.

Federal involvement in urban affairs consists mainly of financial assistance for programs administered by the state or local government. This type of aid was provided in three of the case studies: Boulder, San Diego, and New Orleans. Because the number of federal aid programs for metropolitan areas has increased considerably in recent years, the cities have largely been bypassing the state government when attempting to secure financial aid. Yet, as the Advisory Commission on Intergovernmental Relations points out in its report on metropolitan America, without active state participation in urban policy, it is doubtful whether local government can be reorganized to perform more effectively in metropolitan areas. Local governments derive their powers from the states, and they need state authorization for structural reforms. Coordinating the efforts of all levels of government appears to be essential if government action in metropolitan areas is to be effective.

Basically then, the question raised in the introduction to this chapter of the best institutional arrangement to serve the needs of urban residents is paramount, even though the answer is not readily apparent. Judging from the six case studies of this chapter, current institutional arrangements are not the best solution to today's urban area problems. Nor is relying upon citizens' actions or even citizens' interest going to be able to keep up with the burgeoning needs of America's metropolitan areas. The difficulty of passing the bond issues required to supply these areas with necessary public services was discussed in the San Diego and Louisville case studies. While citizen involvement is the key to effective government, the quality of urban life in the United States appears certain to decline unless local, state, and federal agencies are reoriented so that policy becomes more responsive to the public welfare.

Readings

American Society of Planning Officials. *Nongrowth as a Planning Alternative* [Advisory Service Report #283]. Chicago: American Society of Planning Officials, 1972.

Derthick, Martha. *New Towns In-Town*. Washington, D.C.: The Urban Institute. 1972.

Duhl, Leonard, ed. *The Urban Condition: People and Policy in the Metropolis.* New York: Basic Books, 1963.

Jacobs, Jane. *The Death and Life of the Great American Cities.* New York: Random House, 1961.

Lynch, Kevin. "The City as Environment." *Scientific American,* 213 (September 1965), 209–214.

McHarg, Ian. *Design With Nature.* Garden City, New York: The Natural History Press, 1969.

National Committee on Urban Growth Policy. *The New City.* Edited by Donald Canty. New York: Praeger Publishers, 1969.

Scientific American. Cities: Their Origin, Growth, and Human Impact. San Francisco: W. H. Freeman and Company, 1973.

10

Institutional Behavior

Introduction

In the United States, the principal managers of environmental matters traditionally have been state and local governments. The police powers granted them by the Constitution have enabled these governments to deal with problems such as pollution control, waste disposal, and land-use management. State governments have been responsible for water rights, air and water quality, and standards for public health and sanitation. On the other hand, the federal government has been involved mainly with wildlife, national parks, forests, minerals, the environmental management and custody that affects energy, and the care of the public domain. In addition, environmental policy questions are involved in federal public works programs administered or sponsored by the Bureau of Reclamation, the Civil Works Division of the Army Corps of Engineers, the Federal Highway Administration, the Federal Aviation Administration, and the defense agencies.

During the later sixties and early seventies, federal environmental legislation increased dramatically. The EPA was given control and enforcement responsibilities, some of which overlapped with responsibilities formerly handled by state and local bodies. Many of the control and enforcement functions of the EPA occur at the state and local level. For example, to receive federal funds for municipal sewage treatment programs, local governments must meet EPA standards. State and local governments also play a critical role in implementing policies for clean air, water quality, new transportation systems, solid waste disposal, and land-use planning.

In addition to enforcing federal environmental standards, many states have initiated their own programs for dealing with environmental problems. California has been a leader in establishing air pollution controls. Wisconsin had banned DDT before the federal government took action. The first comprehensive wild and scenic rivers system in the nation was established in Tennessee. Minnesota's comprehensive Pollution Control Agency was established years before the EPA. In an effort to improve environmental quality, the Michigan Environmental Protection Act gave every citizen the right to sue public or private institutions thought to be degrading the quality of life. Numerous state and local governments have also taken the initiative in problems of open-space protection, waste recycling programs, wildlife protection, and in some aspects of energy policy. While states have reorganized their environmental management in a number of different ways, their primary aim has been the same: to establish agencies capable of dealing with interrelated environmental problems.

Despite the changes in policy and institutional arrangements during the sixties and early seventies, many Americans are not satisfied that existing institutions and laws will guarantee the quality of life they demand. The primary institutions for environmental management, besides the CEQ and EPA, are Congress, the laws and the judicial system, executive agencies (federal, state, and local), some independent agencies, and certain boards, committees, and commissions. Standing committees are working units of Congress; environmental bills are subject to control by the powerful chairmen of these committees. In addition to the EPA, independent federal agencies with environmental impacts or concerns are the Nuclear Regulatory Commission (NRC), the Energy Development and Research Administration (ERDA), the Federal Power Commission (FPC), the Tennessee Valley Authority (TVA), the Federal Maritime Commission, the Interstate Commerce Commission (ICC), the National Aeronautics and Space Administration (NASA), and the National Science Foundation (NSF). Some of the chief select advisory councils dealing with environmental matters are the Citizens' Advisory Committee on Environmental Quality, the Advisory Council on Historic Preservation, the National Water Commission, the Water Resources Council, and the Migratory Bird Conservation Commission.

Each of these sets of institutions has, at times, not fulfilled its responsibility regarding the environment. The specialized committee structure in Congress has reduced the effectiveness of the legislature acting as a committee of the whole. The relative novelty of the environmental quality issue has inhibited bargaining and compromise across a broad range of controversies and has complicated the process of choosing among competing priorities. The public is now demanding action toward a quality of life that formerly acceptable policies for economic development did not take into account. Legislatures have not comprehended these new goals quickly enough to avoid costly confrontations. The CEQ has made little progress in improving procedures and policies for choosing between development and preservation, and the EPA's performance in certain areas of responsibility has been challenged in a number of suits filed by environmentalists. Independent federal agencies such as the AEC (now the National Regulatory Commission), FPC, and TVA have been the targets of intense protest by environmentalists for short-sightedness and bias in the interpretation of their mandates. Although they are often broadly representative of the public, environmental and conservation boards and councils seem to have limited impact on governmental decision making. Nevertheless, the judicial system and government agencies at every level are under increasing public pressure to recognize environmental values. Counterpressures, however, are also strong and frequently well financed.

The nation's governmental organization for managing the environment seems, in many ways, to be unsuitable for handling environmental problems. Existing legal and institutional arrangements have been criticized as "archaic," sometimes "unresponsive," at other times "irresponsible." Many mission-oriented agencies have been accused of being indifferent to the general public and to the environmental dimensions of their activities. Some government agencies have even been "hostile" toward the public's demand to participate in environmental policy processes, but they appear to be very responsive to the wishes of their special clientele.

Since the 1960s, environmentalists have increasingly turned to the judicial system to challenge government agencies. Public-interest groups have called on the courts to stop agencies from carrying out policies that had formerly been acceptable, and to compel these agencies to conform to procedures specified in the new laws such as the NEPA. But the use of the courts has been restricted by numerous procedural roadblocks before, during, and after the administrative process. The law can help stop the administration of old policies, but it cannot devise new goals; they must be set through the legislative process. Litigation is a stopgap measure, not a substitute for fundamental policy reorientation. Moreover, because the legal system moves so slowly in its deliberations, the devastation of the environment can continue while the issue is being decided.

Environmental management in the United States requires a national land-use policy. Many states have already enacted land-use policies, and in Congress the proponents of a national land-use policy have come close to passing a new act. Numerous citizens' groups have helped draft state land-use bills, proposed national ones, and lobbied with varying effectiveness in legislatures. Citizens' groups have also played a leading role in requiring agencies to disclose their processes and criteria for making decisions. A number of states have drafted "full disclosure" or "government-in-the-sunshine" acts to force such disclosures, and U.S. Senator Lawton Chiles (D-Florida) has led a drive to pass a similar full disclosure law for federal agencies. In a number of instances throughout the nation, citizen groups have participated in the planning of new institutional arrangements. In some instances, their primary goal has been to prevent mission-oriented programs from continuing beyond the point of general usefulness.

An analysis of the tasks of environmental protection reveals that some can be best performed by agencies, some only by legislatures, and others by the courts. Legislatures are the appropriate bodies to enact the comprehensive environmental policies that guide agencies and courts. Public pressure has guided and motivated state legislatures to add environmental quality legislation to constitutional and statutory law. Recently, the courts have succeeded in opening up administrative processes to review by citizens and environmental groups. The perseverance of citizens has helped to improve the machinery for environmental management and to fix responsibility in governmental agencies.

Agencies of government with missions to develop, alter, or exploit the environment have been the primary targets of citizen action. The Bureau of Reclamation, the Army Corps of Engineers, the (former) AEC, and state and federal highway agencies afford notable examples. Other targets are those agencies which have lost sight of their original missions and developed narrower economic goals. The Tennessee Valley Authority stresses its efforts to supply cheap electricity; the Soil Conservation Service promotes dam and dredging operations; and the Forest Service is strongly influenced by the commercial timber industry. The Department of the Interior has often proved to be an unreliable custodian of the nation's natural resources, frequently engaging in behind-the-scenes deals with private economic interests while neglecting environmental considerations. With astonishing arrogance, state and federal agencies have often resisted public interference with their established procedures and their relationships with favored clients in the private economic sector. There are numerous instances of citizen groups protesting the secret arrangement between agencies and industry and the covert development of policies and plans, which often are announced publicly only when they are too far advanced to be modified or reversed without great cost and effort.

These cases record a degree of wrongdoing, of connivance, of dereliction of duty, and of disregard for the law at all governmental levels that should be disheartening to those who believe in the honesty and integrity of the American public services. But these cases also reveal the power of voluntary citizen action when it is intelligently organized and led and when it perseveres in the face of repeated reverses. The cases do not and should not suggest that government is inherently venal and irresponsible. Rather, they show that in government, as in all human institutions, there is no substitute for accountability. Self-government is an art that must be practiced to be maintained. Dereliction in government is almost always a consequence of dereliction among the citizens.

CASE I   Conflicting Responsibilities: Black Mesa and the
Southwest Power Complex

In the Four Corners area of New Mexico, Colorado, Arizona, and
Utah some 6.5 billion tons of coal lie barely 30 to 100 feet below the surface. These vast reserves of strippable coal are in a semiarid expanse
hundreds of miles from any cities. Since the mid-1960s, huge consorti-
ums of utility companies and development-oriented agencies of the federal government have jointly created an energy complex in the area.
When completed, the total system of generating plants will produce almost 14,000 megawatts of electricity. Utilities plan to sell the power to
rapidly growing urban areas such as Los Angeles, Las Vegas, Tucson,
and Phoenix. The U.S. Bureau of Reclamation (Burec) wants some of the
power to pump water from the Colorado River to its mammoth
reclamation project in central Arizona. Excess power from Burec's
quota would be sold to private utilities, with the revenues going to the
federal treasury.

The Southwest Power Complex exemplifies the inadequacy of institutional structure in the United States for affixing responsibility for
environmental damage. This huge energy project was never specifically
authorized or fully reviewed by the Congress or by any other representative public body. Its legal basis was derived from a variety of au-
thorizations which were combined to produce an arrangement that has
been almost beyond the reach of popular control. The principal authorization was derived from the Colorado River Basin Project Act (Public
Law 90–537) for regulation of the flow of the Colorado, control of
floods, improvement of navigation, storage and delivery of water for
the reclamation of land, improving conditions for fish and wildlife
and *the generation of electrical power incidental to the foregoing
objectives*. This act also authorizes the secretary of the interior to enter
into agreements with nonfederal interests for the construction of coal
field generating power plants, whereby the United States government
acquires the rights to electrical power in relation to its investment in
the plants. The federal role in the Southwest Power Complex has been
solely one of energy production and economic development. No government agency made any preliminary attempt to evaluate the environmental and social consequences of the development, and seldom did
any agency—federal, state, or local—apply the environmental controls
available to it.

The impact of the vast complex of strip mines and coal-burning power plants upon the Southwest's Big Sky environment, famous for its 100-mile visibility, has been devastating. Much of the coal is beneath tribal lands of the Navajo and Hopi, and the scarce artesian water, mostly in aquifers, is beneath tribal reservations. To cool electric generating plants, enormous quantities of water must be extracted from the fragile ecosystem that has been the home of Indians for a thousand years. Emissions of sulphur oxide and nitrogen will exceed the combined quantities of Los Angeles and New York, and long-term weather inversions concentrate smog in the region. Thousands of miles of transmission lines, roads, and rails are quickly lacing the former wilderness. Coal dust, pipelines, ash dumps, poisonous runoff from industrial plants, and leached soils are rapidly destroying sacred Indian lands. Ancestral lands have been taken or tempted from the Indians in the name of increased incomes and employment opportunities for the industrial and agricultural development of the Southwest.

Within the mammoth mining and generating complex lies the Black Mesa highland, which is particularly sacred to the Indians. Here the Peabody Coal Company plans to strip coal from four seams at a rate of 400 acres per year. Peabody's mining leases allow the extraction of 400 million tons of coal over thirty-five years. Royalty payments to the Navajo and Hopi for the destruction of their sacred mountain will amount to about $100 million. Some Black Mesa coal is pumped through an eighteen-inch coal-slurry pipe 270 miles to the Mohave electric plant. Indian water also has been leased for the slurry pipe operation. Coal from Black Mesa also serves the Navajo plant eighty miles away in Page, Arizona, where Burec is one of the major participants.

Planning for the development of the Black Mesa area and the Southwest in general began early in the 1950s. The consortium of utilities and government agencies released very little information about leases, negotiations, and contracts, and in their decison making they ignored such concerned public opinion as existed. State and local agencies and private conservation interests had almost no direct knowledge of plans to develop the region. Although some information about the proposals was printed in newspapers, it was not comprehensive. Even sister agencies within the Department of Interior knew little or nothing of the plans of the Bureau of Reclamation, or if informed, they did not oppose them. Citizen participation in policy making has generally come too late to influence plans begun by developers in the 1960s. But since 1970 there has been a dramatic increase in attempts by the public to alter or improve more recent development proposals. These activities may be broadly divided into attempts (1) to protect the rights of the Indians and (2) to influence a broad range of environmental policies.

The Actors

Federal agencies have the key role in determining resource development in the Southwest. The Department of Interior owns half the coal reserves and holds authority over the Colorado River and much of the region's public lands. Within the Department of Interior, Burec had long sought to stimulate the economic development of the region through its Central Arizona Project. The Burec's policies dominated federal policies for the region, and its development plans complemented those of the coal and generating companies. The Department of Interior's Bureau of Indian Affairs (BIA) has a trusteeship duty to manage all Indian affairs and to protect Indian rights and welfare, but the BIA acquiesced to Burec's policies. The Interior Department's National Park Service (NPS) manages six national parks, more than twenty national monuments, and a number of national recreation areas within 200 miles of the region, but NPS, by interpreting its mandate to conserve natural areas, deferred to Burec's development plans. Neither the Bureau of Land Management nor the U.S. Geological Survey (both within the Interior Department) advocated development alternatives to the options pursued by the Burec.

State and local authorities were excluded from (or indifferent to) early decision making, but in response to increasing public demand for local participation late in the 1960s, the state and local agencies attempted to face the problems. The chief problem was the enormous complexity of related problems of escalating energy demand, urban growth, air and water pollution, landscape degradation, and the lack of information on federal policies. Making effective decisions was temporarily beyond the resources of state and local authorities. Very few institutions were suited to handling environmental problems of any character, and there were very few adequate laws on which to base agency action. By the early seventies, however, state and local authorities gradually began to implement and extend their powers, and were beginning to attempt to cope with some problems.

Indian tribal councils played a significant role in policy formation regarding Black Mesa. Tribal government apparatus, although not recognized by all the Indians or by the traditional leaders and elders, has been dominated by "progressives," Indians who have been urbanized and Anglicized. The minority of progressives, which has advocated developing the coal resources of the Indian reservations, has agreed to leasing arrangements with private utilities through the BIA and Interior. The tribal councils, however, had not been given authority to lease or sell tribal lands when they were created by the Indian Reorganization Act of 1934.

A number of citizens' groups have attempted to influence policy in the region. The principal defenders of Indian rights have been the Committee to Save Black Mesa (CSBM) and two supporting legal advisers, the People's Legal Services and the Native American Rights Fund (NARF). The CSBM was a coalition of Hopi and Anglos devoted to stopping strip mining on Black Mesa and controlling related power projects. The CSBM also disseminated information to Navajo people, presented testimony at hearings, initiated legal actions, and attempted to end tribal council advocacy of mining operations.

The Sierra Club, the Natural Resources Defense Council, the Environmental Defense Fund, and the National Wildlife Federation have supported local citizens' groups in litigation. The Sierra Club in particular was very active at the state level. The Central Clearing House (CCH), a Sante Fe-based environmental group, has played a leading role in drawing local, state, and national attention to the issues in the Southwest. By participating in lawsuits, disseminating information on a national scale, participating in state and federal hearings, and lobbying for environmental legislation in the New Mexico legislature, the CCH has done much to build political support for programs of ecologically sound land use in the Southwest. The New Mexico Citizens for Clean Air and Water (NMCCAW) and, to a lesser extent, the Black Mesa Defense Fund have also lobbied actively for more adequate environmental legislation in the region.

The Policy Process

As previously indicated, the decison-making process has been characterized by secrecy and the absence of public participation. The federal agencies, private utilities, and tribal councils had negotiated most agreements and plans without informing tribal members or the general public. The third characteristic of the decision-making process in this case has been the multi-purpose role of the Department of Interior. Interior and its agencies faced a dilemma. By mandate, the agencies were required to develop resources and enhance the economic prosperity of a region that historically had experienced low income levels and high unemployment rates. At the same time, the agencies had the authority and responsibility to protect Indian rights, preserve the quality of the environment, and evaluate the full impact of alternative policies. None of the agencies vigorously advocated alternative policies intra-departmentally.

By 1970, vigorous debate about policy options had been stimulated by citizens' groups and the press. But even by the mid-seventies, the policies remained basically the same as those established by the utilities and federal developers. Citizens' groups had generally focused their protests on individual plants and mining operations. By challenging air and water pollution regulations and the efficiency of antipollution devices, they had improved policy somewhat. Utilities accommodated incremental changes and federal agencies improved the conditions of some later leases. But the public had only token success in efforts to open administrative decision making to scrutiny; the total costs and benefits of development goals and the exponential increase in energy consumption have not been debated publicly.

Early in 1971, citizens' groups made desperate attempts to publicize the issues in the Southwest. In May, the Central Clearing House placed an advertisement entitled "Like Ripping Apart St. Peter's in Order to Sell the Marble" in the *New York Times,* the *Los Angeles Times,* and the *San Francisco Chronicle* to alert the nation to the issues. The combined efforts of CCH, the Black Mesa Defense Fund, the Sierra Club, Friends of the Earth, Zero Population Growth, and NMCCAW aroused interest in the Four Corners and Black Mesa programs as a national environmental issue. Development programs in the Southwest threatened to become an issue disputed with as much intensity as the Alaska pipeline (see Chapter 6, Energy). Environmental litigation increased dramatically from May 1971 onward.

On May 11, 1971, five Navajo Indians sued to invalidate the Department of Interior's approval of 1960 and 1966 contracts permitting construction of the Four Corners energy complex. The suit alleged also that the Department of Interior permitted the plant to operate in violation of pollution control provisions (mostly inadequate) in the leases.

The suit was also filed against the secretary of the Department of Health, Education and Welfare for failing to carry out health studies of families affected by the plant, and thus violating its trust responsibilities.

Fifty-nine Hopi traditional and religious leaders, including the four Hopi Kikmongwi (chiefs) filed suit on May 16, 1971, against the secretary of interior. The suit sought to invalidate the department's approval of leases by the Hopi Tribal Council to the Peabody Coal Company for strip mining on Black Mesa. The secretary of interior was accused of failing to perform his duty to insure compliance with the Hopi constitution. In February 1973, Judge Craig of the Arizona district court granted the government's motion to dismiss the case. The Native American Rights Fund appealed the decision in the Ninth Circuit Court of Appeals in San Francisco and is waiting for a decision.

U.S. Senator Clinton P. Anderson of New Mexico had been an outstanding supporter of citizens' groups in the region for some time. In late 1969, he had supported the NMCCAW in their successful drive to have environmental protection included in the criteria for determining the public convenience and necessity (under authority of the New Mexico Public Service Commission) in the construction of coal-burning power plants in New Mexico. Anderson was primarily responsible for having the Senate Committee on Interior and Insular Affairs hold public hearings in five southwestern states from May 24 to 28 in 1971. The hearings discussed problems of electric power production in the Southwest. Citizens' groups mustered enormously influential testimony from scientists, lawyers, and Indians. The nationally publicized consensus of participants at the hearings was that federal agencies had handled the issues irresponsibly and inadequately.

On June 2, 1971, the Jicarilla Apache tribe, National Wildlife Federation, Environmental Defense Fund, and the Committee to Save Black Mesa, represented by the Native American Rights Fund, filed suit against the secretary of interior. It was alleged that the development of the Four Corners, Navajo, Mohave, San Juan, and Huntington Canyon projects all violated the National Environmental Policy Act (NEPA), because the Interior Department had failed to prepare environmental impact statements on the plants. But the district court decided against the plaintiffs on the grounds that the plants were initiated prior to the enactment of NEPA. The U.S. Court of Appeals for the Ninth Circuit also decided against the plaintiffs' appeal in a decision rendered early in 1973.

The rush of litigation, the unfavorable attention brought on federal agencies by the Senate hearings in the Southwest, and a desire to stem a repetition of the Alaska pipeline hold-ups persuaded the Interior Department to propose a one-year task force study to begin in late May 1971. With the exception of some participation by the Environmental Protection Agency (EPA) and the National Oceanic and Atmospheric Administration, the study was almost entirely conducted by agencies within the Department of Interior. The Council on Environmental Quality (CEQ) did not intervene and ask for a comprehensive environmental impact statement on the strip mining and power plant complex. Interior proceeded with the intradepartmental study. While environmentalists were pleased that the issues had been given higher priority within the department, many citizens' groups felt its strategy in proposing the study was to postpone public controversy.

The Interior Department was unsympathetic to citizens' demands for a moratorium on electric energy production in the Southwest. Thousands of coupons from environmentalists (promoted by CCH in its May 1971 nationwide advertisement) called on the chairman of the Federal Power Commission (FPC) to help stop exploitive and excessive energy production in the area. The FPC chairman responded that the agency's mandate gave him no jurisdiction over the construction or operation of the Southwest power facilities. Moreover, the FPC's main duty, he explained, was to promote and encourage an abundant supply of energy for the nation. Curtailing energy production, as demanded by citizens' groups, was not conceived by the FPC to be necessary. When drafts of the Interior Department's *Southwest Energy Study* were released, they showed the overriding concern for satisfying energy demands. Federal agencies favored regional exploitation for the benefit of national energy needs.

Citizens' groups continued to use litigation in the hope of altering policies in the region. In a suit filed in January 1972 by the Native American Rights Fund on behalf of the Chemehuevi and Cocopah tribes, the Committee to Save Black Mesa, the Sierra Club, and several Navajo individuals, the FPC was asked to assume licensing jurisdiction over the six major power plants. Although the language of the Federal Power Act is not limited to hydroelectric plants, the FPC has traditionally taken jurisdiction only over these plants. Citizens' groups realized that the FPC had to consider a broad range of impacts in its licensing decisions. If Southwest coal-fired plants became part of FPC control, full consideration of environmental, recreational, aesthetic, historical, and cultural values would be required before licensing. When an Indian reservation is involved in an FPC licensing, the commission must be certain that proposed developments do not interfere with the purposes for which a reservation was established. Predictably, however, the FPC denied it had jurisdiction. The citizens' groups were awaiting a decision of the U.S. Court of Appeals for the District of Columbia almost two years later.

At the local and state level, CDNA, the Navajo legal services program, and NARF have had success in litigation on behalf of a number of Navajo allotment owners, Navajo tribal chapters, and grazing permittees. The citizens' groups protested the violation of trust expressed in rights-of-way agreements for power line routes between the Tucson Gas and Electric Company (TG&E) and Navajo allotment owners in the vicinity of Black Mesa. In a related issue, the citizens' legal groups opposed a TG&E application to the New Mexico Public Service Commission for permission to construct the power lines. Although the commission approved the line and the New Mexico district court upheld the approval, intervention by the citizens' groups helped shape policy. The commission ordered TG&E to follow a stringent set of environmental guidelines to move the power lines to a less environmentally fragile area, and as a consequence the rights-of-way issue no longer exists.

Through 1972 and 1973, the citizens' groups maintained their advocacy of improved policies through litigation. In July 1972, the EPA disapproved certain portions of state implementation plans to meet primary and secondary air quality standards concerning emissions from electric power plants for Utah, Arizona, and New Mexico. Five of the six Southwest plants met with EPA disapproval. Power companies filed suit to reverse EPA's disapproval of original state plans. The NARF, on behalf of the Jicarilla Apache tribe, the Committee to Save Black Mesa, and some Navajos, together with NRDC and the Sierra Club, opposed the power companies and moved for a dismissal of the case. The citizens' groups were once again represented by NARF in litigation during mid-1972. The EPA was ordered by the U.S. District Court for the District of Columbia to issue final implementation plans (originally required by July 31, 1972, under the Clean Air Act) no later than March 15, 1973. One major permit, for the Kaiparowitz plant, has been deferred as a result of the tireless citizens' group activities.

Outcome

The continual advocacy, lobbying, and community education programs of environmentalist interests has had an unquantifiable, but significant, impact on policies for pollution, land use, and strip mining in the Southwest. They have monitored state and local agencies' performances in administering the law. Part of the credit for the adoption of an amendment increasing state control over the use of natural resources to the New Mexico constitution in 1971 has been attributed to citizen action. Late in 1973, citizens' groups were the primary supporters of New Mexico's proposed House Bill 63, the "government-in-the-sunshine" law, which would require state and local governments to conduct public meetings on all matters of policy and guarantee public access to agency information. If the Department of Interior had been subject to a similar law, the Big Sky's 100-mile visibility, Indian ancestral grounds, and the unique ecological features of the Southwest might have been considered along with development proposals.

The environmental irresponsibility characterizing the Southwest Power Complex is perhaps as much a consequence of institutional failure as of distorted priorities. The Bureau of Reclamation has been given sweeping powers that, when combined with authorities exercised by the Bureau of Land Management, the Bureau of Indian Affairs and the secretary of interior are extremely difficult to challenge effectively. The institutional arrangements through which projects such as the Southwest Power Complex were conceived and executed are highly effective and were intended to expedite the growth and development goals of the participating agencies. But these arrangements are not easily subject to redirection on behalf of social or environmental objectives. The probability of environmental degradation, thus, is built into the system by which the United States government promotes economic growth and energy development.

CASE II   Resistance to Public Control: The Tennessee Valley Authority

The Tennessee Valley Authority (TVA), established in 1933 as an independent agency (technically a government corporation) of the federal government, was designed as a model social-environmental planning agency. Its primary functions were flood control, power, and navigation, but resource planning, conservation, and wise land use were among its major objectives. It was to cooperate with and help coordinate the work of local, state, and federal planning. Within a few years of its establishment, the TVA had achieved many of its goals, and President Roosevelt proposed to Congress that it should be considered a model for regional environmental planning agencies. Environmental management, generally called "resource management," was recognized as a vital need in the 1930s, was given low priority for the next quarter century, and then was seemingly rediscovered in the 1960s.

At the time of its establishment fears were expressed, chiefly by conservative critics, that the TVA would not be amenable to public control. Its early history appears to have allayed many of these fears. But with the industrialization of the Southeastern states and the diminution of the fervor for social reform characterizing the New Deal years of the 1930s, the TVA began to behave more and more like the huge power generating system that it had, in fact, become. Its powerful role in the economy of the region fortifies it against attack, and it is not easily subject to the regulatory controls that can be applied to private public utilities which are dependent upon profits for survival.

The TVA appears to have gradually lost its ability to adjust its goals to changing national priorities. Although it spends a lot of money on public relations and makes extensive investments in lakes and lakeshore housing developments and recreation projects, the TVA has become less and less responsive to environmental concerns. Efforts by the public to have the TVA bring its dam building projects and its support of strip mining within the realm of sound environmental planning have been met with bureaucratic resistance or resentment. Public criticism of the agency during the 1960s has had little impact on its policies. Frustrated by the agency in their attempts to participate in decision making during the early 1970s, citizens have been forced to resort to the courts in an effort to open up TVA's decision-making process and to publicize information disregarded by TVA in its self-serving planning. As an independent agency of the federal government, TVA is obliged to consider environmental protection in accordance with the National Environmental Policy Act (NEPA), but citizens' groups have had to take the agency to court to make it fulfill its legal obligations.

The TVA has been involved in water resource and hydroelectric projects since its establishment. Many critics feel the agency has become a compulsive dam builder. Citizens' groups have played a significant role in at least two of TVA's plans for dams since the late 1960s. One of the best known conflicts was over the Tellico Dam on the Little Tennessee, or "Little T," River. Another conflict over dams on the Duck River drew national attention. In this instance, two dams, the Columbia and the Normandy, were declared by environmentalists to be the least justifiable—on ecological and economic grounds—in the history of the TVA. The Columbia Dam was to be built further downstream on the Duck River than the Normandy Dam and would have impounded a larger reservoir. The cost of the joint project was to be $75.5 million. Within a radius of twelve miles, the Tims Ford and Woods dams were holding back rivers of the Tennessee watershed and were already providing most of the benefits claimed in justification of the Duck River dams. Citizens' groups protested the inundation of scenic areas and archaelogical sites. The combined benefit-cost ratio for the Columbia-Normandy project was barely 1.3 : 1.0 (and therefore marginal), even when calculated by TVA itself. Analysis by environmentalists showed the ratio to be much lower than 1 : 1.

The public's image of the TVA has changed dramatically since it was founded. The TVA has evolved from the nation's model resource planning agency to one of the most unresponsive and development-oriented agencies in the country. As the nation's largest purchaser of strip-mined coal for electricity production, the TVA dominates mining policy in Tennessee, Kentucky, Virginia, and Alabama. It also dominates the Appalachian coal mining industry through its coal contracts. Supreme Court Justice William O. Douglas, the General Accounting Office, and the nation's leading environmental organizations have criticized the TVA for its poor record in the regulation of surface mining. Environmentalists have deplored TVA's vigorous lobbying in Congress and in many states against strip-mining legislation. Because the TVA continues to destroy Appalachia by favoring the short-term goals of low-cost electricity and economic growth over the long-term goals of environmental management, suits against the agency filed by preservationists and public-interest law firms have increased dramatically during the 1970s.

The Actors

The federal government has proprietary as well as legislative control over federally owned and financed utility systems such as the Tennessee Valley Authority. The TVA's goals are determined by its three-man board of directors. During the 1960s, the directors set policies that increased TVA reliance on strip-mined coal. Although coal operators who sell to TVA are required by their contracts to prevent water contamination and to carry out revegetation, the TVA has exercised little of its power to compel good mining practices. The state of Tennessee, and in particular its Department of Conservation and the Division of Water Quality Control, have generally followed the lead of TVA and have also opposed strong strip-mining legislation.

The Tennessee Citizens for Wilderness Planning (TCWP) and Tennessee Scenic River Association (TSRA) have directed public pressure for river preservation. The Duck River Preservation Association (DRPA), Save the Duck Committee, and the Environmental Defense Fund (EDF) gave vigorous support for forces protesting the dams. The Natural Resources Defense Council (NRDC) and the Sierra Club provided legal counsel to citizens' groups advocating more effective TVA strip-mining controls. Two local groups, Save Our Cumberland Mountains (SOCM) and Save Our Kentucky (SOK), assumed the lead with TCWP in coordinating citizen participation in strip-mining policy formation by drafting legislation, filing suits, and engaging in public education and lobbying.

The Policy Process

By mid-1966, citizen efforts to prevent the TVA from constructing Tellico Dam on the last remaining free-flowing stretch of the scenic "Little T" had almost been exhausted. A revival of the Association for the Preservation of the Little T (APLT) during the following four years had a significant impact on the TVA project in 1971. By mid-1971, the TVA had spent about $25 million on land acquisitions and about $5 million on construction of the $70 million dam. Citizens' groups were convinced the cost-benefit estimates of the TVA were in error and publicized the issue.

Publicity about the unfavorable consequences of the project elicited some political support for the conservationists. In December 1971, Governor Dunn of Tennessee declared his opposition to Tellico Dam and promised to seek state scenic river status for the "Little T." The chairman of the TVA replied that the project would continue. Realizing the TVA was determined to proceed, some local citizens' groups and the Environmental Defense Fund (EDF) filed suit against the TVA on the grounds that the agency had failed to file an environmental impact statement. The implementation of the NEPA (signed January 1970) during this early phase of the Tellico project provided citizens with an instrument of review. The citizens secured a temporary injunction in January 1972 against the Tellico Dam. After analyzing TVA's formal environmental impact statement, filed with the CEQ in February 1972, the APLT and other citizens' groups strongly criticized it.

The APLT and its supporters worked industriously to mobilize political backing and publicity at the state and national levels during the year. A petition against Tellico Dam, circulated by TCWP, was signed by 7,200 people within a few months. In June 1972, the House Public Works Appropriations Subcommittee cut $7.5 million from TVA's Tellico Dam request. Publicity and political lobbying had won the citizens' groups considerable support in the state legislature and Congress. The courts also gave the citizens' groups extra credibility by the end of 1972. The Sixth District Court of Appeals in Cincinnati denied TVA's appeal of the preliminary injunction against construction of Tellico Dam. But on October 25, 1973, the federal court at Knoxville reversed the ruling, declaring that TVA's environmental impact statement met the requirements of NEPA. The injunction that the citizens' groups had used since January 1972 to halt Tellico Dam construction was lifted. The plaintiffs appealed and asked for the injunction to be reinstated, but the appeal was denied.

To prevent construction of the Columbia and particularly the Normandy dams, which were more expensive and less justifiable, citizens' groups at first attempted to win political support and publicity. Subsequently, they intervened in legislative hearings and conferences with principal decision makers in Congress and the White House. Finally, the citizens took TVA to court.

The Tennessee Scenic Rivers Association and Tennessee Citizens for Wilderness Planning had some success in interventions in policy late in 1969. Through pleas to a Senate subcommittee for appropriations, they managed to have $1.3 million deleted from funds previously appropriated by the House for TVA land acquisitions. But a conference committee of the Senate and House—on which Congressman Joe L. Evins of Tennessee's Fourth District (which included the Duck River area) held a powerful senior position—restored the money in December. Citizens' groups protested immediately to the president. In February 1970, when the budget was sent to Congress, the $1.3 million was designated as "frozen" for the fiscal year. Then the Bureau of the Budget agreed to release the money to the TVA on July 1, 1970, and Congressman Evins even managed to appropriate additional funds for this pork barrel in his own district.

In August 1970, citizens' groups broadcast publicly TVA's failure to submit an environmental impact statement on the dams to the CEQ, even though it had started acquiring land. The citizens' analysis of the benefit-cost estimates revealed that the TVA's original ratio of 1.2: 1.0, only marginal in itself, really should have been less than 1: 1. The preservationists also worked diligently to inform the public, legislators, and various agency officials that the TVA's projects would destroy agricultural, archeological, biological, recreational, and scenic values and that the claimed benefits of the dams could be obtained by alternative, less destructive, means. The Duck River Preservation Association (DRPA) was formed in Normandy in November 1970.

During 1971, numerous citizens' groups cooperated in efforts to turn the political tide against the destructive and uneconomical dams. In May, the DRPA and TCWP testified at both House and Senate appropriations committee hearings in Washington, D.C., and again opposed funding the dam projects. The citizens' representatives also conferred with the Tennessee congressional delegation and alerted them to the impending threat to the Duck River watershed. Governor Dunn conferred with a delegation of citizens in Nashville, but he still supported the project. The commissioner of the Tennessee Department of Conservation also went on record in favor of the dams, even though the environmental statement had yet to be filed. The TCWP and DRPA were successful in obtaining the support of the Coffee County Farm Bureau and the Southeastern Indian Antiquities Survey. The 700-member Tennessee Archaeological Society also joined citizen forces, because the dams threatened to inundate 100 valuable sites, some over 3,000 years old. The various citizens' groups used scientific, economic, and recreational information to compile a Citizens' Environmental and Economic Impact Report on the Normandy project.

TVA filed its draft environmental impact statement in June 1971 and held hearings in August, choosing Columbia, the center of prodam sentiment, as the hearing site. Citizens from the Normandy area, where opposition to the dam ran high, had to travel a considerable distance to appear, and they had to testify after working hours, by which time the press had gone home. The antidam citizens' groups presented a massive array of scientific and economic facts, while one prodam testimony after another repeated the patently false and illogical statement that the river was running dry and that dams were needed for water supply. The TVA made its own "summary" of testimony for the final statement which was released in May 1972.

A month later, TVA began constructing a diversion channel on the Duck River in preparation for building Normandy Dam. The DRPA, TSRA, and TCWP reacted immediately by coordinating letters of protest to President Nixon, to the CEQ, and to Tennessee legislators and the governor. Public meetings, television reports, and petitions were quickly organized, and politicians were invited to take a float trip on the Duck River. In September, Lynn Seeber, general manager of the TVA, publicly embarrassed the agency on television by mentioning that "enhanced employment," one of the main benefits claimed for the dams, was in fact only a "secondary" benefit. The interviewer was quick to realize that secondary benefits are not allowable in benefit-cost calculation and that, as a result, the ratio would drop to $0.8:1.0$. TVA requested that this part of the tape be deleted from the television interview.

In mid-1972, the EDF, DRPA, and others filed suit against the TVA in an effort to halt the feverishly proceeding construction of the Normandy Dam. Groups favoring the dam, such as the Upper Duck River Development Association, Tennessee River Valley Association, four local towns, and two of the watershed counties, intervened on behalf of the TVA. The citizens' group plaintiffs had filed suit on the grounds that the TVA had violated NEPA, the Tennessee Valley Authority Act, National Historical Act, Public Trust Doctrine, and the U.S. Constitution. In December 1972, Judge Charles G. Neese of the federal district court of Winchester upheld the plaintiffs' allegations under NEPA but dismissed the other grounds.

The trial was set for January 14, 1974. In the meantime, the TVA doubled its daily working hours on the dam's construction. During 1973, citizens' groups coalesced to form the Save the Duck Committee which concentrated on lobbying and publicizing the issues. In September, when the EDF was forced to withdraw as a principal co-plaintiff for the citizens due to heavy professional commitments throughout the country, the coalition raised enough money to proceed with the lawsuit. During the trial, which concluded on January 18, 1974, citizens' groups argued that the TVA environmental impact statement was inadequate and inaccurate. A former employee who had compiled the agency's impact statement revealed information that critically jeopardized TVA's

credibility. The TVA had suppressed important information: the conclusions of the agency's own agricultural economists who predicted that
the region's economy would lose $6 million annually if the dams were
completed. This information reduced the benefit-cost ratio of the dam
project even lower than the citizens' estimate.

Some of the documents filed in court were used later that month in
a Tennessee newspaper to show that the TVA had secretly supplied
specific "appropriate techniques" and information to local groups
favoring the dam for use in "combatting" efforts of the preservationists.
Apparently scornful of the public it was supposed to serve, the TVA
had considered the citizens' groups seeking to preserve Tennessee's last
free-flowing river an enemy to be combatted. On March 7, 1974, the
court ordered all work on the Normandy and Columbia dams halted
as of March 30 until TVA filed an acceptable impact statement. The
judge found that TVA had not used "good faith" considerations and
had suppressed information on real costs. According to information revealed in court, the cost of the TVA dam project is known to have increased from $78.5 to $120 million. Citizens realize the court decision
only provides a breathing space. In fact, the court has already delayed
the date of the injunction several times. A permanent stop to the unjustifiable project can only be guaranteed through legislation.

Another of the TVA's activities—its encouragement of destructive
strip mining—has been criticized by citizens since the mid-1960s. The
TVA has been the single biggest factor encouraging this environmentally
degrading practice, because it buys the cheapest coal possible for its
mammoth electric power production. Only in very recent years have
TVA coal contracts even required reclamation of soils. After almost
twenty-five years of unregulated strip mining, the Tennessee Strip Mine
Law of 1967 was enacted. The TCWP and TSRA were lauded in *Field
and Stream* (October 1968) for their leading role in the passage of this
act. The Tennessee Department of Conservation and the TVA strongly
opposed all subsequent attempts to strengthen surface mining laws.
Years after the 1967 act, Tennessee's were considered weak, and even
those were not strictly enforced. In May 1970, the TVA accepted a coal
contract that permitted the producer to strip the banks of the Obed
River in violation of the Wild and Scenic Rivers Act (see Chapter 5,
Natural Areas and Wildlife). Citizens' groups "watchdogging" the TVA
have been demanding that the state strip mine law, as well as TVA's
contract regulations, be enforced.

During 1971, in an effort to strengthen Tennessee's surface mining law, TCWP wrote an amended version of the 1967 law. Known as the Citizens' Bill, the amended version was opposed by TVA, the Tennessee Department of Conservation, and by much of the state administration. When William Jenkins was named the new commissioner of conservation, citizens' groups publicized his previous record as speaker of the house, when he had opposed strip-mining laws. The TCWP persistently tried to confer with Governor Dunn on this appointment, but to no avail, even though the governor had previously assured conservationists he would consult them before appointing a commissioner or deputy commissioner.

In December 1972, citizens' groups were forced to resort to the courts in an effort to make the TVA legally accountable for the environmental effects of its coal purchasing activities and to force the TVA to examine alternative methods of mining coal. The plaintiffs—NRDC, Sierra Club, EDF, SOCM, TCWP, and SOK—filed a motion for either a preliminary injunction or a partial summary judgment against the TVA. The plaintiffs alleged that TVA had not adequately prepared impact statements evaluating the full effects on the human and natural environment of its $100 million contracts for strip-mined coal; that the true cost of the coal should include the enormous effects of strip mining on the landscape, people, ecology, and safety of the region; that TVA had not realistically investigated the cost and feasibility of land reclamation; and that it had not thoroughly investigated alternative methods for producing power. Citizens lost the suit in a judgment issued in the summer of 1973. The judge ruled that filing environmental impact statements for individual coal contracts conflicted with Section 8 (b) of the TVA act that requires competitive bidding. He further ruled the TVA's impact statement was adequate.

While the lawsuit was in progress, citizens continued their efforts on the legislative front. TCWP drafted and stimulated introduction of another set of amendments to the 1967 state law, the Citizens' Bill of 1972. The state administration, influenced by TVA and the strip mine lobby, introduced a rival bill which borrowed heavily from the earlier Citizens' Bill of 1971, though it was weakened considerably. A direct ban on strip mining in Tennessee was proposed this same month in legislation drafted by SOCM. The Mountain People's Mine Law of 1973, sponsored by State Representative Mike Murphy in the 88th General Assembly, provided that all strip mining must cease within six months of enactment of the law. SOCM bused forty-five citizens from five coal counties to Nashville on March 7, 1972, to confer on the proposed law with Governor Dunn, but it did not move out of committee. The administration bill was finally passed, slightly strengthened by some TCWP-supported amendments, and it replaced the 1967 law.

During 1972, citizens' groups received a great deal of direct and indirect support in their fight against the TVA. Indirectly, they received favorable publicity when the TVA took members of the Senate Subcommittee on Minerals, Materials, and Fuels (which was working on federal strip-mining legislation) on a tour of mining areas. TCWP discredited the TVA by proving that the tour had been biased and devoid of public participation. More direct support came from U.S. Senator Fred Harris (D-Oklahoma), who was invited to visit Petros by the SOCM. Senator Harris was shocked by the evils of strip mining and TVA's role in it, and he supported SOCM's proposal to ban it entirely. In April, the unpopular (with environmentalists) Commissioner Jenkins of the Tennessee Department of Conservation was nominated as a director of TVA. SOCM protested the nomination in a five-page letter to U.S. Senator Jennings Randolph (D-West Virginia), chairman of the Senate Public Works Committee, which was holding confirmation hearings on this nomination. As conservation commissioner, they argued, Jennings had continued to lobby against many environmental proposals.

A report from the Environmental Policy Center in Washington, D.C., in May 1972 greatly strengthened the credibility of citizens' arguments against strip mining, and provided data which SOCM and TCWP circulated widely. Then, overwhelming victories for candidates against strip mining in West Virginia's political primary on May 9, gave citizens' groups valuable political backing in Appalachia. In September 1972, the U.S. General Accounting Office (GAO) of the comptroller general issued an alarming report on the federal regulation of strip mining. GAO documented several cases showing that the TVA frequently failed to implement and enforce regulations. Its inadequate procedures for inspection resulted in ineffective reclamation. The GAO alleged, moreover, that TVA's inspection reports were not in accord with the facts.

The Tennessee Surface Mining Act of 1972 required that an operator show he had applied for (but not necessarily obtained) a water discharge permit from the state's Division of Water Quality Control (DWQC) when applying for a strip-mining permit. Of eighty applications submitted since that act was made law, the DWQC had acted on none, according to a TCWP investigation. When the DWQC did not respond to a request of citizens' groups to fulfill its statutory duty, SOCM, TCWP, TSRA, and the Sierra Club filed suit in the Chancery Court of Davidson County for a writ of mandamus to compel the DWQC to perform its duty. Late in 1973, the plaintiffs were granted standing, and the DWQC was ordered to follow administrative procedures specified by the court. Although this case had not been directly related to the TVA, it illustrates the difficulties the public has faced in insisting simply that existing laws be enforced.

Critics charge that TVA also has had an unfortunate effect on local law enforcement. Because of the TVA's influence over the livelihood of major coal producing counties, many of them waive the law in favor of cheap coal. One example is Morgan County, one of Tennessee's biggest coal producers. Morgan County has the duty to enforce the state's truck weight laws, but the general sessions court judge has refused to penalize overweight coal delivery trucks that ruin road surfaces, create unbearable noise levels, and lower the quality of life in mountain towns. Citizens have been forced to ask the courts to terminate this destructive practice. In September 1972, SOCM sued the TVA, alleging that the TVA should assist in controlling overweight trucks by refusing to accept excessive coal deliveries at the Kingston Steam Plant and alleging that TVA's lack of enforcement places unnecessary financial burdens on county governments and also contributes to dangerous driving. The courts dismissed the complaint and also the subsequent appeals.

Throughout 1973, citizens' groups launched a number of strategies in an attempt to change TVA's policies relating to strip mining and kept watch on political maneuvers intended to favor cheap electricity at the price of environmental quality. In June, progrowth Tennessee Valley congressmen, who wanted cheap power for the region, proposed a critical amendment to the TVA act. They proposed that future costs incurred by TVA in complying with environmental laws and regulations should not be included in the costs of the electric power program. This proposal would have required all taxpayers in the United States, not just the consumers of TVA power, to pay for electrostatic precipitators, taller smoke stacks, scrubbers, and possibly even land reclamation. Citizens' groups mounted a publicity campaign to expose the implications of the proposal. TVA was also shown to be lobbying aggressively against strong features of federal strip-mining regulatory bills. Prior to House debate in 1972, and again prior to Senate debate in 1973, TVA circulated a letter to key figures in the Congress claiming that passage of the bill would jeopardize electric power production in the region. This TVA letter was quoted in the Senate debate. TVA also issued several news releases about the supposedly dire economic effects of stringent federal legislation and implied that coal shortages and blackouts were imminent. Citizens' groups countered each argument put forward by the TVA. TCWP emphasized that there is forty times more deep mineable coal than strippable coal in the present TVA purchase areas and that deep mining employs more people. (SOCM's research revealed that only 854 people in Tennessee, only 1.8 percent of the total employment of the five main coal producing counties, worked in strip mines.) This data undermined the TVA forecasts of disastrous coal shortages and of unemployment consequences of abandoning strip mining.

Outcome

The history of the TVA by now clearly documents its self-selected priorities: energy is to be produced as cheaply as possible, regardless of the environmental consequences. Although the act creating this federal agency required it to manage natural resources, it has consistently exploited them and persistently resists all efforts to redirect its activities.

The TVA is an example of misapplied success. Its energy mission overwhelmed its broader objectives, and its charter and institutional status did not provide adequate means for review and reorientation of its purposes and priorities. The extent of the energy development that has occurred under TVA management could not have been foreseen when the agency was created in the 1930s. Hence, no adequate provision was made to prevent a warping or distortion of agency objectives as a consequence of greatly increased opportunities and successes. If there is a lesson to be learned from the evolution of the TVA, it is that institutional arrangements for correcting the course of agency development—and even for reorganizing or abolishing the agency—should be built into whatever legal instrument (statute, executive order, charter, etc.) is used to establish the agency.

CASE III   Mission Fixation: The United States Forest Service

The public lands controlled by the U.S. Forest Service include 187 million acres of national forests and national grasslands. Controlling 18 percent of the nation's total commercial forests, the Forest Service is the largest manager of commercial forests in the United States. In total, public lands under supervision of the USFS contain about one-half of the nation's old-growth timber resources. Gifford Pinchot, the first chief of the USFS, believed that the nation's forest resources should be utilized for the country as a whole. During the past half century since Pinchot's time, and particularly since the 1950s, the concept of multiple-use of forest lands has dominated USFS policies. The multiple-use goal has meant managing the forest for sustained yields of timber, forage, watershed protection, wildlife, fish, and recreation. The Multiple Use–Sustained Yield Act of 1960, and implicitly the Organic Administration Act of 1897, required the USFS to manage the national forests so that each of these resources is available to the nation and to insure that the supply of each will be sustained and the productivity of the lands will not be impaired.

The Forest Service has, however, tended to give priority to the growth of commercial timber, to logging, and to road building. During the 1960s, the Forest Service was under great pressure by the lumber industries to permit increased logging on public lands. There was also a professional predisposition within the Forest Service to increase logging. Appropriated funds for the agency are grossly inadequate and are earmarked for timber sales, road building, and fire prevention. Little funding is made for ecologically sound resource management. President Richard Nixon, in the early 1970s, further constricted the narrow focus when he directed the Forest Service to increase timber production. But during the same time, the heightened environmental conscience of the American public led to serious protest of a number of policies affecting the national forests. Environmentalists alleged that clear-cutting practices were dramatically increasing habitat destruction, erosion, floods, landslides, and landscape degradation. The Forest Service appeared to be dominated by the production goals of the lumber companies. Citizens' groups complained that the multiple-use doctrine was being violated or distorted. The Sierra Club sued the Forest Service in an attempt to stop clear-cutting in the Tongass National Forest in southeastern Alaska, and the West Virginia legislature passed a resolution to stop clear-cutting in national forests in that state. A nationwide effort by conservationists culminated in the enactment of a major piece of nonexploitive legislation, the Wilderness Act of 1964. Conservationists pressed for the act in an effort to remove wildlands from the administrative discretion of the Forest Service.

In a nation traditionally committed to the primacy of economic values and to the treatment of land as a commodity, the removal of significant tracts of undeveloped land from economic exploitation or management was certain to provoke conflict. Efforts to break down or restrict the Wilderness Act have continued. Protracted disputes have occurred over the use and status of areas such as the Quetico-Superior region on the Minnesota-Ontario border and the Magruder Corridor between the headwaters of the Selway and Bitterroot rivers on the Idaho-Montana border.

The Magruder Corridor is essentially a wild area. Although the area is not spectacular alpine and peak, it is mountainous and cut by steep fast-flowing streams. The headwaters of the Selway River are located in the corridor. These waters are of incomparable clarity and purity. From headwaters in the corridor this wild free-flowing stream stretches an estimated 100 miles to join the Locksa River to form the middle fork of the Clearwater River. These free-flowing and wild rivers make up the only major drainage system in Idaho that has not been "developed," or developed in part, except for a few undesignated wilderness areas, such as the Selway-Bitterroot Wilderness Area. The soil on the slopes of the Magruder Corridor is loose and extremely erodable. Logging would lead to severe sedimentation and erosion of the critically important headwaters of the Selway River drainage system. Water quality would be drastically reduced, the habitat of black bear, elk, deer, Rocky Mountain goat, and Rocky Mountain sheep would be degraded, the wilderness would be disrupted, and the valuable anadromous steelhead and salmon resources would be impaired once the corridor was "developed." A meager cut of 12 million board-feet of timber annually would appear to be little gain in return for heavy losses to the environment.

Preservationists have tried by a number of means to halt the USFS plans and protect the Magruder Corridor. The USFS had remained consistently insensitive to public concern for the greater part of the controversy, but it has made a major institutionalized effort to include public involvement in decision making since the Magruder issue demonstrated the perseverance of organized citizen protest.

The Actors

The Forest Service, presently located administratively within the U.S. Department of Agriculture, has jurisdiction over the management of forest lands in the Selway-Bitterroot region. Changes in policy regarding wilderness status for Magruder Corridor must be made either through the administration of USFS or through congressional action via the Wilderness Act of 1964.

U.S. Senators Lee Metcalf of Montana and Frank Church of Idaho, who have responded to the environmental concern of citizens, have had an important influence on policy outcomes for the corridor. By introducing protective legislation, corresponding with Forest Service and Department of Agriculture officials, and prompting of management studies, they took significant steps in the policy formulation process.

National conservation organizations, the Sierra Club and Wilderness Society in particular, have assisted local and state organizations favoring preservation in Idaho and Montana. The Save the Upper Selway Committee (SUSC) and North Idaho Wilderness Committee (NIWC) have consolidated the efforts of dozens of local and state preservation organizations. The citizens' groups have led the defense of public interest in the environment by calling for the USFS to consider more of the ecological values in making decisions about the corridor.

A majority of the local communities in the area, however, have supported Forest Service development plans. Chambers of commerce, county commissioners, certain newspapers, and the lumber industry have lobbied extensively in favor of the economic development of the public lands.

The Policy Process

During the 1930s, citizens' groups and a few preservation-conscious government officials had two occasions to influence forestry policy in the Selway-Bitterroot area. In 1931, the Forest Service, on the recommendation of some Idaho citizens and Governor Baldridge, established the 1.2 million-acre Idaho Primitive Area, south of the Magruder Corridor. In 1936, through the efforts of the Wilderness Society and one of the society's chief organizers, Robert Marshall (who was also chief of the Division of Recreation and Lands in the Forest Service), the service established the Selway-Bitterroot Primitive Area, which included the Magruder Corridor. But in 1934, a large fire in the Magruder Corridor area prompted the construction of a road from the Bitterroot Valley to Elk City, Idaho. Nearly thirty years later this road passing through Magruder Corridor was to be used by the USFS to justify excluding the corridor from the wilderness area. The road is still open and still maintained.

In 1939 new regulations were adopted within the Forest Service that attempted to define more clearly policies on primitive areas. The new regulations, known as "U," superseded the vague "L-20" regulations. This step in policy was to have serious implications for the Magruder Corridor. On the chief of the Forest Service's recommendation, national forest lands in tracts not less than 100,000 acres could be designated as "wilderness." Tracts of 5,000 to 100,000 acres could be designated as "wild" areas, and regulations were established to define nonwilderness lands or "roadless" areas. The new "U" regulations prohibited roads and commercial timber cutting.

World War II interrupted wilderness classification in the region. Early in the 1950s, conservationists feared that the Forest Service would declassify a number of "wilderness" areas in which roads had been built in order to permit development. The Wilderness Society, the Sierra Club, the National Wildlife Federation, the National Parks Association, and the Wildlife Management Institute drafted a federal wilderness bill in 1955. In 1956, conservationists recommended to the Forest Service that the area north of the road be included in the soon-to-be-established Selway-Bitterroot Wilderness Area. The area south of the road was already recommended to be included in the Idaho and Salmon River Breaks Primitive Areas. Conservationists recommended the combined tract be known as the River of No Return Wilderness Area, with the ribbon of road through the Magruder Corridor being the only interruption in the vast wilderness.

On June 12, 1960, the Multiple Use–Sustained Yield Act became law. This was another turning point in policy for Magruder Corridor. The new act authorized a formal commitment toward multiple-use management throughout national forest lands. This same year the Forest Service announced reclassification proposals that critically affected the future of Magruder Corridor. The Selway-Bitterroot Wilderness Area was reduced by a half million acres including the road, Magruder Corridor, and much of the surrounding upper Selway watershed country.

The Sierra Club, the Wilderness Society, the Western Montana Fish and Game Association, the Montana Wilderness Association, and supporting citizens' groups attended reclassification hearings held in 1961 by the Forest Service. The conservationists stated that the enormous deletion of hundreds of thousands of acres was not justifiable merely because of the road in Magruder Corridor. They recommended re-classifying only a narrow corridor parallel to the road and placing all other acreage south and north of the road in wilderness classification. The Forest Service received 4,000 recorded views from organizations and individuals on the controversy. The Inland Empire Multiple Use Committee, backed by the Idaho forest products industry, fought to reduce all wilderness classification. The conflict was so intense that the Forest Service reviewed its earlier decision, but the practical impact conservationists had had on policy was minimal. In 1963, the secretary of agriculture announced an increase in the Selway-Bitterroot Wilderness Area of about 6 percent, but Magruder Corridor was still to be placed in multiple-use development status. After the Wilderness Act of 1964 was passed, the Selway-Bitterroot Wilderness Area was auto-matically included in the National Wilderness Preservation System, but the act reinforced Magruder Corridor's status as a declassified area. Only congressional approval could preserve the corridor as wilder-ness.

Between 1960, when the Forest Service announced the declassifica-tion of the corridor, and 1963, when the final decision was issued, agency decision making was shrouded in secrecy. No information was given to the public, and efforts by the Wilderness Society and other representatives of the public to participate in policy formation were rebuffed by the Forest Service. Insensitivity to environmental values at this point in the corridor controversy may have exacerbated public distrust of the agency, distrust that has grown since the early 1960s. Since the efforts of conservation groups were being directed primarily toward the passage of the national wilderness legislation in the early 1960s, there was little organized protest in the corridor controversy until late 1964. The Forest Service confirmed its intentions to develop the corridor in the fall of 1964, when it awarded a road construction contract.

Preservation-conscious citizens promptly organized to discuss the possibility of returning the corridor to a protected classification. In September 1964, the Save the Upper Selway Committee was formed in Montana, largely under the leadership of Mrs. Doris Milner. In Lewis-ton, Idaho, the North Idaho Wilderness Committee, under the leader-ship of Morton R. Brigham, was organized to oppose the development plans of the Forest Service. The SUSC and NIWC worked together closely as the Selway Committee without a formal merger.

During the mid-1960s, citizens' groups worked primarily to include the corridor in the National Wilderness Preservation System. But intermediate steps were required because the Wilderness Act of 1964 had set difficult obstacles in the path of attempts to protect new wilderness areas. Citizens focused on two intermediate goals. The first was to stop reconstruction of the corridor road so that further studies could be pursued during the delay. To this end, the citizens disseminated brochures describing the issues, broadened support through numerous community action groups, and conducted massive letter writing campaigns. Forest Service officials, the president of the United States, and national and state legislators were informed and urged to address the problem. Using cost and timber data, Morton Brigham of NIWC demonstrated that logging would not be feasible in the corridor and would not benefit game management. Second, citizens' groups focused on winning the support of Senators Church and Metcalf. The conservationists believed that the Forest Service, as an administrative agency, would try to avoid political interference with its administrative decision making. Metcalf and Church were continually pressured to call for new hearings, to approach the secretary of agriculture personally, and to propose an Upper Selway Wilderness Bill.

By mid-1965 the preservationists, through the news media and activities of national conservation organizations, had drawn national attention to the Magruder Corridor issues. In June, Senator Metcalf reported that development in the corridor was to be delayed two years. Citizens' groups were pleased when the entire Selway River was included in the Wild Rivers Bill as it was passed by the Senate. Watershed protection and preservation of the anadromous fish resources in the Selway had been continually encouraged by the citizens' groups. But the Forest Service continued to express its intention to manage the corridor as a multiple-use area. Citizens' groups were now protesting the policy of the Forest Service from two points of view. Besides the participants who demanded wilderness preservation, an increasing number of citizens expressed their lack of confidence in the ability of the Forest Service to execute an acceptable management plan without exhaustive ecological research beforehand.

Conservationists had succeeded in winning the support of Senators Metcalf and Church. Before introducing wilderness legislation, the senators were prepared to call for a feasibility study of the Forest Service's management program. In August 1966, a precedent was set in the Department of Agriculture when the secretary agreed to establish a nongovernmental study committee to review the Magruder Corridor plan and general land-use problems in the area. The Magruder Corridor Review Committee (MCRC), led by Dr. George Selke, a special consultant to the secretary of agriculture, held meetings in Grangeville and Boise, Idaho, and in Missoula, Montana, during December 1966 to obtain public viewpoints on the issues. The meetings and subsequent submissions to the committee revealed the widespread conflict. Local chambers of commerce and county commissioners supported development proposals. Wildlife experts, ecologists, and well-organized citizens' groups were part of the two-thirds majority that opposed the development plans. The Forest Service forecast loss of jobs and economic depression if wilderness proponents succeeded in locking land away from development.

On June 1, 1967, the Magruder Corridor Review Committee report was released, and it severely criticized the studies and decisions of the Forest Service. The report recommended deferring logging and road building until a comprehensive evaluation of the total impact of the plans was made public. It also recommended that the Forest Service needed to strengthen public confidence in its ability to manage wild areas as a primary use without being formally designated. Conservationists had won a temporary stay of execution for the corridor, because the secretary of agriculture immediately directed the Forest Service to carry out the recommendations of the MCRC report. In the meantime, citizens' groups again urged Senators Metcalf and Church to introduce protective legislation for the Magruder Corridor, but the senators preferred to wait for the outcome of the Forest Service program review before proposing legislation.

Late in 1970, the Bitterroot National Forest supervisor released a new management plan for the area that recommended continued road building and logging. In what was interpreted by active development interests as an appeasement to preservationists, the Forest Service also declared a moratorium on development for at least five years. The service rejected as a management alternative the narrow corridor (primarily wilderness) concept previously suggested by conservationists. Two reasons were given: first, the timber was needed by the American people, and second, the proximity of the road would compromise the Wilderness Act of 1964. But in justifying its plan to log and build roads in the wild area, the Forest Service stated that there would be little effect on wilderness solitude.

Outcome

Conservationists were convinced that the Forest Service had no intention of preserving Magruder Corridor. With the Forest Service apparently insensitive to conservationist concern, the citizens' groups had no alternative other than to continue urging legislative protection for the corridor. In August 1971, Senators Metcalf and Church, at the instigation of citizens' groups, introduced a bill in the Senate calling for the roadless area of the corridor to be included in the National Wilderness Preservation System. This legislation did not pass, however, and as of early 1976 the issue was still in a stalemate.

CASE IV   Administrative Discretion: Navarre Marsh, Ohio

In May 1967, the federal government acquired Navarre Marsh adjoining Lake Erie in northern Ohio. Some of the 530 acres in the marsh were a valuable wildlife area and part of the national avian flyway system. Navarre Marsh was subsequently dedicated as a part of the National Wildlife Refuge System. Yet six months later, the secretary of the interior agreed to transfer Navarre Marsh into the hands of two electric utility companies so they could use the marsh as a site for a nuclear generating plant.

The two public utilities, the Toledo Edison Co. and the Cleveland Electric Illuminating Co., proposed jointly to construct the Davis-Besse nuclear power plant in the Navarre Marsh. Their previous plans to acquire land in an area ten miles east at Darby Marsh, where the utilities owned about 480 acres, had been thwarted by overly eager land speculators. The secretary of interior and the utilities secretly negotiated a land exchange deal to permit a pressurized water reactor to be built in Navarre Marsh. In the exchange completed in October 1968, the Department of Interior received the Darby Marsh plus some engineering improvements in the marshland. The first information of the exchange that reached the public (May 1969) was that the deal had been consummated, the appropriate permits secured, and that the utilities would soon begin construction of the reactor.

Environmentalists and citizens' groups reacted immediately, because Darby Marsh was not as valuable as Navarre Marsh as a wildlife refuge. The citizens' groups asserted that the federal government had betrayed the public trust and violated a number of federal statutes protecting natural areas and wildlife. Conservationists and citizens promptly organized to file suit against the secretary of interior, the two public utilities, the director of the Atomic Energy Commission (AEC), and the AEC itself. This conflict between the opponents and promoters of the exchange provides insights into administrative ambivalence regarding environmental values and into the limitations of turning to the courts for administrative review.

The Actors

Federal authority in the policy process was dominated by the Department of Interior and the AEC. The Interior Department, through its Fish and Wildlife Service and its Bureau of Sport Fisheries and Wildlife, had the authority to approve or disapprove the exchange of marshes. The AEC had the authority to license both the construction and operation of the Davis-Besse reactor.

The environmental interests were represented in the Navarre Marsh dispute by the Sierra Club and the Citizens for Clean Air and Water (CCAW). The CCAW, an environmental group of about 500 citizens, had a majority of its membership in the Cleveland area of Ohio. Formed in 1968 to pursue greater control of air and water pollution in the state, the CCAW also became a base for the organization of the Coalition For Safe Electric Power (CFSEP). The CFSEP played a leading role in litigation and citizens' participation in the controversy over AEC licensing procedures. In the Navarre Marsh–Darby Marsh controversy, the CCAW gave moral and financial support to the nationally organized Sierra Club which led the interveners in filing suit to reverse the Navarre Marsh land exchange.

The burden for deciding this case was thrust upon the courts. Administrative procedures in the Interior Department and AEC were alleged to have betrayed a public trust. The public turned to the courts in order to examine the administrative process and agency unresponsiveness. The problem of gaining access to the courts, however, hampered citizens attempting to defend the public interest. The Sierra Club and CCAW's efforts to have the courts open up agency decision processes were not successful. Agency-utility conspiracy dominated the policy process and placed environmental management out of the public's reach.

The Policy Process

The process of decision making was confined to the actions of three institutions, the AEC, the Department of Interior, and the courts. Each of these institutions was unresponsive to public demands for including environmental criteria in decision making. An examination of the role of the courts demonstrates some of the problems of access to environmental litigation.

In the first complaint filed in October 1970, plaintiffs sought relief on the following four grounds: (1) Plaintiffs sought to nullify the two-year old exchange agreement of Navarre Marsh for Darby Marsh. They alleged that the agreement was in derogation of the statutory duties of the secretary of interior. (2) Plaintiffs also sought to enjoin the director of the AEC from holding construction license hearings and to revoke the previous construction variance granted utilities by the AEC. (3) The citizens' groups also claimed that the exchange of lands violated the official Convention Between the United States of America and Mexico for the Protection of Migratory Birds and Game Mammals. (4) Plaintiffs further alleged that the law pertaining to the National Wildlife Refuge System under which the exchange was made (16 U.S.C. 688 dd) was unconstitutional. Motions to dismiss these four claims were filed by the secretary of interior and the two utility companies in federal district court.

At this point the citizens were confronted with legal doctrines and procedural rules which protracted the controversy. The first was the standing issue. Established conservation organizations, such as the Sierra Club, in recent years have been deemed by the courts to have sufficient economic and legal interests on which to sue. The court held that plaintiffs had standing because they had sufficient stake in the outcome. The motion to dismiss, however, was granted by the court on April 5, 1971, on the grounds of sovereign immunity (i.e., the government is immune from suit) and reviewability (decisions committed to agency discretion are not reviewable by courts).

Most authorities agree that the doctrine of sovereign immunity works an undue hardship on plaintiffs and has no relevance today. Environmentalists are particularly handicapped by the doctrine of sovereign immunity because it has special relevance to the disposition of public lands (sovereign property). Plaintiffs are also denied access to the court on other grounds resulting from interpretations of the sovereign immunity doctrine. In requesting that the marshes be swapped back, the citizens raised the issue of disposition of unquestionable sovereign property which necessitated affirmative action by the government. As mentioned earlier, citizens had not discovered the plans for the agreement until after the exchange had taken place. If the citizens had learned of the proposed disposition of public lands before the exchange took place, they could have sought an injunction and perhaps have circumvented the disposition of property and related agency action.

The court employed the doctrine of reviewability as a basis upon which to dismiss the citizens' complaint. The courts have held that decisions committed to agency discretion are not reviewable, even though legal precedents have been set establishing that abuses of discretion are reviewable. The citizens pointed out that there was no specific technical limitation on the secretary of interior's discretion to conduct the exchange of marshes, but that various federal statutes required the secretary to manage and protect wildlife. The citizens' attempts to protect these resources in Navarre Marsh were prevented, however, because they could not point to a specific provision impinging on the secretary's discretion in this instance.

The Sierra Club and Citizens for Clean Air and Water then filed an amended complaint, the sole allegation being that the transfer of title to Navarre Marsh was an arbitrary and capricious act and constituted an abuse of discretion. Further, plaintiffs asked that the court issue an order directing the two utility companies to return the title of Navarre Marsh to the federal government. The court declared it could not return title without ordering the government to return Darby Marsh to the two utilities. In September 1972, the case was dismissed on the grounds of reviewability and sovereign immunity.

Had the dissenting views of Judge John Feikens prevailed, a substantial increase in the citizen impact on policy would have occurred. In Judge Feikens' view, the standing requirement had been met and the plaintiffs should have been allowed to assert the public interest. He also noted that the secretary of the interior failed to consider the intent and purpose of a number of statutes under which he is required to act. Quoting from the Endangered Species Conservation Act and the National Environmental Policy Act (NEPA), the judge cited congressional intent to preserve the environment and wildlife populations and habitats. He challenged the defendants' claim that the secretary of the interior had total discretion to dispose of land, regardless of the harmful effects it may have on wildlife refuges. Judge Feikens pointed out that the Interior Department may not exercise unbridled discretion and, furthermore, that declaring the case unreviewable does not resolve the question of administrative discretion. Judge Feikens called for a trial to resolve the issue of whether the secretary acted illegally (i.e., his action was *ultra vires*). Feikens argued strongly that sovereign immunity should not be used as a shield to prevent the review of government agency rulings.

The citizens' groups, on behalf of the public, had little or no influence on the decisions of the Department of Interior. The fact that it was not required to hold public hearings before making exchanges of land, pursuant to 16 U.S.C. 688 dd (b) (3), helped the Interior Department and the utilities maintain secrecy. The public could not discover whether environmental implications of the land exchange were included in decision making. The Interior Department seemed insensitive to environmental criteria. The record of the less-than-efficient decision-making system within the department was revealed by citizens' probing through the courts. In an affidavit in district court, Secretary of Interior Stewart Udall declared that he had received only a superficial explanation of the proposed land exchange. According to Udall, he had not been informed of the ecological consequences of the exchange, nor, it seems, had his departmental officials investigated them. He noted that had he known the facts, he would not have approved the exchange. Despite this cumbersome and inefficient decision-making process, the marsh exchange transaction was approved by Secretary Udall. Citizens' inquiry, although unsuccessful in changing the course of policy, did reveal a classic example of administrative irresponsibility.

Besides bringing suit over the Department of Interior's actions in the Navarre Marsh and Darby Marsh exchange, citizens' groups intervened later in AEC hearings. The AEC had granted the utilities an exemption that permitted them to commence construction late in April 1970. The original construction license hearings to determine whether the plant could be built safely were held between November 30, 1970, and February 12, 1971, for a total of seventeen days, and the construction license was formally issued on March 24, 1971. But construction had already been underway for almost a year.

Outcome

The citizen action in the hearing phase of policy formation incurred the hostility exhibited by the AEC towards other public interveners (see Chapter 8, Case VI, Environmental Health). Environmental claimants were, in effect, opposing the agency policy of promoting nuclear electric generation as rapidly as possible. But the procedural obstacles placed in the path of interveners by the AEC and its rules used to limit public participation in hearings were to be reversed by the judiciary in a critical case involving Calvert Cliff's Coordinating Committee and the AEC (see Case V).

The Navarre Marsh case illustrates the risk of conflict between the public and the government when agreements affecting the public interest are made between government agencies and private corporations without public notice or consultation. It is not uncommon for government agencies to transfer or exchange public lands, for example, to eliminate isolated privately owned tracts surrounded by national parks or forests (in-holdings). These transactions are governed by law to protect the public financial interest, but criteria or policy guidelines to indicate the need for, and character of, public involvement in the decisions have been inadequately developed. The Gettysburg National Battlefield case (see Chapter 1, Land Use) represents a closely related issue in which environmental decisions of great public concern are made behind the closed doors of high government offices, with minimal consultation even within the agency primarily concerned. The Navarre Marsh case presents the problem, but not its solution. Possibly some type of review or mediation procedure is needed before such transactions can be consummated.

CASE V   Enforcing NEPA: Three Examples

There is no truly comprehensive national environmental policy in the United States. Although the National Environmental Policy Act of 1969 provides a foundation for broadly inclusive and consistent environmental policy, far more effort has been made to narrow the scope of NEPA than to strengthen it, and to allow exemptions when its provisions are inconsistent with other laws and policies.

There has never been a consensus on the priorities for the use of natural resources in the United States. Decisions about optimum growth rates in population, technology, and the economy have to be made before priorities concerning resource use can be ordered. In the absence of a consensus about fundamental issues, there have evolved a number of conflicting policies on development and conservation. Environmental considerations had been consistently underrepresented in governmental decision making before the early 1970s. Government agencies had been established to control the nation's natural resources consistent with a long-standing growth ethic which encouraged development and "progress" at the expense of the environment.

Environmental considerations became prominent during the 1960s, when students of environmental policy and critics in the Congress pointed out how inadequately the nation managed the environment. They criticized the traditional segmental approach to resource utilization and called for comprehensive policies upon which to base environmental management. The fragmented authority of numerous mission-oriented federal agencies defied comprehensive management. A series of reports prepared for Congress stressed the need for new legislation that would create a more rational process for evaluating government actions possibly detrimental to the environment.

The outcome of the drive for inclusion of environmental considerations in national policies was the enactment of the National Environmental Policy Act (NEPA) of 1969. (See Appendix A.) Signed into law by President Nixon on January 1, 1970, NEPA became a symbol of the nation's effort to incorporate ecological values in government decision making. The act was more than a general declaration of national goals; it also authorized procedures to force compliance. The imposition of procedural safeguards provided a basis for judicial intervention in the administration of NEPA. Section 103 of the act required agencies to review their enabling legislation to determine whether or not they could fully comply with NEPA. The NEPA did not arrange priorities for use of the nation's resources, nor did it alter the fundamental missions of existing agencies, but it did provide the first mechanism in the nation for improving the environmental impact of agencies within the federal government.

It was not foreseen that the courts would play a major role in enforcing the NEPA. Because agencies were expected to implement the act, it was hoped that their narrow, mission-oriented decision-making processes would be broadened to include ecological considerations. But environmental interveners soon became aware that many agencies either were not complying with the act, or were mocking the full intentions of the act, or were using internal regulations to inhibit a full examination of environmental criteria. The courts were inundated with interveners' requests for decisions on whether NEPA could be enforced retroactively or whether particular agencies were in full compliance with the law. Three of the most important cases that tested the scope of NEPA and demonstrated a significant public contribution to environmental management involved suits by citizens' groups against the U.S. Army Corps of Engineers, the Atomic Energy Commission (AEC), and the Federal Power Commission (FPC).

The Actors

In the first case, the Civil Works Division of the Army Corps of Engineers (see Chapter 7, The Economy and Growth), under the direction of the secretary of the army, is responsible for planning, engineering, and maintaining waterways for navigation, flood control, and the improvement of rivers and harbors. In 1958, the corps had been authorized to build the Gillham Dam across the Cassatot River in Arkansas. Late in 1970, the Environmental Defense Fund (EDF), the Ozark Society, the Arkansas Audubon Society, the Arkansas Ecology Center, and some individuals filed suit against the corps in an attempt to block construction of the dam.

The second case involves the AEC, which was established to guide the development of nuclear energy. The AEC was responsible for both promoting and regulating civilian use of nuclear materials and nuclear reactors. The congressional Joint Committee on Atomic Energy was a leading supporter of the AEC in Congress and strongly promoted nuclear energy (see Chapter 7, The Economy and Growth). In 1968, the AEC permitted the Baltimore Gas and Electric Company (BG & E) to begin construction of its $347 million nuclear power plant in the Calvert Cliffs area of Maryland. The Chesapeake Bay Foundation led public opposition to the BG & E proposal except in the legal battles. The Chesapeake Environmental Protection Association (CEPA), founded in January 1969, was established to oppose the Calvert Cliffs project because property owners objected to transmission lines crossing their land. In September 1968, the Calvert Cliffs Coordinating Committee was established and served as representative for all opposition groups except CEPA.

The third case concerns the FPC, which was created in 1920 to ensure that the nation's needs for adequate electric power and natural gas services would be met. The FPC has jurisdiction over permits and licenses for nonfederal hydroelectric power projects, and it also regulates rates for interstate transactions in natural gas and electric power. In August 1968, the Power Authority of New York applied to the FPC for authorization to construct and operate a one million-kilowatt pumped storage power plant in the towns of Blenheim and Gilboa. Some local government authorities and citizens' groups protested the plans for the Gilboa-Leeds transmission line, a part of the project. Motions to intervene were filed by the Greene County Planning Board, the town of Durham, the Sierra Club, several individuals, and the Association for the Preservation of the Durham Valley (APDV). The APDV had been organized in 1960 to preserve the scenic ecological and historical values of Durham Valley. The Durham Valley groups had more than 100 members in 1970, and among them they owned over 5,000 acres of land in the Durham Valley and nearby vicinity.

The Policy Process

1. *Army Corps of Engineers: Gillham Dam, Arkansas.* In this confrontation between the Environmental Defense Fund and the Army Corps of Engineers, the citizens' groups strengthened the future role of NEPA in environmental management. Two main principles were established as a result of the court's decision to enjoin construction of the dam. First, a clearer definition of the sufficiency of an environmental impact statement was established. Second, retroactivity was established. Since this case, the courts have generally held that NEPA does apply to projects started before the enactment of the legislation.

The citizens' groups called for a judicial evaluation of the sufficiency of the corp's environmental impact statement filed pursuant to Section 102 (2) (C) of NEPA. The citizens had discovered that the corps had submitted a mere twelve-page abbreviated statement, certainly not a detailed study of the environmental factors involved in the project. The court's first hearing of the suit revealed that the corps had omitted or only briefly examined a number of crucial factors: recreational losses, expected changes in water quality as a result of the Gillham Dam, the dam's effects on fish, marine, and plant resources, and the economic benefits claimed by the corps. Further construction of the dam was enjoined pending submission of a revised impact statement. The court had shown that superficial compliance with Section 102 (2) (C) was unsatisfactory.

The corps later submitted a second environmental impact statement after conducting public hearings in Arkansas in August and September 1971. This voluminous interdisciplinary statement, estimated to have cost $225,000, was deemed adequate by the court and the injunction was dissolved.

The second contribution of citizens' groups to the strength of NEPA as a result of the Gillham Dam case was to have the courts declare the retroactive applicability of the act. Congress had authorized the Gillham Dam project in 1958. At the time EDF and others filed suit, 63 percent of the total $14.8 million cost estimate of the project had been expended. The court ruled that the corps should objectively evaluate all projects regardless of the amount spent or the degree of completion of the project. This ruling established a precedent on retroactivity that has since been generally followed by the courts.

2. *Atomic Energy Commission: Calvert Cliffs Nuclear Plant, Maryland.* On May 29, 1967, BG & E announced its intention to construct a nuclear power plant on Chesapeake Bay at Calvert Cliffs, Maryland. In order to apply for a provisional construction permit from the AEC, BG & E was required to submit a preliminary safety analysis report, which they filed on January 25, 1968. Final AEC approval and the granting of an operating license would not be given until later, after the filing of a final safety analysis report. The preliminary report was distributed by the AEC to the Division of Reactor Licensing (DRL) and to the Advisory Committee on Reactor Safeguards (ACRS) for examination and approval. The ACRS was established by Congress to give independent advice to the AEC's Division of Reactor Licensing, but it has no power to compel the AEC to adopt its findings. Problems mentioned in the routine ACRS comment on the project apparently had not been considered by either BG & E or the DRL in subsequent planning. An exemption request allowing BG & E to commence certain construction activities was granted by the DRL in January 1969. The ACRS abdicated its responsibility to defend the public welfare and safety by assuming BG & E or the DRL should solve any problems at a later stage in construction.

On March 28, 1969, the AEC announced that public hearings would be held before an Atomic Safety and Licensing Board (ASLB) to consider a construction permit. The hearings opened on May 12, 1969, and ASLB chairman Arthur W. Murphy reminded participants that comments on zoning, transmission lines, thermal effects, and power costs would not be accepted. The hearing was to consider only radiological problems. The Chesapeake Environmental Protection Association (CEPA) actively contested the safety of the proposed nuclear generator, the issue being radiological discharges of tritium. BG & E argued that if the concentration of tritium did not exceed AEC standards, then the discharge was safe, but the citizens' groups challenged the adequacy of AEC radiation standards. Nevertheless, on July 7, 1969, the ASLB issued the construction permit to BG & E.

In January 1970, almost one year after the enactment of NEPA, the AEC published Appendix D to its regulations in order to comply with the requirements of NEPA. Soon after, the Calvert Cliffs Coordinating Committee decided to contest the weaknesses and flaws in the AEC decision-making process. The AEC had failed to consider adequately and defend the public interest in ecological balance and safety. The committee filed two suits: the first challenged four aspects of the AEC Appendix D regulations, and the second challenged the application of the regulations in granting the construction permit for the Calvert Cliffs nuclear reactor.

The decision of the U.S. Court of Appeals for the District of Columbia in July 1971 declared that the AEC's regulations for implementing NEPA in licensing nuclear power plants did not comply with congressional intent implied in NEPA. The court declared that the AEC's biased and narrow interpretation of NEPA made a mockery of the act. Further, the AEC's rules were shown by the court explicitly to exclude from full consideration a number of environmental issues: AEC rules prohibited the ASLB from considering environmental factors raised by persons outside of AEC regulatory staff; the rules prohibited examination of nonradiological environmental issues where a notice of the hearing was published prior to March 4, 1971; they prohibited reconsideration of water quality impacts if certification of compliance with state standards had been obtained; and finally, AEC regulations did not provide for environmental review of cases in which construction permits had been issued prior to NEPA's effective date but the operating license had not been granted. The court ordered the AEC to revise its regulations in these four respects so as to consider environmental issues, and on September 9, 1971, the AEC complied by publishing a revision of Appendix

D, subsequently amended on September 30. In the preface to its new regulations, the AEC stated that it would be responsive to the conservation and environmental concerns of the public.

Calvert Cliffs was a landmark case in the interpretation and application of the NEPA. But it could not have happened if the law had not provided for public review of the government's environmental impact statements. And it is uncertain whether a case against the AEC would have been won had the concerned citizens of the area not formed a coalition to protect their environment from inadvertent degradation by a government-licensed electric generating plant.

3. *Federal Power Commission: The Blenheim-Gilboa Project in New York.* In August 1968, the Power Authority of New York filed an application with the Federal Power Commission to construct and operate a one million-kilowatt pumped storage power project to cost $160 million. The project was to include two reservoirs (one of them a dam across Schoharie Creek), a power plant, and three 345-kilowatt transmission lines. On June 6, 1969, the FPC granted the license, but with certain restrictions that required the Power Authority to prepare a specific plan that considered some aspects of environmental protection along the transmission line routes. The authority prepared the required report and on November 24, 1969, applied to the FPC for construction authorization for three transmission lines. As there were no protests or petitions regarding two of the lines, Gilboa-New Scotland and Gilboa-Fraser, the FPC approved the application for those two lines without a hearing.

But the FPC did receive several protests about the Gilboa-Leeds transmission line. This line, which would run from the plant in Schoharie County through the Durham Valley to the Leeds substation near Catskill, required a path thirty-five miles long and 150 feet wide. Intervention was granted in May 1970 to the Greene County Planning Board, the town of Durham, the APDV, the Sierra Club, and a number of individuals. The petitions requested detailed consideration of the environmental impact of the Gilboa-Leeds line on Durham Valley and Greene County. The FPC limited participation to this one issue raised by the public.

Before the intervention was granted, but after the Power Authority applied for the transmission line permits, NEPA became effective on

January 1, 1970. During the following December, the FPC issued regulations in accordance with NEPA. Section 2.81 (b) of FPC regulations required the Power Authority and other future applicants to file an environmental impact statement on the basis of NEPA Section 102 (2) (C). The NEPA regulations required the FPC to prepare a detailed statement for uncontested applications, but not for applications such as the Gilboa-Leeds line which were contested. In accord with the new regulations, the Power Authority filed an environmental impact statement on March 21, 1971, for the proposed Gilboa-Leeds line and two alternative routes.

A prehearing conference on these proposals was held the following June by the FPC. At this conference, Greene County requested the presiding examiner to set a date for the FPC to file its own impact statement pursuant to NEPA. Soon after, in July 1971, the interveners moved for a court decision vacating, rescinding, or suspending the license for the entire project that had been granted by the FPC in June 1969. The interveners alleged that the FPC had not complied with the mandates of NEPA, in particular Section 102 (2) (C). At this time 75 percent of the $160 million total cost had been expended or committed on the project. In effect, the citizens' groups and the local, town, and government bodies asked the courts to assess the licensing procedures of the FPC.

The FPC held that the Power Authority's impact statement would suffice and had it circulated for the purposes of satisfying Section 102 (2) (C) of NEPA. The FPC refused to prepare its own environmental impact statement until its final decision on the project was rendered. Preservationist interveners argued that the FPC must file its statements prior to hearings, and the court agreed with the petitioners' interpretation of NEPA. The court declared the FPC had primary and nondelegable responsibility for considering environmental values at every stage of the agency's decision-making process. The FPC was found to have abdicated part of its duties by substituting the Power Authority's statement for its own, a procedure that could be dangerous since the applicants' statements might be based on self-serving assumptions.

The petitioners also asked the court to stay construction of the pumped storage plant and the two previously approved transmission lines pending compliance with NEPA. In its ruling, the court referred to the Gillham Dam case that sanctioned retroactive application of

NEPA, but it declared that there was no basis for applying NEPA retro-actively in this instance, because the project had been completed six months prior to the effective date of NEPA.

Outcome

These three cases illustrate the reluctance of federal agencies to assume voluntarily a responsibility for environmental protection. The National Environmental Protection Act is one weapon citizens can use to insist that agencies do not ignore environmental concerns.

CASE VI   Institutional Reform: Wisconsin

Vast highway systems and the extensive use of private automobiles are the dominant features of American transportation. The state of Wisconsin, like most states, has devoted the greater part of its public works, planning, and transportation budget in the last two decades to extending its highway network. Wisconsin's highway expenditures were second only to those for education in per capita state and local funding in the early 1970s. These expenditures were 16.7 percent above the national level and were much higher than per capita welfare spend-ing in Wisconsin.

Automobile drivers have been subsidized heavily by public funds. Over $200 million annually from gas tax and vehicle registrations, and more than another $200 million from local property taxes, have been used in Wisconsin to pay for road maintenance and traffic control. These costs—together with the costs of lost air quality, the loss of land taken from tax rolls for roads, 1,200 deaths and 50,000 injuries an-nually, and over $200 million lost due to fatalities, injuries, and prop-erty damage—were seldom made public. Skyrocketing property tax rates, the demise of rail and bus systems, and the fact that a large minority of the state's population was not served by the expensive high-way system prompted the formation in 1972 of a Madison-based citi-zens' group to address the issues.

The Wisconsin Coalition for Balanced Transportation (WCBT) first met in early 1972 as a group of alert citizens aware of the seldom recog-nized threat to the quality of life posed by the state's existing transpor-tation system. The WCBT set two main objectives: to inform the public about the need to change patterns of use of public transportation and to draw attention to the folly of encouraging continued reliance on the automobile. Holding the view that building more highways only exacerbated traffic congestion, the WCBT set about reversing the trend of failing bus systems. One of the prime institutional objectives of the citizens' coalition was to restructure the Wisconsin Department of Transportation in order to achieve more balanced planning, to increase public input in decision making, and to have alternative modes of transportation during policy formation. The WCBT has had remarkable success in mobilizing public opinion on transportation issues. Its main goal—institutional reform—now seems well within the grasp of this well-organized and industrious citizens' group.

The Actors

The leading citizens' group has been the Wisconsin Coalition for Balanced Transportation, which was organized in February 1972. Its original 250 members represented twenty-two counties, fifty-two different organizations, and included individuals from another fifty-seven organizations outside Dane County. Within a year, the membership of the WCBT had reached 6,000. Other groups that offered various means of support to the coalition included the Environmental Education Council of Greater Milwaukee, Environment Wisconsin, the Wisconsin League of Women Voters, the Wisconsin Resource Conservation Council, and the Highway Action Coalition of Washington, D.C.

The state Department of Transportation and the state Highway Commission have been the targets of the WCBT's efforts to reform transportation. The Federal Highway Administration was an indirect influence on some aspects of policy reform through its call for a State Action Plan that required public participation in transportation planning. The governor's Mass Transit Study Committee was instrumental in establishing a focal point for discussion of the issues.

The Policy Process

From its beginning, the coalition attempted to create a strong constituency by publicizing transportation issues statewide. Realizing that widespread urban and rural support were essential aspects of their plan, the citizens' organization attempted to involve community members like the management of the railroad and bus companies, civic leaders, elected officials, business and professional people, school officials, merchants, media representatives, union leaders, environmental and conservation organizations, the American Association of Retired Persons, students, and others. In addition to building a constituency, the coalition planned to participate in state and local projects and to conduct research programs aimed at legislative change.

National Balanced Transportation Week, May 15–19, 1972, provided a focal point for the WCBT's early efforts. The coalition created and implemented the statewide observance of "UnCar Day" on May 17, 1972. The objective of the UnCar Day program was to encourage Wisconsin residents to leave their automobiles at home for a day in order to dramatize both the need for improved public transit and the environmental benefits of reducing the number of cars on the road. The WCBT's compilation and widespread distribution of a model resolution for declaring Balanced Transportation Week had a positive effect in several communities. UnCar Day was observed in Green Bay, Eau Claire, Madison, Milwaukee, Oregon, Sheboygan, and Fond du Lac, where people resorted to horse and buggy transit, massive biking, and walking brigades.

The coalition's thorough organization for UnCar Day ultimately proved effective. The Bus Utility Commission, the Madison City Council, and other town and city councils, mayors, and county boards agreed to observe the day when approached by the coalition. The WCBT also encouraged chambers of commerce and merchants to advertise the program by offering shoppers discounts and tokens. Madison Metro was asked to reduce fares on UnCar Day and to advertise on its buses. The WCBT generated considerable advertising to promote car pools and encouraged civic leaders—judges, mayors, doctors, and newspaper editors—to use public transportation for the day. Of particular concern to activist citizens was a demonstration to show the imbalance between expenditures for mass transit and highways. On UnCar Day, the coalition made special efforts to advertise the fact that automobiles do not pay their own way. Its research showed that Madison taxpayers subsidized each car driver $100 per year, because property taxes paid for highways and streets, thoroughfare maintenance, and traffic control. The citizens also planned to measure noise and air pollution and to count traffic before and during UnCar Day. Capitol Square became a highlight of community attention as it was closed off to vehicular traffic and open only to pedestrians, buses, and bicyclists.

Immediately following UnCar Day and the Balanced Transportation Week projects, the WCBT sponsored a statewide meeting on May 20, 1972, to further strengthen the organization and hold workshop sessions on research directions and legislative proposals. Guest speakers were Mayor Wallace Burkee of Kenosha, the president of the Wisconsin Alliance of Cities, who had successfully established Kenosha's municipal bus system, and Ms. Linda Katz of the National Highway Action Coalition, who spoke on national issues and highway legislation. By June 1972, the coalition had established clear-cut objectives for future action and had created eight subcommittees within its structure to pursue specific aspects of those objectives. The subcommittees divided up the tasks of information gathering and dissemination, monitoring and designing state legislation, consulting with local and state citizens' groups, monitoring the positions of legislative candidates on transportation issues, and preparing research for participating in agency hearings. Through this specialized division of labor, the WCBT set out to achieve a number of objectives aimed at institutional reform:

1.   To greatly strengthen the mass transit planning capabilities of the Wisconsin Department of Transportation.

2.   To incorporate citizen participation into all stages of planning and decision-making related to transportation projects, including streets and highways.

3.   To institute transportation hearings at which the Department of Transportation would present alternative solutions to a given transportation need.

4.   To make money from the segregated highway fund and other sources available for any valid surface transportation use, especially modern mass transit facilities within and between our urban centers.

5.   To bring about revision of the 1990 State Highway Plan to include all modes of transportation and reorientation to emphasize use of existing roadbeds rather than new corridors.

6.   To restructure the Wisconsin Department of Transportation to create a balance in planning and implementation of the various transportation modes.[1]

Workshops at the statewide meeting of May 20 and on-going research carried out by coalition subcommittees laid out programs and means by which institutional reform could be achieved. The WCBT identified specific problems that required legislative innovation and

[1] Wisconsin Coalition for Balanced Transportation, *By-Laws* (May 20, 1972), 2–3.

supported transportation bills. These bills proposed establishing a mechanism for spending state aid to mass transit, establishing a Transportation Fund to replace the Highway Fund, raising the gas tax and automobile registration fees to provide money for mass transit, and reorganizing government agencies in such a manner that the Highway Commission be placed under the secretary of transportation or the commission itself be reorganized into a balanced transportation commission.

By the end of 1972, the WCBT had increased its public support considerably and had gained significant recognition by some policy makers. The coalition was one of two nonuser groups invited to be represented on the statewide Wisconsin Airport Systems Plan Advisory Committee. The coalition had also strengthened its network of connections by becoming affiliated with the Highway Action Coalition of Washington, D.C., and by joining Environment Wisconsin and the Wisconsin Resource Conservation Council, two statewide federations of environmental groups. The governor's Study Committee on Mass Transit included two coalition members, and a number of the issues the committee addressed had been raised by the WCBT, specifically institutional reform in Wisconsin.

Within a year of its creation, the WCBT had influenced a number of issues related to transportation. By lobbying and testifying, the coalition had participated in discussions on the advisability of studded snow tires, advocated reduced transit fares for the elderly, opposed abolishing the Merrimac Ferry, and helped address highway corridor and design problems. The WCBT's pre-election survey of candidates for the state legislature revealed that two-thirds of the sixty respondents supported greater financial assistance for bus and rail transit and lower subsidies for automobiles—or even making cars pay their own way. The coalition also amassed information on national energy shortages and the role transportation played in the energy policies of the nation. The coalition then adapted the information to circumstances at the state level so that it had meaning and relevance for the Wisconsin public.

With the release of the Phase I Report of the governor's Mass Transit Study Committee early in 1973, it appeared that the WCBT had influenced transportation planning. Many of the WCBT's institutional reform objectives were supported in the report's recommendations to the governor: the state Highway Fund should be replaced by a state

Transportation Fund to be used for all transportation-related purposes, and the system of dedicated revenues favoring automobiles should be abandoned; the secretary of transportation should assume responsibility for the statutory duties formerly assigned to the Highway Commission and other divisions of the department; the state Highway Commission should be replaced by a five-man Transportation Commission that would develop an all-mode state transportation plan; and a Division of Mass Transit should be created within the Department of Transportation to coordinate mass transit programs.

While the governor considered these recommendations, the WCBT moved ahead on other issues. The Federal Highway Administration had requested the Wisconsin Department of Transportation to develop an Action Plan that would include citizen participation in transportation planning. To continue receiving federal highway funds, the state transportation agency had to comply with the Action Plan directive. The WCBT analyzed and criticized the draft Action Plan thoroughly, and it drew extensive publicity to the undesirable aspects of transportation planning in the state.

The 1990 State Highway Plan, the only plan operative for the Highway Commission, was viewed by the citizens' organization as the fundamental stumbling block in the path of efforts to reform Wisconsin's transportation planning. The plan called for 2,093 miles of freeways and 1,644 miles of expressways to be built in Wisconsin by 1990. As of 1972, 31 percent of the freeways and only 4 percent of the expressways had been completed. The WCBT sought to inform the people of the state of the extensive and unfavorable impact the 1990 plan would have on the environment if it were carried out. The coalition was convinced that the social, environmental, and economic costs of implementing the 1990 plan could not be justified by the predicted benefits, that alternatives were not being considered, and that the 1990 plan should be subject to an environmental impact statement to enhance the likelihood of rational decision making.

Outcome

With continued advocacy, rigorously documented contributions to hearings, and a strengthening constituency throughout the state, the WCBT made significant strides toward achieving its general and specific objectives. Its successful publicizing of UnCar Day on September 19,

1973, the sponsorship of a 1990 Revisited Symposium in late September 1973, and the joint sponsorship with other citizens' and environmental groups of a symposium on railroads in February 1974 all helped the WCBT establish widespread credibility among citizens, businessmen, and government officials in Wisconsin. There is widespread recognition of the central role the WCBT is playing in institutional reforms on transportation matters in the state.

This case again illustrates the potential effectiveness of organized citizen action in influencing public attitudes and policies. To change deeply entrenched positions on public transportation policies is a long term task. But the WCBT has already demonstrated that combinations of political power as traditionally unchallengeable as the highway lobby can be put on the defensive and can be defeated on specific issues. The WCBT understood that the structure of state government in Wisconsin, providing for an independent highway commission, was an obstacle to the goal of balanced transportation. Accordingly, it directed its efforts toward a reorganization of the transportation agencies of the state government.

Conclusion

Although there is no general agreement about the best institutional system for managing the environment, citizen groups have revealed a number of critical weaknesses in the existing system. Government agencies have been criticized for neglecting environmental concerns and, at the same time, pressured by economic and political interests to minimize environmental obstacles to "progress." The cases in this chapter illustrate the need to open up administrative procedures so that basic questions and assumptions can be discussed publicly. Government agencies should present resource allocation or land-use policy alternatives to the public rather than making decisions behind closed doors, the procedure preferred by financially interested clients. Even if the technical and scientific expertise of the agency is essential for reaching a decision, as it often is in the case of atomic energy, there seldom is a justifiable excuse for administrative secrecy. Opening agency decision processes to public scrutiny could prevent serious controversy, increase the rationality of natural resource decisions, and strengthen public confidence in the honesty and integrity of government.

The cases considered throughout this book make it apparent that society must be able to disband or reorient an agency after it has completed its original mission. The external success of a government agency too often has been measured solely by its contribution to material growth, and the internal indications of its success are too often considered the development of new facilities, the addition of personnel and administrative units, and the extension of its authority or domain. The agency's own survival and growth tend to become more important than its stewardship of public goods. Hence, agencies are often motivated by goals no longer relevant to the needs of society. As time passes, these agencies often become conservative defenders of the status quo. Most of the agencies discussed in this chapter—the Forest Service, the TVA, and the Bureau of Reclamation—have mandates that require them to secure community economic stability. But they also have regulatory responsibilities that conflict with the economic goals of their mandates. Eventually, most of these administrative bodies have developed a symbiotic relationship with the groups they regulate.

Citizens have been frustrated by the narrow vision and inertia of administrative bodies at each level of government. The Department of Interior, the Department of Agriculture, the Department of Transportation and other institutions at both federal and state levels have become complex bureaucratic entities. Large, complex organizations with specialized goals and personnel, fragmented internal authority, and complicated channels of communication are not always responsive to broad public interests. Their responsiveness to changes in the political climate, such as the growing national awareness of ecological values, is constrained by bureaucratic tendencies toward routines, traditional assumptions, and legalisms.

Their hostility and resistance to public participation in established procedures are separate but related problems of organizational behavior. To a public official dedicated primarily to his technical mission, the would-be participant is an obstructive busy-body, an uninformed nuisance. The public official may believe that because of his position he represents the public interest, and that organized citizens are merely private parties with no lawful authority to question his official judgments.

Altering the basic missions of existing departments and agencies is a formidable political task. Although providing a comprehensive set of resource-use priorities is a pressing responsibility of legislatures, they are poorly organized to perform this function. The enactment of NEPA was an effort to get around these difficulties by restructuring the processes of government planning. NEPA was intended to assure the examination of second order consequences of decision making. The impact statement procedure was a step in the right direction, but its effectiveness is limited unless it is vigorously reinforced at highest administrative levels. Citizens' groups have forced interpretations of NEPA in the courts and have thereby extended its effectiveness, but the success of NEPA relies heavily on the willingness of courts to require full compliance. Without continuous citizen initiatives, the role of the courts is limited, and in many cases, they are too late to prevent irreversible damage.

The Black Mesa and Southwest Power Complex case is a symbol of what is becoming a rapidly spreading environmental disaster in America's western open lands. While the energy demands of industry, commerce, and affluent urban centers grow unchecked, cities such as Los Angeles and New York will not permit more polluting generating plants in their environs. Consequently, suppliers have turned to low-sulfur content, strippable coal from the Southwest and the Great Plains of Montana and Wyoming (see Chapter 1, Land Use). Economies of scale and strip mining in these regions could lower the costs of electricity. The near absence of pollution controls in the western states during the 1960s was an added incentive to developers, who planned huge mine-mouth generating plants. But the institutional circumstances that have prevailed in the West also influenced the course of events.

Federal agencies and industry dominated policy for development of the Southwest Power Complex. The area directly affected, predominantly public lands, was primarily within the jurisdiction of the Department of Interior's agencies. The mandates of these agencies, however, posed a dilemma: they had responsibilities for both development and protection. When citizens turned to the Department of Interior for help in environmental controversies, they found the agency locked into commitments for development. The development goals were pursued far more vigorously than were responsibilities for resource conservation or protection of Indian rights and lands. Within the Department of Interior, the Bureau of Reclamation dominated policy; other agencies in the Interior Department did not dispute Burec's objectives and alternatives. The department also had little regard for the important public debate needed to help resolve differences between interests in the region. The development policies for Black Mesa and the Southwest Power Complex were devised largely without state and local participation from New Mexico, Arizona, Utah, and Colorado. State governments were ignorant of the interrelated problems that would stem from federal policies for energy generation, water management and use, and the resultant widespread pollution and landscape degradation, and were not prepared for the mammoth tasks of planning and regulation. The development of the Four Corners region was well established before state authorities could begin to focus on the issues.

The Tennessee Valley Authority began as an institution designed for the dual purposes of conserving resources and developing the regional economy. The TVA has provided low-cost electric power, flood control, and increased river traffic and it has created vast recreational waterways in its plan to provide a healthy economy in the Tennessee Valley. Like the Department of Interior, TVA has a conflicting mandate. On the one hand, the TVA must buy coal as cheaply as possible (strip-mined coal costs less than deep-mined coal), but on the other hand, it must also protect the environment. Both the purchase of cheap coal and reclamation enforcement are required of the TVA by law, and within the TVA there is disagreement on policy matters. Agency conservationists are in conflict with the fuel purchasing division, which is not responsible for land reclamation. So far, the agency's economic objectives appear to have outweighed its ecological objectives.

The Magruder Corridor case concerns an area that occupies less than 1 percent of the land area under control by the Forest Service, but the controversy drew national attention. It appears that Forest Service administrators firmly believed that continued multiple-use development best serves the long-run public interest. The agency lost the confidence of a majority of the concerned public by constantly resisting the efforts of citizens and environmental groups to participate in policy formation for the corridor. The public was not confident that the Forest Service could or would execute a multiple-use management plan for the area without eventually destroying the Upper Selway watershed, because the agency's development orientation has been much stronger than its concern for the environmental responsibilities of its mandate. The Forest Service became noticeably distressed about the deterioration of its image as a result of the unfavorable publicity regarding Magruder Corridor. Citizen groups in the Magruder Corridor case have been credited with stimulating the Forest Service to greatly expand activities designed to involve the public in its policy processes.

The Navarre Marsh case illustrates an instance of low-visibility decision making; the Department of Interior and the utility companies had minimized public awareness and participation. Unfortunately, this case is not exceptional. Administrative agencies throughout the country have time and again participated in secret deals involving the use, sale, or transfer of public lands for private convenience. In many of these instances, citizen groups have challenged the failure of administrative agencies to protect the public interest and have filed suits against the government agencies supposed to protect the public interest. The Navarre Marsh case illustrates the process and causes of official dereliction in the continuing collusion of government and private economic interests. It is typical of numerous cases where citizen groups have turned to the courts for a response to the immediate needs of resource management. But the courts often respond, as they did in this land exchange case, by asserting that protection of the public interest has been vested in public agencies and it is up to them to decide what action is in the public interest. Furthermore, some courts have asserted that it is not appropriate for the public or for the courts to involve themselves in the administrative procedures of public agencies. Nevertheless in some states, such as Massachusetts, the courts have forced agencies to seek approval for any actions that may betray the public trust.

Fortunately, in many other instances, the courts have been amenable to assisting the growth of new theories of environmental law. The three cases examined in this chapter concerning NEPA illustrate such developments. Generally the courts have asserted that NEPA does apply to projects initiated prior to passage of the act. Furthermore, the courts have decided the act also creates judicially enforceable duties. Court decisions have developed some definition of the duties imposed on federal agencies by the act. The sufficiency of impact statements and the adequacy of consideration of environmental factors in decision making have also been addressed and clarified by court interpretations. Agencies must be prepared to change internal procedures and organizations to ensure full compliance with the act. The courts have also concluded that environmental impact statements must contain sufficient quantified data to support the conclusions drawn in cost-benefit claims, as in the Tellico Dam case. Environmental and citizen groups, by and large, have initiated the intervention that has secured these increases in the effectiveness of NEPA.

Citizen groups, through the courts and NEPA, have been successful in modifying the environmental posture of some agencies, but significant pressures have built up to revise NEPA or to exempt certain actions or agencies from its application. For example, litigation introduced by environmentalists against the Amchitka Island nuclear blast was not successful. In this case, citizens sued to enjoin the blast mainly on the grounds that the AEC's environmental impact statement was inadequate, but the AEC contended that certain data could not be included in the statement for reasons of national defense and security and executive privilege. By granting this exemption, the court's ruling in the Amchitka case undercut the broad application of NEPA which the Calvert Cliffs court recognized as necessary. The exception from NEPA granted the trans-Alaska pipeline proposal (see Chapter 6, Energy) by Congress was another precedent that may also dilute the potential of NEPA.

The Wisconsin Coalition for Balanced Transportation case illustrates the inertia of powerful public programs with strong economic and development implications. The Federal Highway Act of 1956 and the Highway Trust Fund resulted in a greatly unbalanced system of transportation in the United States. Citizen groups, such as the National Highway Action Coalition and the WCBT, challenged the justification for narrowly conceived national and state highway policies that are decades out-of-date. Generally, the trust funds rigidly limit appropriations to road construction and have become prized and uncontrollable public pork barrels. The objectives of the trust funds have not changed with changing societal needs. Furthermore, institutional structures established to administer the planning of road systems have generally shown a reluctance to adjust their goals to suit new needs. Efforts by the Wisconsin citizens' group to abandon outdated institutions and to establish new structures are typical of attempts being made across the country to improve the instruments of environmental management.

The cases in this chapter have shown that legislatures, in the main, have been slow to respond to rapidly changing needs for comprehensive environmental management. The executive administrative departments and agencies have been shown to be largely inadequate—and often unwilling—to implement effective policies for environmental protection. Preservationist interveners and a rapidly growing, ecologically alert public have turned to the courts seeking judicial remedies for the lack of effective administrative response. During the late 1960s and early 1970s, the burden of prompt response to environmental degradation fell to the public. The cases in this chapter support the view that well-organized citizens' groups have provided a significant impetus for the establishment of more effective machinery for environmental management.

Readings

Caldwell, Lynton K. "Environmental Policy as a Catalyst of Institutional Change." *American Behavioral Scientist,* 17 (May–June 1974), 711–730.

—————. *Man and His Environment: Policy and Administration.* Edited by John E. Bardach, Marston Bates (Deceased), and Stanley A. Cain. New York: Harper & Row, 1975.

Council on Environmental Quality and Federal Council for Science and Technology. *The Role of Ecology in the Federal Government: Report of the Committee on Ecological Research, December 1974.* Washington, D.C.: U.S. GPO, 1974.

Edmunds, Stahrl and John Letey. *Environmental Administration.* New York: McGraw-Hill, 1973.

Green, J. Thomas, Harold Leventhal, et al. "Environmental Decision-Making: The Agencies Versus the Courts." *Natural Resources Lawyer,* 7 (Spring 1974), 337–371.

Haefele, Edwin T. *Representative Government and Environmental Management.* Baltimore: The Johns Hopkins University Press, 1973.

Haskell, Elizabeth H. and Victoria S. Price. *State Environmental Management: Case Studies of Nine States.* New York: Praeger, 1973.

Henning, Daniel H. *Environmental Policy and Administration.* New York: Elsevier, 1974.

Howard, A. E. Dick. "State Constitutions and the Environment." *Virginia Law Review,* 58 (February 1972), 193–229.

Tobin, R. J. "Some Observations on the Use of State Constitutions to Protect the Environment." *Environmental Affairs,* 3 (1974), 473–493.

SOURCES

The sources of data for the studies contained in this volume varied greatly from case to case. For many, newspapers or newsletters were the principal sources. Personal communication—by letter and word-of-mouth—were important sources in a great many cases. So far as was feasible, actual participants in the cases were interviewed. Other frequently used sources include statutes, court reports, administrative documents, and, in a few instances, other books dealing with particular cases, case-studies techniques, and citizen action generally. In brief, all pertinent sources were sought, whether printed or oral, official or informal.

The following notes indicate some of the key sources of *published* information for each case. For many cases, they represent fewer than half the sources used, but those cited are the more comprehensive and less dispensable. A complete and detailed bibliography for each case would have added materially to the cost of the book without commensurate benefit to most users. The authors will, however, provide more complete information on request.

Introduction

The People versus the Duly Constituted Authorities

From a very large literature on citizen activism and voluntary organizations, the following were found to be especially useful in the preparation of this volume:

Arnold W. Bolle, "Public Participation and Environmental Quality," *Natural Resources Journal*, 11 (July 1971); Citizens Advisory Committee on Environmental Quality, *Citizens Make the Difference* (Washington, D.C.: Citizens Advisory Committee on Environmental Quality, 1973); M. Rupert Cutler and Daniel A. Bronstein, "Public Involvement in Government Decisions," *Alternatives*, 4 (Autumn 1974); Lloyd C. Ireland, "Citizen Participation—A Tool for Conflict Management on Public Lands." *Public Administration Review*, 35 (May–June 1975); Michael Kitzmiller and Richard Ottinger, *Citizen Action: Vital Force for Change* (Washington, D.C.: Center for a Voluntary Society, 1971); Melvin B. Mogulaf, *Citizen Participation: A Review and Commentary on Federal Policies and Practices* (Washington, D.C.: Urban Institute, 1970); James A. Riedel, "Citizen Participation: Myths and Realities," *Public Administration Review*, 32 (May–June 1972); and Roger M. Williams, "The Rise of Middle Class Activism: Fighting City Hall," *Saturday Review* (March 8, 1975). For a "how to" account of citizen action on behalf of the environment, see James Robertson and John Lewallen, *The Grass Roots Primer: How To Save a Piece of the Planet—By the People Who Are Already Doing It* (San Francisco: Sierra Club, 1975).

CHAPTER 1 *Land Use*

CASE I. *Preserving Open Space: Jefferson County, Colorado*

Garden Daily Transcript (1972–1974); Jefferson County League of Women Voters, *Open Space—A Background Sheet* (October 1971); *Denver Post* (1973–1974); and *Plan Jeffco Publications* (1972).

CASE II. *Wilderness Preservation: Mineral King, California*

Peter Browning, "Mickey Mouse in the Mountains," *Harper's* magazine (March 1972), 65–71; Arthur B. Ferguson, Jr., and William P. Bryson, "Mineral King: A Case Study in Forest Service Decision Making," *Ecology Law Quarterly*, 2 (Summer 1972), 493–531; "Mineral King Valley: Who Shall Watch the Watchmen?" *Rutgers Law Review*, 25 (Fall 1970), 103–144; and Sierra Club *Bulletin* and *News Reports* (1970–1972).

CASE III. *Landforms Degradation: The Northern Plains*

Alvin Josephy, "Agony of the Northern Plains," *Audubon Magazine*, 75 (July 1973), 71–83 ff.; *Billings Gazette* (1973); *Casper Star-Tribune* (1973); and Northern Plains Resource Council *Newsletters* (1973).

CASE IV. *Protecting Historical Sites: Gettysburg National Military Park, Pennsylvania*

Charles F. Roe, "Land Use: The Second Battle of Gettysburg," *The Appraisal Journal*, 42 (January 1974), 90–102; "The Second Battle of Gettysburg: Conflict of Public and Private Interests in Land Use Policies," *Environ-*

mental Affairs, 2 (Spring 1972), 16–63; issues of the *Gettysburg Times* (September 1970–September 1971); *Philadelphia Inquirer* (August 9, 1971); and *Washington Post* (July 23, 1971).

CASE V.   *Highway Building: Overton Park, Memphis, Tennessee*

For newspaper accounts, see *Memphis Press Scimitar* and *Memphis Commercial Appeal* during 1972. See also Harry Rice, "Overton Park–Interstate 40 Conflict," in *Citizens Make the Difference: Case Studies of Environmental Action* (Washington, D.C.: Citizens Advisory Committee on Environmental Quality, 1973), 43–53; Irma O. Sternberg, *Overton Park is YOUR Park* (Memphis, Tennessee: Tri-State Press, 1971); and William A. Thomas, "The Road to Overton Park: 'Parklands Statutes' in Federal Highway Legislation," *Tennessee Law Review*, 39 (Summer 1972), 433–458.

CASE VI.   *Limiting Urban Growth: Petaluma, California*

Frank S. J. Bongs, "Petaluma Controlled-Growth Law is Voided by Federal District Court," *Planning* (March 8, 1974); City of Petaluma publications, *A Unique Approach to Control Growth* (1972); *Environmental Design Plans* (March 27, 1972); "Petaluma Growth Control Ordinance Struck Down by Federal Court" and "Fairfax Measure Challenged," *Housing and Development Reporter* (Bureau of National Affairs), 2 (January 23, 1974), No. 19, A–1; and William C. McGivern, "Putting a Speed Limit on Growth," *Planning* (November 1972), 263–265.

CASE VII.   *Land-Water Interface: Santa Barbara, California*

Lee Dye, *Blowout at Platform A: The Crisis that Awakened a Nation* (Garden City, New York: Doubleday, 1971); Get Oil Out, Inc., *Reports; Santa Barbara News Press* (1973–1974); and Harvey Molatch, "Santa Barbara: Oil in the Velvet Playground," *Ramparts* (November 1969), 43–51.

CHAPTER 2   *Coastal Zone*

CASE I.   *Land-Use Problems: Filling in San Francisco Bay*

Harold Gilliam, "The Rape of San Francisco Bay," *Audubon Magazine*, 70 (March–April 1968), 45–48 ff.; Rice O'Dell, *The Saving of San Francisco Bay* (Washington, D.C.: The Conservation Foundation, 1970); "A Classic Confrontation in California: Citizens Move to Save San Francisco Bay," The Conservation Foundation *Newsletter* (June 9, 1969); *San Francisco Chronicle* (1962–1970); and Sierra Club *Bulletin* (March–April 1964, and June 1967).

CASE II.   *Salt Marsh Conservation: Udall's Cove, New York*

The issue was publicized in the *Great Neck Record, Long Island Press, Ledger,* and *New York Times* (1969–1972). See also Al Reinfelder, "You Must Save This Marsh," *National Fisherman Yearbook* (1973), 2.

CASE III.   *Water Pollution: San Diego Bay, California*

Roy E. Dodson, "Cleanup of San Diego Bay," *Civil Engineering—ASCE*, 42 (March 1972), 62–63; Richard Greenbaum, "How San Diego Cleaned Up Its Bay," *Ocean Industry*, 4 (July 1969), 55–56; Ellen Stern Harris, "To Clean a Harbor," in *Citizens Make the Difference: Case Studies of Environmental Action* (Washington, D.C.: Citizens Advisory Committee on Environmental Quality, 1973), 27–33; and E. W. Kenworthy, "San Diego Cleans Up Once-Dirty Bay as Model for U.S.," in *Eco-Solutions: A Casebook for the Environmental Crisis*, edited by Barbara Woods (Cambridge, Massachusetts: Schenkman, 1972).

CASE IV.   *A Continuing Struggle: Galveston Bay, Texas*

Luther Carter, "Galveston Bay: Test Case of an Estuary in Crisis," *Science*, 167 (February 20, 1970), 1102–1108; The Conservation Foundation, *The Decline of Galveston Bay* (Washington, D.C.: The Conservation Foundation, 1972), p. 127; "Galveston Bay, An Estuary in Distress. . . ," The Conservation Foundation *Newsletter* (July 1972), entire issue; and Bob Eckhardt, "How We Got the Dirtiest Stream in America," *Texas International Law Journal*, 7 (Summer 1971), 19.

CASE V.   *Development versus Conservation: Hilton Head, South Carolina*

Marshall Frody, "The View from Hilton Head," *Harper's* magazine, 240 (May 1970), 103–112; and Bostwick H. Ketchum, ed., "The Hilton Head Case," in *The Water's Edge* (Cambridge, Massachusetts: M.I.T. Press, 1973); and "The Fight at Hilton Head," *Newsweek*, 75 (April 13, 1970), 71.

CASE VI.   *Industry versus Environmental Quality: The Indiana Dunes*

Thomas E. Dustin, "The Battle of the Indiana Dunes," in *Citizens Make the Difference: Case Studies of Environmental Action* (Washington, D.C.: Citizens Advisory Committee on Environmental Quality, 1973), 35–41; James J. Kyle, "Indiana Dunes National Lakeshore: The Battle for the Dunes," in *Congress and the Environment*, edited by Richard A. Cooley and Geoffrey Wandesforde-Smith (Seattle and London: University of Washington Press, 1970), 16–31; Harold M. Mayer, "Politics and Land Use: The Indiana Shoreline of Lake Michigan," *Annals of the Association of American Geographers*, 541 (December 1964), 502–523; and William Peeples, "The Indiana Dunes and Pressure Politics," *Atlantic Monthly*, 223 (February 1963), 84–88.

CASE VII.   *Planned Coastal Protection and Development:*
Rookery Bay, Florida

The Conservation Foundation, *Rookery Bay Area Project* (Washington, D.C.: The Conservation Foundation, 1968); "Development and Conservation can Coexist," *Environmental Science and Technology*, 3 (January 1969), 24–

27; and Carl W. Buchheister, "The President Reports," *Audubon Magazine*, 68 (July–August 1966), 212–213.

CASE VIII.   *Beach Preservation and Public Access: The California Coast*

Janet Adams, "Proposition 20—A Citizens Campaign," *Syracuse Law Review*, 24 (Summer 1973), 1019–1026; California Coastal Alliance *Publications*, especially *Save Our Coast—The Story of the California Coastal Alliance* (Woodside, California: California Coastal Alliance, August 17, 1971); and T. H. Watkins, "To Save the Golden Shore," *Cry California* (Spring 1970), 34–39; *Los Angeles Times* (1972); *Redwood City Tribune* (1972); *San Francisco Chronicle* (1972); and *Sacramento Bee* (1972).

CHAPTER 3   *Inland Waters*

CASE I.   *Channelization: Oklawaha River, Florida*

Office of the White House Press Secretary, *Statement by the President* (January 19, 1971); The Conservation Foundation, "Conservationists and Nixon Stop Cross-Florida Canal," *Conservation News* (February 1, 1971); and *Gainesville Sun, Miami Herald, Ocala Star Banner, Orlando Sentinel, St. Petersburg Times, Florida Times-Union* (Jacksonville), and *Tampa Tribune* (1970–1974).

CASE II.   *Dam Construction: Hells Canyon, Idaho*

Boyd Norton, *Snake Wilderness* (San Francisco: Sierra Club, 1972), and "The Last Great Dam," *Audubon Magazine*, 72 (January 1970), 15–27; R. Staines, "Chapter and Verse on the Dam Builders," *Field and Stream*, 76 (March 1972), 10; "Disaster on the Snake," *Outdoor Life*, 149 (May 1972), 70–71; "FPC Examiner Reviews Hells Canyon Dam Threat," *Living Wilderness*, 35 (Spring 1971), 46; and A. Tussing, "Fight to Save the Snake," *Field and Stream*, 76 (October 1971), 22 ff.

CASE III.   *Saving a Lake: Lake Washington, Washington*

Earl Clark, "How Seattle is Beating Water Pollution," *Harper's* magazine (June 1967), 91–95; W. T. Edmondson, "The Lake that Came Back," *Newsweek*, 76 (November 16, 1970), 98; E. W. Kenworthy, "How Seattle Cleaned Up," *Audubon Magazine*, 73 (January 1971), 105–106, and "How Seattle Beat Pollution," *Water and Wastes Engineering*, 9 (February 1972), 30–40; and D. Shaw, "Thanks to Jim Ellis, You Can Go Jump in the Lake, With Pleasure," *Today's Health*, 51 (September 1973), 28–33 ff.

CASE IV.   *Saving a River: The Willamette, Oregon*

James E. Bylin, "Oregon's Tough Policy Revives the Willamette: Pollution Drops by 90%," *Wall Street Journal* (October 25, 1972), 1, 10; Council on Environmental Quality, "Cleaning Up the Willamette," in *Council on Environmental Quality Annual Report—1973,* 43–71; George W. Gleeson, *The Return of a River* (Corvallis, Oregon: Water Resources Research Institute, Oregon State University, 1972); Anthony Netboy, "Cleaning Up the Willamette," *American Forests,* 78 (May 1972), 12–15 ff.; and Ethel A. Starbird, "A River Restored: Oregon's Willamette," *National Geographic,* 141 (June 1972), 817–820 ff.

CASE V. *Agricultural Water Supply: Kern County, California*

League of Women Voters, "The Big Pipe Dream?" in *The Big Water Fight,* by the League of Women Voters (Brattleboro, Vermont: Stephen Green, 1966), pp. 15–24.

CASE VI. *Water Quality and Watershed Protection: Lake Tahoe, California*

P. H. Abelson, "Long-Term Efforts to Clean the Environment," *Science,* 167 (February 20, 1970), 1081; William W. Bronson, "It's About Too Late for Lake Tahoe," *Audubon Magazine,* 73 (May 1971), 48–52 ff.; David Holmstrom, "Overdevelopment Threatens Lake Tahoe," *Christian Science Monitor* (January 11, 1973), p. 15; "Plan Prepared for Lake Tahoe," *New York Times* (May 25, 1971), p. 15; and "Tahoe Draws the Line on Growth," *Business Week* (April 8, 1972), 60–61.

CASE VII. *Ecological Conservation: Thompson Pond, New York*

George B. Bookman, "The Thompson Pond Story," *The Nature Conservancy News,* 23 (Winter 1973), 9–12.

CHAPTER 4   *Air Quality and Weather Modification*

CASE I. *Dust Pollution: Fernley, Nevada*

Richard E. Ayres and James F. Miller, "Citizen Suits under the Clean Air Act Amendments of 1970," Natural Resources Defense Council, Inc. *Newsletter,* No. 4 (Winter, 1971), reprinted by the Environmental Protection Agency, updated; *Nevada Cement Company v. Timber,* 514 *Pacific Reporter,* 2d Series 1180; and Parry D. Sorensen, "Pollution Fallout: Cash for Citizens," *National Observer* (December 25, 1971), 9.

CASE II. *Industry Resists Controls: Chicago, Illinois*

James Cannon, "South Works—U.S. Steel," in *Environmental Steel,* by James Cannon (New York: Council on Economic Priorities, 1973), pp. 456–463; The Conservation Foundation, "On the Shore of Lake Michigan, Citizens Fight with a Wide Range of Tactics to Protect the Environment," *The Conservation Foundation Letter* (September 1971), entire issue.

CASE III. *Air Quality and Rail Transportation: Harlem Valley, New York*

Harlem Valley Transportation Association *Newsletter* (December 1970–August 1973); "Lettie Saves the Rails," *Time* (July 9, 1973), 52; Lewis Mumford, "In Praise of Trains," *Harper's* magazine (August 1972), 22–26.

CASE IV. *Air Quality and Road Construction: New York City*

Robert H. Silver, "Lower Manhattan Expressway," *Architectual Forum*, 127 (September 1967), 66–69; and *New York Times* (March 8, April 2 and 18, and December 24, 1968; January 9, February 2 and 13, April 4, June 20, July 13, 17, and 18, and August 21 and 22, 1969).

CASE V. *Controlling Automobile Emissions:
Two Suits against Lead Pollution*

Environmental Defense Fund Memorandum dated June 30, 1973; *EDF* v. *California Air Resources Board*, Superior Court of the State of California, County of San Francisco, No. 633673 (Filed July 1, 1971) and Court of Appeals of the State of California, First Appellate District, No. 1/CW. 32024 (Filed June 29, 1972); and Norman Landau and Paul Rheingold, *The Environmental Law Handbook* (New York: Friends of the Earth/Ballantine, 1971).

CASE VI. *Offensive Odors: Bishop, Maryland*

Abatement Conference Proceedings, *Selbyville, Delaware–Bishop, Maryland Interstate Air Pollution Abatement Conference, November 9–10, 1965*; John Esposito, *Vanishing Air: The Ralph Nader Study Group Report on Air Pollution* (New York: Grossman, 1970); and U.S. Department of Health, Education and Welfare, *Report on Interstate Air Pollution in the Selbyville, Delaware–Bishop, Maryland Area* (November 1965).

CASE VII. *Pollution Standards: Allegheny County, Pennsylvania*

Group Against Smog and Pollution, *GASP—Hotline* (especially, Vol. 3, 1973); Ted O. Thackery, "Pittsburgh: How Our City Did It," in *Ecology and Economics: Controlling Pollution in the 1970's*, edited by Marshall Goldman (Englewood Cliffs, New Jersey: Prentice-Hall, 1972); University Health Center of Pittsburgh, *Communique*, 2 (Spring 1973); and *Voluntary Action News* (April 1972).

CASE VIII. *Rainmaking: Two Cases—New York and Texas*

"Battle of the Clouds," *Time* magazine (August 31, 1966); *Slutsky* v. *City of New York*, 97 N.Y.S. 2d 238 (1950); *Southwest Weather Research, Inc.* v. *Rounsaville*, 320 S.W. 2d 211 (Tex. Civ. App., 1958); and *Southwest Weather Research, Inc.* v. *Duncan*, 319 S.W. 2d 940 (Tex. Civ. App., 1958);

aff'd subnom. Southwest Weather Research, Inc. v. *Jones,* 327 S.W. 2d 417 (Tex., 1959). Robert S. Hunt, "Weather Modification and the Law," in *Weather Modification: Science and Public Policy* (Seattle and London: University of Washington Press, 1969), pp. 118–137.

CHAPTER 5   *Natural Areas and Wildlife*

CASE I.   *Wild and Scenic Rivers: Tennessee*

Tennessee Citizens for Wilderness Planning *Newsletter* (1970–1973); and U.S. Bureau of Outdoor Recreation, Southwest Region, *Obed National Wild and Scenic River Study—A Summary of the Federal-State Field Task Force Study Findings* (Atlanta, Georgia: U.S. Bureau of Outdoor Recreation, Southeast Region, August 1973).

CASE II.   *Wildlife Refuge: Great Swamp, New Jersey*

"Rescue of the Great Swamp," *Audubon Magazine,* 64 (November–December 1962), 312–314; Brooks Atkinson, "Critic at Large—A Salute to Those Near and Far Fighting for the Great Swamps of Morris County," *New York Times* (October 29, 1963) and "Great Swamp is Good For Nothing But Life, Knowledge, Peace, and Hope," *New York Times Magazine* (February 12, 1967); Joseph Gale, "How the 'Great Swamp' of New Jersey Was Saved," *National Parks Magazine,* 37 (August 1963), 11–14; *Newark Evening News,* "A Challenge" (October 23, 1962); and *Newark Sunday News,* "Untamed Land" (March 31, 1963).

CASE III.   *Wetlands Preservation: The Everglades, Florida*

John Hartke and Robert H. Socolow, "The Everglades: Wilderness Versus Rampant Land Development in South Florida," *Environmental Affairs,* 1 (April 1971), 140–164; John Edwin Laird, *The Politics of Arrogance: A Case Study of the Controversy over the Proposed Everglades Jetport, 1967–1970* (Miami: University of Florida Press, 1972); and James R. Wagner, "Search for Florida Jetport Site Provides Lesson for Environmental Disputes," *National Journal* (October 2, 1971), 1998–2004.

CASE IV.   *Protecting the Natural Character of Small Localities: Berkshire Hills, Massachusetts*

Berkshire Natural Resources Council—Five Years in Review (Pittsfield, Massachusetts: Berkshire Natural Resources Council, Inc., 1973); *Berkshire Courier* (April 13; February 9, 12, and 24; and October 5, 1972); *Berkshire Eagle* (February 9, 12, 19, 21, and 24, March 29, June 24, September 23, and October 7, 1972); and Susan Watters, "Monterey Political Firecrackers Set Off by Antihighway Coalition," *Christian Science Monitor* (August 24, 1972).

CASE V.   *Open Beachlands: Padre Island, Texas*

Primary sources have been the *Corpus Christi Caller, Houston Chronicle, Houston Post,* and *Houston Press* (1958–1972); Public Law 87–712 *Padre Island Seashore Act* (September 27, 1962); Texas Conservation Council, Inc., *Statement for the Record of the Hearing on the Padre Island National Seashore Plan* (March 25, 1972), and *House Document No. 92–357, 93rd Congress, 2d Session,* Washington, D.C., 1972.

CASE VI.   *Habitat Preservation: Lower Keys, Florida*

Sources include *Reports* of the Boone and Crockett Club of New York; *News Releases* of the U.S. Department of the Interior (October 11, 1955; December 30, 1960; and October 29, 1963); and *News Releases* of The North America Wildlife Foundation (July 20, 1961).

CHAPTER 6   *Energy*

CASE I.   *Power Plant Siting: Bodega Head, California*

Joel W. Hedgpeth, "Bodega Head—A Partisan View," *Bulletin of the Atomic Scientists* (March 1965), 2–7; and *Petaluma Argus-Courier, News Call Bulletin, San Francisco Chronicle,* and *Santa Rosa Press Democrat* (1960–1964).

CASE II.   *Economics of Nuclear Energy: Eugene, Oregon*

Joseph A. Holiday, "Atomic Power: Some Unanswered Questions," *Oregon Democrat* (September 1969); *Eugene Register-Guard* (1970); and Eugene Future Power Committee *News Bulletins* and *Reports.*

CASE III.   *Offshore Energy Development: Penobscot Bay, Maine*

Coastal Resources Action Committee *Bulletins and News Releases, New York Times* (March 21, 23 and April 18, 1971); Frank Graham, Jr., *Oil and the Maine Coast: Is It Worth It?* (Augusta, Maine: Natural Resources Council of Maine, 1970); *Maine Sunday Telegram, Maine Times, Portland Evening Express,* and *Portland Press Herald* (1971–1973).

CASE IV.   *Priorities for the Scenic Hudson:*
The Storm King Mountain Project

William M. Goodman, "Scenic Hudson Revisited: The Substantial Evidence Test and Judicial Review of Agency Environmental Findings," *Ecology Law Quarterly,* 2 (Fall 1972), 837–865; Irving Kaufman, "Power for the People —And By the People: Utilities, the Environment and the Public Interest," *New York University Law Review,* 46 (November 1971), 867–878; and

Lawrence Pringle, "Storm over Storm King," *Audubon Magazine* (July–August 1968), 59–73.

CASE V.   *Energy in America's Last Frontier: The Trans-Alaska Pipeline*

Alaska Public Interest Coalition *Reports, National Journal Reports* (1971–1973); Alyeska Pipeline Service Company, *Hearing Testimony* (March 1971); Charles J. Cicchetti, *Alaska Oil: Alternative Routes and Markets* (Baltimore: The Johns Hopkins University Press, 1972); Peter M. Hoffman, "Evolving Judicial Standards under the National Environmental Policy Act and the Challenge of the Alaska Pipeline," *Environment Law Review*, 4 (1973), 287–334; and Sierra Club *Bulletin, National Observer, Wilderness Society,* and *Pipeline Alert* (1971–1973).

CASE VI.   *Pricing Policies and Energy Demand:*
Connecticut's Public Utilities Commission

Berkshire-Litchfield Environmental Conservancy Council and Connecticut Citizen Action Group v. *Public Utilities Commission of the State of Connecticut,* Court of Common Pleas of Hartford County, *Brief in Support of Petition and Appeal* (January 15, 1974) and *Memorandum of Decision* (June 17, 1974); Natural Resources Defense Council *Docket* (New York: Natural Resources Defense Council, 1974), 46–47; and "Utility Rates," *Progress Report—Selected Cases* (New York: Natural Resources Defense Council, 1973), p. 3.

CHAPTER 7   *The Economy and Growth*

CASE I.   *Technology: The Supersonic Transport*

Citizens League Against the Sonic Boom, *Fact Sheets* (1970–1973); Leo A. Huard, "The Roar, the Whine, the Boom and the Law: Some Legal Concerns About the SST," *Environment Law Review*, 1 (1970), 68–107; *National Observer* (March 29, 1971), 3; *Wall Street Journal* (September 9, 1970), p. 16; and *U.S. News and World Report*, 69 (September 7, 1970), 1–6.

CASE II.   *Subsidized Growth: Rampart Dam, Alaska*

Alaska Conservation Society, *News Bulletin* (1961–1965); Paul Brooks, "The Plot to Drown Alaska," *Atlantic Monthly*, 215 (May 1965), 53–59; *Audubon Magazine,* 68 (May–June 1966); and U.S. Department of the Interior, *Alaska Natural Resources and the Rampart Project* (June 1967), 44.

CASE III.   *Nuclear Economy: Breeder Reactors*

Claude E. Barfield, "U.S. Retains Commitment to Breeder Reactor Despite Environmental, Economic Challenges," *National Journal Reports* (December 15, 1973), 1864–1873; Thomas B. Cochran, *The Liquid Metal Fast Breeder Reactor: An Environmental and Economic Critique* (Baltimore, Maryland:

The Johns Hopkins University Press, 1974); and "Stopping Nuclear Power," *Environment Action Bulletin*, 5 (April 6, 1974), entire issue.

CASE IV. *Restricting Throwaways: Bowie, Maryland*

Peter W. Schrath and Walter Mugdam, "Bottling Up the Throwaways: An Improved Bill and Some Thoughts for Future Drafters," *Journal of Urban Law*, 51 (November 1973), 227–246; *Environment Action Bulletin*, 5 (April 20, 1974), whole issue; Don Waggoner, "Oregon's Bottle Bill," *Oregon Environmental Council Progress Report* (February 15, 1973), p. 28; and Ellis L. Yochelson, "Teaching Geology with Bottles and Cans," *Journal of Geological Education*, 22, No. 3 (May 1974), 97–100.

CASE V. *Private Property and Public Goods: Big Thicket, Texas*

Big Thicket Coordinating Committee *Fact Sheets, Chicago Tribune Magazine* (October 10, 1971), 61–62 ff.; *Wall Street Journal* (June 10, 1973), p. 8; and issues of the *Beaumont Enterprise, Dallas Morning News*, and *Houston Post*, etc.; E. C. Fritz, "The Big Thicket: This Year's Park for the Future," *Outdoor America*, 38 (July 1973), 1 ff.; and A. Y. Gunter, *Big Thicket: A Challenge for Conservation* (New York: Viking Press, 1972).

CASE VI. *Cost-Benefit Analysis: Allerton Park, Illinois*

Roger Findley, "The Planning of a Corps of Engineers Reservoir Project: Law, Economics and Politics," *Ecology Law Quarterly*, 3 (Winter 1973), 1–106; Bruce Hannon and Julie Cannon, "The Corps Out-Engineered," *Sierra Club Bulletin* (August 1969), 8–12; and The Committee on Allerton Park, *"Battle for the Sangamon: The Struggle to Save Allerton Park"* (Champaign, Illinois: The Committee on Allerton Park, November 1973), p. 47.

CHAPTER 8   *Environmental Health*

CASE I. *Occupational Health: Black Lung Disease*

Articles by Lorin E. Kerr, M.D. in *Archives of Environmental Health*, 16 (April 1968) and 37 (October 1973), and *The Virginia Medical Monthly*, 46 (March 1969); *New York Times* (January 7 and 27, February 12, 27, and 28, March 4 and 30, May 28, and December 31, 1969); and United Mine Workers of America, *Black Lung* (Washington, D.C.: United Mine Workers of America, 1970). See also *United Mine Workers Journal* (1973–1974), and National Tuberculosis and Respiratory Disease Association *Bulletin* (October–November 1972).

CASE II. *Noise Control: New York City*

Robert A. Baron, *The Tyranny of Noise* (New York: St. Martin's Press, 1970); *New York Times* (July 8 and November 14, 1971, and September 13 and October 5 and 19, 1972); City of New York Environmental Protection

Administration, *A Guide to 1972 New York City Control Code* (1972) and *The Noise We Hear in New York* (1973).

CASE III.   *Pesticides Regulation: People for Environmental Progress*

Frank Graham, Jr., "Pesticides, Politics and the Public," *Audubon Magazine,* 69 (July–August 1967), 54–62; Vito Mussomeli, "Herbicides Attacked in Canada, California," *Environment Action Bulletin,* 5 (February 23, 1974), 4; and *People for Environmental Progress,* Press Release, July 9, 1973; *People for Environmental Progress* v. *Douglas R. Leisz, Regional Forester, et al.* Civil No. 73–1405–LTL *Stipulation for Compromise Settlement* (September 10, 1975).

CASE IV.   *Drug Policy and Public Health: Food Additives*

Donald Carr, "Food Additives," in *The Deadly Feast of Life* (Garden City, New York: Doubleday, 1971); Environmental Defense Fund, Inc., *Petition for Repeal of the Regulation Prescribing Conditions under Which Diethyl Pyrocarbonate May Be Used as a Food Additive* (New York: Environmental Defense Fund, Inc., 1972); and James S. Turner, *The Chemical Feast* (New York: Grossman, 1970).

CASE V.   *Questionable Drinking Water: Reserve Mining*
Company, Lake Superior

Duluth News Tribune (1972–1973); *Minneapolis Tribune* (1973); *Milwaukee Journal* (November 11, 1973); *Time* magazine (October 22, 1973 and May 6, 1974); Stanley Ulrich, Timothy J. Berg, and Deborah Hedlund, *Superior Polluter* (Duluth, Minnesota: Save Lake Superior Association and Northern Environmental Council, 1972); and David Zurick and Marcy Benstock, "Better Late Than Never: The Lake Superior Story," in *Water Wasteland* (New York: Grossman, 1971).

CASE VI.   *Nuclear Radiation: The Davis-Besse Reactor, Ohio*

Citizens for Clean Air and Water, Inc. *Newsletter* (1970–1971); Coalition for Safe Electric Power *Newsletter* (1973); and Coalition for Safe Nuclear Power, *Summary Statement in the Matter of the Toledo Edison Company on the Cleveland Electric Illuminating Company* [Davis-Besse Nuclear Power Station] Docket No. 50–346, Atomic Energy Commission Construction Hearing, February 12, 1971.

CHAPTER 9   *Quality of Urban Life*

CASE I.   *Quality versus Size: Boulder, Colorado*

American Society of Planning Officials, *Nongrowth as a Planning Alternative,* Advisory Service Report #283 (Chicago: American Society of Planning

Officials, September 1972); Eric Johnson, "Is Population Growth Good for Your City?" *ZPG National Reporter* (October 1971), 3–4; and *Summary Workshop Reports, National Conference on Managed Growth* (September 16–18, 1973).

CASE II.   *Solid Waste Disposal: Louisville, Kentucky*

See *Louisville Courier-Journal* (September 12 and 13, October 31, and November 8 and 15, 1972); "Town on the Spy for Polluters," *Life* magazine, 73 (August 4, 1972), 32–33.

CASE III.   *Housing and Lead Poisoning: New York City*

Robert J. Bazell, "Lead Poisoning: Combating the Threat from the Air," *Science,* 174 (November 1971), 574–576; Diana R. Gordon, "Getting the Lead Out," in *City Limits: Barriers to Change in Urban Governments* (New York: Charterhouse, 1973), 17–62; Ann Koppelman Simon, "Citizens vs. Lead in Three Communities," *Scientist and Citizen,* 10 (April 1968), 58–64.

CASE IV.   *Urban Transportation: San Diego, California*

San Diego Transit Corporation, *We're Going Your Way* (July 1973); San Diego News Release, *A Look at San Diego Transit* (April 12, 1974); and D. W. Scarr, "City Has Longest 25-Cent Bus Ride," *San Diego Union* (November 14, 1972).

CASE V.   *Historic Preservation: Vieux Carré, New Orleans, Louisiana*

Richard O. Baumbach, Jr. and William Borah, *The Second Battle of New Orleans: History of the Vieux Carré Riverfront Expressway* (to be published); Priscilla Dunhill, "An Expressway Named Destruction," *Architectural Forum* (March 1967), 54–59; Russell Kirk, "The Bureau of Public Roads, Devastation," *National Review,* 202; *New York Times* (1966 and 1967); "The New New Orleans: Comeback of a Southern City," *U.S. News and World Report* (July 25, 1966), 78–80; "Threat to New Orleans' Famed Quarter," *U.S. News and World Report* (February 28, 1966), 10; and "Will Success Spoil the Vieux Carré?" *Architectural Forum* (June 5, 1969), 79–83.

CASE VI.   *Recreation versus Development: Seward Street Mini-Park, San Francisco, California*

San Francisco Chronicle, San Francisco Examiner, San Francisco News Call Bulletin, and *San Francisco Progress* (1964–1971); *Unanimous Resolution of the San Francisco Board of Supervisors Congratulating the Residents of Corwin-Seward Street Area,* Resolution No. 130–66 (February 18, 1970).

CHAPTER 10   *Institutional Behavior*

CASE I.   *Conflicting Responsibilities: Black Mesa and
the Southwest Power Complex*

Malcolm F. Baldwin, *The Southwest Energy Complex: A Policy Evalua-
tion* (Washington, D.C.: The Conservation Foundation, 1973); Black Mesa
Defense Fund *Publications* (1971); William Brown, "The Rape of Black
Mesa," *New Mexico Review and Legislative Journal,* Nos. 8 and 9 (August/
September 1970), p. 3 and p. 5; Central Clearing House [Santa Fe, New Mex-
ico] *Publications* (1971–1974); Alvin M. Josephy, Jr., "The Murder of the
Southwest," *Audubon Magazine,* 73 (July 1971), 55–67; and New Mexico
Citizens for Clean Air and Water *Newsletters* (1971–1974).

CASE II.   *Resistance to Public Control: The Tennessee Valley Authority*

Clinchmore Citizens, Claryville, Tennessee, *Letter to Chairman Wagner
of* TVA (September 7, 1973); Comptroller General of the United States, *Opportunities for Improvements in Reclaiming Strip-Mined Land Under Coal Purchase Contracts* (Washington, D.C.: United States Government Printing Office,
1972); Save Our Cumberland Mountains, *Florence Times/Tri Cities Daily*
(April 17, 1972); *The Nashville Tennessean* (1971–1973); and Tennessee Citizens for Wilderness Planning *Newsletter* (1968–1974).

CASE III.   *Mission Fixation: The United States Forest Service*

William P. Cunningham, "The Magruder Corridor Controversy: A Case
History," Missoula, Montana: unpublished M.S. Thesis, University of Mon-
tana, 1966; Joel Frykman, "The Bitterroot Dialogue Continues," *American
Forests,* 78 (March 1972), 28–30; and Boyd Norton, "The Oldest Established
Perennially Debated Tree Fight in the West," *Audubon Magazine,* 74 (July
1972), 61–69.

CASE IV.   *Administrative Discretion: Navarre Marsh, Ohio*

Citizens for Clean Air and Water *Newsletters and Reports* (1970–1971);
Coalition for Safe Nuclear Power *Newsletter* (May 1973); Donald W. Large,
"Is Anybody Listening? The Problem of Access in Environmental Litigation,"
Wisconsin Law Review, No. 1 (1972), 62–113; and *Sierra Club* v. *Hickle,* Civil
No. C70–971 (Northern District of Ohio, September 16, 1971).

CASE V.   *Enforcing* NEPA: *Three Cases*

Daniel A. Bronstein, "The AEC Decision-Making Process and the Environment: A Case Study of the Calvert Cliffs Nuclear Power Plant," *Ecology Law
Quarterly,* 1 (Fall 1971), 689–725; *Calvert Cliffs Coordinating Committee* v.
AEC, 449 F., 2d 1109 (D.C. Cir. 1971); *Environmental Defense Fund* v. *Corps
of Engineers,* 325 F., Supp. 728 (E.D. Ark. 1971); *Greene County Planning*

Board v. *Federal Power Commission,* 455 F., 2d 412 (2d Cir. 1972); and Irving Like, "Multi-Media Confrontation—The Environmentalists' Strategy for a 'No-Win' Agency Proceeding," *Ecology Law Quarterly,* 1 (Summer 1971), 495–518.

CASE VI.   *Institutional Reform: Wisconsin*

Sources were almost entirely publications of the Wisconsin Coalition for Balanced Transportation (e.g., *News Bulletin, Interchange,* and study papers). But see also *Wisconsin State Journal* and *Capital Times,* Madison, Wisconsin.

INDEX